Cambridge studies in medieval life and thought

Edited by WALTER ULLMANN, LITT.D., F.B.A.
*Professor of Medieval Ecclesiastical History
in the University of Cambridge*

Third series vol. 2

MONARCHY AND COMMUNITY

CAMBRIDGE STUDIES IN
MEDIEVAL LIFE AND THOUGHT
THIRD SERIES

MONARCHY AND COMMUNITY

POLITICAL IDEAS
IN THE
LATER CONCILIAR
CONTROVERSY
1430‚1450

ANTONY BLACK

Lecturer in Political Science
University of Dundee

CAMBRIDGE
AT THE UNIVERSITY PRESS
1970

Published by the Syndics of the Cambridge University Press
Bentley House, 200 Euston Road, London N.W.1
American Branch: 32 East 57th Street, New York, N.Y.10022

Library of Congress Catalogue Card Number: 72-108101
Standard Book Number: 521 07739 7

Printed in Great Britain
by Alden & Mowbray Ltd
at the Alden Press, Oxford

FOR MY GRANDMOTHER

CONTENTS

Contents

PREFACE

The struggle between the Council of Basle (1431-49) and the papacy under Pope Eugenius IV (1431-47) and Pope Nicholas V (1447-55), raised questions of lasting importance. The central issue was, Who holds authority over them, and for what reasons? This was partly a theological debate, but it also developed into a debate about political theory. For both Council and pope claimed authority not only on the basis of revealed truth, but also of secular political norms. This book is about the political theory of Conciliarism (Part I) and of papal monarchy (Part II), and, since this dispute involved a power-struggle for the actual machinery of church government, about the influence of contemporary politics and diplomacy on the theories advanced by each side (Part III). Though inter-related in various ways, each Part could be considered separately. In order to minimize footnotes, full bibliographical details have been relegated to the Bibliography.

The dispute between the Council of Basle and the papacy has previously been studied chiefly from the point of view of political history, in the general opinion that this was a time when the doctrines of Conciliarism and of Papalism respectively—the earlier development of which has received so much attention—had become ossified. The academic popularity of Nicholas of Cusa, and Carla Eckermann's brilliant and too little-known work, *Studien zur Geschichte des monarchischen Gedankens im 15. Jahrhundert*, are notable exceptions. In recent years, furthermore, increasing attention, much of it biographical, but some also concerned with doctrine, has been paid to certain of the participants. But the works of many individual thinkers are still virtually unexamined (though aspects of Turrecremata's theology have been studied). Above all, the importance, and even existence of Baslean Conciliarism and Eugenian Papalism as distinctive political doctrines of vital interest in themselves, and full of significance for later political thought, has never been brought to light. Further, the intricate and in some ways unique inter-relation between theory and practice in this dispute, noticed by Eckermann, has never been expounded.

This book, then, sets out to examine Baslean Conciliarism and mid-fifteenth century Papalism as schools of political theory, and the interaction in them between doctrine and diplomacy. John of

ix

Preface

Segovia among the Basleans, and John Turrecremata among the Eugenians, emerge as political thinkers of primary significance by any standards.

The original writings in this dispute, as even contemporaries acknowledged, were voluminous. It has therefore been necessary to concentrate on political theory at the expense of other, no less, intrinsically important, aspects of the dispute. Above all, the theology of each side, which certainly predominates in the actual sources, is here considered only as it bears on their political theory (with the exception of the *Epilogue*). This has meant a certain amount of distortion, since this was the period when the true, theological notion of the papacy was obscured by an almost neo-pagan theory of absolute monarchy. The issue of reform, which was hardly less important than that of conciliar supremacy (and about which a good deal has been written), and the influence of the renaissance, are only touched on. Naturally, the themes that I at first selected for consideration have constantly had to be re-weighed and re-stated in the light of actual sources; in fact, this work began with the question, To what extent did the papacy seek an alliance of monarchical powers against subversion?—which is now only dealt with in the last Part of the book.

We of today are fortunate in being able to utilize centuries of patient work by men whose names are too easily forgotten. Not only were many of our sources for the thought of this period actually printed in the sixteenth century, but also a great number of the treatises and documents have been published in the sturdy collections of the eighteenth and nineteenth centuries. And, since the early nineteenth century, commentators have been sifting the evidence. The modern enquirer has tremendous facilities at his disposal.

I would like first to offer my sincere and lasting gratitude to Professor W. Ullmann for the kindness and inspiration which he has given to me in this work. My thanks are also due to the Department of Political Science in the University of Dundee for their help and encouragement; I am also most grateful to the librarians of the Cambridge University Library, particularly of the Anderson Room, and of Dundee University Library, for the way they have facilitated research. Above all I want to thank those friends who have made this work possible.

Dundee, 1969 ANTONY BLACK

ABBREVIATIONS

Ampl. disp. Segovia, Joannes de. *Amplificatio disputationis* in *id.*, *Historia gestorum generalis synodi Basiliensis*, XVII, 25–60; ed. C. Stehlin in *MCG*, III, 695–941

Auct. ep. Segovia, Joannes de. *De magna auctoritate episcoporum in generali concilio*, Universitätsbibliothek, Basle, B.V. 15.

Barb. lat. Codices Barberini latini

CB Haller, J. and others, edd. *Concilium Basiliense, Studien und Quellen zur Geschichte des Conzils von Basel*, 8 vols. (Basle, 1896–1936)

CBC Piccolomini, A. S. (Pius II). *De gestis concilii Basiliensis commentariorum libri II*, ed. and trans. D. Hay and W. Smith (Oxford, 1967)

CMH VIII *Cambridge medieval history*, VIII: *The close of the Middle Ages*, ed. C. Previté-Orton and Z. Brooke (Cambridge, 1936)

Conc. cath. Cusa, Nicholas de. *De concordantia catholica*, ed. G. Kallen (Hamburg, 1959–65)

Dec. advis. Segovia, Joannes de. *Decem advisamenta*, Vat. lat. 4039, fos. 192r–231v

FM, XIV. Fliche, A. and Martin, V., edd. *Histoire de l'église depuis les origines jusqu'à nos jours*, XIV: *L'Eglise au temps du grand schisme et de la crise conciliaire (1378–1449)*, by E. Delaruelle, E-R. Labande and P. Ourliac, 2 vols. (Paris, 1962–4)

Gub. conc. Escobar, Andreas de. *Gubernaculum conciliorum*, H.v.d. Hardt, *Magnum oecumenicum Constantiense Concilium*, VI (Leipzig, 1700), 139–333

MCG Palacky, F. and others, edd. *Monumenta conciliorum generalium seculi decimi quinti, Concilium Basiliense. Scriptorum*, 4 vols. (Vienna–Basle, 1857–1935)

Mon. Pol. *Monumenta medii aevi res gestas Polonias illustrantia*, II (Cracow, 1876), XII (Cracow, 1891), XIV (Cracow, 1894)

Panorm. Panormitanus or Nicholas de Tudeschis

Rayn. Baronius, C., Raynaldus, O., and Theiner, A. edd. *Annales ecclesiastici*, XXVIII–XXIX (Barri-Ducis, 1874–6)

HISTORICAL INTRODUCTION

The medieval church in some ways resembled a super-state. It had a universal legal system, recognized legislative procedures, and a fairly centralized bureaucracy. Universal sovereignty was claimed for the pope and his court; the medieval theorists of papal monarchy leaned heavily on the terminology and ideology of Roman imperial law and precedent. This was, to be sure, only one aspect of the medieval church; unlike a state, for example, its membership depended, not on birth and region, but on baptism and faith. But, viewed politically, as one organization among others in the course of history, the church in the Middle Ages seems to have emphasized, more than the church in early or indeed modern times, the elements of law, formal organization and authority.

During the later Middle Ages, the fourteenth and fifteenth centuries, this way of thinking and behaving was challenged from two sides. Many Christian reformers rebelled against the formalization of religious life, against the centralization of church government, and against the wealth and political power of the clergy; they wanted to return to a simpler, more personal type of religious community, and to reassert the New Testament ideals of equality and brotherhood in ecclesiastical and in secular life. This did not necessarily lead them to reject the doctrines or institutions of the church as it stood; though, with economic and social grievances added to the spiritual, there was often a strong incentive to do so.

Secondly, under the drive of national kings and territorial princes, the legal, military and administrative organization of society was being developed and centralized; the modern state, and modern political theory, were being born. The rulers of these new states wanted to assert their independence and leadership in ecclesiastical as much as in other spheres.

The conciliar reform-movement was a constitutionalist reaction

I

to the centralization of church government, which had itself—paradoxically—been the (only partly intentional) result of the eleventh-century reform-movement against secular domination over the church in feudal conditions. This idea, that a council could override a pope, correct his behaviour and even overhaul his administrative system, was developed in the early fourteenth century in response to the increased administrative power acquired by the papacy. It was at the same time an attempt to solve the theological problem of the possibility of papal error, and the location of infallibility. It entered the scene of ecclesiastical and international politics during the Great Schism (1378–1417), when, with two 'popes' contending for the same office, conciliar arbitration seemed necessary, and conciliar sovereignty, at least over the existing 'popes' in their existing circumstances, seemed right. This solution was attempted, first at the Council of Pisa (1409), which only made things worse by appointing yet another 'pope', and then at the Council of Constance (1414–18), which succeeded in deposing two of the claimants, persuading the third to retire, and electing a new, undisputed pope, Martin V (1417).[1]

But the Council of Constance did not quite stop there. Many wanted it to go on to reform the Roman curia and other ecclesiastical institutions; and, what was more, to assert the general right of a council to do so, whatever the pope might say. To this end they passed two decrees of historic importance: *Sacrosancta* (1415), which asserted the supremacy of a council over all, even the pope, in matters of heresy, schism and reform;[2] and *Frequens* (1417), which said that councils must in future meet at stipulated intervals. But, once elected, Martin V bypassed substantive reforms by concordats with the secular rulers (1418), which gave general recognition to the decrees of Constance, named one or two reforms, but in effect gave the rulers a freer hand in domestic church affairs.

The next Council, due to meet in 1423, assembled at Siena, but was dissolved by Martin V before it had achieved anything. Mean-

---

[1] For this period, cf. esp. FM, XIV, part 1; W. Ullmann, *Origins of the Great Schism;* E. F. Jacob, *Essays in the Conciliar epoch*, ch. 2.

[2] For the text of this and the following decree, see *Conciliorum œcumenicorum decreta*, 2nd ed., 384 f. and 414; see on the former now B. Tierney, in *Essays presented to Bertie Wilkinson*, 354 ff.

while, Bohemia, under the influence of John Hus and his more radical followers, was going much further much more quickly. A revolution in Prague in 1419 had spread throughout the country; pope and emperor were dispossessed, clergy and lords humiliated, the Germans expelled. Now, it was the very idea of the clergy's possession of wealth and power, and the very idea of the priesthood as a separate category with unique functions, which was under attack. The extreme group of Hussites, the Taborites, preached a new social as well as religious order of things; thus secular authority too was endangered. Three times papal–imperial armies were defeated by the Bohemians, the last in 1431; after this, the victorious revolutionaries swept Central Europe with forays, and circulated their views far and wide by letter. Secular and ecclesiastical authorities were alike terrified.[1]

It was now that the next Council, due to meet in 1431, assembled at Basle. Pope Eugenius IV, elected only a few months previously, immediately tried to dissolve it, as his predecessor had done Siena; but the secular powers, who now saw Basle as their last hope of stemming revolution by timely reform, and of negotiating with the successful Hussites, would have none of this. By 1432, there had assembled at Basle a number of ecclesiastics, including many ordinary priests, who were determined both to reform the church and to make the pope accept the authority of a council, as declared by Constance, whose decrees were re-promulgated. Their combined opposition compelled Eugenius, who soon after lost Rome itself to a citizens' rebellion, to recognize the Council of Basle (December 1433). The Council now began a blast of reform-decrees, the most important of which was the reduction of papal power over benefices and revenues. But these were rendered ineffective by the non-co-operation of the pope, and of other parties to whom the reforms applied.[2]

Eugenius IV, meanwhile, ignoring the Council, began to canvass support among the secular powers. In March 1436, Basle issued a

---

[1] On Hussitism, cf. H. Kaminsky, *A history of the Hussite revolution*; M. Spinka, *John Hus' concept of the church*; and R. R. Betts, 'Some political ideas of the early Czeck reformers', in *Slavonic and East European Review*, XXXI (1952–3), 20 ff.

[2] For this, and what follows, see FM, XIV, part 2; N. Valois, *Le Pape et le Concile*, vol. II *passim*; H. Jedin, *A history of the Council of Trent*, I, ch. 1; P. Ourliac, 'La sociologie du Concile de Bâle', in *Revue d'Histoire Ecclés.* LVI (1961), 2–32.

summons that he should attend trial for disobedience to its decrees; Eugenius replied with a *Tract of self-defence*, which appealed to kings to take the lead in supporting monarchical authority in the church. The Greeks, meanwhile, were in desperate need of military aid against the Turks, for which the West made ecclesiastical reunion with Rome a condition. The Greek Church had thus been negotiating for years with the papacy, and more recently with the Council of Basle, for a council to resolve the centuries-old schism. The Greeks, however, were unwilling to travel beyond the Adriatic seaboard of Italy, where Eugenius IV was prepared to meet them. But Basle preferred to hold a Council nearer home, north of the Alps. On 7 May 1437, the Council was split between those who were prepared to go to Italy to meet the Greeks, and those who refused; the former were in a minority, but included many of higher rank; the latter, though a majority, were mostly of low rank. According to the rules of the Council, which operated on the basis of rule by a majority of incorporated members regardless of status, the majority decree prevailed. This refusal to accommodate the Greeks lost Basle the support of many enlightened ecclesiastics, who were already impatient with the ineffectiveness of the reforms decreed by the Council.

Eugenius transferred the Council to Ferrara in September 1437, where the Greeks arrived soon after; having moved to Florence on account of the plague, this Council achieved, in July 1439, the celebrated Union of Florence between the Latin and Greek Churches. Not long afterwards, however, this was rejected by the Greeks; Constantinople fell in 1453. But the effect in the Western Church was enormously to strengthen Eugenius's hand.[1]

The Council of Basle, meanwhile, consisting now mainly of lower clergy but with some prelates still supporting it and many others undecided, continued with the 'process' against Eugenius. Lack of bishops did not disturb it, for its organization was not dependent on them. It suspended Eugenius in January 1438, and after protracted delays and heated debates finally deposed him, after reaffirming in greater detail the doctrine of conciliar supremacy, in June 1439. In November it elected in his place Amedeus, a former Duke of Savoy, as Pope Felix V.

[1] Cf. J. Gill, *The Council of Florence*, 46 ff., 293 ff.

This schism, which officially began with Eugenius's transference of the Council in 1437 and lasted until Basle dissolved itself in 1449, differed both from the Great Schism and from the schism of 1431–3. First, it was ideological as well as personal; it was rival views on church government, as well as rival popes, that claimed allegiance now. Secondly, the secular powers, whom Basle had indeed gratified by reaching agreement with the Hussites in 1433–4, maintained for the most part a studied neutrality, in particular France, the German emperor, nearly all the German princes, and Poland. On the one hand, this enabled them to increase their power over the church at home; certain reform-decrees were accepted by France in the Pragmatic Sanction of Bourges (1438), and by Germany in the Acceptatio of Mainz (1439) (though this implied no acceptance of the continued legitimacy of Basle itself). These two measures transferred power over the crucial spheres of ecclesiastical appointments and revenues, not to the chapters and other bodies stipulated by canon law and confirmed in their role by the Council, but to the secular authorities themselves. At the international level, the neutral powers exerted pressure, directly and through prelates whom they had appointed and could therefore control, for an end to the schism on their own terms. One observer summed up the situation thus:

Basle too provides material for a joke. Those cardinals, who have been preaching the authority of the church and of general councils with such conviction that they seemed willing to die for it, on one letter from their king, which threatened them not with death but with loss of benefices, have left Basle; they know better than to be without a flock...The purse binds more strictly than honour; for what is disgrace with plenty of money![1]

The chief exceptions to neutrality were England and Burgundy on the one hand, who supported the pope; and Aragon and Milan on the other, who supported the Council. It is noticeable that England already possessed, and Burgundy soon obtained, extensive influence in domestic church matters.

Throughout the height of the dispute, *c.* 1438–44, the neutral powers demanded a 'new, third council', to resolve the question. But the continued reluctance of either side to accept this proposal,

---

[1] The German Chancellor Schlick, in *Mon. Pol.* XII, 442–3.

the increasing willingness of the papacy to exchange domestic ecclesiastical powers for allegiance, and the conversion of the Emperor to Eugenius's cause in 1444–5, swayed them in favour of abandoning Conciliarism and accepting separate agreements with the papacy. After lengthy negotiations at the Diet of Frankfurt (1446) and other meetings in France (1447), the emperor persuaded the princes to join him in supporting Eugenius, which led to the Concordat of Vienna (1448). Aeneas Sylvius Piccolomini had long before predicted that, whichever way Germany as a whole went, others would be likely to follow;[1] and indeed the end of Basle soon came. The imperial ban forced it to move to Lausanne. In 1449, Felix V agreed to resign, the Council formally elected the reigning pope, Nicholas V, and disbanded itself. It was the end of Conciliarism as a movement, but not of reform.

[1] 'Mea opinio fert, tanti ponderis tantique nominis esse Germaniam, ut in quamcumque partem declinet, reliquam christianorum portionem ad se trahet, dummodo integra sit. Non dicam plura': *Der Briefwechsel des Eneas Silvius Piccolomini*, ed. R. Wolkan, I, 502.

Part I

CONCILIARISM

THE CHURCH AS A SELF-GOVERNING COMMUNITY

Conciliarism was the doctrine that the council held supreme authority in the church. It could override the judgment of anyone, including the pope; its own judgment and decrees were infallible, and must be obeyed by all, including the pope. All may appeal to the council, none may appeal from it; it is 'the supreme tribunal of God on earth'.[1] It derived its power from no other human source, but directly from God; when Christ gave his authority to the church, he gave it to the council. The Conciliarists held this as a divinely-revealed truth, and the Councils of Constance and Basle proclaimed it as a doctrine to be held by all Christians.[2]

It was the Council of Basle, and the Baslean Conciliarists, who took this view to its logical conclusion. Whereas Constance claimed that the council was the pope's superior in the specific cases of heresy, schism and the need for reform, Basle and its supporters, we shall see, claimed for the council the unlimited sovereignty previously claimed by popes:

the power of the church is greater than that of the pope absolutely...
and not in those three cases only.[3]

But, in arriving at this view, and in presenting it to others, they inevitably had recourse to political ideas; not only because ecclesiastical and secular ideas on government were so intertwined, but also because this was the obvious, perhaps the only, way of talking about aspects of church government and society not plainly prescribed in the documents of revelation. The doctrine of conciliar sovereignty,

[1] *MCG*, III, 131, 160, 533–4.   [2] Mansi, XXVII, 590 ff., 1159 ff.
[3] Escobar, *Gub. conc.* 301–2; on him see J.-B. Sägmuller, 'Der Verfasser der Traktates De modis uniendi ac reformandi Ecclesiam in Concilio universali vom J. 1410', in *Hist. Jahrbuch*, XIV (1893), 562–82; and L. Walters, *Andreas von Escobar*.

like that of papal sovereignty, was the result of a conflation of religious and political ideas.

As Hallam, Figgis and others have long since recognized, the Conciliarists were in a position remarkably similar to that of later Constitutionalists.[1] Oakley, in his attempt to produce evidence for the direct influence of Conciliarism on sixteenth- and seventeenth-century secular thinkers, has cited cases of similar views being expressed, and even of references to the fifteenth-century councils as precedents.[2] But the truth probably is rather, that constitutionalist and democratic ideas arose in response to certain political problems, in the minds of men whose concept of justice was steeped in the beliefs of their ancestors. It is, moreover, on the Constance period that attention has focussed when considering Conciliarism from this angle. It is hoped to show here that it was at Basle that the implications of Conciliarism as a political theory were fully developed; and that the Basleans did indeed evolve ideas which, already latent in European tradition, were to be developed on a similar pattern on many future occasions.

The Conciliarists maintained that Christ had given authority to 'the church' and that this meant the council: 'the general council *representing the Catholic church* holds power immediately from Christ'.[3] The strategy of conciliar theory, aimed at subjecting the pope to the council, rested on the idea that the church was the real sovereign; they related this to the sovereignty of the whole people in secular government, and thus became involved in a broad tradition of popular sovereignty.[4] This political idea stemmed partly from citizen rule in the ancient city-state, inherited through Aristotle; and partly from the folk-sovereignty of the Germanic tribes. It had

---

[1] H. Hallam, *View of the state of Europe in the Middle Ages*, II, 105, 110; J. N. Figgis, *Studies in political thought*, 31, 34, 42, 47; H. J. Laski, *Political theory in the later Middle Ages*, in *CMH*, VIII, 638; P. Sigmund, 'Cusanus' Concordantia', in *Polit. Studies*, X (1962), 180.

[2] F. Oakley, 'On the road from Constance to 1688', in *Journal of British Studies*, I (1962), 1–32; *id. The political thought of Pierre D'Ailly*, 211 ff.

[3] Mansi, XXVIII, 590 ff.

[4] For explicit statements that supreme power belongs to the church as such, see Panorm. in *RTA*, XVI, 485–6, 506; Segovia in *MCG*, III, 804; Escobar, *Gub. conc.* 309. Most simply, 'the universal church is superior': *RTA*, XV, 226. Turrecremata himself saw the importance of community sovereignty to his opponents' programme, below, pp. 54 f.

struck firm roots in European society in the Middle Ages, in village organization, town self-government, in the rules generally applied to the working of corporations, such as guilds, monasteries and universities. 'Corporation theory' by the fifteenth century comprised a body of constitutional precepts, such as the regular assembly of all, majority voting, the appointment and accountability of officials, and the association as a legal entity ('person' or 'subject'). Such concepts—like those applied nowadays in trade unions and social clubs—were largely directed towards implementing the sovereignty of the group as a whole, of the *universitas*.[1] Meanwhile, claims made by barons and parliaments over the king, reviving the notion of tribal or national sovereignty originally expressed by the *Thing* or folk assembly, denoted a similar outlook. This is shown in such terms as 'the *universitas* of the realm'; some corporation rules, such as majority voting, were being introduced in national assemblies.[2]

The Conciliarists asserted the sovereignty of the church first of all on the basis of Christ's gift of power to the apostles; power had been given to them all, and, when Peter was singled out, he was acting only as the representative agent of them all.[3] Zabarella had expressed this view in the terms of the corporation theory of the canon lawyers; as in an ecclesiastical corporation (a cathedral or monastic chapter), so too in the universal church, power lies basically with the *universitas*, of which the pope is the agent or *minister*.[4] This view was repeated, as the legal basis for conciliar sovereignty, by Andrew of Escobar in 1435, and again in 1442 by a pupil of Zabarella's, Nicholas de Tudeschis (d. 1445), known as Panormitanus. Panormitanus was perhaps the greatest canonist of the fifteenth century, his *Commentary on the Decretals* being generally cautious and meticulously traditional. But his speeches of 1442 and 1444 expounded, on the basis of canon and civil law, a thoroughly Baslean conciliarist viewpoint. In that of 1442 he said:

[1] Cf. O. von Gierke, *Political theories of the Middle Age*, 27 f., 37 f.; W. Ullmann, *Principles of government and politics*, 215 ff.; B. Tierney, *Foundations of conciliar theory*, 96 ff.

[2] Cf. Gierke, *Political theories*, 24, 64; G. Post, *Studies in medieval legal thought*, 247, 311, 328.

[3] Panorm. in *RTA*, XVI, 504; Escobar, *Gub. conc.* 147; cf. Tierney, *Conciliar theory*, 36.

[4] Cf. W. Ullmann, *The origins of the Great Schism*, 211–12; Tierney, *Conciliar theory*, 225–7.

Conciliarism

When it is said that the pope has fullness of power, this should be understood as referring not to him alone, but to him as head of the *universitas* (corporation): so that power itself is in the *universitas* itself as foundation, but in the pope as principal minister, through whom this power is applied.[1]

Escobar also used an argument for communal sovereignty derived from some civil (Roman) lawyers: the church, like the Roman people, transferred only limited power to the ruler,

because they could not alienate the whole jurisdiction from themselves... the power of the people is greater than that of the government.[2]

Conciliarists on several occasions supported the sovereignty of the *universitas* by referring to the example of the city-states, in which sovereignty was frequently claimed for the whole people. Again, Zabarella had taken the lead, but it was during Basle that this vital analogy was most often used. Both Escobar (1435) and Panormitanus (1442) repeated what Zabarella had said:

The power of the universal church seems to reside in the whole church itself, just as the philosophers say that the government of a city belongs to the assembly of the citizens, or its weightier part, an opinion gathered from Aristotle, *Politics*, III, c. 8. And in the same way we should say that the government of the world belongs to the assembly of the men of the whole world, or its weightier part.[3]

Panormitanus himself was considerably influenced by Bartolus, who had established the right of cities to self-government, often in a

---

[1] 'Illud quod dicitur, quod papa habet plenitudinem potestatis, debet intelligi, non solus, sed tanquam caput universitatis; ita quod ipsa potestas est in ipsa universitate tanquam in fundamento, sed in papa tanquam in principali ministro, per quem haec potestas explicatur': Panorm. in *RTA*, 506. Cf. *ibid.* 483, 499, 521; Escobar, *Gub. conc.* 261. Cusa says that 'habitus et potestas' reside with the *universitas*: *Conc. cath.* II, 13. On Panormitanus, see J. Schweizer, *Nicolaus de' Tudeschis, seine Tätigkeit am Basler Konzil*; K. Nörr, *Kirche und Konzil bei Nicolaus de Tudeschis*; C. Lefèbvre, 'L'Enseignement de Nicolas de Tudeschis et l'autorité pontificale', in *Ephem. juris canon.* XIV (1958), 312 ff.

[2] *Gub. conc.* 267. See also Panorm. in *RTA*, XVI, 521.

[3] Escobar, *Gub. conc.* 260: 'Cum ergo potestas universalis ecclesiae videatur residere in ipsa tota ecclesia, sicut dicunt philosophi quod regimen civitatis consistit penes congregationem civium vel ipsius congregationis partem valentiorem, quae sententia colligitur ab Aristotele III Politicorum, c. viii. Et conformiter dicendum est quod regimen orbis penes congregationem hominum totius orbis, vel ipsius partem valentiorem consistit.' See also Panorm. in *RTA*, XVI, 456. Cf. Ullmann, *Great Schism*, 197; Tierney, *Conciliar theory*, 223.

democratic form, in terms of civil law.[1] Panormitanus seems to echo Bartolus's famous dictum, 'the city is its own sovereign (*civitas sibi princeps*)', when he declares that, 'the general council has the rights of sovereign (*iura principis*)'.[2] He made an even more explicit reference to the city, on his own initiative, in defending the council's power to depose the pope on analogy with the (alleged) constitution of Venice:

> jurisdiction is in the whole body of the church...and in Peter as chief minister...We can observe the same in the government of the Venetians. The duke is first in council and among individual citizens; but if he errs, he is resisted by the city, and if necessary deposed. This is because the foundation of jurisdiction is in the body of the city, and in the duke as chief minister.[3]

We shall see later how he used the analogy with the city, with references to Bartolus, in defence both of conciliar supremacy and of majority rule.

But it was upon John of Segovia, a theologian from the subsequently famous school of Salamanca, a patient but conciliatory advocate of Baslean doctrine, that the civic milieu made its deepest impression. He defended his contention that, 'supreme power... belongs to the church continuously, permanently, invariably and perpetually', by saying:

> There is a useful example in any large community not recognizing a temporal superior; its supreme power...resides first of all in the community itself, then in rectors, magistrates, consulate or senate...and lastly in the executor, podesta (*potestas*), dictator or governor...supreme power resides first of all in the community, like a personal emotive or moral force.[4]

---

[1] Cf. W. Ullmann, 'De Bartoli sententia: concilium representat mentem populi', in *Bartolus de Sassoferrato*, II, 703 ff.; C. N. S.Woolf, *Bartolus of Sassoferrato*, 153 ff.

[2] *Comm.* VII, fo. 242r on 5.40.27; see also *RTA*, XVI, 468.

[3] *RTA*, XVI, 521.

[4] *Ampl. disp.* in *MCG*, III, 802: see below, p. 150. For the civic terms, cf. *ibid.* 713, 736, 803; for the endorsement of civic sovereignty, cf. *ibid.* 845, and *id.* in *RTA*, XV, 682. The Italian city-states were, it seems, regularly cited by fifteenth-century legal writers as examples of popular sovereignty.

  On the connection between the city and Taborite ideas, see H. Kaminsky, *A history of the Hussite revolution*, 483–94. On Segovia, cf. R. Beer, *Urkundliche Beiträge zu Johannes de Segovia's Geschichte des Basler Conzils*; J. Haller in *CB*, I, 20 ff.; U. Fromherz, *Johannes von Segovia*.

Conciliarism

Again, he argues the church's intrinsic right of self-preservation, 'by comparison with other *universitates*: every household, village, town or city has the intrinsic power to maintain its own *status*'.[1] Segovia too uses the city to justify majority rule, and (as we shall see later) his whole notion of government seems, not unlike Marsigilio's, to depend upon the model of the city-state.

Lastly, some Basleans appealed to the analogy between council and parliament. During debates on the deposition of the pope, the Bishop of Burgos introduced the argument that a king is 'greater than each but less than all',[2] and developed it on the basis of a remark made by Aristotle:

With respect to individuals, the pope could be judged by no-one, but this was not so with respect to the *universitas* of the church. This could be argued on the basis of *Politics*, III, where Aristotle says that a good monarch should be more powerful than any individual in the kingdom, but not more powerful than the kingdom itself. The words of Aristotle are these: 'the king should hold power, but such a power as to be greater than that of individuals, one or several, but less than that of the people (*multitudo*) ...' it is the same for the pope with respect to the church in the case of legal power: he is more powerful than individuals, not more powerful than the church.

The next speaker drew the conclusion that the deposition of king by realm, and of pope by church, was legitimate; Aristotle's statement on military power was thus made to apply to jurisdiction.[3] This new defence of their position in terms of a familiar political norm was rapturously received by the Council.

The Basleans then advocated communal sovereignty as an extension of the form of government in the small *universitas* onto a universal scale, and also in its traditional parliamentary form. They were tending more and more to think of the *universitas* model as everywhere applicable, and indeed as the only legitimate disposition of power. At the same time, they were developing it in their own

[1] *Ampl. disp.* in *MCG*, III, 781. Cf. Rousseau, *Du Contrat social*, II, 4. Cf. below, p. 151.
[2] Cf. Gierke, *Political theories*, 48.
[3] *MCG*, III, 261. See also *CBC*, 28 ff.; *Ampl. disp.*, 736. Gerson and D'Ailly had previously compared the occasional sovereignty of the council to that of the French Parlement, 'by which [the king] does not refuse to be judged': below, pp. 107 f. Cf. Aristotle, *Politics*, III, x, 1286b; cf. below, pp. 49, 92.

12

specific way. This they did by elaborating the distinction, implicit in the dictum that a king was 'greater than each but less than all', between the community as a series of individual members and the community as a unified group. This again derived from the view that the *universitas* was a legal person, so that, when acting as a whole, it possessed rights and powers not possessed by any of its members acting individually.

> In reality, the college is nothing other than its individual members. But in jurisdiction college is one thing and individuals another.[1]

It was in accordance with 'the nature of *universitas* and individuals'[2] that the government should be superior to the latter, but subject to the former. Conciliarists, beginning with Gerson but more generally during Basle, used the terms *collective* and *dispersive* to describe this distinction when applied to the universal church. The pope was, they argued, certainly superior (as the traditional texts alleged) to the church in its separated form, but not to the church considered as a whole.[3] It was to the church collectively, not to any individual part of it, that sovereignty was ascribed: this again marked off the Conciliarists of Basle from those of Constance, who had generally based conciliar authority on the *ex officio* authority of those present.

But the conciliarist identification of the church as a whole as the ultimate power-bearer was the culmination of much previous canonist and theological thought. It was evolved from the notion of the ecclesiastical corporation (cathedral chapter, etc.) as 'a fictional and represented body' or 'person', which had been applied by Zabarella to the universal church.[4] It was also a jurisdictional

---

[1] 'Secundum veritatem, collegium non est aliud a singulis de collegio, sed secundum jurisdictionem aliud collegium, aliud singuli': *Comm.* VII, fo. 98v on 5.3.30. See also *RTA*, XVI, 468, where he says: 'Nam aliud universitas, aliud singuli de universitate; nam factum singulorum non attribuitur universitati.' And Segovia: 'aliud universitati, aliud singulis suppositis illius competere dicitur': *Ampl. disp.* 736.

[2] Segovia, *Dec. advis.*, Vat. lat. 4039, fo. 224r.

[3] Below, p. 14 f. Cf. Gierke, *Political theories*, 72, 171.

[4] Panormitanus says: 'praelatus et canonici sunt unum corpus, et est unum corpus fictum et representatum de singulis de corpore': *Comm.* VI, fo. 90v on 3.10.4. And again: 'collegium seu universitas est quaedam persona ficta et representata': *Comm.* VII, fo. 98v on 5.3.30. Cf. Gierke, *Political theories*, 29–30; Tierney, *Conciliar theory*, 99, 221–2; M. J. Wilks, *The problem of sovereignty in the later Middle Ages*, 24, 354–5; E. H. Kantorowicz, *The king's two bodies*, 209, 305.

application of the idea of the church as a spiritual person, as an invisible group entity, with a life, mind and will of her own—in short, of the Pauline notion of the church, as 'the mystical body of Christ'. Such terms as 'mystical body', 'congregation of the faithful', had once referred primarily to a spiritual unity, though even this had its visible side in the relations of Christians with each other, and with God in the sacraments. Canon lawyers of the thirteenth and fourteenth centuries had tended to think of these terms as implying that the church was a legal person, with certain defined legal powers.[1] Since ecclesiastical judgments and decrees were frequently made in the name of 'the church', it was easy for the Conciliarists to finalize this whole process by ascribing jurisdictional sovereignty to the church in person.

The church as a whole, the mystical body of Christ, was jurisdictional sovereign; the church in its dispersed form, which they called a 'political body' (meaning that in this respect the church was just like any other society) was subordinate to the pope. This view was expounded most fully by Cracow University in 1442:

The church may be regarded in two ways: *first*, as a *mystical body*, and in that way it is regarded as ruled by Christ...this is a true body living by a spiritual life...*Secondly* the church may be regarded as a *political body*, in which case it is regarded like any other society or state...in that it depends on human judgment. In *this* sense, it could be considered proper to call the pope the head of the church. But insofar as the church is a *mystical body*, his rôle is not head of the church, but rather its vicar and servant.

Put forward by Escobar (1435), Segovia (1441) and Panormitanus (1444) this doctrine may be said to constitute the essence of Baslean Conciliarism.[2]

---

[1] Cf. especially Tierney, *Conciliar theory*, 131 ff.

[2] Cracow University: 'Ecclesia universalis consideratur dupliciter. Uno modo est corpus mysticum; isto modo consideratur prout a Christo regitur...quae est corpus verum vivens vita spirituali...Alio modo consideratur ecclesia ut est corpus politicum, secundum quod consideratur sicut alia communitas aut societas politica...quantum est ex humano iudicio...Isto modo posset dici, quod papae competeret dici caput ecclesiae: sed prout ecclesia est corpus mysticum, non proprie sibi competit esse caput ecclesiae, sed posset dici vicarius et minister capitis': C. Égasse du Boulay, *Historia Universitatis Parisiensis*, v, 489. This doctrinal *memorandum* was based on five tracts, among which those by Thomas Strempinski and

This notion of a 'social whole' was already embedded in secular social thought: people generally thought of the community as a real thing, so that they could speak of 'the soul of our city which is composed of the souls of all its citizens',[1] or of a national kingdom as a 'mystical body', articulated like a human body. Baslean Conciliarists contributed to this outlook a renewed emphasis on the unique jurisdictional quality of the whole. The effect on secular thought, then, was that the ancient notion of a ruler as 'less than each but greater than all' was now strengthened by corporation law and theology. In the hands of Cusa and Segovia, this formed a basic element in a theory of government as such, whether in church or state. Cusa, speaking of any society, said that a ruler stood as 'father over individuals, so long as he recognizes himself as creature of his subjects collectively'.[2] According to Segovia, the ruler may override 'particular' persons or groups, but is subject to 'the whole multitude'.[3] The Conciliarists of Basle, then, were at once extending the meaning of 'mystical body', as a description of the sum total of Christians, into the sphere of government, and giving new theoretical reasons for the legitimacy of claims made on behalf of the whole body of citizens, or of the realm, to sovereignty.

THE PROBLEM OF REPRESENTATION

That, quite simply, was the basis for the claim that the council was sovereign: the council constituted the church, in its collective aspect, for purposes of legal status and jurisdictional power. It was in this sense that the council 'represented' the church: it simply *was* the church in its jurisdictional form. The Conciliarists made this claim

Jacob za Paradyz were particularly important: cf. *Universitatis Iagelloniae 1364–1764 Historia*, I, 115–26, 457; J. Fijalek, *Mistrz Jakob za Paradyza*, I, 428—where he quotes an identical passage from Strempinski. See, for other identical passages, Escobar, *Gub. conc.* 305; Segovia in *RTA*, xv, 682; and Panormitanus in *RTA*, xvii, 351: 'The church represented in general councils is considered in one way as a mystical body, and in another way as a political body. Insofar as it is the whole church represented in the council, it is ruled by the Holy Spirit immediately. And insofar as it is considered as a series of parts (partialiter), it is ruled by the pope; for thus the pope is head of all members of the church, but not of the whole church.' Below, pp. 51 f., 110, 120.

[1] Cf. W. Robertson, *A history of the reign of Charles V*, I, 36 ff.
[2] *Conc. cath.* III, 4.
[3] *Ampl. disp. MCG*, III, 720.

long before they rationalized it. The council is 'the assembled church'; its decrees constitute 'the judgment of the church'.[1] In the early days of the conciliar movement, it was easy for people to think that a council, containing leading church rulers and thinkers from every country, 'represented' the church more 'really' than a pope; but was there a basis in law or in political theory for this general impression?

The Conciliarists of Constance seem to have thought of the council in traditional ecclesiastical terms, as the meeting-place for the established church authorities: bishops, abbots and secular rulers. These 'represented' the church *ex officio*, regardless of how they had been chosen. The Conciliarists of Basle, partly because of circumstances, shifted the bases of legitimacy from the office-holders onto the council itself, which co-opted new members as it wished, and where all members had equal voting power, so that the majority ruled.[2] But this left an unexplained hiatus between council and church: why should the former be authorized to act in the latter's name? (Cusa was alone in suggesting (1433) that all church rulers should be elected, so that the council would, indirectly, 'represent' the church by election.)[3] Their attempt to rationalize their position seems to have rested on a particular conception of the relation between society and assembly as such.

This originated partly in the *universitas*, where all members met periodically to discuss important business; when they did so, they lost their individual status, and acted 'as the *universitas*', 'as comprising the college'.[4] Once again, Conciliarism put the universal church on the same plane as the ecclesiastical chapter, or the city-state; the council *was* the *universitas*, the 'priestly college', its members acted 'as comprising the council'.[5] It was 'the church in conciliar assembly', 'the church legitimately assembled in the Holy Spirit'.[6] Escobar said that it was 'the Christian people itself' which 'makes general councils';[7] Segovia likened the council to 'an assembled

---

[1] For example, *MCG*, III, 276, 534, 536; *CB*, V, 154.
[2] Cf. Ourliac, 'La sociologie', 24 ff.   [3] *Conc. cath.* II, 18.
[4] Panorm., *Comm.* VI, fo. 35r on 3.5.15. Cf. Gierke, *Political theories*, 67, 168.
[5] Panorm. in *RTA*, XVI, 504. For 'collegium sacerdotum', see *MCG*, II, 208; *MCG*, III, 390; *CBC*, 72 ff.
[6] Above, p. 14; Escobar, *Gub. conc.* 329; Segovia, *Ampl. disp.* 806.
[7] Escobar, *Gub. conc.* 329: 'ipsa sacra generalia concilia faciat ipse populus christianus'.

people'.[1] Panormitanus was even more explicit in his analogy with the council of a city: Basle had been 'legitimately assembled for making a council, just as we say of the people of a city'. He said that the rival council at Florence could not represent the church any more than citizens their city, 'unless they were legitimately assembled, and the matter discussed *in universitate*'.[2]

According to this outlook, derived from the small *universitas*, the community expresses its sovereignty in person in the assembly. Baslean propagandists transferred this notion to the universal church, by saying that the council exercised powers that were only 'latent' or 'potential' with the church in its 'dispersed' form. The abstract notion of the church 'taken collectively', or as a 'mystical body', was identified with the concrete phenomenon of the council, by sliding from the abstract to the concrete meaning of such terms as *collective, congregatio*. It was in the council that the church actually existed in its collective form; and without the council the church could not realize the power ascribed to it, for 'the dispersed church does not speak'.[3] This was most explicitly put by some university delegates in 1444:

the whole church, dispersed as it is over the world, cannot have the exercise of its power, which it holds immediately from Christ, for that activity which properly belongs to the whole church; for the whole church is assembled out of different members and hierarchical ranks, which cannot come together for the exercise of any one activity, unless they are joined together; and this cannot happen except by means of the assembly of a general council. Thus the power of the universal church is brought into activity through the existence of the general council. Such power exists in the dispersed church in the same way that the seed exists in the grass, or wine in the grape; but, in the general council, it exists in its formal and complete essence. Nor can it be said that such power can only be exercised through the pope; for then the universal church could not

---

[1] *Ampl. disp., MCG*, III, 720.

[2] *RTA*, XVI, 513: 'nam etsi totus clerus orbis esset in uno loco congregatus, non propter hoc ibi diceretur esse congregatum concilium, nisi essent ibi legittime congregati ad faciendum concilium; sicut dicimus de populo civitatis...nisi fuissent legittime congregati, et fuisset in universitate illud deliberatum'. For the civic analogy on this point, see also Segovia, *Dec. advis.*, Vat. lat. 4039, fo. 225r; and *Auct. ep.*, fo. 9r.

[3] 'Ecclesia dispersa non loquitur, sed dumtaxat concilium generale ipsam representans': tract of a Paris doctor, in Du Boulay, *Historia*, v, 450; cf. *ibid.* 454, 457.

exercise its power through itself and in the first instance (*per se ipsam* 🙄 *primo*), but only through a part and in a limited way (*per partem et* 🙄 *modum*).[1]

An important consequence of this view was that it bypassed the very notion of legal or political 'representation'. The church does not delegate its powers to anyone; church and council are, from the point of view of legal status and political power, identical, a single legal entity or power-bearer (*Rechtssubjekt*).

The whole church *itself* exercises *its own* jurisdiction *through* the council representing it.[2]

Conciliar jurisdiction is an 'activity which properly belongs to the whole church'; it is in the council that the church enters upon 'the active exercise of *its own* jurisdiction and power'.[3] The council is no proxy, but a living and necessary development of the church itself, without which its claim to sovereignty would be meaningless. In the words of Segovia, it is 'a sort of transfusion or extension rather than a new creation' of power.[4]

Thus the idea, current in medieval society, of the collective mind or will of a community, attained political realization in the thought of Basle. The council embodies 'the judgment of the church' both in the legal and in the moral sense. The community takes its own decisions in the council; it is politically self-determining.[5] Gierke seems to miss the point in saying that conciliar doctrine viewed the church-community as nothing more than a 'legal fiction', precisely because he assumes that his own notion of the 'real personality' of the group, of which the individual members are but varied reflections, constituted the only alternative.[6] The church-community was, to them, a living unity, first in the traditional theological sense of

---

[1] *RTA*, XVII, 367; cf. above, p. 14. On the notion of the *latent* power of the church, see also Cusa, *Conc. cath.* II, 19.

[2] 'Ecclesia ipsa universalis exercet jurisdictionem suam per concilium ipsam representans': *RTA*, XVI, 499.

[3] Du Boulay, *Historia*, V, 492; see also above, n. 1.

[4] *Ampl. disp.*, *MCG*, III, 803: see below, p. 150. The community may in fact 'exercise through itself its own intrinsic power' (*ibid.* 802).

[5] Above, p. 15, esp. n. 1; see also Segovia, *Ampl. disp.*, *MCG*, III, 720, 726.

[6] See Gierke, *Political theories*, 29–30, 67–8, 72; and *id.* cited in E. Barker's introduction to his translation of O. Gierke, *Natural law and the theory of society*, lxviii–lxix.

he 'mystical body', united in faith and the sacraments and foresha-
owing a real unity in the world to come; secondly in the theological
nd also general social sense of a common mind and will, directed at
a single 'common good'; and thirdly in the concrete realization of
this through the decisions of the sovereign council. The community
is no mere string of individuals; it is a political reality.

The difficulty with this whole outlook was that it made no
provision for the very obvious fact that a small community could
literally assemble itself, whereas the universal church could not.
The notion of the assembly as *ipso facto*, by its very existence, representing, i.e. *constituting*, the community in jurisdictional form,
depended on the small number of citizens; beyond a certain size,
either the citizens must become an élite, or there must be a mechan-
ism whereby some represent the views of others. Basle perhaps
occasionally leaned towards the former tactic, with its emphasis on
itself as consisting of priests and learned men. This was certainly one
implication of the statement frequently heard, that the council
represented the church 'virtually', that is in all its essential qualities,
of leadership, learning and the like. In particular, functional qualifi-
cation for special power in the church was extended, beyond the
traditional boundaries of the episcopate and the priesthood, to those
who had graduated as 'doctors', a group which Segovia called 'as it
were outstanding in the church',[1] and which Basle itself declared to
have a share with bishops in the teaching function of the church.[2]
This claim was perhaps inspired partly by the circumstance that
Basle became increasingly comprised of university delegates, whose
chief claim was their rank in the world of learning; but it was also a
development of a view common among canon lawyers, that knowledge as well as official power was essential for a valid act.[3] Certainly,
it was no accident that Basle was open to the charge of academic-
ism;[4] it wanted to rule by a kind of seminar which would contain
'fullness of knowledge'.[5]

But Basle evolved no consistent theory or practice on this basis. Nor

---

[1] *MCG*, III, 267; see also *RTA*, XIV, 9; XV, 725; XVI, 58; Auct. ep. fo. 23r.
[2] *RTA*, XIV, 410.
[3] See Panorm., *Comm.* I, fo. 143v on 1.6.6; VII, fo. 174r on 5.31.18. Cf. Gratian, D.20, pars I and II.   [4] See below, p. 114, n. 5.
[5] Segovia, *Auct. ep.* fo. 172r. Cf. Ourliac, 'La Sociologie', 12, 20.

did it ever contemplate electoral representation. It simply carried on as if the universal church were really like an ecclesiastical chapter, in which the assembly comprises all except those who, for accidental reasons of time and place, cannot come. It is 'virtually' the whole church, but unfortunately only 'certain elements' can actually attend;[1] and 'those present represent those absent'.[2] As Segovia put it:

Though the general council, compared to the universal church, is restricted in four ways [*sc.* in time, place, and in number and condition of persons], it is not so restricted in regard to virtue and power.[3]

The legal or moral relationship between those present and those absent was never stated or worked out. It was a disastrous vacuum.

In fact, Basle was here to some extent merely reflecting a general trend in 'representative' assemblies of this period, in which electoral representation seems to have been the exception rather than the rule. Assemblies 'represented' a city or a national kingdom to a large degree on the basis of the customary standing or qualifications of their members, according to legal rules fixed in custom. In the secular sphere, too, the application of the corporation-model, regardless of the difference in scale, blocked the path to true representation by perpetuating the view that the assembly could act *ex officio* (not unlike a king or bishop) in the name of those it claimed to represent. Parliament was often referred to as 'the corporation of the realm' or its 'mystical body'; the vagueness of such titles must surely have contributed to the weakness of late medieval parliaments.[4]

---

[1] Cracow University (1442): 'ut (ecclesia) possit exire in actum exercitivum suae jurisdictionis et potestatis, opertet eam interdum congregari in suis certis suppositis et membris principalioribus et aliis': Du Boulay, *Historia*, v, 492. See also Paradyz, cited in Fijalek, *Mistrz Jacob za Paradyza*, I, 374.

[2] Segovia, *Auct. ep.* fo. 5r. The loose, perhaps opportunist, element in conciliarist thought here is shown by the way they invoke *universitas* rules only when it suits their case: if the church were really considered the *universitas*, why does Panormitanus not apply to it the majority principle he invokes so loudly within the council? Cf. *Comm.* I, fo. 160v on 1.6.10; VI, fo. 90v on 3.11.1.

[3] *RTA*, xv, 681; similar passages in *MCG*, III, 729 and *Auct. ep.* fo. 11v.

[4] Above, p. 9, n. 1. Cf. Thomas Smith on the English Parliament: 'For every Englishman is entended to be there present . . . from the prince to the lowest person. And the consent of Parliament is taken to be every man's consent': cited in J. W. Allen, *A history of political thought in the sixteenth century*, 264. And R. Hooker,

Segovia in fact endorsed this view of the council's claim to represent the church 'by way of identification'. It is like the 'consulate' of a city which 'uses the name and power' of the city. He explicitly generalized the dispersed-collective distinction, and applied the latter to the assembly:

Any empire, kingdom, dukedom or princedom is customarily described in this twofold manner, especially in discussing its virtue and power... That the title 'the church' belongs to such an assembly is shown first of all by *the political manner of speaking*: not only all the inhabitants, but the consulate with power of ruling others, is termed 'the city'.[1]

We may call this the collegiate version of the tacit or mechanical notion of representation.

This, then, was the political rationalization used to defend the conciliarist thesis that 'the general council representing the Catholic church holds power immediately from Christ'.[2] The sovereignty attributed to the church is monopolized by the council, because church and council form a single juridical person, or political entity. It was at this point that the powers latent in the community were conceived, not only as being concentrated for jurisdictional action in the council, but as forming the recipient, in the case of the church council, of the unique divine gift of teaching authority, given by Christ to the original church, and by the Holy Spirit to successive councils. The purpose of the elaboration of the church-in-council as a political–legal structure was to create a fit receptacle for the theological power.

This political theory produced a form of Conciliarism radically different from that of Constance. The council is now no mere

Of the laws of ecclesiastical polity, I, 10, 194. On the whole question of the relation between secular and ecclesiastical ideas on representative assemblies, see G. Lagarde, 'Les Théories représentatives des xive–xve siècles et l'Église', in *Studies presented to the International Committee for the History of Representative and Parliamentary Institutions*, XVIII, 63 ff.

[1] 'Sic enim imperium, regnum, ducatus vel principatus magnus quicumque hoc duplici modo accipi consuevit, presertim quando sermo est de virtute et potestate eius...Quod autem eiusmodi congregationi nomen ecclesie competat, ostendit primo *politicus loquendi modus*; quia non solum omnes habitantes, sed et consulatus potestatem habens regendi alios civitas dicitur': *Ampl. disp., MCG*, III, 729. The notion of absorptive representation is thus transferred from prelate to council: cf. Tierney, *Conciliar theory*, 125; Wilks, *Sovereignty*, 488 ff.; and below, pp. 64 f.
[2] Cf. above, p. 8.

emergency weapon with 'occasional' power in time of papal heresy or schism; it is the normal vehicle of the church's supreme authority, and the regular ecclesiastical superior of all. Papal theory had indeed been turned on its head; it is now the church-in-council which has 'total power'.[1]

JOHN OF SEGOVIA AND THE COMMUNAL ETHIC

As well as the doctrine of communal sovereignty, worked out through corporation theory, Baslean Conciliarism enshrined the spiritual and political ideals of the commune. Moral aspirations for the application of the communal spirit of government formed an integral part of its constitutional programme. The whole mystical body has a single common will, which is expressed in the decisions of the council; this view involved concurrently theological belief, moral aim, and a constitutional plan.

To say that sovereignty resided 'with the community and not with the individuals' meant also that everybody (that is, again, everybody within the commune, in this case the council) must be considered in decision-making, that the common good is the criterion of right action, and also that the community is generically different from a mere mass of individuals. In the case of the church community, this meant more than the agreed common goal and common procedural rules (which may be said, broadly speaking, to have constituted the communal unity of the aristotelian *polis*): it meant also the presence of Christ himself. Few texts can have been quoted more often by the Conciliarists than that in which Christ promised to be present 'whenever two or three are gathered together in my name'; one reason often given for the council's sovereignty is the fact that it constitutes such a group, 'legitimately assembled in the Holy Spirit', so that 'the divine majesty is present'.[2] The fact of community produces a spiritual and constitutional power, such as

---

[1] Panormitanus says: 'ipsum concilium generale representat *totam ecclesiam* quoad *totalem sui potestatem*, quia tota potestas ecclesiastica est in ecclesia tanquam in fundamento...in (ecclesia) est fundamentum plenitudinis potestatis ...ecclesia universalis tanquam maior et comprehendens in se omnem potestatem ecclesiasticam': *RTA*, xvi, 483, 485, 506. Zabarella had said that the pope held power *principaliter* but not *totaliter*: cited in Ullmann, *Great Schism*, 212 n.

[2] 'The council itself is ruled and governed by the Holy Spirit': *MCG*, iii, 279; see also Aleman, *RTA*, xvii, 85; Segovia in *CBC*, 146.

can belong to no individual. In this way, Conciliarism may be seen as in part an extension of the 'Common Life' movement of the fourteenth century:[1] hence, perhaps, Cusa's emphasis on 'concordance' as the basis of authority. 'Fraternal correction' was the first method to be applied to an erring pope.[2]

Again, Conciliarism was partaking in an aspect of medieval European culture in which Christian ideals had been grafted onto older traditions of thought, and in which secular and ecclesiastical institutions shared the same type of aspiration. It drew both on the Northern piety of the type found among the Brethren of the Common Life, and on the republican spirit of the Mediterranean city-states; it was perhaps most of all Cusa who represented the former, and Segovia the latter strand. Both elements pointed towards the primacy of the community and the public ownership of political power. Escobar said, as an argument for equal votes in the council:

Fraternity among Christians is based on charity...charity makes everything to be held in common, and puts common things before private... Therefore also there must be one charity, one will, *one intention* in the council.[3]

Again, Escobar suggests the intertwining of a religious and a civic ideal:

The universal church is a certain mystical body, a *certain public thing (res quaedem publica)* of the Christian people...and thus it is the *common property (res communis)* of the Christian people.[4]

Segovia adds:

Our Saviour wished the church to be governed *in common*.[5]

The medieval university was perhaps the institution closest, in temper and also personnel, to the Council of Basle in this respect.

---

[1] Escobar calls specifically for a restoration of *vita communis*: *Gub. conc.* 195–6.
[2] Cf. L. Buisson: *Potestas und Caritas*, 214–15.
[3] *Gub. conc.* 265: 'Omnes Christiani sunt fratres spirituales...Et ideo debent esse tanquam fratres carnales...Ergo aequalem in (ecclesia) habent portionem. Ergo ad (ecclesiae) salvationem et gubernationem omnes Christicolae debent habere in ea aequalem vocem. Item haec fraternitas inter Christicolas est ratione caritatis... caritas facit omnia esse communia...una esse debet caritas, una voluntas, una intentio in concilio.' On the church's indefectibility in charity and therefore in power, see Segovia, *Ampl. disp.*, *MCG*, III, 804.
[4] *Gub. conc.* 328.   [5] *CBC*, 144. See also below, p. 35.

23

Conciliar doctrine had from its beginning owed much to university men, and to the university environment; and during Basle the universities played an increasingly important part, both through their delegates, and by their independent action, in support of the Council. A glance at the constitutions of medieval universities suggests that these might well have been one important channel for the impact of the *universitas* model upon Conciliarism, whose lifespan coincided with a period of phenomenal university expansion, especially in Central Europe. There too the communal pattern of decision-making corresponded to the communal pattern of life.[1] In the intimate quadrangle of old Cracow University one can feel close to the spirit of Conciliarism which inspired its doctors. On the refectory door, in faint lettering, are the words 'stuba communis'.

These doctrines and ideals received their most explicit development from John of Segovia who, like Nicholas of Cusa, paid careful attention to the underlying principles of Conciliarism. Considering himself as merely 'the least of the advocates of the conciliar doctrine', he summed up better than anyone the mentality of his colleagues, and seems to express more fully what they were feeling their way towards. As in the case of Cusa, his reflections led him to expound a social philosophy which shed light both on the theology of the church and on the political theory of the state. The social ideals of the New Testament and the political norms of Aristotle were, in his work, more closely interwoven than ever, and he made perhaps the most whole-hearted attempt yet to give them constitutional embodiment. He referred frequently to historical and contemporary methods of government, as both legal and empirical evidence for his case, and so may be said to be bridging the distance between medieval and modern types of political reasoning.[2]

---

[1] Cf. H. Rashdall, *The universities of Europe in the Middle Ages*: some thirty-three new universities were founded in Europe *c.* 1350–1450, and of these Prague (1348), Cracow (1364), Vienna (1365), Erfurt (1379), Cologne (1380) and Leipzig (1409) played a prominent part at the Council of Basle; the author suggests that Conciliarism owed much to ideas stemming from these institutions, particularly from Paris, from the constitution of which, he claims, originated the idea of voting by nations, practised at Constance (*Universities*, I, 572, 576). Cf. P. McKeon, 'Concilium generale and studium generale', in *Church History*, XXXV (1966), 24 f. on relations between the medieval universities and the universal church; and also *Les Universités européennes du xive au xviie siècles*, publ. by Inst. d'hist. de Genève.

[2] See esp. *Ampl. disp.* 707–13: below, pp. 144 ff.

Segovia makes it clear that he is concerned with the nature of society as such: 'if anyone duly considers the nature of association (*universitas*) and individuals...'[1] What he says is deliberately designed to apply to 'the president of *any* people', to '*any* supreme president, such as pope, emperor or king'; it is set forth as 'the rationale of presidency (*presidentiae ratio*)'.[2] What he seeks to do is to establish the personal sovereignty of the community, that is, of all its assembled members, on the basis of the communal goal, interpreted on analogy with the 'interest' of a legal person in private law.[3] The ruler's office is to act as legal proxy for the whole community by promoting its corporate interests; he 'represents' the community, in the strict private-law sense of being entrusted with the care of its interests.

He ceases to be a private and is made a public person; he loses in a sense his isolated unity, and puts on the united people, so that he may be said to bear the person not of one but of many. He acts the part of a good ruler just so long as he intends the public utility of many.[4]

Whoever is made ruler or president of any people puts aside his private and takes on a public person, in that he must seek not, as before, what is useful to himself, but what is useful to all. He carries two persons; he is a private person, and by legal fiction a public person.[5]

The community, however, is considered not, as in theocratic doctrine, as a 'minor' incapable of acting on its own behalf;[6] but as a normal legal person, who deliberately chooses to entrust his interests to another, for reasons of convenience, while retaining ultimate responsibility for them himself. It is those whose interests are at stake, therefore, who are the sole ultimate judges of what their own interests are. According to this analogy, then, the whole people are the judges of the common good, which is expressed as 'the intention of all'.[7] Therefore, if the ruler's moral title depends upon whether

---

[1] *Dec. advis.*, Vat. lat. 4039, fo. 224r: below, p. 142.
[2] *Ibid. Ampl. disp.* 720: below, p. 148.
[3] Cf. below, p. 29, n. 1.　　　　　　　　　[4] *Dec. advis.* fo. 224r: below, p. 143.
[5] *Ampl. disp.* 720: below, p. 148. Cf. Tierney, *Conciliar theory*, 113, for the notion of the bishop's dual personality, 'as prelate' and 'as canon', in the cathedral chapter; and Baldus in Kantorowicz, *The king's two bodies*, 445 n.
[6] Cf. below, p. 66, n. 4.
[7] 'Intentio omnium': *Ampl. disp.* 720; below, p. 148. Cf. 'intentio universalis ecclesiae', *ibid.* 726.

or not he is representing this common good, his legal title depends upon the actual approval or contradiction of the whole people. This state of affairs, Segovia assumes, exists both *de facto* and *de iure*.

Here Segovia introduced the notion of government as a trust (to which we shall return shortly), in the legal sense of an explicit mandate from a *principal* to an *agent*. The principal entrusts the agent with the care of his interests; but, being himself a full legal person, retains ultimate responsibility in himself. Segovia seeks to establish this relationship, which was in this period also being applied in the spheres of diplomacy and commerce, as the model for the political relationship between people and government. Private law, we might say, is being taken as the model for public law. The ruler's *de iure* ability to act on behalf of all derives solely from their *de facto* trust in him.

His judgment is presumed to conform to the intention of all over whom he presides, for the welfare of the republic and of themselves. This is the highest power granted to any president, that what he thinks right, all should believe to be the intention of all.[1]

It is presumed that he must procure only the public good; and because of this legal fiction his commands and judgments are trusted as being for the common good, and are obeyed...It is presumed that his judgment conforms to the intention of all over whom he presides, or the greater number of them. This is the highest point in a ruler's excellence, that the subjects should deem that the judgments made by him proceed from the intention of the whole people, or the greater part.[2]

The distinction between whole and parts now enters the scene. The ruler, in virtue of his position, may override any 'particular' person or group within the community, since he derives his authority from the whole which is greater than any part. But, for exactly the same reason, he is subordinate to the whole community whenever it decides to act in person. Since it is the good of all that confers public power, and since it is assumed (as in private law) that the good of the principal is what he deems it to be, not what his agent may imagine it to be, therefore the whole people can override the judgment of the ruler whenever they wish to do so. Furthermore, because the good in question is theirs, they themselves as a whole *are*

[1] *Dec. advis.* fo. 224v: below, p. 143.   [2] *Ampl. disp.* 720: below, p. 148.

26

the true 'public person', while the ruler is a public person only by legal fiction, as promoting their interests for them. Whenever, therefore, they disagree with his interpretation of their good, they can override him; he (*ipso facto*) ceases to be their representative, and they act on their own behalf.

To implement this, Segovia merely had to introduce the corporation notion of the spontaneous self-assembly of the people. It is the model of the small community, which can physically assemble together, so that its 'intention' can be immediately recognized, which lies behind his whole theory:

If it occurs that the whole people assembles itself together, and asserts or desires something contrary to what the president himself says; then the people will deservedly prevail, since truth itself is preferred to fiction. For the truth is that this people is many persons; while the fiction is that the president himself, who in truth is a single person, is said to be many by representation. But, when someone is said to have authority simply on the ground that he represents one or many others, by the very fact that those represented are present, their authority, and not his, is heeded. Therefore, the authority of the president is not considered to hold good, as before, in the presence of the whole people... When the whole people is itself present *principaliter* [*sc.* as principal or, here, sovereign] and judges something to be in their interest, while the president says the opposite; it is perfectly clear that the reason why more assent should be given to him than to others, namely the belief that his judgment conformed to the intention of all, has ceased to exist. Rather, since he demonstrably holds an opposite opinion, it is quite clear that his judgment does not conform to the intention of all, who now expressly declare what their judgment is.[1]

When he compares himself to the whole people, his judgment is not preferred to theirs, since it is a comparison between truth and fiction, and truth is preferred to fiction... When the whole people decides that (his decision) is not in its interests, there ceases to be any reason why more assent should be given to him than to others, on the grounds that it was presumed that his judgment conformed to the intention of all. Rather, the opposite is obviously the case; therefore he is not preferred to them.[2]

It is the people as a whole then, or their majority, which creates the legal fiction of government, and which is the ultimate arbiter of the

[1] *Dec. advis.* fo. 224r–v: below, pp. 143 f. [2] *Ampl. disp.* 720–1: below, pp. 148 f.

political good. The people as a whole constitute the true sovereign, the *Rechtssubjekt*; and, in their assembly, they express in person their own political will.

Not only does this passage summarize the entire development of Conciliarism at Basle as a political theory; resting upon a fusion of corporation theory with the communal ethic, it is a unique statement of popular sovereignty. Ultimate political power belongs to the whole people, because its sole purpose is to promote their interests. Perhaps, if we want a term for the concept 'state' in its nascent form, we could not do better than Segovia's 'public person', as meaning in one sense the government, and in another the people, according to their relation to the public interest.[1] This was probably, apart from Marsigilio, the clearest statement of the democratic ideal in the late Middle Ages; and it anticipated Rousseau in advocating the model of the directly self-governing small community as the ultimate political ideal. The notion of representation in both Locke and Rousseau bears so close a resemblance to Segovia's, that one can only suggest that they were implicitly using the same analogy with the same private-law notions. Rousseau says that,

À l'instant que le peuple est *légitimement assemblé* en *Corps souverain*, toute juridiction du Gouvernement cesse, la puissance executive est suspendue ...*parce qu'où se trouve le représenté il n'ya plus de représentant.*[2]

Locke says that the ruler commands obedience so long as he acts as 'public person' by following 'the will of society declared in its laws'.

But when he quits this representation, this *public will*, and acts by his own *private will*, he degrades himself, and is but *a single private person*, without power and without will, that has any right to obedience; the members owing no obedience but to the *public will* of the society.[3]

Thus both Locke and Rousseau seem to follow Segovia in attempting to apply the private-law notion of representation to the relation

[1] Cf. Pufendorf's notion of the state as a 'moral person': Gierke, *Natural law*, 118 f. It seems most unlikely that Segovia owed anything to Ockham, as Dempf suggests: A. Dempf. *Sacrum imperium*, 554–5. But perhaps Panormitanus did, for example in the view that the church's infallibility may be maintained by a single faithful Christian. Cf. G. de Lagarde, *La naissance de l'esprit laïque*, v, 333.
[2] J-J. Rousseau, *Contrat social*, III, 14. (My italics.)
[3] J. Locke, *Second treatise on civil government*, ch. 13. (My italics.)

between government and people; the former is the trustee, the latter are the (adult and responsible) trustors.[1]

The whole notion of government and association in both Locke and Rousseau seems to owe more than has been acknowledged to the credo of the *universitas*, a phenomenon which may help to explain the recurrence in European thought of such notions as the will of society and such ideals as direct democracy.

THE CONCEPT OF TRUST

Segovia proceeded to broaden the notion of power as dependent on trust. What we have seen so far is that the ruler's legal status depends on the actual trust placed in him by the people: 'through this legal fiction, the belief is given [*creditur*] to his commands and judgements, that they are for the common good'. Elsewhere, he develops this notion of government as a legal fiction, by saying that both law and political power (*dignitas principatus*) are 'things of reason', as opposed to 'actual things' (such as natural or supernatural power), and are the creation of human will.[2] This is consonant with his view that tenure of political power depends upon what people actually think.

Segovia's notion of trust is closely related to that of theological belief. People believe the authors of the gospels, not because they can check up on all they say, so much as because, insofar as they can check up, they are found to be true. This seems to be his basis for ecclesiastical authority in general; people extend their belief from statements that can be proved to statements which cannot, on the grounds that these statements come from a person who has previously been found to be reliable.[3] A similar reliance, he goes on, was placed on certain philosophers.

[1] Cf. E. Barker in his ed. of Gierke, *Natural law*, addition to Gierke's notes on p. 299: 'In public law (Staatsrecht), to which Locke may be said to transfer the doctrine of trust, the People or "Public" (which is both trustor and cestui que trust) acts in its capacity of trustor by way of conferring a "fiduciary power" on the legislature (which thus becomes a trustee), for the benefit of itself, and all its members, in its other capacity of *cestui que trust* or beneficiary of the trust.' Cf. *id. ibid.* 348.

[2] *Ampl. disp.*, MCG, III, 853–5: below, pp. 154 f.

[3] *Ibid.* 843–6: below, p. 152; cf. *ibid.* 838. For an explicit analogy between theological and political trust, see below, p. 31 n. It was commonly said that faith was the constituent element of the church; in the Cracow University memorandum (1442) faith is called the 'mystical form' of the mystical body: Du Boulay, *Historia*, v, 483.

The more it is believed (*creditur*) that someone cannot err from the truth, the greater is his authority, that is, the more reverence is shown to his statements.[1]

Such trust, then, means the reasonable and willing assent given by one person to the judgments of another, because they trust the person rather than because they can check up on everything he says.

Segovia sees a close resemblance between trust in this sense, and the relation between people and ruler; he considers trust to form the basis not only of political power, but of the social bond itself. Authority, therefore, in all its forms, depends upon something like the modern notion of 'credibility'; and this in turn, as a matter both of fact and of right, depends upon the actual performance of the claimant. This alone enables others to have confidence in him, even when they cannot know for themselves. This was a new interpretation of the very force which creates society and political power, as the ability of one man to trust another.

In every polity, so that men may live rightly, virtuously, usefully and peacefully, it is necessary for them to believe (*credere*) firmly even those things which hardly or never can be known for certain.[2]

This, he asserts, is a necessary element in all human relationships. A son respects his father as such, without certain knowledge that he was his father; the law of contracts could not exist without mutual faith (*fides*); and people recognize the authority of officials without having seen their authorizing documents. Only on this basis are stable and continuous social relationships possible.

Thus it was more than well-known that no state could exist without the mutual trust (*credulitas*) of men in each other, in those matters which are not seen. Reason itself dictates that human society should be preserved, since it is by force of reason that nature brings one man towards another . . . and human society is unable to exist, unless mutual trust (*credulitas*) is present.[3]

---

[1] *MCG*, III, 843–5: below, pp. 152 f.
[2] *RTA*, xv, 652: 'In omni politia, ut recte virtuose utiliter ac pacifice homines vivant, necesse illis est firmiter credere etiam illa que vix aut numquam certitudinaliter possunt cognosci.'
[3] *Ibid.*: 'Itaque plus quam notorie constabat nullam politiam posse consistere absque hominum invicem in hiis, que non videntur, credulitate; evidentia dictante rationis, cui resisti nequit, ad hoc, ut societas hominum conjunctioque servetur, cum vi

When we turn to political relationships, we find that this notion worked in two directions. On the one hand, Segovia used it as an argument for the necessity of authority and obedience, in the church as well as in secular society. In arguing against those who adopted neutrality in the dispute between pope and council, he said:

It is well-known to all who know the elements of moral or political philosophy, that, to achieve orderly government in any group of men, some supreme authority or power has to be designated; by means of which simple men, who are more numerous than wise, must regulate their actions according to written or verbal laws... This is necessary in any city or kingdom. Just as presidency is necessary for the proper government of a group of men, so too subordination to that supreme power is necessary on the part of subjects.[1]

Again he defended the superiority of the council as legislature over the pope as executive in the following terms:

subjects are bound to trust (*credere*) the judgment [*sc.* of a superior authority] rather than their own, and in a sense to enslave their minds into obedience to the superior... In every civil or criminal adjudication... inferiors are bound to assent to, and conform their actions to, the declaration [*sc.* of a superior authority], and to carry out its commands.[2]

On the other hand, as we have already seen, this view made all authority and obedience dependent upon the relation of mutual trust between people and ruler, in the church as in secular society. In following Aristotle's description of the origin of kingship, Segovia says that the first king was like a philosopher, a man whose proved excellence made people trust him:

rationis natura hominem homini conciliet... societate humana alias sistere nequeunte nisi invicem credulitas assit.'

[1] *RTA*, xiv, 375: 'Est namque notorium scientibus principia philosophie moralis seu politice, quod pro regimine ordinato alicuius multitudinis hominum est necessario assignanda aliqua suprema auctoritas vel potestas, per quam legibus scriptis aut verbo datis simplices homines, quorum maior est multitudo quam sapientum, debeant suas actiones et opera regulare... Simili modo videmus esse necesse in quacumque civitate vel regno. Et quemadmodum ad debitum regimen multitudinis hominum necessaria est presidentia, ita etiam ex parte subditorum necessaria est subjectio ad illam potestatem supremam.'

[2] *Dec. advis.* fo. 216r: 'subditi teneantur illius potius quam suo proprio credere iudicio, ac in superioris obsequium suos quodammodo captivare intellectus. Exponitur sic in omni iudicio civili aut criminali... inferiores tenentur assentire et iuxta illorum diffinitionem conformare actiones suas et exequi illorum mandata.'

Just as they believed the statements of philosophers, because they understood that what they said conformed to reason, so too they believed the commands of kings, having experienced the wisdom of their rule.[1]

Public 'credit' is placed in the ruler, who is 'presumed' to be working for the public good; but this presumption depends not (as in Roman law) on his office, but on his actual 'credibility', on the degree to which the subjects are prepared to trust him. This in turn depends on his actual performance.

Rule, then, is legitimate so long as it can command respect (*veneratio, reverentia*); and it can do so just so long as it is oriented towards the public good. Rule by mere force, which (as in the case of the Roman Empire and its epigones) demands allegiance to the ruler's will or office as such, is illegitimate; and Segovia expresses approval of those who reject it:

royal power came to many not by wisdom but by force...This was another meaning of the term, when the name of authority was attributed to their commands, so that they should be believed and obeyed as if they were true and just, prior to rational agreement. The view gained force that 'whatever pleased the prince had the force of law', and so, reason set aside, the determination of the prince's will, reduced to writing, was held as law; it gained force not, as with previous laws, by evidence of reason, but by the power of the founder. But no violence is permanent, and this view lost acceptance as it had gained it: whoever did not recognize their dominion refused to use princes' laws. So there is a most clear difference between that authority which depends on the teaching of reason, and that which depends on the command (*imperium*) of prince or governor; the former demands the subjects' respect (*venerantiam*), the latter does not.[2]

Similarly, he distinguished between political and servile authority as depending on reason and will respectively.[3]

Segovia, working within the school of Baslean Conciliarism, was also giving the (mainly Thomist) appeal for reason as the criterion of good government a certain constitutional reality. He assumed (as did Marsigilio) that the sovereign decision of the whole people will

---

[1] *MCG*, III, 844: Cf. below, pp. 152 f. Aristotle, *Politics*, III, x, 1286b.
[2] *Ibid.*: below, p. 153. The phrase 'quicumque non recognoscebant eorum dominium' suggests an approving reference to the independence of city-states from the empire, though this speech was originally made at a Reichstag! Cf. above, p. 11, n. 4.　　　　　　　　　　　　　　　　　　[3] See below, p. 38.

express their spontaneous recognition of what is in fact in their own interest. Rationality plays an even more prominent part in his discussion of aristocratic monarchy, in which (as we shall see later) the emphasis shifted from popular sovereignty to consultation with wise and virtuous counsellors, as the best way of obtaining the trust and obedience of subjects. His view of authority, in church and state, as dependent upon the reasonable trust of the whole people, was a challenge to the whole notion of unconditional sovereignty implicit in the Roman concept of government as command (*imperium*), and of the ruler's official status as inviolable. This involved both a new distribution of constitutional power, and a new attitude towards authority as such, whoever wielded it.

The Roman-law notions of the prince as above the laws, of the prince's will as valid law, of the obligation to accept the 'mere word' of the prince on the 'presumption' that he is right, are all dismissed as arbitrary, tyrannical, and therefore illegitimate. His solution is, in the first place, a constitutional one; it is 'through the said decree (on conciliar supremacy)' that the church 'has been liberated'.[1] The ideal of the ruler as servant of the common good is given teeth because the ruler is subjected to the legal expression of the will of the common people. But the very location of sovereignty with the whole society, or even merely with the whole assembly, implied a new relationship between those who command and those who obey. In the former case, the people as a whole are themselves both sovereign and subject; in the latter case, the degree of consultation and consent is considerably widened. This new relationship was perfectly expressed in Segovia's notion of rational trust, which could be made to fit both cases. The very word 'sovereign (*princeps*)' tends to disappear from Segovia's writings, and to be replaced with the term 'president', implying the chairman of a committee.[2]

Segovia's political notions led to the same conclusion, on the question of final jurisdictional power, as the legal arguments of Zabarella and Panormitanus. But he also introduced an emphasis not

---

[1] *MCG*, III, 283; cf. *ibid*. 282.

[2] In *MCG*, III, 723 he deliberately destroys the analogy between divine and princely omnipotence: 'It is only God, on whom all things depend, who is set above all *absolutè*.' The notion of government as trust was of course to be elaborated by many political thinkers; the analogy with private law does not here seem as strong in Segovia as, for example, in Locke.

to be found in the writings of the canonists. Segovia shows a profound interest in the state of mind of subjects and rulers; but this does not lead him away from reform of the external working of government, for in him moral and constitutional reform do not part company. If, on the other hand, we compare Segovia's trust with Cusa's concord and consent, we find that the former retains Cusa's emphasis on the need for mutual harmony between rulers and ruled, but goes beyond Cusa in backing it with constitutional sanctions. It was in Segovia that Baslean Conciliarism found at once its most typical and its most effective spokesman.

THE COUNCIL AS SOVEREIGN AND THE POPE AS MINISTER

We must now turn to the actual constitutional programme of the Council of Basle. Once we accept that the council is the *universitas*, the application of the *universitas*-model to the council and its relationship with the pope follows a logical pattern.

First, the council is self-substantiating, autonomous; it exists on its own authority.[1] Its assembly and validity depend, not on the pope, but on constitutional rules formulated by the council itself. This meant primarily the decree *Frequens*;[2] but Basle also decreed that the council could not be dissolved except by itself, and that the assembly of the next council must be determined before dissolution. It was claimed to be 'a truth of both divine and human law, that the council could not be dissolved without its own consent'.[3] Panormitanus compared this procedure with the 'legitimate assembly' of a city.[4] While sitting, the council regulated its own procedure and

---

[1] Its authority is *ordinaria*, not *delegata*: Escobar, *Gub. conc.* 303; Segovia, *Ampl. disp.*, *MCG*, III, 803: below, p. 151. Again, Segovia says: 'Christ stands among those assembled in *his* name, not in the name of the emperor or any other secular authority, of the pope or any primate in the church': *RTA*, XVII, 157. The point was most clearly established in the May 1439 debate, by Aleman in particular: below, pp. 35 f.

[2] This decreed the intervals at which the council must meet: above, p. 2, n. 2.

[3] Mansi, XXIX, 57D. Cf. the 'decree of the stability of the council': *CB*, VI, 551; Cf. *ibid.* 544; Mansi, XXX, 1234; *MCG*, II, 251; *MCG*, III, 536. Escobar discusses the opinion of 'many moderns' that 'the convocation of a council belongs and should be performed by general councils, in such a way that one council convokes another, and that another, and so on continuously': *Gub. conc.* 273.

[4] Above, p. 17, n. 2; cf. *RTA*, XVI, 472, where he cites Bartolus on this point.

agenda, and regulated the function of the pope within the council.[1] This notion of constitutional rules for assembly, dissolution, and conduct of business, made for itself by the council, was both a reflection of corporation practice, and an anticipation of parliamentary claims; here as elsewhere, Conciliarism seems to provide a stepping stone from the one to the other.

In its rules for the composition and procedure of the council, Basle departed radically from previous conciliar tradition, and reflected clearly the influence of the corporation. Members were 'incorporated' into the council by oath: though this involved the quasi-oligarchic practice of co-option, it also meant that, once sworn in, all members of the council became equal, since their legal status stemmed from their incorporation into the council, not from their prior rank. This was a revolutionary procedure which, though criticized by prelates and princes, was but a new application of corporation and civic principles. A parliamentary claim was again anticipated by making conciliar members exempt from external jurisdiction.[2]

If all members are equal in status, differences can only be resolved by counting heads: the majority principle lay at the core of Baslean thought. It was the practical application of the communal ethos of corporation and city; to act as an *universitas* meant to act as a whole. Panormitanus defended this precisely on the grounds that 'ordinary jurisdiction lies not in individuals *but with the community itself*',[3] and that the *universitas* '*by common right* received *in common* its power'.[4] Other Basleans defended the majority principle as a 'most evident' and a 'most familiar' legal norm.[5] Cardinal Louis Aleman, the active leader of the Council during the schism, who, having lost his post at the Curia to one of Eugenius's relations in 1431, focused the senti-

---

[1] Aleman says: 'The universal church assembled at Basle has made certain rules for conducting a general council': *CB*, VI, 452. Cf. *CBC*, 174; and *MCG*, III, 489, where the Council established 'rules and regulations for the conduct of the papal office in the council' (1440). [2] *MCG*, III, 477, Cf. Ourliac, 'La sociologie', 11, 13, 17.

[3] *Comm.* (Lyons, 1534) III, part 2, fo. 84v, on 2.27.26. (Panorm.)

[4] *Ibid.*; see also *Comm.* (Venice, 1571) I, fo. 170r on 1.35.1: 'regularly in the affairs of a *universitas* the opinion of the most prevails'; and *ibid.* I, fo. 160v on 1.6.19. See also his defence of the majority decree of May 1437 in *RTA*, XVI, 439 ff., 456, 473, 483 and *passim* (cf. below, p. 114); and Segovia, *Ampl. disp.* 726, where he refers to 'actiones communes...*simul invicem ab omnibus aliquando procedentes*'. Cf. above, p. 23. [5] *RTA*, XVI, 438.

ments of the educated of low status who dominated the Council after 1437—he was beatified in 1517—refused to allow himself or anyone else to represent the Council in virtue of rank or influence. He appealed rather to the sovereignty of the council as a whole:

the whole council [he said] was the spokesman (*procurator*) of the faith... it was the method of councils that everything should be decided, not in the name of prelates or doctors, but in the name of the council.[1]

In answer to an invitation to negotiate with Eugenius, he replied that 'the matter concerned not himself, but the whole council, and it would have to be seen to in the deputations'.[2] It was in defence of this principle, too, that the analogy with the city-state was most often invoked. Segovia (using for the 'greater part' an argument used by Zabarella for the 'stronger part') declared that majority decisions must be final in communities without a superior, and that they drew their validity, not from the individuals present, but from the application of an impersonal legal rule. He appeals for precedent both to the exempt cathedral chapters, and to 'many imperial cities, from whose judgments there is no recourse to the Emperor', and concludes that,

the most appropriate example is in *the great communities* of Italy.[3]

Panormitanus frequently refers to Bartolus and the city-states in his defence of majority rule.[4] Conciliar sovereignty at Basle always meant the sovereignty of the majority within the council.

But the majority principle did not altogether exhaust the meaning of communal government for Basle, and in particular for Segovia. It was because its decisions were taken by a particular social and spiritual process of communal discussion, as well as because they followed the legal formula of majority rule, that the council could claim supremacy. It was the fact of common discussion, as well as

---

[1] *MCG*, III, 276; cf. *id. ibid.* 65. On Aleman, see G. Pérouse, *Le Cardinal Aleman, Président du Concile de Bâle, et la fin du Grand Schisme*; C. F. Savio, *Il Cardinale d'Arles, beato Ludovico Alemandi (1382–1450)*.

[2] *RTA*, xvii, 13.

[3] *RTA*, xv, 699; see also his discussion of equality and democracy in Aristotelian terms, *Auct. ep.* fo. 173r-v. On the civic milieu in relation to equality and 'fraternization', cf. M. Weber, *The city*, trans. Martindale and Neuwirth, esp. 107 ff. On Zabarella, cf. Ullmann, *Great Schism*, 214; Tierney, *Conciliar theory*, 229.

[4] *RTA*, xvi, 439 ff., esp. 456.

the formula of majority rule, that stamped conciliar decisions as authentic 'judgments of the church', in the view of Segovia. In a passage which might be seen to anticipate Rousseau's distinction between 'the general will' and 'the will of all', Segovia says:

if all members of the city as individuals, or their greater part, perform some action, the city is not deemed to perform it... unless it is preceded by common discussion or common consent, tacit or explicit, because the actions of the community and those of individuals are not the same.[1]

He supports this with the argument (taken from Aristotle), that in an assembly the wisdom of each participant is increased by mutual contact, that 'by common concourse each one's virtue is increased'; 'the nature of the assembly [*sc.* the fact of coming together] increases the virtue [*sc.* also strength] of any community'.[2]

Thus, by 'conciliar enactment (*synodale iudicium*)', Segovia, and often Basle as a whole, meant both a formal legal process, and an actual social and spiritual event. The council's decisions were inspired by the Holy Spirit because they were taken in the spirit of community; they were identified by means of the legal majority rule. The council's judgment is considered to be at once a scholarly conclusion arrived at by those skilled 'in the knowledge of the faith', and a legal enactment by a sovereign body. 'Conciliar justice' embodies both a legal and a moral claim.[3] Basle, and especially Segovia, was in line with Aristotle and much late medieval political dissent, in that they sought to relate the tenure of power to moral qualities (*virtus*).[4] They developed the conventional notion of the moral

---

[1] 'Etenim, si omnes et singuli de civitate vel maior pars aliquid agant, non ideo censetur civitas agere vel illa actio civitati imputatur, nisi antecedat commune consilium aut communis consensus tacitus vel expressus propterea quod, aliae sunt actiones universitatis et aliae singulorum': *Ampl. disp. MCG*, III, 736. Cf. above, p. 13, n. 1.

[2] *Ampl. disp.*, *MCG*, III, 711, 713, 806. Cf. Aristotle, *Politics*, III, vi, 1281b; and x, 1286a.

[3] See for example, *MCG*, III, 326; *RTA*, xv, 682; xvI, 118, 122; xvII, 85, 351. One writer says that the Holy Spirit 'presides' at the Council, and adds that in cases of unanimity, 'we know that the Holy Spirit dictates the decision' (Prior of Dijon, ed. G. Kallen in *Sitzungsber. d. Heidelb. Akad. d. Wiss., phil-hist. Kl.* 1935-6, 24, 102).

[4] For example, 'on the throne of the militant church there sit just men to judge the great with the small according to their merits': Basle's *Warning* of 1436, Mansi suppl. IV, 1292. Cf. *RTA*, xv, 183, 319; xvI, 524 (Panorm.). We may note the dual meaning of the term *virtus*, frequently also coupled with 'power' by Segovia.

obligation of the ruler into a legal obligation; but it was no individual but the community as a thinking subject, that was to be set up as moral, and also legal, judge. This culminated in the familiar conciliarist claim that in the council 'the principal agent, Christ, works through himself and immediately'.[1]

The common spirit of government was also expressed by emphasizing the ruler's duty towards the common good, or, as Panormitanus called it for the church, 'the political spiritual good'.[2] This was stressed in the summonses appealing for attendance at the beginning of the Council, on the grounds that its business 'concerned all', and that 'the universal good should be provided for by universal attendance'.[3] Segovia restated the distinction (made by Aristotle and Aquinas) between government 'directed to the common end' and government 'directed to a private end' as differentiating monarchy from tyranny, and political from servile authority.[4] But he also felt his way towards converting this abstract distinction into a constitutional reality for, if the good of the community is the supreme aim and the sole justification of government, then government is a matter of serving the community. Christ had said that, 'he who wishes to be great in [His] people should be the minister and servant of all'; this, said Segovia, was meant to indicate both the *raison d'être* and the actual pattern of church government, its *forma regiminis*.[5] This could also be expressed by saying that the pope was a 'part' of the whole body of Christians, and so must act as 'one of them'.[6] Segovia's classic phrase for the position of the pope was that he was the 'first minister (*primus minister*)' of the church.[7]

[1] Cracow University (1442) in Du Boulay, *Historia*, v, 490.
[2] *Comm.* VI, fo. 55r on 3.5.30.
[3] Mansi, xxx, 62D, 67D; Mansi Suppl. IV, 286B.
[4] *Ampl. disp.*, MCG, III, p. 707, 722 (where he says, 'the servant exists for the sake of the lord...whereas political rule exists for the sake of the ruled, so that their president should govern them not by will but by reason'), 878.
[5] *Ibid.* 709–10, 724. He brings together Aristotle and the New Testament, when he says, 'if every right state should be directed towards the common good, and the rule of the pope was established by Christ not for his own but for others' sake... (The pope) should follow Him whose vicar he is: and He came not to be ministered to but to minister' (*ibid.* 709 f.).
[6] *Ibid.* 722–3; *Dec. advis.* fo. 225r, where he says, 'the ecclesiastical president should rule not like a lord, but as if made one body and one soul with the people themselves'.
[7] *Ampl. disp.* 733, 802, 850, 879.

This idea of the ruler as the community's servant found full constitutional realization through the use of corporation theory as a model for the relation between council and pope. Just as the council was seen as a legally self-subsistent *universitas*, so the pope was seen as the elected and accountable *rector*. The view that the *rector* was subordinate to the *universitas*, and could be sanctioned by it for disregarding its interests, was derived from notions of government that had been developed in the context of the corporation. Basle was here drawing the full implications from Zabarella's statement that power lay 'fundamentally in the *universitas*, and in the pope as chief minister', which had itself been but a direct application to the whole church of the constitutional relations within ecclesiastical corporations, as interpreted by some canonists.[1] But Zabarella, when he said this, had been concerned only to establish the superiority of the council over the pope in certain exceptional cases, particularly in the crises of schism and heresy. Basle, on the other hand, was using his doctrine as a basis for saying that the relation between the pope and the church–council was, *in every respect*, like that between *rector* and *universitas*. This meant a radical development of that relation, far beyond anything dreamed of at Constance; it brought about the constitutional realization of the doctrine that the whole community-in-assembly was sovereign.

Above all, this view transformed the relation between council and pope from one of ordinary judicial superiority to one of general governmental sovereignty. It was not only that, as claimed by earlier canonists and by the Conciliarists of Constance, an erring pope was subject to conciliar jurisdiction like any other individual Christian. It was the papal office itself which was made subordinate, in its public role, to the council: here they turned to the canonists' notion of a diocesan *administrator*, and to the civilians' notion of a civic *rector*,[2] whose function it was to ensure the implementation of decrees made in assembly, and whose performance was liable to review at each meeting of the assembly. In fact, such an office existed only because it was impractical for the assembly to meet continuously:

---

[1] Cf. Ullmann, *Great Schism*, 211 f.; Tierney, *Conciliar theory*, 225 f.; Rashdall, *Universities*, I, 404 ff.

[2] Cf. Tierney, *Conciliar theory*, 117 ff.; Ullmann, 'De Bartoli sententia', 718 f.

The council when assembled can undertake any action like the pope. But, when it is not assembled, the pope with the cardinals takes the place of the council, so as to *execute* what the council has decided, and to avoid what it has forbidden.[1]

Segovia frequently styled the pope as 'the chief *executor* of the decrees'.[2] The pope is conceived as performing a task defined for him, a limited commission.[3] This was partly forced on the Council of Basle by the situation in which it found itself; it wanted full papal co-operation in the implementation of its reform decrees. But it seems to have been primarily the *universitas-rector* model of government which inspired the Basleans' thinking and rationalized their practice. Their views represent a 'reading-off' of the respective power of council and pope according to the original model of the small corporation. The pope acquires the status normally assigned to the executive official of a sovereign body: he is the church's 'vicar', 'first minister', 'chief servant', 'political and ministerial head'.[4] The judicial superiority of the council had left the way open for its precedence in every aspect of government.

This new conception of the pope's role came out most clearly in some of the justifications offered for the deposition of Eugenius IV (June 1439). He was deposed for the political crime of bad government, as well as for the ecclesiastical crime of heresy. Here, yet again, Basle tended, partly through lack of ecclesiastical precedents, to elevate secular precedents to the level of a general principle. Some, for instance, defended the deposition on analogy with the barons' power in a feudal monarchy:

Just as kings who administrate badly or exercise tyranny are sometimes excluded and ejected by the whole kingdom, so too there is no doubt that popes can be deposed by the church, that is by general councils...If we see a king despise the laws, steal his subjects' property...and subject all to his lust...surely the nobles of the realm would assemble, remove him,

---

[1] 'Concilium congregatum *potest in omnen actionem* sicut papa; sed non congregato concilio papa cum cardinalibus *tenet locum* concilii; ut que constituit concilium *exequantur*, que inhibuit caveantur': *RTA*, xvii, 351; Cf. Du Boulay, *Historia*, v, 492.

[2] *Ampl. disp.* 879; *Auct. ep.* fo. 179r.

[3] Cf. Cusa, *Conc. cath.* ii, 9, 13; iii, 6.

[4] *CBC*, 72 (*vicarius*); above, p. 38 (*primus minister*); Du Boulay, *Historia*, v, 460 (*capitalis servus*); Escobar, *Gub. conc.* 305 (*caput politicum, civile et ministeriale*); Segovia, *Ampl. disp.* 704, 724, 805.

and another would be set up, who would swear to govern well and obey the laws? Well then, what reason suggests, practice teaches.[1]

Panormitanus appealed to the supposed constitution of the Venetian city-state:

> If the duke errs, he is resisted by the city and if need be deposed.[2]

The possibility of deposition was implicit in the notion of the pope as 'vicar of the church'; the *rector*, being subject to the assembly's jurisdiction, could in the last resort be dismissed. Public crimes of a general nature were mentioned among the reasons for Eugenius's deposition: perjury, breaking the laws, alienation of public property, rebellion, tyranny, arbitrary government, 'useless' administration.[3] Once again, what Marsigilio had already said of the small state, Conciliarism applied to a larger community; the notorious weakness of 'medieval' constitutionalism, namely the lack of sanctions enforceable by a legal process without recourse to arms, seems to have been overcome.

The function of the pope, as *rector*, thus came increasingly to be confined to the execution of conciliar decrees. Here, Basle could appeal, from the canonist tradition that placed the pope above positive law,[4] with the power to dispense and amend positive laws, to the current secular tradition, derived from the Germanic past and feudal practice, and sanctioned by Aristotle, that the ruler is bound to observe the laws, which issue from the community and may only be altered with its consent.[5] This doctrine of the sovereignty of the laws was applied by Cusa to the church, and then stated as a general political norm.[6] The secular analogy was boldly stated at Basle in the debate of May 1439, with an explanation (derived from Cicero) that laws were introduced with the specific purpose of restraining the arbitrary government of kings.[7] But, while the in-

---

[1] *CBC*, 32–4. Cf. above, p. 12.

[2] *RTA*, xvi, 521.

[3] Mansi, xxix, 180; also in *MCG*, iii, 325–7. Cf. *Monitorium* (1436), Mansi, xxx, 1047D.　　　　　　　　　　　　　　[4] Cf. Tierney, *Conciliar theory*, 48 ff.

[5] Cf. F. Kern, *Kingship and law in the Middle Ages*, 73–4, 181–7; Aristotle, *Politics*, iii, vi, 1282b; x, 1286a; xi, 1287a.

[6] *Conc. cath.* iii, Preface and c. 12; see also *Monitorium* (1436), Mansi, xxx, 1047A; and Prior of Dijon, *Sitzungsber.* 97.

[7] *CBC*, 28–34. Cf. Cicero, *De officiis*, ii, 12.

violability of laws was often associated with a general notion of their originating from the sovereign community, Basle went much further than most secular thinkers had done, in extending the ruler's subjection to laws to his subjection to the assembly as a source of law.

It was, again, on the basis of corporation concepts that the Council of Basle was able to justify the validity of conciliar legislation without papal consent. Although, from the start, it had legislated on its own initiative, its supporters, when speaking in traditional terms, showed themselves wary of excluding the pope from valid legislation, which (as in the case of 'the king-in-parliament') was looked upon as an act of the whole community, the power of the pope co-operating with that of others; so that all that could be said was that the decrees of the pope with the council were of greater authority than those of the pope acting alone.[1] It was the notion of the church as a self-determining legal person, capable of acting on its own behalf, that enabled Basleans to justify unilateral legislative and executive acts by the council as normal practice. Panormitanus (1442) seems to have been echoing Bartolus when he made the claim that:

those incorporated in the council...all together as comprising the council and representing the universal church, have the power of the church, and *can make statutes and precepts, and exercise all the jurisdiction* of the church.[2]

Similarly, in 1444, he said that 'the assembled council can *undertake any action* just like the pope'.[3]

The result of all this was a considerable step in the direction of constitutional government in the modern sense. A number of conciliar decrees were in effect constitutional rules: the pope is 'bound' to follow 'a certain formality' in the convocation and dissolution of councils, which must be assembled at stipulated times,

---

[1] Cusa, *Conc. cath.* II, 13; Panorm., *Comm.* VII, fo. 242r on 5.40.27; see also his early *Quaestio* I in *Consilia*, fo. 199r, dub. 2, n. 20; Segovia, *Ampl. disp.* 711, 714; Denis Rickel in *Opera omnia*, XXXVI, 626 (citing D'Ailly on mixed government).

[2] '*Possunt facere statuta* et precepta et *omnem iurisdictionem* ecclesiae exercere': *RTA*, XVI, 504. Cf. Bartolus: 'Quando populus habet *omnem iurisdictionem, potest facere statutum*': cited in Ullmann, 'De Bartoli sententia', 713. On the basis of strict canonist corporation theory, Panorm. could say this only when the rector was 'dead or disabled': *Comm.* II, fo. 190v on 1.38.15.   [3] Above, pp. 34 f.

'according to a definite legal method'.[1] He must accept the council's reform of his financial system and the restoration of election as the normal system of appointment to ecclesiastical offices; he must consult the cardinals on stipulated matters, and abide by the specific guarantees he has made in his electoral pact.[2] The council, as we have seen, is to function regularly as the supreme court, the legislature, and the supervisor of the pope's administration. The provision for the regularity of councils was perhaps the most significant point in the Conciliarist programme; and it was applied to provincial and diocesan synods as well as to the general council.[3]

Finally, we find, as in Marsigilio, the beginnings of a distinction between the notions of legislature and executive, corresponding to the actual constitutional pattern being implemented by the Council. This distinction may owe something to that, made by canonists when writing on the respective temporal power of pope and emperor, between power 'in tenure' and 'in execution'.[4] Cusa (1433) distinguished a divinely-bestowed power of 'jurisdiction' (in which all bishops, and perhaps priests too, were equal), and a man-made power of 'administration' or 'execution' (in which there was a hierarchy with the pope at the top).[5] This seems to correspond broadly to the familiar Baslean differentiation between the powers of the community itself, represented in the council, and of individuals within it, governed by the hierarchy. This emerged more clearly in a statement made by Heinrich Campo (who had been Cusa's teacher) in 1440:

The keys of the church are twofold; priestly, which the council uses in the judgment of distinction and definition; and ruling (*regales*) or pastoral, which each hierarch of the church uses.[6]

Similarly, Segovia (1439) related this distinction to the different aspects of the church as a mystical and as a political body, as well as pointing out that, according to Aristotle, legislation confers greater authority than execution:

[1] *MCG*, II, 251; and Paradyz, cited in Fijalek, *Mistrz Jacob za Paradyza*, I, 374 ('secundum *certum* modum et *legitimum*'). Cf. above, p. 17.
[2] Above, p. 3, n. 2.
[3] *MCG*, III, 306 ff.; *RTA*, XIV, 186 ff., esp. 193 ('temporibus *statutis*...concilia provincialia et synodalia frequentabuntur').
[4] Cf. Wilks, *Sovereignty*, 306, 537.   [5] *Conc. cath.* II, 13.   [6] *RTA*, XV, 469.

on the point that there is more authority *in defining than in executing,* much in favour of the general council can be gathered from the book of Politics...Through the councils...decrees are universally *laid down*... the pope is the first minister of the church...Therefore he is bound above all others to *obey and execute* the decrees of general councils.[1]

The ascription of sovereignty to the council, which could only operate from time to time, virtually necessitated some such distinction between the functions of legislation and execution; this had already been drawn explicitly by Marsigilio in the civic context, and was to some extent implicit in the rules commonly assigned, at least by those in the populist tradition, to *universitas* and *rector.* But in this, as in other things, Basle seems to have been the first to have applied the model of the *universitas* to government on a large scale; and in doing so, it drew implications which could have pointed the way for constitutionalism in the national or territorial state.

THE ROAD TO CONSTITUTIONAL MONARCHY

Segovia himself undertook a discussion of the implications of conciliarist principles of government for the national or territorial monarchical state. He sought to define conciliarism in the light of the aristotelian types of government, particularly aristocracy and monarchy. At first, in 1439, he described the conciliarist position as closest to aristocracy; because, as Aristotle said, 'where there are men strong in temperament and virtue, it is better for a community to be ruled by many wise and virtuous men than by one'.[2] But this did not mean that the papal office was dispensable; for he remarked that Aristotle's types were not supposed to be mutually incompatible, so that there could be a place for a monarch in the church's aristocracy.[3] In 1441, however, though his ideas had changed little in other ways, we find Segovia emphatically denying that the church is an aristocracy, and asserting that it is a monarchy. This, as we shall see at length later, was because the pope's propaganda had been accusing Conciliarism of subverting monarchy in the secular order too, in order to convince kings and princes that Conciliarism was wrong. The change in Segovia's views, then, is verbal rather than

[1] *Dec. advis.* fo. 215v, 231v.
[2] *Dec. advis.* fo. 218v: below, p. 141. Cf. Aristotle, *Politics*, III, x, 1286a–b.
[3] *Ibid.* fo. 219v: below, p. 142.

substantial. He still viewed the church as a mixture of monarchy and aristocracy:

The aristocratic form can by no means be properly attributed to the general council, except in the sense that many virtuous and wise men assemble at it...It is surely one thing to behave in an aristocratic way in governing, and another thing to be an aristocratic state.[1]

In 1450, Segovia re-emphasized the monarchical element in the church, this time partly because his notion of Conciliarism itself was changing. But he still insisted that monarchy and aristocracy both played a part in the church's constitution:

Conciliar guidance does not obstruct but perfects monarchical rule...it is in no way repugnant to the monarchical government of the church, that the pope should heed conciliar decrees and carry out their judgements.[2]

But in 1441 and in 1450, he added the general reservation that the church could not strictly speaking be compared with any aristo-telian types, because it was a unique society, and in it authority meant service. All that could be said was that the church's consti-tution was the opposite of tyranny, and was most similar to mon-archy.[3]

He proceeded, nevertheless, to give his own views on monarchy as such, secular and ecclesiastical; and he applied, in a muted way, his notions of trust and reason. First, he emphasized that, as Aristotle had said, monarchy differs from tyranny in that it seeks the good of the subjects, and accepts the rule of law over the monarch himself:

Looking at the teaching of Aristotle, one readily perceives that to reject laws pertaining to the common good, and to govern according to one's own desire, brings no special glory, rather perhaps no glory at all, to monarchical sovereignty. Where laws are not sovereign, there is no state ...monarchy with complete power can but be tyranny; for rightly-established laws should be the rulers.[4]

Next, he emphasized very strongly the role of consultation with wise and experienced men in monarchy: here he argued both from

[1] *Ampl. disp.*, MCG, III, 707–9: below, pp. 144 f. Cf. below, p. 48, n. 5.
[2] *Auct. ep.* fos 172v–173r: below, p. 157.
[3] *Ampl. disp.* 707: below, p. 144; *Auct. ep.* fos 106r, 174r, 176r: below, pp. 157 ff.
[4] *Ampl. disp.* 709: below, p. 145; *Auct. ep.* fo. 176r: below, p. 159. Cf. above, p. 41.

accepted practice and from the need for rational trust in the ruler.
All rulers, he pointed out, both secular and ecclesiastical, take advice,
and this enhances rather than weakens their standing in the eyes of
their subjects. It would seem to follow that if (as Segovia supposes)
all rule is based on trust in the superior rationality of the ruler,
then the more a ruler consults, and is seen to consult, numerous
and expert counsellors, the greater authority (*de facto* at least) will he
have.

It greatly helps the subjects, both to *perceive* the justice, necessity or expediency of commands, and to obey them, when they can *observe* their
president using the advice of wise men...for no one dares to call unjust
what has issued from the advice of wise men. The greater the number of
them that are in agreement, the greater the *respect* for their decision...
The government that deliberates with wise men is *esteemed* (*reputatur*) just.[1]

Segovia here employs the term 'credit (*creditus*)' to describe the quality contributed by consultation.[2] For the same reason, decrees made
jointly by pope and council have greater 'weight and authority'
than those made by the pope alone.[3] He adds the practical point
that consultation with leading men ensures the speedy execution of
laws (which, like Cusa, he sees as especially important for the
empire):

Those who have greater acquaintance (*notitia*) with the laws are in a better
position to have them carried out.[4]

Every president approaches and pursues a difficult task with greater
confidence that he will accomplish it, when the prominent men of his
realm have given their consent that it should be so.[5]

A king or any monarch is thought to have most sovereignty when his
judgments are executed without any resistance; and this happens when the
subjects are aware that they have proceeded from the advice of wise men.
The greater the number of wise who are known to have taken part, the
greater the respect in which the decisions are held and the ease with which
they are executed.[6]

---

[1] *Ampl. disp.* 711: below, pp. 146 f.; cf. *ibid.* 710: *Auct. ep.* fo. 176v: below, p. 160.

[2] *Auct. ep.* fos 176v, 177r: below, p. 159. The government of some cities was called
the *credenza*.

[3] *Ampl. disp.* 711: below, p. 147; *Auct. ep.* fo. 182r: below, p. 161.

[4] *Dec. advis.* fo. 219r: below, p. 142.   [5] *Ampl. disp.* 711: below, p. 147.

[6] *Auct. ep.* fo. 176v: '...maiori habentur veneratione et facilius executioni demandantur': below, p. 160.

Consistent consultation meant, in effect, regular councils, selected however on the basis of status or merit rather than of popular election. Segovia once again appeals to an alleged general custom:

In every state governed by royal or monarchical rule, this same practice is observed (*observatur*), that general assemblies are frequently held.[1]

This was as far as Segovia's comparison between conciliar doctrine and secular monarchy took him. Perhaps because he wanted to persuade the kings and princes themselves that Basle offered no threat to their own position, there is a marked lack of constitutional firmness in what Segovia had to say about the national kingdom and the territorial state; he is apparently content to rely on what he takes to be existing custom. Quite contrary to what he said of the church and the city-state, he now refrained from making his constitutional views legally enforceable. It is a ghost of his main theory; whatever superiority the laws made by the ruler-in-assembly may have is *de facto* rather than *de iure*, and the community itself becomes a mere purveyor of consent. Again, he observed that, 'as is clear from the teaching of Aristotle, this aristocratic rule could and should reasonably be introduced to correct another rule, when it becomes tyrannous'; and he defended deposition in the church on the grounds that it no more detracted from the papal office than natural death.[2] But he never mentioned sanctions against bad government in the context of secular monarchy itself. Segovia here displayed in full the characteristic weakness of 'feudal' constitutionalism;[3] this is all the more remarkable when one considers that the legal sanction of deposition evolved for church government was just what was lacking in secular constitutional thought and practice. A writer like John Fortescue, for example, who viewed consultation and legality as part of the constitution, i.e. as necessary for certain acts to be valid, could usefully have borrowed this from Conciliarism.[4] The contrast between Segovia's doctrine of ecclesiastical power, derived from the commune, and his views on secular monarchy, is flagrant. But it can probably be explained, partly by the diplomatic situation, partly by the tendency on the part of Conciliarists, and of Segovia

[1] *Ampl. disp.* 894; cf. *ibid.* 803.   [2] *Dec. advis.* fo. 219v: see below, p. 142.
[3] Cf. C. H. McIlwain, *Constitutionalism: ancient and modern*, 90–3.
[4] Cf. S. B. Chrimes, *English constitutional ideas in the fifteenth century*, 304 ff.

himself, to maintain that ecclesiastical and secular government were different in kind; and partly also by the fact that Segovia eventually modified his own views on the council.

The whole emphasis, in Segovia's writing on national and territorial monarchies, lies on the compatibility of Conciliarism with monarchy. He takes the argument onto the offensive, by proclaiming the advantages a monarch will gain by following legality and consultation.

The use of many wise men for advice on difficult matters in no way derogates from, but rather enhances monarchical rule, both in secular and in ecclesiastical government.[1]

The use of wise men for advice is not opposed to royal or monarchical government, nor does it obscure it but glorifies it with great splendour... it in no way derogates from monarchical power, which rather, by holding a general council, receives the greatest splendour, special strength and increase.[2]

This was not far removed from the viewpoint of a moderate papal theorist, such as Pierre de Versailles, who maintained that, though the pope's intrinsic authority remained unchanged, a council could increase his 'authority of repute'.[3] Segovia does, however, come close to saying that a monarch is only a true monarch when he follows these prescriptions; it is the tyrant who rules without law or advice. Similarly, Paris University (1440) defended its adherence to Basle against the king's attempt to bring it into line with his official policy of neutrality, by saying that, if the king suppressed the University's 'liberty of advice'—'it would be a tyranny and not a royal monarchy'.[4] Thus, in certain ways Segovia points towards Jean Bodin: the distinction between tyranny and monarchy, between the actual constitution and the way it is operated,[5] and above

---

[1] *Ampl. disp.* 710: below, p. 146; cf. *ibid.* 711, 713, 718. It is here that he makes most use of (alleged) contemporary experience.

[2] *Auct. ep.* fo. 173r: below, p. 157.

[3] Below, p. 170.

[4] Cited in Valois, *Pape et Concile*, II, 240. Below, p. 107.

[5] Segovia says, 'aliud nempe est secundum aristocraticum se habere in regimine, aliud esse aristocraticum principatum': *Ampl. disp.* 708. Bodin distinguishes the 'form of state' from the 'form of government', so that the monarch may be sovereign but use a popular machinery of government: J. Bodin, *Six books of the commonwealth*, trans. Tooley, II, c. 2, p. 56 and c. 7, p. 75.

all the attempt to combine a monarchical constitution with consultative practice, are all intimated by Segovia. Bodin indeed echoed Segovia's argument that consultation enhances monarchy, when he said that royal sovereignty, though legally complete on its own, is 'most fully manifested...in no way qualified or diminished' by an assembly of the estates: 'his majesty appears more illustrious when formally recognized by his assembled subjects'. He, too, added the argument that the estates' consent, though not necessary, was helpful 'for the purpose of securing obedience'.[1]

Segovia thus contributed something to the process whereby modern 'monarchy' inherited some of the moral obligations of medieval 'mixed monarchy', such as consultation and legality: arbitrary rule denotes not a monarch but a tyrant. Out of this was to develop, in many parts of Europe, a type of 'parliamentary' or 'conciliar' monarchy, in which consultative bodies were used, but remained dependent for their legal existence upon the royal will.[2]

As we have seen, the doctrine applied to the church by Segovia, as by others, was far more stringent, with constitutional norms backed by the sanction of deposition. In both theory and practice, Conciliarism provided a potential arsenal for secular constitutionalism; and some Basleans were quite prepared to relate their ideas to the national kingdom, as well as to the city-state. For example, the Bishop of Burgos asserted the legal sovereignty of the 'whole kingdom' over the king; others derived the council's power to depose the pope from the alleged power of a 'whole kingdom' to depose a bad king.[3] Nicholas of Cusa not only formulated a general theory of power, as stemming from the people through wise legislation, and as responsible to them; he also gave this philosophy its strongest constitutional application in the context of the German Empire, using analogies from church government.[4] For example, he advocated regular councils; he compared the proper function of the emperor or monarch to that of an archbishop who 'can make no decrees without the consent of the other bishops'; the emperor

---

[1] Bodin, *Six books*, I, 8, pp. 31–2; cf. *ibid.* IV, 4, p. 200.

[2] See J. Major, *Disp. de auct. conc.*, in Gerson, *Opera*, II, 1141; and G. W. F. Hegel, *The philosophy of history*, trans. Sibree, 113–14, 317. Cf. F. L. Carsten, *Princes and parliaments in Germany*, 428 ff.

[3] *CBC*, 28 ff.   [4] Cf. P. Sigmund, *Nicholas of Cusa*, esp. 121, 188 ff.

should carry out what the council of the realm has laid down, and in doing so should consult a 'daily council', like the college of cardinals, 'chosen from every part of the realm'.[1] Cusa in fact here displays the opposite tendency to Segovia: he goes further in applying responsible government in the secular than he does in the ecclesiastical sphere; though he spoke of no legal sanction against an erring pope, he suggested that the prince 'should be punished according to the laws' for serious offences.[2]

CONCLUSION

We may see Segovia's tract as evidence that Conciliarism not only resembled, but was to some degree conscious of itself as, constitutional monarchy; and helped to develop ideas and mechanisms to that end. If we have rightly assessed the importance of the *universitas* theory throughout Conciliarism, we may say that, while Zabarella and Panormitanus transferred it from the cathedral chapter and city-state to the universal church, Segovia developed it into a general theory of government. Conciliarism, therefore, facilitated the age-long process whereby the principles of the *universitas* came to be applied to large states.

Above all, it gave wings to the doctrine that the assembly is superior because it represents the whole community *ex officio*, by transferring to the universal church the distinction between the community *ut universitas*, 'taken collectively', and the community *ut singuli*, 'taken dispersedly'. It was in the former sense, as an assembly, that the community was sovereign; in the latter sense, while still consisting of the same actual people, it was subject. The community could play two roles, active or passive, public or private. They took this central idea, the distinction between the society as a whole and its constituent parts, from the legal theory of corporations, and worked it up into a general political theory. Political theory owed this distinction, and much of the doctrine contained in it, to the efforts of Conciliarism. We find Almain, for instance, applying it to the secular kingdom in the course of his defence of Conciliarism (1512).[3] The *Vindiciae contra Tyrannos*, in asserting the

---

[1] *Conc. cath.* III, 12, 32.
[2] *Conc. cath.* III, preface and c. 12.
[3] J. Almain, *De auct. eccl. et conc.*, in Gerson, *Opera*, II, 996C.

estates' broad powers of deposition, drew directly on conciliar precedent:

> Now if, according to the opinion of most of the learned, by decrees of councils and by custom in like occasions, it plainly appears that the council may depose the pope...; who will make any doubt or question, that the general assembly of the Estates of any kingdom, who are the representative body thereof, may not only degrade and disthronize a tyrant, but also even disauthorize and depose a king, whose weakness or folly is hurtful or pernicious to the State.[1]

In Suarez, the idea found general form in terms similar to those of the Basleans:

> A group of men can be considered in two ways: in one way, as a certain aggregate without any order...in another way, insofar as they are assembled by special will or common consent into one political body with one bond of society...In this way, they make up one mystical body, which can be said to be morally one in itself.[2]

Here we may quote one of Gierke's magnificent summaries:

> It is in the ecclesiastical systems of Natural Law, which culminated in the theories of Molina and Suarez, that we find the most vigorous attempts to use the idea of the organic nature of the State in order to vindicate for the social Whole, when once it has been called into existence, a power of control over its parts.[3]

In Basle, as in Marsigilio, the political rationale of the *universitas*, corporation or commune, found vital expression: society is a whole, into which individuals are incorporated, it possesses a single will, which is determined by the majority. The concept of trust as the basis of society and government was also an inherent part of that pattern; and Segovia emerges as the first thinker to formulate it as such. Certainly, he uses it as a way of rationalizing monarchy, as well as making it the philosophical basis for direct popular sovereignty. In its monarchical form, it would turn up again in Thomas Eliot (1531),[4] in Bodin[5] and in Hegel.[6] But the more attention that

---

[1] *Vindiciae contra tyrannos*, by P. de Mornay, 142. For this and further examples of the influence of Conciliarism on secular constitutionalism, see above, p. 8 and n. 2.
[2] Cited in Gierke, *Natural law*, 243.   [3] *Ibid.* 54.
[4] Allen, *Political thought*, 248.   [5] Bodin, *Six books*, I, 8, p. 34.
[6] Hegel's *Philosophy of right*, trans. Knox, 163–4.

was paid to it, the more, it seems, did it betray its origin in the *universitas* environment, as well as in private and corporation law. While such ideas were to find new application in America, and to be developed more fully by Locke and Rousseau, their basic pattern would change little.[1]

[1] See also B. de Jouvenel, *Sovereignty*, esp. 115–16.

Part II

PAPAL MONARCHY

THE RESPONSE TO CONCILIARISM

To say that doctrine and politics were interwoven in the history of the medieval papacy would be a truism. But it is important not to emphasize either to the exclusion of the other; here was an institution which drew its strength from religious beliefs, but which was faced with organizational problems of historic dimensions. Throughout the Middle Ages, the papacy became intertwined with civilization; medieval 'papalism' has long been recognized as having the elements of a political theory; but what this meant in terms of 'the evolution of an idea' has only been fully examined in the works of Ullmann.[1] It is proposed here to continue this study into the fifteenth century, to this aspect of which historians, overwhelmed perhaps by the presence of renaissance and the absence of reformation, have paid relatively little attention.

Whereas late medieval writers on canon law and ecclesiology seemed almost to revel in the repetition of every conceivable text and argument, regardless of the increasing 'confusion' that resulted,[2] the advocates of papal monarchy during the 1430s and 1440s were faced with a new ideological challenge, Baslean Conciliarism. In the first place, they attacked with ruthless logic the central doctrine of communal sovereignty; here as elsewhere John Turrecremata (Torquemada) led the way. A Dominican from Castile (and not to be confused with his infamous nephew of the Spanish Inquisition, Thomas Torquemada), he was energetic both as a writer and as a diplomat. His views were developed in a series of powerful speeches, often before secular audiences; he completed his massive *Summa on the church* in 1449. He may be said to have begun the task, con-

---

[1] W. Ullmann, *The growth of papal government in the Middle Ages; id. Medieval papalism; id., Papst und König* (Munich-Salzburg, 1966), 9–41.

[2] M. J. Wilks, *The problem of sovereignty in the later Middle Ages*; L. Buisson, *Potestas und Caritas*.

tinued by Cajetan in the next century, of rescuing ecclesiology from the canonists; but in so doing he gave Thomism an increasingly authoritarian orientation.[1]

Turrecremata attacked the contention that sovereign jurisdiction belonged to the church 'taken collectively', 'in all its members together', and the analogy with the civic doctrine that power belonged 'to the assembly of the city or its weightier part'.[2] (Indeed, he saw this as an extension of Marsilian views, whereas in fact we have seen that it more probably had a common source in civic and other associations.) He called the argument that the church is superior to the pope because it is 'a certain whole', and the pope but a part, 'their Achilles'.[3] Having first countered this by saying that a king was superior to his whole kingdom,[4] he went on to attack the view that a 'mystical body' constituted a united real entity to such a degree that it was capable of bearing and exercising jurisdiction.

Though there is a certain likeness between the mystical body of the church and the natural body of a man, namely that both have many members... nevertheless there is a manifold difference...the members of a human body constitute a certain substantive whole with a single identity (*unum numero reale totum*), which as a subject in its whole self is capable of receiving a certain form or quality or substantive influx. But what are called the members of a mystical body are not the same...Since they consist of different persons in different places, they are not said to constitute any substantive whole with a single identity, capable as a subject in itself of receiving any form or quality or any influx of substantive effect.[5]

He supported this attack on the 'realist' interpretation of the corporate analogy by adapting Baldus's civil-law maxim, that 'the empire does not have a mind, therefore it cannot will or renounce', into a more general statement, that 'an association does not have a mind'.[6]

---

[1] See esp. S. Léderer, *Der spanische Cardinal Johann von Torquemada*; K. Binder, *Wesen und Eigenschaften der Kirche bei Kardinal J. de Torquemada.*

[2] *SE*, II, c. 24–6, fos 137v–139v; esp. c. 25, fo. 139r; c. 70, fo. 193r, 195r: below, pp. 165, 169 f. Cf. above, pp. 8 ff.   [3] *SE*, II, c. 83, fo. 215r: below, p. 171.

[4] *SE*, II c. 26, fo. 139v.   [5] *SE*, II, c. 71, fo. 195v: below, p. 169.

[6] 'Universitas non habet animam [prob. for *animum*]': *SE*, II, c. 71, fo. 195v; *ibid.* c. 82, fo. 214r; c. 83, fos 215v–216r: below, p. 169; see also Poggio Bracciolini, *De pot. papae et concilii*, argt. 8. Cf. Baldus: 'imperium non habet animum, ergo non habet velle neque nolle, quia animi sunt': cited in Gierke, *Political theories*, 70. Cf. Lagarde, 'Les théories représentatives', 72 f.

This reasserted Innocent IV's theory that the personality of associations is a legal fiction invented by the sovereign, and it did so in such a way as to exclude its being anything else. It struck at the keystone of Baslean Conciliarism, by claiming that it rested on an exaggerated conception of social unity. This amply supports Gierke's contention that the theory of sovereignty began by destroying the traditional notion of corporate association.[1]

Turrecremata went on to argue that the specific character of ecclesiastical jurisdiction, as a gift of divine grace, meant that it could reside only with individual men, not with an imagined group-entity. It is only individuals who can receive the sacrament of ordination, and with it the power of binding and loosing, which is what ecclesiastical jurisdiction means. The whole idea of community sovereignty in the church seemed to be struck down by the simple remark, 'The whole community of the church cannot undertake the exercise of the power of binding and loosing from sins.'[2] Again, speaking of the gifts of teaching and prophecy, Turrecremata declared: 'Every informed person knows that the community itself cannot be a subject capable of receiving such graces.' His opponents commit the verbal error of applying to the whole what belongs to the part.[3] Though he put this forward primarily as an argument about ecclesiastical jurisdiction, Turrecremata elsewhere showed that it coincided with his view of authority in the secular sphere too:

Often the term 'community' is used, when what is meant is its prelate or prince...as Aristotle says in *Ethics* IX: 'The city is what is most sovereign in it'. Hence, what the prelate does, the church is said to do; what is meant is the part of the association which is capable of jurisdiction, not the whole which is not capable of it.[4]

At the same time, Turrecremata attacked with gusto the application of corporation theory to the church as a whole, on the grounds that it was unrealistic. So too did Poggio Bracciolini, the renaissance humanist who was in papal service and employed his wit against the

---

[1] Gierke, *Political theories*, 97–100; cf. Tierney, *Conciliar theory*, 106–8.

[2] *SE*, II, c. 71, fo. 196r: below, p. 169.

[3] 'Nullus enim doctus ignorat quod talium gratiarum subiectum capax esse non potest ipsa communitas': *SE*, II, c. 72, fo. 199v.

[4] '...intelligitur de ea parte universitatis quae iurisdictionis est capax, non de tota quae non est capax': *SE*, II, c. 92, fo. 225r. Cf. below, p. 65, n. 2.

Council. If ecclesiastical jurisdiction belongs to the whole church, it belongs to all individual Christians; but these could never assemble together to exercise their supposed power, and if they did the majority would consist of lay men and women.[1] This again struck at a weak link in conciliar theory, namely its lack of a proper theory of representation.

But Turrecremata and his colleagues did not stop at mere refutation. As was necessary if they were really to surmount the challenge, they gave the political theory of the papacy a new emphasis and direction. Like a lone shoot in autumn foliage, there is one factor which stands out among the mounting recital of old material: the comparison between the church and a state. Since early times, the pope had occasionally been styled 'prince', and more recently he had been titled 'emperor', 'monarch' and 'king'; this had to some extent been inspired by the need to emphasize the superiority of the church over the secular powers, who were often regarded as its 'subjects'.[2] In the mid-fifteenth century, these analogies ceased to operate in isolation, and were built up into a single, coherent and generally applicable doctrine of sovereignty. At the same time, they were trained not so much on the secular powers as on the council; Turrecremata himself has hitherto been famous largely for his *modification* of papal claims over the secular powers.

This new development was due to both internal and external pressures. It was natural that the advocates of papal supremacy, when faced with Basle's claims, should turn to the idea of monarchy in secular institutions. It was a simple solution to the ambiguities of late medieval ecclesiology, and attractive to the renaissance mind. But it also owed its prominence to the need to attract kings and princes themselves (on whose support or indifference the conciliar movement seemed so largely to depend for its political force) back to Eugenius's allegiance: the people, and even the clergy, would mostly follow their royal masters. This was surely why some Eugenians, at the same time as intensifying their own notion of

---

[1] *SE*, II, c. 71, fo. 197r–v; see also *ibid.* c. 92, fo. 223v; Poggio, *De pot. papae*, argt. 35. On Poggio, cf. H. Baron, *The crisis of the early Italian Renaissance*, 54 f.; D. Hay, *The Italian Renaissance*, 158 f.

[2] Cf. Ullmann, *Papal government*, 139, 193 ff., 276, 313 ff.; Kantorowicz, *The king's two bodies*, 193; Wilks, *The problem of sovereignty*, 45 f., 278, 334 f., 377.

sovereignty, presented it as applying no less to the secular 'sovereign', and also modified papal claims in the temporal sphere.

HIERARCHY

The fifteenth-century papal philosophy of power derived its unique character from the tradition of Christian Neoplatonism which viewed the world as a 'hierarchy', or 'holy order of rule'. All beings received both their origin and their continued existence from the One, God. Emphasis was placed, first on the absolute power of God as the source of all being, secondly on the mediation of being and power through a chain from the highest angels to inanimate matter. It was thought that this 'hierarchical' pattern must be ubiquitous in every subordinate sphere of life, including above all nature and human society. The result was that each type of governmental authority was continually being likened to the effluence of creative power from God to creatures, and of sacramental gifts from Christ to the church. Society, secular or ecclesiastical, was a microcosm of the universe; king and pope were the unique sacred channels through whom God bestowed gifts on His, and their, subject peoples. This philosophical outlook, deriving above all from Pseudo-Denis, had for centuries permeated papal thought and Christian theology. During the rebirth of Aristotelianism in the thirteenth century, Albert the Great and Thomas Aquinas had combined it with the new ideas; in the fourteenth and fifteenth centuries, it was elaborated in the mystical theology of such thinkers as Eckhart and Denis Rickel ('the Carthusian'). During the Renaissance, it received new impetus from the interest in Plato and in Byzantine Platonism, which the Council of Florence itself helped to transmit to the West.[1]

The theocentric constitution of the universe was thus, in the fifteenth century more than ever, commandeered to underpin a hierarchical and monarchical conception of society. The principle of hierarchical order was inherent in the cosmos, as perceived through eyes trained in neoplatonism:

[1] Cf. E. Gilson, *A history of Christian philosophy in the Middle Ages*, 81 ff., 431 ff., 528 ff.; W. Ullmann, *Principles of government and politics in the Middle Ages*, 46 f.; A. O. Lovejoy, *The great chain of being*, chs 3–4. On Rickel (1394–1471), who himself wrote on ecclesiology in our period, cf. FM, xiv, 375, Jedin, *Council of Trent*, I, 43.

[God] laid down this as a natural law in everything, that the last should be perfected through the middle, and the middle through the first.[1]

God had created the heavenly macrocosm and the earthly microcosm according to one and the same primordial pattern, so that hierarchical order was a 'natural law' of universal application; the ecclesiastical and secular 'hierarchies' must imitate the cosmic. This omnipresent influence of neoplatonism may be illustrated by a passage from Albert, which was quoted by both Turrecremata and Carvajal:

This unification (*adunatio*) shines in heaven, is demonstrated in nature, is typified in the works of Christ, is commanded in the divine laws, and is maintained in the whole body of Christ.[2]

The universe, nature, the church and secular society; there is a valid analogy possible between each of these.

The effect of this was to supply an inexhaustible reservoir of analogies between cosmos and polity, and between secular and ecclesiastical government. The lawyers' principle of analogy, neatly expressed in the adage 'empire and papacy seem to walk in step',[3] thus attained philosophical status. This trend is perhaps best illustrated in Cusa's *Catholic Concordance* (1433) and Roselli's *Monarchy* (1433), which both—despite their quite divergent standpoints—emphasized the parallelism between the various rungs of the ecclesiastical and secular hierarchies of government.[4]

Both popular and official language reflected this mentality. The very terms generally used to describe secular and ecclesiastical offices, such as '*ordo*', '*gradus*', '*status*', '*honor*', imply hierarchical ranks. Indeed in the popular mind the hierarchical outlook could lead to a

---

[1] Turrecremata, *SE*, II, c. 1, fo. 116r; see *ibid.* fo. 116r–v, for the notion of the earthly imitating the heavenly, explicitly derived from Pseudo-Denis: below, p. 162 f.

[2] *SE*, II, c. 2, fo. 118r; Carvajal in *RTA*, XVII, 144. On Carvajal, cf. L. G. Canedo, 'Juan de Carvajal y el cisma de Basilea', in *Archivo Ibero-americano* (1941), 29 ff., 209 ff., 369 ff.

[3] Monte, cited in Eckermann, *Studien*, 108. The lawyers' saying was, 'divine and public law walk in step'; and Bartolus', 'church and fisc walk in step': cited in Kantorowicz, *The king's two bodies*, 177 n. Cf. Monte to Henry VI, below, p. 101.

[4] See esp. Cusa, *Conc. cath.* I, 6; Roselli, *Monarchia*, in Goldast, *Monarchia*, I, 312. Cf. P. Sigmund, 'Cusanus' Concordantia, a reinterpretation', in *Political Stud.* X (1962), 191–2.

58

certain confusion, sometimes reflected by the theorists, whereby spiritual and jurisdictional values were conflated, and the pope or king was credited with both. In general, under the influence of neoplatonism, there was an ever-increasing tendency for theological notions to take on political meanings, and for political power to escalate into theocracy. In the fifteenth century this was as true of kingship as of the papacy. The jurisdictional initiative of pope or king is described as *'gratia'*, *'favor'*, *'mansuetudo'*, all acts of *condescension*. The corresponding act of the subjects is seen as *'obedientia'*, *'fides'*, *'reverentia'*, *'gratitudo'*. Almost imperceptibly, but with compelling insistence, the hierarchical mentality transmuted spiritual into governmental concepts, and demanded in terms of law a moral acquiescence. Such confusion was encouraged by the ambiguity of terms like *'virtus'* (which Turrecremata, as well as Cusa and Segovia used to denote both legal and moral authority), and by the cosmological analogy in which the two aspects were actually concurrent in God Himself. This intersection also led to the belief that hierarchy and morality were interdependent, together forming 'the bond of society'.[1] It was sometimes supposed that men became virtuous by accepting their hierarchical rung; that 'royal virtues', like the papal 'holiness', inhered in the office; and that moral decline was the direct result of attempts to modify the ecclesiastical or political structure.[2] Besides, without hierarchical order, 'political discipline' would itself be lost.[3]

The effect of this outlook on formal political theory was ensured by the papal writers under Eugenius IV, among whom Turrecremata was but an extreme example in his consistent recourse to the neoplatonic world-view. His debt to Aristotle and Aquinas seems almost reduced to the selection of convenient quotations. Aquinas's distinction between nature and grace was, at least in the sphere of government, subsumed by Turrecremata into the hierarchical pattern, in which they were simply twin examples of the same universal principle. There is nothing human or empirical about his references to 'nature', which was simply a divinely-ordained unit,

---

[1] Pierre de Versailles in Martène-Durand, *Thes. nov. anecd.* I, 1736; Monte in Vat. lat. 4145, fo. 51v. On Versailles, cf. A. Coville, 'Pierre de Versailles (1380?–1446)', in *Bibl. de l'École des Chartes*, XCIII (1932), 208 ff.

[2] Cf. below, pp. 71 f.   [3] Henry VI in *RTA*, XVI, 553. Below, p. 98.

obedient to the hierarchical rhythm. 'Hierarchy' was a single 'natural law' pervading cosmos and polity.[1]

This outlook, first, enabled the papal theorists to lay new emphasis on the hierarchical and monarchical interpretation of the corporate analogy. Monarchical thinkers, no less than the Conciliarists, called society a 'mystical body', and meant by this an organic, articulated whole; but they took the principle of functional differentiation, 'cohesion in diversity',[2] to apply above all to the tenure of jurisdiction. Not only is the 'head' the origin of all powers, but the power deriving from it is channelled through, and belongs exclusively to, a 'hierarchy', meaning (in today's sense) the upper echelons of society, those 'set above (*praelati*)', whether in church or kingdom. The quality of 'animation', that is of jurisdiction, was thus monopolized by the prince and his hierarchy, together forming a closely-knit unit, an inner 'mystical body'. Jurisdictionally, they *were* the community.[3]

In this way the principle of hierarchy was made to signify a stratification of society into ranks subordinate to each other; and in this respect the church is like any 'state (*politia*)'. The cosmic rule already quoted, that 'the last are perfected by the middle, and the middle by the first', is stated as the necessary postulate of any society:

In any society it is necessary to have order. And order comes about by the arrangement of many in grades.[4]

In this way, the neoplatonic model resulted directly in the statement of a general political norm. As Turrecremata put it, 'Power (*praelatio*) is reckoned according to ascending and descending levels, not according to equality'.[5] He emphasized the analogy from secular government, whose organization, he argued, the church must reflect to an even higher degree, since grace is more 'orderly' than nature.[6]

---

[1] Turrecremata, *SE*, II, c. 1, fo. 116r: below, p. 162; and *id.* in Mansi, XXXI, 75A, 87E; and in Mansi Suppl. V, 238; and Monte, Vat. lat. 4145, fo. 59v.

[2] Turrecremata, *SE*, II, c. 1, fo. 116v: below, p. 163; Cusa, *Conc. cath.* II, 32. Cf. Ullmann, *Papal government*, esp. 289.

[3] Eugenius IV in Raynaldus, *Annales ecclesiastici*, XXVIII, 88, 322; and others in *RTA*, XVII, 265, 451. On the notion of government as animation, cf. Ullmann, *Principles*, 92 f.   [4] Versailles, Vat. lat. 4140, f. 30r; Turrecremata, *SE*, II, c. 1, fo. 116r.

[5] *SE*, II, c. 2, fo. 116v: 'Praelatio attenditur secundum ascensum et descensum, non secundum aequalitatem': below, p. 163.

[6] *SE*, II, c. 1, fo. 116r: below, p. 162.

In the church too, therefore, there must be 'an order of superiority'; as a 'glorious kingdom', it must express in a transcending way the order of other kingdoms. And:

The order of a kingdom consists in this, that there are different grades of men, distinct ranks of preferment, and a diverse distribution of offices.[1]

What emerges is a clear statement of political principle: it is the hierarchy which creates society, not society which makes its own hierarchy. Society depends for its very existence upon hierarchical order. The series of members is bound together, not by a force evenly distributed through the whole mass, but by a force transmitted from the top through hierarchical organs:

An army results from its parts considered in their order with one another, and with their leader. So too the political structure of the church results from the subordination of its ministers to one another and their being oriented towards the first.[2]

The power-bearing hierarchy is conceived as being welded onto a society not at the will of its members, but as a postulate of their very existence as members of one society. The 'praelati' or 'more principal members'[3] are vital and irreplaceable organs of power, given to a community, concurrently with its own existence, by a superior power.

This could be deduced both from neoplatonic cosmology and from contemporary experience, which furnished the salutary example of anarchy. As the German princes, at the imperial election of 1440, quoted Gregory I:

No association could by any means subsist unless held together by a great

---

[1] *SE*, I, c. 34, fo. 40v; Poggio, *De pot. papae*, argt. 9.

[2] 'Exercitus *resultat ex* suis partibus consideratis in ordine adinvicem et ad suum ducem. Sic politia ecclesiae *resultat ex* subalternatione ministrorum adinvicem et ordinatione eorum ad primum': Versailles in Vat. lat. 4140, fo. 30v. On the unity of the people as deriving from the prince, cf. Rickel: 'qui eidem subduntur, unus sunt grex unaque plebs, et quasi unum corpus per reductionem et comparationem ad suum presidentem': *De auct.*, in *Opera omnia*, XXXVI, 659.

[3] Turrecremata, *SE*, I, c. 95, fo. 109r; they form, as in the case of the cardinals or senate, a single inner body politic with the ruler: Rayn. XXVIII, 88, 322; *RTA*, XVII, 265, 451. Cf. Ullmann, 'Eugenius IV, Cardinal Kemp and Archbishop Chichele', in *Stud. pres. to A. Gwynn*, 359 ff.

order of differentiation; so that the lesser show respect for the more powerful...[and] true concord and union is constructed out of diversity.[1]

MONARCHY

In the thought of the fifteenth-century supporters of papal monarchy, the principle of monarchy was implicit in that of hierarchy itself. Just as the hierarchical order of the universe flowed from, depended upon, and culminated in, the supreme 'Hierarch', so too, it was argued, every earthly order of society depended upon its supreme monarch. Just as all life flowed from the divine source, so too all governmental authority flowed from the ruler:

In every state, the power of jurisdiction devolves upon any person in that state from the monarch or prince of the state. This is clear from the opinion of Denis, who teaches, both on the ecclesiastical and the celestial hierarchy, that the light of illumination flows to all persons of the hierarchy from the hierarch himself...In every system, it is from the one in whom especially fullness of virtue or power originally resides, that the virtue of all following him in that system depends...Hence, it will be so in the ecclesiastical hierarchy, that the power of jurisdiction, according to which is reckoned the order of superiority and inferiority among prelates of the church, *first descends* upon the pope directly from God, and through him is derived to those that follow.[2]

The metaphysic of monarchical unity could also be stated in terms of Aristotle's cosmology: 'there is no such thing as infinite recession', there must be a 'return of the lowest things to the first', a 'convergence in one'.[3]

Turrecremata's doctrine was here faithfully expounded by Piero da Monte:

Since 'prince' implies the nature of origin (*principium*), and origin has the nature of source and causality, then if the pope is the church's prince, it is necessary to admit that he has the role of origin, pouring out (*influens*)

---

[1] *RTA*, xv, 183; see also Turrecremata, *SE*, ii, c. 1, fo. 116v, and c. 78, fo. 210v; and Cusa, *Conc. cath.* ii, 30, 32. Cf. below, p. 98. Both Gregory I and Gregory VII had said this: Ullmann, *Papal government*, 289.

[2] Turrecremata, *SE*, ii, c. 55, fos 171r–172r: below, p. 167; also *id. Oratio synodalis de primatu* (1439), ed. E. Candal, 23–4; and *Comm.* i, 206a on D. 22, c. 1. For the papal doctrine of 'derivation' in general and the descending theme of government, cf. Ullmann, *Principles*, 53.

[3] Turrecremata, *SE*, ii, c. 2, fo. 116v: below, p. 163; *Comm.* i, 190b on D. 21, c. 1; and *ibid.* 352b on D. 40, c. 6; and *id.* in Mansi, xxx, 558B.

and causing every ecclesiastical power...every power of inferiors takes its origin from the fullness which is in the pope alone. For it is certain that, as blessed Denis teaches, the hierarchy of the militant church is formed according to the model (*exemplar*) of the heavenly hierarchy...But in the heavenly hierarchy, as Denis again testifies, no power is given to any by God for the exercise of hierarchical acts, *except through the mediation of the first of that order or hierarchy.* By the same reasoning, then, this must also be the case in the ecclesiastical hierarchy...lower prelates receive from the pope the influx of their divine power...For in all things which have order among themselves...every one which pours down something to others receives the power of pouring down (*virtutem influendi*) from the first.[1]

He goes on to assert the same principle in secular government:

This is also shown by the royal power of the pope. For just as the king gave to the magistrates, commanders and other judges of the realm all the power they employ, why do we not say the same for the pope and the prelates below him?...all their power *descends* from him.[2]

The corporate analogy, meanwhile, was reinterpreted so as to make the head the origin of power for other parts.[3]

By thus stating the traditional papal notion of the 'derivation' of all power from the top as a political universal, Turrecremata and others gave a new philosophical rationale for the monarch's claim to be not only the supreme court, but also the very source of the legal authority of all inferior courts. This was probably the most complete formulation that the 'concession-theory' had so far received. It was the inevitable consequence of expressing legal sovereignty in neoplatonic terms.[4]

Another governmental principle of great importance established by this mode of thinking was the ability of the sovereign to intervene 'immediately' in any subordinate sphere. Already clearly established for the pope, in the traditional view that he was the direct superior of all (he had 'ordinary jurisdiction'), this was now universalized for all monarchs, thanks to the neoplatonic notion that it is *in the nature of things* that all subordinate power derives from, and can therefore

---

[1] Monte, *Contra impugnantes* (c. 1450), Vat. lat. 4145, fos 18v–23r. For this speech, cf. below, p. 128.   [2] *Ibid.* fo. 23r.

[3] Turrecremata in Mansi, xxxi, 87C; Mansi Suppl. v, 238D; *SE*, ii, c. 55, fo. 171v. Versailles in Vat. lat. 4140, fo. 11r. Monte in Vat. lat. 4145, fo. 59v.

[4] Cf. Gierke, *Political theories*, 87 ff.; Ullmann, *Principles*, 54 f., 120 f.

be interfered with by, the supreme power. Turrecremata first states the papal principle in hierarchical terms:

In every order, when the whole power of inferiors depends on and originates from the power of the superior, the power of the superior can extend itself over all those things, over which the power of the inferiors can extend itself.[1]

He promptly assumes this to be a characteristic of royal power too:

Any king can perform immediately in his realm whatever the inferior powers can perform, even without their having been requested.[2]

In furnishing these notions of derivation and immediate intervention (long familiar to the papacy) as general principles of government, neoplatonic cosmology in effect revolutionized the secular notion of what a hierarchy was. Instead of a sequence of self-substantive rungs on the feudal pattern, we have absolute dependence on the monarch; it is the theoretical framework for centralization.

Exactly the same view was expressed in Cusa's later works, after he joined Eugenius in 1437, thinking that the transferred Council of Ferrara–Florence now embodied the church's consent more truly than Basle itself. Despite his change of sides, his social thought seems to have developed little. As has been suggested, it was his neoplatonic notion of hierarchy that inspired and facilitated the transition from the *Catholic concordance*, in which the tendency was to make actual popular consent necessary for valid authority, to his later view that all power resides in essence with the ruler, and only 'in explication' with others:

If in the church there exists the power of judging, it is in [the pope] as prince and source...It flows from the church's head, where there is fullness of power, and where all power in the church is concentrated... All the power which is unfolded (*explicata*) in the church is in the pope as its causal origin implicitly (*complicatorie*).[3]

This outlook also served to express and develop the argument of tacit representation, that a sovereign ruler represents his people by

---

[1] *SE*, II, c. 65, fo. 188v; *ibid.* c. 52, fo. 167v; c. 54, fo. 169v; c. 55, fo. 171v.

[2] 'Quilibet rex potest immediate in regno suo facere quicquid inferiores potestates possunt, etiam eis irrequisitis': *SE*, II, c. 65, fo. 188v. See also Monte, Vat. lat. fo. 27r, for a similar statement.

[3] *RTA*, XVI, 421, 423 (1442); cf. Sigmund, *Nicholas of Cusa*, 266. This provides an exact contrast to Zabarella and Panormitanus: above, pp. 9f.

'tacit consent', absorbing their powers into himself and acting in their name *ex officio*, without any reference to their choice. This followed naturally from the pattern of neoplatonic hierarchy, in which the upper always contain the *virtus* and power of the lower, simply because of their status, and mediate them downwards. This received celebrated expression in Cusa's letter to Arevalo (1440); but the notion that princes 'contain' their peoples was anyway a commonplace among papal thinkers.[1] Turrecremata could further support this by reference to Aquinas's 'nominal' notion of representation that, 'What the ruler of a city does, the whole city is said to do.'[2] This linguistic notion of representation is exactly parallel to what Segovia was saying of the council.[3]

In answering Basle's contention, that Peter had acted merely as ambassador in receiving power from Christ on behalf of the whole church, Turrecremata had simply to expound this hierarchical notion of representation. The fact that Peter and the popes passed power on to their subordinates implied no responsibility to them, but only, in accordance with the hierarchical notion of the downward distribution of power, to Christ in whom the power originated.[4] Since, in any hierarchical system, power came from the top, the ruler as 'the first' contained in himself all the jurisdictional power of his subordinates.

According to the right order of the church, it was necessary that one be placed above and supreme, so that the *status* of all ecclesiastical power might be in him.[5]

---

[1] Turrecremata, *SE*, II, c. 75, fo. 203r–v: 'dicuntur principes continere populos quibus praesunt'; see also below, pp. 82 f. See esp. Cusa's letter to Arevalo (1440) in his *Opera omnia*, 825 ff.; discussed in Sigmund, *Nicholas of Cusa*, 259 ff. Cf., in general, Gierke, *Political theories*, 62–3, 162–3.

[2] *SE*, II, c. 75, fo. 203v. Cf. St Thomas Aquinas, *Summa theol.* I, q. 75, a. 4, ad (1): cited in Ullmann, *Principles*, 255. This was based on Aristotle's general comment that 'a city or any other composite whole is above all identified with its supreme element': *Ethics* IX, viii, 1168b.   [3] Above, p. 21.

[4] 'Dicitur aliquis in receptione alicuius beneficii, gratiae aut auctoritatis alium vel alios figurare in quem, vel in quos derivanda est, ex intentione donantis, talis gratia aut auctoritas; sicut qui a rege accipit castrum pro se, et ab eo *descendentibus* [*sc.* here presumably his heirs], dicitur in receptione castri figurasse omnes ab eo descendentes': *SE*, II, c. 75, fo. 203r; see also *ibid.* fo. 203v and c. 61, fo. 179r; also *id.* in Mansi, xxx, 1085; and in *Oratio synodalis*, 39. Cf. above, p. 9.

[5] '...in quo totius potestatis ecclesiasticae esset status': *SE*, II, c. 2, fo. 116v: below, p. 163.

Versailles said virtually the same:

> It was necessary that there should be one first, set above all, so that the *status* of all ecclesiastical preferment might be in him.[1]

Louis XIV, with his 'L'État, c'est moi', could hardly improve on that. Nothing demonstrates more clearly the intrinsic connection between neoplatonism and absolutism.

The hierarchical principle in this way engulfed the very notion of consent, sterilized in Cusa's 'tacit consent'[2] and purely vestigial in Turrecremata's *complacentia*.[3] The subjects' consent or recognition is seen, not as a condition, but as a consequence, of hierarchical status. This irreducible separation between monarch and people emerged as a dominant attitude enshrined in everyday language. The monarch is 'prince', 'lord', 'father', 'shepherd', *'praelatus* (set above)'; the people are 'underlings', 'subjects', 'servants', 'children', 'sheep'.[4] Monarchy promotes love and concord among subjects; to restrict the pope with laws, said Turrecremata, would 'dissipate the community of the Christian polity'.[5] It was presupposed that there was a moral bond also, which united rulers to subjects as fathers to children, strengthened the blood-ties of nobility, and enabled the ruler to win his people's affection, the only possible expression left for public opinion.[6]

The contribution made by the Eugenians to monarchical doctrine then, stems directly from their tendency to state the primordial pattern of the neoplatonic hierarchy as a universal political norm.

---

[1] Vat. lat. 4140, fo. 30r. Cf. Buisson, *Potestas und Caritas*, 399.

[2] Cf. Sigmund, *Nicholas of Cusa*, 156, 268.

[3] Turrecremata, *Comm.* on D. 22, c. ii, ad (1), àpropos the Apostles' approval of the Petrine commission.

[4] See for example Turrecremata in Mansi, XXXI, 75A, 87C; and the German princes in *RTA*, xv, 184. Also, compare Pius II (1463): '(papa) prefertur (ecclesiae) ut pastor gregi, princeps populo, rector familiae' (Rayn. XXIX, 388) with a sixteenth-century French royalist: 'Quis enim nescit aliud regem, aliud regnum, aliud pastorem, aliud oves, aliud tutorem, aliud pupillum?' (cited in Church, *Constitutional thought*, 321 n.). Cf. W. Ullmann, *Individual and society in the Middle Ages*, for the same idea in earlier times.

[5] Mansi, XXXI, 88A; cf. *SE*, II, c. 2, fo. 118r: 'Principatus ille videtur omnibus aliis praestantior...quo inter subditos caritas et pax ac concordia nutritur...et quo seditio et discordia, quae est cuiuslibet communis corruptio, devitatur.' See also Cusa, *Conc. cath.* II, 32; Denis Rickel, *Opera omnia*, XXXVI, 659.

[6] See for example, *RTA*, xv, 187.

Indeed, it is sometimes stated, not only as the correct constitution, but also as a social necessity, with the implication that not only legal authority, but actual social cohesion flows from the monarch. The existence and harmony of any system depend upon hierarchy and hierarch.

If anything was not subjected to the power of this first and supreme one, unity would be dissolved in some part of that coordination, and the political structure of the church would not be conducted towards one.[1]

THE PERSONALIZATION OF POWER

The papal arguments for monarchical sovereignty now took two paths. First, there was the argument for pure monarchy, that is for the tenure of power by a single person. Secondly, there was the argument for a unitary seat of power, for sovereignty as such (which could apply equally to a person or a group).

To take the first, the personalization of sovereign power arose out of a continuation of the arguments from unity and peace. If political power has as its specific purpose the maintenance of the socio-political order in a state of peace; and if it achieves this purpose by providing a point of resolution for the conflicts arising within a society; then, it must follow, this power itself must be free from the very possibility of conflict. But, just as a plurality of sovereign agencies would be a source of conflict, so would a plurality of sovereign wills. The papalists make all the arguments from unity point, not only towards a single sovereign, but also towards a sovereign individual. They introduce an empirical argument, that conflict will only be avoided, and peace ensured, if all submit to a single will;[2] therefore, of the forms of government offered by Aristotle, monarchy is unquestionably the best.[3] 'Plurality of princes' breeds discord; there must be 'unity of prince'—the argu-

---

[1] 'In aliqua parte istius coordinationis solveretur unitas, si aliquid esset in ea quod non submitteretur potestati huius primi et supremi, nec politia ecclesiae esset continuata ad unum': Versailles, Vat. lat. 4140, fo. 30v.

[2] Turrecremata, *SE*, II, c. 2, fo. 117r: below, p. 163; *id.* in Mansi, XXXI, 88A; Arevalo in Mansi, XXXI, 3B; Roselli in Goldast *Monarchia*, I, 313; also Pius II in Rayn. XXIX, 388 (1463).

[3] Turrecremata, Mansi, XXX, 557 and XXXI, 88C; *SE*, II, c. 71, fo. 196r; Poggio, argt. 9, 13; Versailles in Rayn. XXVIII, 364.

ment goes back to the days of Agamemnon.[1] For the very purpose of government would be frustrated if it were entrusted to a group, which 'quickly divides up into different parts'.[2] To function adequately, the holder of 'fullness of power' must be 'a particular man', 'one subject (*suppositus*)';[3] the seat of sovereignty, the 'head' or 'soul', must literally be an individual mind or will.[4] Most clearly of all, 'supreme power cannot be except one, nor except in one'.[5] The monarch is truly 'the people's foundation';[6] as usual, it was Monte who reduced the papal position to its utmost simplicity:

All power and authority subsists (*consistit*) in the prince...fullness of power rooted in some one [person].[7]

This was supported by references to alleged observations of fact, many of them second-hand from Aristotle or other traditional sources, but some claiming validity from 'experience, which is our daily teacher'.[8] Hierarchical monarchy was shown to be natural by reference to physical and biological examples, as well as to forms of human organization, such as the family and military command.[9] The papal supporters encouraged the tendency among monarchical thinkers to point to existing conditions of anarchy, and in their own case particularly to the ecclesiastical schism and the occasional outbreaks of violence within the Council of Basle itself, as evidence of the need for the unified command of a monarch. Here, perhaps more than anywhere, they could count on profound sympathy among the secular audiences. One of the many reasons for the considerable popularity achieved by the expanding monarchies of the

---

[1] Turrecremata, *SE*, II, c. 71, fo. 198r: below, p. 170; Poggio, argt. 8; others in *RTA*, xv, 187 and xvII, 651; also Pius II in Rayn. xxIx, 388 (1463). Cf. Homer, *Iliad*, II, 204–5; cited in Aristotle, *Metaphysics*, xII, x, 1076a.

[2] Versailles in Rayn. xxvIII, 362; *id.* in Vat. lat. 4140, fo. 31r; Turrecremata, *SE*, II, c. 72, fo. 199v; the German princes in *RTA*, xv, 187.

[3] Versailles in Rayn. xxvIII, 362 and Vat. lat. 4140, fo. 31r; Turrecremata, *SE*, II, c. 2, fo. 117r–v; and *id.* in Mansi, xxxI, 50E–51A; Ebendorfer in *RTA*, xvII, 24; Arevalo in Barb. lat. 1487, fo. 121r.

[4] Cf. Louis XI in Rayn. xxIx, 318: 'ut hominum membra nulla contentione capite uno et una mente ducuntur' (1461, on papal primacy).

[5] 'Suprema potestas non posset esse nisi una et non nisi in uno': Turrecremata, *SE*, II, c. 80, fo. 213r.   [6] *RTA*, xvII, 453.

[7] Vat. lat. 4145, fos 15v, 36v, 109r.

[8] Ebendorfer, in *RTA*, xvII, 651; see also Mansi, xxIx, 484A.

[9] Ebendorfer, in *RTA*, xvII, 651; cf. Aquinas–Ptolemy, *De reg. princ.*, c. 2.

fifteenth century was undoubtedly the generally felt need for a unified political system, orderly succession, and that degree of political stability which was the necessary precondition for commercial and cultural development. This need was particularly felt, and widely discussed, during the Baslean crisis, which provided a focal point for such sentiment. All this simply made the monarchical solution yet more attractive, for both its theoretical and its practical simplicity, to the mentality of the 1440s, weary with disputes. The desire for peace in secular circles was indeed one of the papacy's strongest allies during the 1440s; we find the theme of peace at any price increasingly dominant in negotiations.[1] The ideology of monarchical peace, of peace as the gift specially bestowed by the monarch, and as the goal with which he was most concerned, was enthusiastically canvassed both by the renaissance monarchies, and by the restored but weakened papacy. It was an argument with a great future.

The personal sovereignty of the monarch could also be supported by an analogy with the specifically ecclesiastical notion of jurisdiction. Jurisdiction in the church was viewed as a unique type of 'grace', a divine gift freely bestowed, not in virtue of any human quality, but in virtue of a certain office, established originally by the divine will. Since the gift comes from above, there is no reason why the monarch alone should not exceed all others in this particular quality.[2] Turrecremata proceeds, typically, to claim this as a characteristic, not only of ecclesiastical jurisdiction, but of political authority in general:

This is shown in any prince, with respect to the people over whom he presides. There is no doubt that the prince is a member of the association of the commonweal...and yet, though he does not possess all the virtues and graces which are possessed by all the other members of the association...nevertheless in the power of jurisdiction he is superior to them all, to the whole association.[3]

In this way, the papal notion of the separation between the person and the office, of the immunity of the former in virtue of the latter,

---

[1] Below, p. 126.
[2] Turrecremata, *SE*, ii, c. 82, fos. 214v–215r: below, p. 170; cf. *ibid.* c. 75, fo. 205v and c. 76, fo. 206v.   [3] *SE*, ii, c. 82, fo. 214v: see below, pp. 170 f.

the very notion of official power (so crucial to the modern state) was transferred into the secular sphere.[1] The sovereign may sin, but no man may punish him; it is an extension of St Augustine's attitude to tyranny, a case of governmental *laissez-faire*. Political power, like ecclesiastical jurisdiction, belonged to an objective legal category, into which extra-legal criteria could not be admitted. As Arevalo said:

In a disputed judgment, no attention is paid to superiority in regard to any natural quality in the judge; only the quality of jurisdiction and coercive power is considered.[2]

Both Turrecremata and Versailles distinguished clearly between jurisdiction, in which the pope alone was supreme, and *de facto* influence ('power of reputation') in which the pope with a council could be considered superior to the pope alone.[3] This notion of ecclesiastical jurisdiction confirmed the idea of political power stemming from society's objective need for peace, unity and order, and not from its (subjective) will. This was also no doubt in part a continuation of the analogous development of the abstract 'crown' and the undying 'see'.[4]

The idea of the pope's position depending upon a personal commission or 'vicariate' from Christ was also applied to other monarchs. Power had been bestowed on St Peter personally, like a vocation, and he was personally responsible to God alone for it; his position of holding power from above, not from below, was comparable to that of a king's 'vicar', whose power could be revoked by no one but the king. There are no legal limits to it; he is an 'absolute vicar'.[5] Roselli expressed the pope's position as legally self-substantiating, and compared it to that of the sovereign prince:

[The pope] holds power from himself and directly from God...by his

---

[1] On the papal distinction between person and office, cf. Ullmann, *Principles*, 41, 51, 55, 102–4.
[2] Arevalo in Barb. lat. 1487, fo. 83v. Similarly, Turrecremata in *SE*, II, c. 23, 70, 89.
[3] Turrecremata, *Oratio synodalis*, 36; *Comm.* I, 176a, on D. 19, c. 8; cf. *SE*, III, c. 53–4. Versailles in Rayn. XXVIII, 363.
[4] Cf. Kantorowicz, *The king's two bodies*, 272, 336 ff.
[5] J. Leonis, 'De synodis et eccl. pot.', Barb. lat. 1487 fo. 21v; Turrecremata, above, p. 65, n. 4. For antecedent papal doctrine, cf. Ullmann, *Papal government*, esp. 427 ff.

own right and no-one else's; this is because he holds it according to the law by which [power] is principally founded and rooted in the person of the prince...jurisdiction is principally in him through himself.[1]

In the same way Ebendorfer said of the prince (1442) that

he holds the place of head in the commonweal, subjected to God alone, so that he may be ruled only by the just decision of his own mind.[2]

Just as it was held that the pope could be judged 'by nobody', so royal sovereignty came to be described by a French lawyer as 'the crown, sceptre and empire, which he holds from nobody'.[3] This was, no doubt, the original meaning of 'autocracy'.

We may also observe the emergence, partly under papal influence, of some of the ideas that were to characterize absolute monarchy in its strictly hereditary form, namely 'legitimism'. It is the individual king or prince himself who, by divine predestination, has been personally called to the monarchical office:

The Most High singled out [kings] with special divine grace before others in a more glorious way, and chose, pre-selected and called them out before the foundation of the world, to wield the principates and dominions of this world.[4]

It is this or that individual king or prince who, adorned with the 'royal virtues' of his 'divine predecessors', receives power 'by divine gift...by special grace'—'on them has shone the divine favour'.[5] The view that the king held a 'divine legation' was gaining currency in secular circles. In the effort to secure obedience, governments fostered the popular view of the ruler as 'the image of God on

---

[1] Goldast, *Monarchia*, I, 278–9.

[2] *RTA*, xvii, 40. Similarly on the pope, Arevalo in Barb. lat. 1487, fo. 83r: 'a decision of the Roman pontiff may be changed for the better by himself; but according to no law can he be compelled by any mortal...unless perhaps the rectitude of his own mind and his own conscience move him...out of a certain *gratia*'. On Ebendorfer, cf. A. Lhotsky, *Thomas Ebendorfer*; W. Jaroschka, 'Thomas Ebendorfer', in *Mitt. d. Inst. f. oest. Gesch.* LXXI (1963), 87 ff.

[3] 'Corona vel sceptrum et imperium, quod a nemine tenet': Nicholas Boyer in *Tract. univ. iuris*, xiv, fo. 307v; cf. below, p. 83. Cf. the maxim, 'Le Roy ne tient que de Dieu et de l'épee': cited in Church, *Constitutional thought*, 317.

[4] Nicholas V (1448) in *Regesta*, ed. Chmel, 99; cf. *id.* (1452) in *Bull. Rom. Taurin.* v, 109. Also Frederick III in Mansi, xxxi, 344; Ebendorfer in *RTA*, xvii, 40; and Albert II in *Reichsregister*, ed. Koller, 120, 240.

[5] Eugenius IV in Braun, *Notitia*, vi, 162. Cf. below, p. 72, n. 3.

earth'; there was perhaps a reminiscence of Pseudo-Denis in the statement that the ruler was 'in residence upon an earthly throne in the likeness of the emperor of the heavens'.[1] As well as providing the rationale for the doctrine of monarchical immunity, this galvanized popular emotion; it combined *raison d'état* with popular mystique. Emotional attitudes were reflected in legal *dicta*: the law can only 'presume' that a prince acts rightly, his 'good name' virtually inheres in his office.[2] There was a blatant contradiction here, which was to emerge with full vigour in good time, between the claim of impersonal criteria for office, and the appropriation of personal, mythical qualities in virtue of office; it was a clear paradox that, in the case of the monarch alone is the office necessarily tied to a particular person. Similarly, there are signs of a tendency to glorify, if not divinize, the royal ancestors or predecessors, as 'predecessors of pious memory', or 'our immediate predecessors of divine memory in the holy empire'.[3] Alfonso V, a typical renaissance monarch, came even closer to ancient Roman usage with his 'divine predecessors'.[4]

Finally, religious sanction was bestowed upon the institution of monarchy itself. The ancient doctrine of the divine institution of governments, which had been tempered by Aquinas's interpolation of 'nature' as intermediary, was now revived, by saying that monarchy was the constitution established, not only in the church, but 'according to the general providential plan for the world'.[5] It was monarchy that best fulfilled the task prescribed for government by Augustinian theology, of neutralizing the chaos of a fallen world. Monarchy, furthermore, is the political principle of the Christian society, and is essential to its well-being.[6]

---

[1] German princes (1440) in *RTA*, xv, 183–4; see also *RTA*, xvi, 133; Rickel, *Opera omnia*, xxxvi, 511. For the pope in this sense, cf. Ullmann, *Principles*, 40; and for the king, *ibid.*, 202, 210 n.

[2] Eugenius IV in Rayn. xxviii, 199; Roselli, cited in Eckermann, *Studien*, 106: cf. Buisson, *Potestas und caritas*, 177; and H. Fichtenau, *Arenga*, 187. See also above, p. 59.

[3] Frederick III (1441) in *Publicationen aus d. kön. preuss. Staatsarch.* xxxiv, ed. Hansen, 51. Cf. Fichtenau, *Arenga*, 173–4, 184.   [4] *Dipl. Aragonese*, ed. Rogadeo, 121.

[5] Arevalo, Barb. lat. 1487, fo. 120v; Versailles in Rayn. xxviii, 361; Roselli in Goldast, *Monarchia*, I, 312.

[6] Turrecremata, in Mansi, xxxi, 105B; Mansi, xxxv, 44D; Versailles in Vat. lat 4140, fo. 30r.

These examples indicate the growing pressure of papal ideas upon secular monarchy. The extension of divine sanction and immunity to a particular institution, a particular family and a particular individual, were to become both the constitutional and the emotional basis of royal 'legitimism'. Indeed, the constitutional implications of this whole philosophy of power were to involve, under the auspices of the 'new monarchies', a radical transformation in the relative powers of king and feudatories, of central and local government.

JOHN TURRECREMATA: SOVEREIGNTY AND THE COMMON GOOD

Another series of developments, running parallel to these and often confused with them, pointed towards the doctrine of sovereignty as such, in its general rather than its strictly monarchical form. Though the aim of Turrecremata and others was indeed to establish the need for pure monarchy, some of their arguments were in fact a proof rather of the need for a single sovereign power. The papacy now developed still further its ancient inheritance of the doctrine, implicit in Roman law, that the supreme judicial authority, the *princeps*, is itself immune from judgment.[1] When they decried 'plurality of princes', and advocated 'unity of prince', they sometimes meant, not only that one will creates more order than many, but also that political order requires a clear chain of command, and is incompatible with rival jurisdictions. This was particularly demonstrable in terms of law: both the textbooks and contemporary experience advertised the need for a single supreme court. (The empire at this period provided an eloquent witness that uncertainty in the application of law can damage society.) This was woven into the argument for hierarchy:

Through [one head] [the church] is made more like the heavenly hierarchy, which is its exemplar. Through this, too, it conforms to the order of nature; for the whole universe is under one supreme heaven...In this it conforms to civil order; for there is one principal judge, from whom comes the final decision of cases, lest with equal judges contending litigation should be endless.[2]

[1] Turrecremata in Mansi, xxx, 602B; see also *id.* in Mansi, xxix, 484C. Cf. Ullmann, *Papal government*, 7; *id. Principles*, 37.
[2] Ludovicus Forojulio, *Dialogus de pap. pot.* Vat. lat. 4143, fos 7v–8r. For antecedents,

But, just as law and, increasingly, the ability to make law, was generally considered the basis of all other governmental authority, so too it could easily be argued that principles obtaining in the sphere of legal jurisdiction were applicable to the running of society in every aspect. The evolution of this wider notion of sovereignty out of the strictly legal context is made clear by a statement of Bologna University for Eugenius (1443):

There is one judge, from whom the final decision of cases comes, lest with many judges contending, and no one supreme, litigations would never be finished. Also, no family, no community, no kingdom can remain in its full *status*, unless it has one supreme ruler; because from division of heads there easily arises division and schism among the members.[1]

It was thus clearly established that the supreme judge has to be 'absolute and immune' for the successful functioning of the legal system.

The need for a single seat of sovereign power was stated still more explicitly and cogently by Turrecremata, in the course of his reply to the claim that the same supreme power resided in different ways with pope, council and church.

It is impossible that in any one association the prelate and the subjects should have the same fullness of power. This is clear, because it is unintelligible that what constitutes someone as superior and prelate of others should be commonly held by prelate and subjects in the same fullness; and in the whole Christian association the Roman bishop is prelate, and all the other faithful are subjects... The fullness of power which is located in the church is either one and the same in identity (*numero*) with that which is located in the pope, or it is different. But it cannot be said that it is different, because then there would be two supreme powers, or fullnesses of power, which cannot be... because plurality of princes is not good... also because the church's unity could not endure two supreme powers. This fullness of power cannot be said to be one and the same in identity, because in that case neither would the pope be superior and prelate, nor could it be said that the church was superior in power to the Roman bishop himself... because if 'equal cannot command equal', far less can it do so when there is identity (*identitas*) of power.[2]

see Durandus, cited in Ullmann, *Medieval papalism*, 117 n.; and Ockham, cited in Ullmann, *Papal government*, 456–7.

[1] *RTA*, xvii, 162.   [2] *SE*, ii, c. 71, fo. 198r: see below, p. 170.

It was a straightforward but masterly application of the principle that 'prelacy follows a pattern of ascending and descending levels, not of equality,[1] and it suggests how fertile a ground that principle was for the doctrine of sovereignty in its later secular form.

The very same consideration led to a development in the notion of the sovereign's scope as well as of his supremacy: they were taken to entail the general illimitability of the sovereign's power. The fifteenth-century supporters of the papacy thus developed the legal argument into the wider political doctrine, that the integrity of society depends upon the immunity of the sovereign. General sovereignty, we might almost say, evolved out of legal sovereignty, but retained, as functionally necessary qualities, the unity and immunity of the superior. Sovereignty became more than a legal concept; the sovereign's task is not confined to administering laws, but includes the maintenance of social well-being by any means. Judicial supremacy was being taken to entail the right of legislation and of administrative initiative: modern was developing out of medieval sovereignty.

The provision for extra-legal action by the sovereign had already become current in the notion of 'discretion' (*epieikeia*, 'equity'), taken from Aristotle. This originally meant a judge's right to depart from the letter of the law in exceptional circumstances, and had also been taken to justify the adaptation of law itself, by a sovereign power, to meet new conditions. The doctrine of discretion had thus strengthened the case for the ruler's being 'freed from the laws', for his power to dispense from positive laws, and for his power of legislation.[2] Turrecremata and his colleagues now took discretion to mean the sovereign's ability to take any action, whether or not specified by law, that he considered necessary for the public welfare. He must have full power because he has to react spontaneously to the future exigencies of the 'common good'. Promotion of the 'public utility' was thus monopolized, just as final legal judgment had been, by the sovereign. The scope of the monarch's power was left 'open', in

[1] Above p. 60.

[2] Cf. *Dict. de droit canon.*, *s.v.*; Buisson, *Potestas und Caritas*, 70–1, Ullmann; *Principles*, 294; N. Horn, *Aequitas in den Lehren des Baldus* (Köln–Graz, 1968). Ironically, it had been the early Conciliarists who had themselves invoked this para-legal idea in favour of emergency sovereignty for the council.

order to cater for the unforseeable requirements of the public interest.

In every well-ruled community, it is necessary that there reside with the supreme one, full power extending itself to everything needful and evidently convenient for the good of the commonweal of that community.[1]

In every well-ruled people, it is necessary that there reside with its supreme one, full power,* the potency of which...extends itself to everything necessary and useful for that people.[2]

Above all, this strengthened the growing crescendo of arguments for the legislative power of the prince (which for centuries was to deprive the people of their traditional role in law-making):

This is the reason why [God] wished there to be a pope and princes, so that, when reasons of public utility demanded, on account of the instability of human affairs, there might be [a power] on earth which could change statutes, and cater for public utility.[3]

Turrecremata reintroduced Aquinas's definition of the ruler's function as not only the maintenance but also the 'promotion' of the common good of society which was understood (following Aristotle and Aquinas) as a unitary goal for society as a whole. He argued that the existence of a single social goal demanded a single ruling power:

Wherever there are many directed towards one [end], it is necessary that there be some universal ruling power over particular ruling powers... Therefore over the ruling power which produces a partial good, it is necessary that there be a ruling power with respect to the common good, otherwise there would not be convergence in one. Since the whole church

---

[1] Turrecremata, *SE*, II, c. 52, fo. 166r: see below, p. 166. See also Cusa in *RTA*, XV, 642, and *ibid.* XVI, 431; and Eugenius IV in Rayn. XXVIII, 199. For earlier uses of 'public utility', cf. Ullmann, *Papal government*, 425; *id. Principles*, 67, 84; and G. Post, *Studies in medieval legal thought*, 7 ff., 241 ff.

[2] Monte, Vat. lat. 4145, fo. 36v.

[3] Galganus, Vat. lat. 4129, fo. 28r: '...ut exigenti causa publicae utilitatis, propter instabilitatem humanarum rerum, esset in terris (potestas) que statuta mutare possit, et publicae utilitatis consulere'. Turrecremata, *SE*, II, c. 4, 119r: 'Oportet omnem communitatem habere unum caput sive rectorem, qui visibiliter cum illa conversetur circa personas illius regiminis sui ministerium pro varietate temporum, locorum ac personarum...corrigendo hanc vel illam personam secundum communem cursum.' For the canonistic origin of this, cf. Ullmann, *Papal government*, 371.

is one body, it is necessary, if its unity is to be preserved, that there be some ruling power with respect to the whole church...and this is the power of the pope.[1]

Society, being a single unit in respect of its common good (as Aristotle and Aquinas had said), required a unitary sovereign to motivate the social mass towards its goal, to give it single-minded direction:

In every well ordered commonweal, there was to be granted one president in it, who would be able by his own authority to move the whole commonweal towards everything, especially those things without which it could not remain safe. So too, in the church's community there was necessarily to be granted one prince, who...by his *magisterium* (teaching authority) could move and direct the whole Christian commonweal itself.[2]

Again (perhaps echoing Dante, whom he would have known through Roselli), he said that a secular ruler's aim was to lead his subjects towards 'political felicity', just as the pope's aim was to lead his towards 'beatitude'.[3] Similarly, there was a tendency in monarchical courts to speak as if the king had a unique purview of the needs and aims of society, and unique 'knowledge' to cater for them.[4] Turrecremata, in discussing the purpose of any authority, says that it exists first of all for the sake of society's goal, and only secondarily for the sake of the subjects;[5] the goal is not left to the subjects' choice, but objectively laid down in the nature of things. It was made clear that this notion of public service involved no submission to the public; on the contrary, 'this ministry involves the rationale of sovereignty (*hoc ministerium importat rationem principatus*)'.[6]

[1] *SE*, II, c. 2, fo. 117r–v: see below, p. 164. Cf. Roselli on society's goal as 'finis unius, cuius est totius etiam civitatis...' (*Monarchia*, in Goldast, I, 313). Cf. Buisson, *Potestas und Caritas*, ch. 7.
This doctrine derives from Aristotle, *Politics*, III, iv, 1278b; Aquinas, *Comm. on Ethics*, lect. 2, and *Comm. on Politics*, lect. 1.
[2] *SE*, II, c. 107, fo. 248r: see below, p. 172. Cf. *ibid.* c. 52, fo. 167r; and others in *RTA*, XVII, 453. Cf. Aquinas, *De regimine principum*, c. 15, for the idea that it is the ruler's task to 'promote' the common welfare.
[3] *SE*, II, c. 84, fo. 217r: see below, p. 172.
[4] Cf. Kantorowicz, *The King's two bodies*, 455 n.; Ullmann, *Papal government*, 433; Fichtenau, *Arenga*, 185.   [5] Above, n. 3.
[6] Versailles, Vat. lat. 4140, fo. 30v; cf. the papal title 'servant of the servants of God', Ullmann, *Principles*, 39. Cf. Buisson, *Potestas und Caritas*, 398–9.

This is because it is on the sovereign power that the good of the commonweal depends. The monarch becomes the beneficiary of the common good; nothing must hinder the scope of either; the monarch's power is as illimitable as are the potential requirements of the common good.[1] We may summarize this as the monarch's illimitable responsibility and power over the political structure as a totality, in virtue of its public interests.

The gulf between the sovereign and the rest was a qualitative one. The Leonine distinction between the pope's 'fullness of power' and others' 'share in responsibility' was heightened, according to the neoplatonic–hierarchical notion of influx from a god-like superior. The pope has a *totalitas* of power, because all subordinate power flows from him, and is absorbed in him. According to Turrecremata's neoplatonism, therefore, it is the pope, not the church, which has 'the rationale of a whole'; fortified by a quotation from Pseudo-Denis, he declared:

In the question of power, it is rather to be said that the pope *is* the whole church virtually, since in him alone is the wholeness (*totalitas*) and fullness of the whole ecclesiastical power...For the order between powers has this characteristic, as Boethius says, that whatever authoritative (*potestativa*) virtue exists in inferiors, exists in the superior. Hence, the quantity of all other inferior powers is included in the supreme power. Thus, since the papal power is supreme, in it are contained in virtue all other powers of the church; and so, in the question of power, it has the rationale (*ratio*) not of part, but of whole.[2]

Turrecremata thus used the Basleans' notion of a totality of power existing in the community, against themselves; since whatever the community possesses flows from the top, this totality is already contained more fully in the pope. More specifically, he reversed the meaning of Cracow University's declaration of 1442. Whereas this had stated that power resided in the church, not 'as in an integral whole...but as in a jurisdictional whole', meaning that it could be

---

[1] 'Princeps, lex et finis videntur sic commensurata ut subinvicem paris sunt universalitatis': Turrecremata, *SE*, II, c. 15, fo. 130r.

[2] Turrecremata, *SE*, II, c. 83, fo. 216r: see below, p. 171. See also above, pp. 66 f. Contrast above, p. 22, n. 1. For the notion of 'totality' previously, cf. Ullmann, *Papal government*, 209, 277; id. *Great Schism*, 212. Cf. St Thomas Aquinas, *Comm. in quartum lib. sent.* d. 24, q. 2, a. 1.

diffused among different parts and still be effective, Turrecremata, using the term *integratum* in the opposite sense, said that the church's jurisdiction was not something 'integrated out of particular parts... but is as it were a jurisdictional whole', meaning that it must be perfectly unified to be effective.[1]

It is clear that Turrecremata, thanks largely to Neoplatonism, viewed this total power as an abstract whole, which must be 'preserved in its fullness and integrity'.[2] By the same token, since the principle of hierarchy characterizes every system in the universe, this type of power belongs to every sovereign, to king as well as to pope:

> Sovereignty (*principatus*) is a kind of jurisdictional whole, in the nature of which it is that it exists, according to the complete version (*ratio*) of its perfection, in one alone, that is the prince; and for others, upon whom it is distributed through grades of different ranks and offices, there is a kind of participation in it; just as the sovereignty of a kingdom exists in one man, the king, and in others according to a kind of participation.[3]

We have travelled a good way towards that notion of sovereignty as an abstract universal (which 'either is or is not'), which was to play such a leading part in secular thought in the centuries to come. We find, in fact, that the Eugenians eagerly applied the notion of fullness of power to secular rulers. This was, at least partly, because (as we shall consider in Part III) they were courting the allegiance of kings and princes against Basle on the basis of political as well as theological ideas; to do so, they tended to argue that the papal case against Basle was but an application of universally valid monarchical principles. It was partly this that led them to assert that fullness of

---

[1] Turrecremata, *SE*, II, c. 83, fo. 216r: see below, p. 171. Above, p. 20 n. (Several chapters in this part of the *SE* appear to be a direct refutation of the Cracow memorandum.)

[2] 'in sua plenitudine et integritate': Turrecremata in Mansi, xxx, 557D.

[3] *SE*, II, c. 53, fo. 169v: see below, p. 166. Turrecremata goes on to cite Aquinas's analogy between the way in which the whole power of sacramental order resides in one rank, the priesthood, and the whole sovereignty resides in one man, the king; the point being that in both cases the whole power resides in one part, and others share in it: Turrecremata, *SE*, II, c. 53, fo. 169v, and again in *SE*, II, c. 83, fo. 216v: see below, p. 171. Cf. St Thomas Aquinas, *Comm. in quartum lib Sent.* d. 24, q. 2, a. 1, ad. 2, whence this doctrine is closely and explicitly derived. For the origin of the fullness-participation distinction in Leo I, see W. Ullmann, 'Leo I and the papal primacy', in *Journal of Theol. Stud.* XI (1960), 25 ff.

power belonged to the pope precisely because an all powerful monarch was politically necessary. Aquinas's remark that a king has fullness of power, was repeated and elaborated by Turrecremata and others. The long interwoven papal and secular ideas were at last stated as a general theory of monarchy and sovereignty, as a single 'royal, sovereign principle'.[1]

PAPAL AND SECULAR MONARCHY: THE BIRTH OF AN IDEOLOGY

The *de facto* triumph of papal monarchy over Conciliarism in the 1440s, and the 'restoration' of the papacy in its medieval form in the latter half of the century, symbolized by the Jubilee pageantry of 1450, coincided with the beginning of a widespread expansion of monarchical power in European states. These 'new monarchies' needed constitutional and popular acceptance of their claims. They could rely a good deal on legal titles and national feeling; but the very laws that gave them the throne as their birthright, also hemmed them in, and provincial loyalties might often outweigh national. What they really required was a justifying 'ideology'.[2]

It has often been pointed out that 'the theory of sovereignty', particularly as elaborated by Jean Bodin, gave the centralizing monarchies the basis they required in legal and political theory. It now seems clear, as has often been suggested,[3] that much of this was already created for them by papal theory. Certainly, long before this period, Roman imperial doctrine had been used by national kings and territorial princes to justify the overriding of positive laws, and a centralized system of legislation and appointment. Papal doctrine both endorsed this (as Monte's tract of *c.* 1450 amply illustrates),[4] and also supplied something of the more abstract and more generally applicable notion of sovereignty which was to be fully developed in the works of Bodin.

[1] 'Ratio regalis, principalis': Turrecremata in Mansi, xxx, 1080D.
[2] For this and what follows, cf. below, pp. 112 ff.
[3] J. N. Figgis, *Gerson to Grotius*, 60; *id. Divine right of kings*, 49; Laski in *CMH*, VIII, 642; Wilks, *Sovereignty*, p. VIII.
[4] Monte, Vat. lat. 4145, fos 18v–19r, a fulsome passage, and *ibid.* 38v–39r; cf. below, p. 128. See also Eugenius IV in Rayn. XXVIII, 199; and Turrecremata in Mansi, xxx, 1093A and XXXI, 93A. Cf. Gierke, *Political theories*, 37, 77; Ullmann, *Principles*, 198 ff.

Neoplatonism helped the supporters of the papacy under Eugenius IV to evolve a notion of sovereignty that was abstract, total and universally applicable. Once again we must concur with Gierke, when he says that 'in this direction [*sc.* state sovereignty] Philosophy with giant strides was outstripping Jurisprudence'.[1] The supporters of Eugenius universalized, as natural and necessary, the claims previously made specifically, and in mainly legal terms, for the empire or papacy. Monarchy was the best form of government because it coincided at once with the experienced need for unity and order, and with the divine pattern of the universe. Sovereignty was necessary for the monarch, both because without it he could not promote public interests, and because the hierarchical principle postulated that all power descends from a totality at the top. Roman law might provide a rationale for absolute sovereignty in the negative sense of power unrestricted by legal coercion. But papal doctrine provided its rationale in the positive sense of a universal power of initiative. In this process, the ancient analogies between pope, emperor and king were fused into the modern doctrine of sovereignty.[2]

Papal theory also provided an answer to the immediate problem of the respective claims of monarch and assembly to represent the general interest. For, as a result of their refutation of the specific doctrine of Baslean Conciliarism, the Eugenians could and did claim to establish the sovereignty of the monarch in general over representative assemblies. He is sovereign over the community in its collective form, as well as over each of the individuals composing it.[3] Again, the specifically ecclesiastical notion of jurisdiction as a gift bestowed in its totality on the individual solely in virtue of his office, was transferred by Turrecremata to the general political sphere. Such power, being a gift of grace, can only belong to specific individuals, never to the supposedly supra-personal community. Such an argument furnished an overriding reason why the jurisdictional status of the community was nothing more than that of the individuals composing it. Hence, if a monarch is sovereign over the individuals, he is no less sovereign over the collective or assembled

---

[1] Gierke, *Political theories*, 98.
[2] See esp. above, pp. 67 ff., 73 ff., 80 ff.
    See esp. Turrecremata, *SE*, II, c. 82–3; Monte, Vat. lat. 4145, fo. 99r; Versailles, Vat. lat. 4140, fo. 30v; Rickel, *Opera omnia*, XXXVI, 584, 598, 657–8.

community.[1] This seemed a definitive answer to the age-old dictum, that the king was 'greater than each but less than all', and, at the theoretical level, to the threat contained in general assemblies.

The influence of Eugenian ideas on monarchical thought in this period was facilitated by the fact that (as will be discussed in Part III) they had diplomatic reasons of their own for wishing to press home to secular rulers the political implications of the dispute between Eugenius and Basle.[2] But it seems probable that secular monarchies were more than willing to help themselves to a theory which so lucidly expressed, and so grandly endorsed their own ambitions and policies. We have already noticed cases of this; and a cursory glance at contemporary royal sources suggests, at least, that papal monarchical ideas were beginning to infiltrate secular courts, most noticeably, it is true, in the terminology of official documents. Alfonso V of Aragon illustrates this with the *cedula*: 'on our certain knowledge and our own proper initiative, out of pure grace and liberality, out of the fullness of our royal, lordly and absolute power'.[3] Antonio Corseto, in a work *On royal power*, used both papal and imperial precedents, and made the general claim that '(kings) can act and legislate in the same way as pope and emperor'.[4] Just as 'the church' had been absorbed into 'the prelate', so now 'the kingdom' was becoming identified with 'the king', and national honour with 'the royal estate'.[5] It seems that, as the medieval papacy declined, others appropriated its ideology.

The hunger for papal monarchical ideas is perhaps best demonstrated by the very fact that the imperial court itself thought it could enhance its status by the addition of titles and arguments taken from the contemporary papacy. Aeneas Sylvius Piccolomini, above

---

[1] Above, p. 12.

[2] See below, pp. 87 ff.

[3] *Diplomatico Aragonese*, ed. E. Rogadeo, III: 'de certa nostra scientia, libera mera propria gratuita et spontanea voluntate ac ex plenitudine nostra regie, dominice et absolute potestatis'; cf. *ibid.* 112, 122.

[4] 'Possunt idem facere et statuere sicut papa et imperator': Antonio Corseto, *De pot. regia*, in *Tract. ill. iurisconsult.* XVI, fo. 138r a. For this late fifteenth-century author, cf. Hove, *Prolegomena*, 508 n.

[5] Cf. the Polish royal title, 'rex regnum et corona'; above, pp. 56, 63, 70 f., 79 f.; and below, p. 83, n. 2. On the tendency of the prince as 'public person' to absorb the community as 'mystical person', and to contract with it a moral union, cf. Kantorowicz, *The King's two bodies*, 96, 214 n., 312.

all, himself ex-Conciliarist and future pope, completed the circle of
analogies by applying papal claims to the emperor: 'Just as in
spiritual matters there is one head, from whom no-one may appeal,
and to whom all may appeal, is it not fitting to practise this in
temporal affairs too? It is not right for anyone to revoke and nullify
the decree of the Roman pontiff; no-one may impugn the will of
the Roman prince'. Like the pope in spiritual affairs, the emperor is
'as it were holding the place of God in temporal affairs'.[1]

Nicholas Boyer, a French lawyer of the early sixteenth century,
in defending the sovereignty of the king's court over Parlement,
while he relied mostly on imperial precedents from civil law, also
turned to papal doctrine. He applied to France the ecclesiastical notion
of absorptive representation: 'Just as the church is in the prelate, and
the prelate in the church...so the prince is in the commonweal and
the commonweal in the prince.'[2] He went on to draw a direct
parallel between the jurisdictional sovereignty of the pope in the
church, and of the king in France:

It must be that the kings of France and their great council are above the
parlements, since they have superiority and supreme power in the whole
realm, as is clear from the crown, which is a body with an indivisible spirit
...In the same way Christ, the highest pontiff, when he went away, left
the divine Peter in his place as bishop, who should be over all the apostles.
Though the power of binding and loosing was given to all the others, as
to Peter himself, nevertheless, so that some order should be made clear
in this power, the power was given to Peter alone first, and it must des-
cend from him. Wherefore, Christ said to him particularly, 'Strengthen
your brethren'. It was for this reason that divine Peter, prince of the
apostles, raised up helpers to share his responsibility (*in partem sollici-
tudinis*)...Therefore the lords of the parlements should not complain
about revocations made by the royal majesty and his great council;
because a proconsul, bishops, and other self-substantive (*ordinarii*) powers
can revoke mandated jurisdiction.[3]

---

[1] *De ortu et auct. Rom. imp.*, ed. Wolkan in *Fontes rerum Austriacarum*, LXVII (Wien
1912), 22–3. See also *id.* cited below, p. 123; Roselli, below, pp. 86 f.; and
Ebendorfer, above, p. 71. On this subject, cf. Eckermann, *Studien*, 46, 106–7;
Widmer, *Enea Silvio Piccolomini*, 113, 130.

[2] Nicolas Boyer, *De custodia clavium* in *Tract. univ. iuris*, XII, fo. 122v. Cf. Tierney,
Conciliar theory, 125.

[3] *De ord. et preced. graduum*, in *Tract. univ. iuris*, XIV, fo. 307r. Cf. above, p. 79, n. 3.

Of course, these are mere pointers, and a full examination of such sources would be required to establish the degree of papalist influence; all we can do here is to establish that there was some influence, and to suggest that it may have been considerable.

We may also observe that Bodin himself cited 'the canonists', and referred to Innocent IV as 'he who best understood the meaning of absolute power', in connection with the sovereign's ability to override positive laws.[1] It has often been suggested that the notion of sovereignty developed in the age of absolutism owed a good deal to the papal notion of 'fullness of power'. Jouvenel has drawn attention particularly to L'Oyseau's description of supreme authority (*c.* 1609): 'It consists in absolute and entire authority at every point, *what the canonists call plenitude of authority*...and just as the crown cannot be a circle if it is not complete, so sovereignty is not if anything is lacking to it.' He remarks that such writers seem to be 'carried away by the idea of perfection'.[2] This seems to be an exact echo of the neoplatonic description of 'fullness of power' as an abstract 'totality' which must be maintained 'in its integrity'.[3] Indeed, a good many of Bodin's arguments for the need for absolute sovereignty in the monarch seem closely to resemble those of Turrecremata. Turrecremata thus to some extent anticipated what has been regarded as the specific achievement of Bodin, namely the elaboration of an abstract notion of sovereignty as necessary for all societies and as the only source of legitimate power.[4] But, in the absence of evidence for direct influence (as with Segovia and Locke), one can only suppose that the prevailing notions of Roman law and a similar constitutional problem—and one should perhaps add the continued influence of neoplatonic theology—enabled Bodin to reach similar formal conclusions in different circumstances.

[1] J. Bodin, *Six books of the commonwealth*, I, 8, p. 28–9, 35.
[2] Jouvenel, *Sovereignty*, 181–2.
[3] See above, p. 79 n. For earlier applications of *plenitudo potestatis* in the secular sphere, cf. Ullmann, *Principles*, 205–6, 254; Buisson, *Potestas und Caritas*, 216–17, 229, 306.
[4] See for example, Bodin, *Six books of the commonwealth*, VI, 4, 197–200. Church, in *Constitutional thought*, 226, describes Bodin's achievement as the elaboration of sovereignty as 'a body of power which was absolute, undivided, perpetual and responsible only to God'; and Allen, in *Political thought*, 423, claims: 'It may perhaps be said that in doing this, in detaching the idea of sovereignty from association with Emperor, Pope or King and attempting to define its nature apart from all circumstance, he was doing what had never quite been done before.'

Part III

DOCTRINE AND DIPLOMACY

THE SPECTRE OF REVOLT

Having considered the ideas in their logical sequence, we must now consider them in their political context. These ideas were not only a means of establishing and justifying certain doctrinal positions, they were also, especially in the case of the papacy, the helpmate of diplomacy. For supporters of the papacy especially, this was not simply a theoretical debate; it was also a contest for men's allegiance, which meant, above all, as we shall see, the allegiance of the secular powers. It was also, in their view, a crisis in the Christian community, which seemed threatened on all sides: the Turks, the Hussites, and now the Conciliarists. Just as the Christian community was a political and social as well as a spiritual entity, so too the crisis seemed to be threatening secular as well as ecclesiastical order. Certainly, the loosening of feudal and ecclesiastical ties of obedience, and the rise of new economic forces and social classes, had led to political instability in the later fourteenth and early fifteenth centuries. Rebellions by distressed peasants and indignant artisans became frequent; the English war in France, and the dismemberment of the German Empire made for anarchical conditions in some parts. Then came Hussitism, which seemed to provide an ideological justification and incitement for all the forces of disorder and violent upheaval. The Hussite victory and propaganda campaign of 1431 had indeed been followed by peasant and urban risings, at once anti-clerical and anti-aristocratic, in France and Germany.

On this issue at least, the secular powers of Central Europe, and the Council of Basle itself, shared the fears of the papacy. The papal legate at Basle, Cesarini, himself warned Eugenius (1432) that the Hussites' aim was 'to overthrow all human authority', and urged him to recognize the Council as a bulwark against 'the open danger of subversion'. The Emperor Sigismund similarly complained that, unless the Council continued, 'they will strengthen their following and infect with this deadly poison the faithful peoples, to whom, we hear, they have dispatched their errors'. Wladislas of Poland decided against Hussitism after a theological debate in the same year, on the grounds that 'such great social disturbances had followed the religious changes in Bohemia, owing to the removal of sacred and lay magistrates'.[1]

Then, in 1434, the people of Rome rebelled; Eugenius himself had a narrow escape by night in a boat. He fled to Florence, where the Medici had only just been restored after a rising against them in 1433. Eugenius tended to see these things in black and white; he had suffered an attack of apoplexy and paralysis in 1431; he was stubborn, and unbending in his attitudes and in his interpretations of events. He stiffened in the face of a crisis in which many of his closest supporters deserted him.[2]

THE MONARCHICAL FRONT

The development of the new papal theory of monarchical sovereignty was to a certain extent a direct response to these alarming events. Like secular monarchs later, the papacy expanded its claims partly in order to survive. It was from Eugenius himself and his immediate circle, including Roselli (a fellow-Paduan) and Turrecremata, that the idea took shape, in the early 1430s, that Conciliarism was but another form of revolution against ecclesiastical and secular authority. Ideas, written down as well as spoken (printing was invented in the 1440s), were a force to be reckoned with. Eugenius's very first bull opened, as if symbolically, with a statement about 'any monarchy, human as well as divine'.[3] By 1433, while Turrecremata was presenting the papal case at Basle in general monarchical terms,[4] Piero da Monte produced his *Monarchy*, which emphasized the analogy between pope and emperor, and asked whether anyone 'would be so foolish as to assert that a king is inferior to his council'.[5] The same year saw the publication of

[1] Rayn. XXVIII, 86, 106, 115, 120; Mansi, XXIX, 401 f.; *id.* Suppl. IV, 399C. For Hussitism, see above, pp. 3, 5.
[2] Cf. J. Gill, *Eugenius IV*, esp. 42, 120, 170, 172.
[3] Rayn. XXVIII, 88.   [4] Mansi, XXX, 557D, 602B.
[5] *Tract. illustr. iurisconsult.* XIII, part 1, fo. 150r. Cf. Haller, *Piero da Monte*, 31*f.; Eckermann, *Studien*, 108.

Antonio de Roselli's *Monarchy*, a celebrated work which combined the parallelism between papal and imperial principles of authority with a diminution of papal claims over the emperor in the temporal sphere.

The significance of this ideological programme, and its practical import, have been brilliantly summarized by Carla Eckermann:

When he made the attempt to set forth a political system in which both powers had a place side by side, living in an amicable partnership with strongly differentiated functions, he was perhaps one of the few men at the Curia who had a particularly clear insight into the existing situation. For it cannot be doubted that all these theories were based upon politically realistic considerations, to the effect that the Emperor and the Pope seemed capable of standing together, in opposition to the Council... This common front against the democratic ideas of the Conciliarists, which makes Roselli put the Emperor on the side of the papacy, is not explicitly stated by him; but there remains no doubt that this is the meaning of his whole tract. Here lies the key to the understanding of Roselli's *Monarchy*.[1]

The development of a general theory of monarchical sovereignty by the supporters of Eugenius was closely related to the diplomatic straits in which the papacy found itself, and to the type of audience to which it had to appeal. It was to the secular powers, with their considerable control over their own churches, and over the religious allegiance of their subjects, that appeal had to be made. The Council itself recognized its dependence upon the 'consistent adherence and good will' of these powers.[2] Whichever side was to regain the allegiance of Christians had to negotiate with them. It was Eugenius's supporters who recognized this situation most clearly; they understood, regretted, and utilized it.

Monarchical ideology and diplomatic expediency pointed in the same direction: all monarchs must combine to rescue the principle of monarchy. In this undertaking, ideology and diplomacy were to go hand in hand; an undertaking for which the papacy's courtly milieu was a better equipment than was the university régime at Basle. To this end, Eugenius employed a team of clerical diplomats,

---

[1] Eckermann, *Studien*, 45–6; cf. *ibid.* 53–4. Sigismund received the imperial crown from Eugenius in Rome the same year (1433).
[2] *MCG*, III, 245; cf. *ibid.* 268, 273.

men such as Piero da Monte, Carvajal and Rodrigo Sanchez de
Arevalo who, though they had temporarily abandoned the pulpit,
combined with their subtle worldliness great faith in the rhetorical
method, whether spoken or written. Renaissance Latinists could
promote the same end; Poggio Bracciolini and others used Ciceron-
ian bombast against the Council. But it was Aeneas Sylvius Piccolomini (who served first Basle, then Frederick III, and only later
the papacy), who most brilliantly typified this new type of ideological courtier.[1]

It was in a work issuing from Eugenius himself that the supposed
threat of Conciliarism was first explicitly suggested to the secular
monarchies. This was his *Tract of self-defence*, written for circulation
to all rulers in June 1436, as an answer to Basle's charges and threat
of deposition. Secular analogies were used to defend the papal power
of appointment and of dispensation.[2] Eugenius went on to compare
Conciliarism to Hussitism, because it championed the rights of
'inferiors' to judge their 'superiors', and published books 'in which a
great deal is said about *the people*, the church and the pope'.[3] Since,
he argued, Basle was placing power 'in the hands of the people', and
trying to replace 'monarchy' in the church with 'the rule of the
people and democracy', it too was a potential threat to all rulers.[4] He
explicitly suggested that the very same ideas could be used against
secular monarchs in their own sphere:

This is fatal for the whole estate of Catholic princes; for in exactly the
same way their own peoples, by assembling together, could claim power
over *them*. This would turn upside down at once the episcopal order and
the Christian polity—which is both unspeakable and insufferable.[5]

A similar kind of warning had been given by supporters of Benedict
XIII in 1398.[6] It seems probable that Eugenius was not only pointing

---

[1] For Piccolomini in this context see esp. B. Widmer, *Enea Silvio Piccolomini in der
sittlichen und politischen Entscheidung.*; and, in general, G. Voigt, *Eneas Silvius
Piccolomini als Papst Pius II.*; and Hay, *The Italian Renaissance*, 191 f. On Poggio,
cf. above, p. 56, n. 1.

[2] Rayn. xxviii, 199.   [3] *Ibid.* 204–5.

[4] *Ibid.* 197, 200.   [5] *Ibid.* 197.

[6] 'To withdraw obedience from the Pope would be to give an opportunity for
subjects or peoples not to obey their sovereigns or temporal lords, from which
rebellions would follow': cited in B. Huebler, *Die Constanzer Reformation* (Leipzig,
1867), 372 n.

out the general parallel between pope and king, but was also seeking to revive the fear of popular revolt through the spreading of insurrectionary ideas, which had permeated ruling circles since the Hussite victory and propaganda campaign of 1431.

In May 1437 there occurred the extraordinary simultaneous reading of two decrees at the Council of Basle. The disagreement was over arrangements for discussing reunion with the Greek church authorities. A minority of prelates and distinguished theologians at Basle agreed with Eugenius, that the Council should be transferred to Italy to accommodate the Greeks—though this was also in Eugenius's interests. The decree adopted by the majority, however, refused to accept this, and suggested various northern cities as the venue for the transferred Council, which were unlikely to be acceptable to the Greeks. This rowdy scene, when the principles of rule by numbers and rule by status, of corporation and hierarchy, clashed visibly, became the focus of future controversy.

When Eugenius eventually transferred the Council to Ferrara in September 1437, the majority remained at Basle, and open schism had once more broken out. Eugenius proceeded to argue that civil war, as well as rebellion, would be likely to result from Basle's activities. Shortly before leaving Basle for Florence in 1437, Cesarini had warned the Council of this possibility:

Once this unhappy schism has started in the church, there will immediately begin violence, domestic and internal strife among citizens and laymen. Alas, because of our division, learned men will begin quarrelling in nearly every province and city.[1]

In other words, schism is liable to escalate from the ecclesiastical into the political sphere. Schism, hardly less than rebellion, was a challenge to monarchical authority. In a letter circulated to rulers (1437) Eugenius himself took up the theme:

Scandals and divisions will pollulate from this accursed seed, not only in the ecclesiastical sphere, but also in kingdoms, principates and temporal dominions.[2]

Eugenius warned the Duke of Savoy (1438) that Baslean doctrine

[1] P. Braun, *Notitia hist.-lit.* 133 f. Cf. FM, xiv, 273; on Cesarini, cf. E. F. Jacob, 'Giuliano Cesarini', in *Bull. of J. Rylands Library*, li (1968), 104 ff., and Gill, *Council of Florence*, 46 ff., 94.   [2] Rayn. xxviii, 239.

and practice were likely to 'accumulate seditions, dissensions, divisions, civil wars and numerous ills among Christian people'.[1] He told Charles VII of France, the most cunning of monarchs, that it would bring 'schism...rebellion and the disturbance of Christians', and warned him against 'this impious contagion'.[2] The relation between schism and the collapse of political authority in general was stated more explicitly in a letter to Albert II (April 1439):

We observe that their efforts open the way to the division of the church's unity, the sedition of peoples, and the destruction of all political discipline.[3]

The deposition of Eugenius took place in June 1439, and in reply Eugenius issued the bull *Moyses* (September 1439), which condemned and deposed Basle and its adherents. In this bull, he described the Council as a rebellious 'conspiracy', and blamed it for 'discord among the faithful, quarrels between peoples...worse than civil wars'.[4] In 1440, Eugenius warned Henry VI of England, to whom Monte had meanwhile been presenting this line of argument, that Basle 'sows among people the causes of civil wars'.[5]

BASLE'S POSITION

The Council of Basle, meanwhile, was both seeking to refute, and involuntarily substantiating, this line of papal argument. Their refutation consisted of the simple assertion that secular and ecclesiastical principles were dissimilar in this respect, and that conciliar supremacy had been specifically prescribed by Christ for the church, and was not intended to apply in the secular sphere. This was first stated, probably in answer to Eugenius's *Tract of self-defence*, in a circular of October 1437:

The general council is not like some assembly of the counsellors of a sovereign prince, over which the pope may, like a sovereign and lord, hold sway.[6]

---

[1] *Concilium Florentinum: documenta et scriptores*, I, ed. G. Hofmann, part II, p. 11.
[2] Rayn. XXVIII, 302, 306.
[3] *Vet. mon. hist. Hungariam sacr. illustr.* ed. A. Theiner, II, 220.
[4] Rayn. XXVIII, 308, 315.   [5] *Ibid.* 332.
[6] *MCG*, II, 1055. In FM, XIV, 339 n. the authors remark of French Conciliarists during the Great Schism, 'Il est notable, qu'on ne veut pas utiliser contre le roi les théories qu'on oppose au pape'.

They also tried to turn Eugenius's argument against himself, by saying that it was he who, by disobeying the Council, was setting a dangerous example for the disregard of authority.[1] On the other hand, the *Monitorium* (March 1436), which initiated the legal proceedings against Eugenius, roundly condemned arbitrary government in political terms, saying that 'the holy church, which God willed to be free, has been made a tributary', and that 'no offence in a commonweal is more grievous than to follow one's own whim, and to overturn the laws'. Arbitrary government entailed automatic self-deposition. Indeed, rulers in general seemed to be the target of attack, when they condemned 'the often-quoted number of crimes of those that rule, which brings all Christendom into many slaughters and many perils'.[2] Again, in 1437 they exclaimed, 'Why should every man yield to one man, and everything be given over to his arbitrary will?'[3] They accused Eugenius (1438) of accumulating wealth 'by tyrannical means', and of treating the citizens of the papal states 'in an inhuman way'.[4]

Secular rulers had from the beginning joined supporters of Eugenius in their attacks on the committee-system of decision-making within the Council itself, which, by giving all members an equal vote and using majority procedure, applied in practice the *universitas* principles inherent in Baslean Conciliarism.[5] Now, in 1439, the independent spirit of Baslean Conciliarism drew down upon it once more the displeasure of several powers. Disregarding their recommendations that an agreement should be patched up with Eugenius 'for the sake of peace', the Council adopted its own course, strong in the claim that, as its great spokesman Cardinal Aleman put it, 'the church is assembled here in the name of Christ, not of the princes... who are subject to the Holy Spirit, not He to them'.[6] The bishops themselves came under attack at the Council for their connivance in the neutral policy of the major powers: 'they would sooner sell the church's liberty to the princes than lose their worldly possessions'.[7]

[1] *MCG*, III, 153. [2] Mansi, XXX, 1046C, 1047A; *MCG*, II, 1010.
[3] Rayn. XXVIII, 240. [4] *MCG*, III, 91.
[5] Cf. above, pp. 16, 35 f., For comments from secular powers, see Mansi, XXX, 883; Suppl. IV, 403; *RTA*, XVI, 555.
[6] *MCG*, III, 271, 276; Piccolomini, *CBC*, 98, 174 f. Cf. Valois, *Pape et Concile*, II, 165 ff. On Aleman, cf. above, pp. 35 f.
[7] *MCG*, III, 268; *CBC*, 108, 120 ff., 176.

The lower clergy carried all before them: the Council owed allegiance to no-one.

All this was given a keener edge in that the Council's policy which the princes were opposing was nothing less than the deposition of a previously undisputed pope. It was Eugenius's insistence on his own absolute powers, and his refusal to reform his administration according to conciliar decrees, that were the main grounds for his deposition; the 'heresy' included in the charge was simply his refusal to accept the doctrine of conciliar supremacy, which was specially repromulgated just before his final condemnation.[1] The constitutional implications of all this, moreover, were not passed over at the Council itself. It was argued by some during debates in May 1439, in support of their demand for immediate deposition, that this procedure was sanctioned by secular precedent, and only reflected the proper distribution of authority in any state.

In a well-organized kingdom, it is necessary that the kingdom have more power than the king; otherwise it would be called a tyranny, not a kingdom.[2]

These words were greeted with unusual enthusiasm by the Council. Other speakers took up the analogy:

Just as kings guilty of maladministration or tyrannical government are frequently overthrown and exiled by the whole kingdom—so too the church, i.e. general councils, has without doubt the power to depose popes...If a king despises the laws, violates his subjects' property... and turns everything over to his own arbitrary whim, surely the magnates of the realm would assemble and depose him, and set up someone else, who would swear to govern well and to keep the laws. What reason tells us, custom teaches us too.[3]

Thus, the charge that Conciliarism threatened the authority of the king as well as of the pope had some validity. In several countries there was conflict, open or incipient, between king and estates. England had not long ago deposed a king, and Germany an emperor; in England, earlier in the century, Parliament had been claiming wide powers of supervision; in France, Charles VII was wearying of the need to consult the Estates General; in Castile the

---

[1] Mansi, xxix, 179 f.   [2] *CBC*, 28; *MCG*, III, 261.
[3] *CBC*, 30–4. Cf. above, pp. 12, 49.

estates' claims to supremacy were supported by rebellious nobles, and in Sweden by rebellious peasantry. Even though Basle directly championed no such movement, its doctrine cannot have gone unnoticed.

THE EUGENIAN OFFENSIVE: BOURGES (1438) TO MAINZ (1439)

So, at least, Eugenius thought. He told Alfonso V of Aragon in April 1439 that Basle disrupted 'the whole earthly hierarchy' by giving power to 'a tumultuous mob', and that this would bring about 'the complete subversion of monarchy, principate and magistracy'.[1] Writing to another ruler who at this time supported the Council, the Duke of Brittany, he gave a more explicit warning:

Who would believe that such a prudent prince as we have always understood you to be would praise or approve the audacious presumption of the Basleans? If the rest took it up, neither princes, nor kings, nor the establishment of any commonweal could exist in this world. For, if opportunity or permission were given to subjects to rise up against their superiors, or to punish them at their own desire, what *status* of princes, what government could be maintained in its own position? Indeed before now subjects have perhaps been able to rise up against secular princes with some right; but on what grounds could inferiors rise up...against the vicar of Christ? It is surely something never heard of in earlier times, and it would give inferiors far too great an opportunity for mischief, if they could pass judgement on their superiors whenever they wished. It would be the destruction of all commonwealths.[2]

This letter provoked sufficient attention for it to be given a public reading at the Council (July 1439), after which an answer was sent to Charles VII himself, to the effect that the comparison between 'the legitimately-assembled church' and 'a secular association' was invalid because the former had special divine authority given by revelation.[3] Two years later, Segovia took the charges contained in this letter as his starting-point for a lengthy disquisition, with the

---

[1] Rayn. xxviii, 317.

[2] *Ibid.* 382; *MCG*, iii, 328 ff. Cf. P. A. Pocquet du Haut-Jussé, *Les Papes et les Ducs de Bretagne*, ii, 563 ff.

[3] *MCG*, iii, 328 ff.; for the same point, see also *RTA*, xiv, 193 (June 1439).

intention of proving that Conciliarism condemned only tyranny, and was fully compatible with true monarchy.

Meanwhile, the King of France and the German Emperor and Princes were seeking their own kind of solution to the schism. This meant, first, following Baslean reform-decrees in reducing papal power over church appointments and finance, but replacing it with their own influence. Secondly, from 1438 onwards, they refused to support either side against the other, but tried to make both agree to attend a 'new, third Council'; this was to be separate from Basle or Florence, and was to be held, significantly, in France or Germany. The German powers drew up an *Act of Neutrality* at the Diet of Frankfurt in March 1438, which they reaffirmed at Mainz the following year.[1] Several other powers adhered to this policy, and from 1438 until 1444 a third Council seemed to many the only feasible and just solution to the crisis. During this period, each side presented its case, for the benefit of the secular powers, at a series of public debates held before the French court and the German Diet. In several of these, the constitutional implications of the whole dispute became the centre of discussion.

The first of these took place at the Assembly of Bourges in July 1438, which eventually promulgated the famous *Pragmatic Sanction* giving royal control over church benefices. The papal delegation, which included Pierre de Versailles, having failed to make much impression on the clergy present,

turned to the secular princes, and expounded to them that the power of the pope was just like that of a secular prince over his subjects; in the same way that all the subjects of a prince, though assembled together, had no power over him, so too the whole assembled clergy had no power over the pope.[2]

It is remarkable that this papal appeal to the king, as summarily reported by their opponent Thomas Courcelles, expressed the Baslean doctrine in terms which its own exponents were to emphasize more and more, and drew attention to the idea of the sovereignty of the assembled community, which was to become a salient feature of

---

[1] Cf. Valois, *Pape et Concile*, II, 135 ff., 247 ff.; FM, XIV, 280 ff.; R. Bäumer, 'Eugen IV. und der Plan eines "Dritten Konzils" zur Beilegung des Basler Schismas', in *Reformata Reformanda* (Münster, 1965), 87 ff. For comments on the general trend of secular policies, cf. FM, XIV, 281, 292, 368, 424.   [2] *CB*, V, 172.

Baslean thought. About the Basleans' reply, Courcelles (who, having been Rector of Arts at Paris University from 1426 to 1431, was a typical and influential Baslean) only says that they 'refuted the allegations of the pope's speakers with most adequate arguments'.[1]

At the Diet of Nuremberg (autumn 1438) Turrecremata expounded his reply to Baslean claims in terms of general political theory. He argued the sovereignty of the pope over the council, on the grounds that the principle of monarchical sovereignty applied to the pope just as it did to any king or prince. The pope's relation to the council was that of 'prince' to 'college'; and it was a commonplace, he maintained, that an assembly required the prince's consent.[2] This was by no means true of Germany at this time; but Turrecremata was anticipating the line that was to be taken increasingly by many German princes later in the fifteenth century.[3] Next, he assigned to the 'king' the papal quality of 'fullness of power', as part of his claim that Eugenius's position rested on universal principles; Aquinas had already done this; but as a comparison not with the pope in person, but with the priesthood as a whole. Turrecremata said:

The pope has fullness of pontifical power, just as a king in a kingdom has the highest power and sovereignty (*principatus*) over the whole kingdom; that power resides in one man alone, the prince.[4]

The qualities of the *princeps* of Roman law were thus once again being applied to all sovereign monarchs; the word *princeps* may now be translated as 'sovereign'. But Turrecremata went on to make the existing notion of princely sovereignty more explicit by extending it to embrace the collective assembly of the people (unknown in Roman law), as well as the individual subjects. In answer to Basle's claim that the people assembled as a whole, though not individually,

[1] *Ibid.* On the Assembly of Bourges, cf. V. Martin, *Les Origines du Gallicanisme*, II, 299; N. Valois, *Histoire de la Pragmatique Sanction de Bourges*, 82. On Courcelles, cf. FM, XIV, 366; and on this speech, *ibid.* 354.

[2] Mansi, XXXI, 54C, 56D, 57 f. On this speech, cf. G. Hofmann, *Papato, conciliarismo, patriarcato*, 9 ff.

[3] Cf. F. L. Carsten, *Princes and parliaments in Germany*, 422 ff.; W. Andreas, *Deutschland vor der Reformation: eine Zeitenwende.*

[4] Mansi, XXXI, 50E–51A; cf. above, p. 71.

have power over the ruler, he replied that princely sovereignty extended no less over an assembly:

Who would contend that a king is head of each province and city, and not of the whole kingdom?...as if the assembly of subjects in one place could bring about a change in the authority of the prince! Who is sovereign over a people when they are dispersed and not also when they come together in one place under the sovereign's authority?[1]

Turrecremata was in fact developing the very notion of secular sovereignty to which he was appealing: and it was a development that must have delighted his audience, if we judge by their subsequent attitude towards their own estates. Turrecremata's intention, however, was to provide a clear-cut case for papal sovereignty over the council. He tried to make his argument even more convincing, by warning the princes that conciliarist ideas could engulf them too:

Indeed the next day somebody could make up a similar error about your Empire, most noble Caesar, and about your Princedoms, most illustrious Princes. This fiction is ridiculous and dangerous![2]

The Council's representatives replied that the question at issue was one of theology, not of political doctrine, and that it had already been decided by the decrees of Constance.[3]

THE DEPOSITION OF EUGENIUS (1439): GERMANY ALARMED

The outcome of this Diet, and its successor at Mainz in the spring of 1439, was the *Acceptatio of Mainz*, in which rulers of Germany followed a course similar to the French king's, accepting Basle's reform-decrees, but increasing their own control over benefices, and remaining neutral on the crucial question of the respective claims of Eugenius and Basle.[4] Indeed, at this point a common front was formed among the major powers, insisting on a containment of the

---

[1] *Ibid.* 46A–C.   [2] *Ibid.* 46C–D.

[3] *CB*, VI, 447. The Baslean representative was the Bishop of Lübeck, on whom see G. Hödl, 'Zur Reichspolitik des Basler Konzils. Bischof Johannes Schele von Lübeck (1420–1439)', in *Mitteil. d. Inst. f. oesterr. Geschichtsforsch.* LXXV (1967), 46–65.

[4] Cf. Valois, *Pape et Concile*, II, 148 ff.; A. Werminghoff, *Nationalkirchliche Bestrebungen in deutschen Mittelalter*, 33 ff., 162 ff.

dispute, and a new Council, in France or Germany, to settle existing differences. They demanded acceptance of their proposals on the grounds that they 'represented the world';[1] whichever side accepted their policy would gain their support; if both sides remained obstinate, 'the princes would find their own way'.[2] Charles VII even suggested that 'a council of princes might intervene as mediator'.[3] This programme of peace meant leaving reform to individual rulers; and the common front, with its determination to remain neutral, to check the progress of the schism, and to prevent measures leading to schism from taking effect within the various states, was probably more inimical to the interests of Basle than of Eugenius. For Eugenius had already transferred the Council, and had his own Council of Florence; while Basle had not yet deposed Eugenius or elected his successor. It halted the initiative of the reform-movement; but it also showed the weakness of Basle, which lacked the confidence to submit to a new Council.

In any case, the deposition, which took place in June 1439 soon after the policy of neutrality had taken final shape, seemed a direct affront to the pacifying attempts of the powers, who expressed their indignation in strong terms, and refused to recognize what seemed to them a new act of aggression. At this point Nicholas of Cusa began wooing the powers, particularly the German Emperor and Princes, with the idea that their dissent invalidated Basle's actions, and that without their consent Basle could not claim to represent 'the church spread throughout the world'.[4] Moreover, the Germans themselves began, like Eugenius, to recognize the public dangers of open schism, which had split the Empire only a generation ago. The princes' Diet at Mainz, in August 1439, expressed their alarm:

---

[1] *MCG*, III, 133.

[2] *MCG*, III, 247; cf. *CB*, VI, 450.   [3] *MCG*, III 250.

[4] 'The Basleans think they are the Council, and can get away with splitting the church in opposition to the Princes...Representation lies in tacit or explicit consent, and on it rests the power of councils. If therefore it has been established through explicit protestations that the Italian nation, Kings and Princes, and the church diffused through the world does not consent, how can they dare to seek support in the decrees of the holy Council of Constance?' In J. Koch, *Cusanus-Texte iv*, in *Sitzungsb. d. Heidelb. Akad. d. Wiss., phil-hist. Kl.* 1942–3, part 2, 46–7. Cf. Turrecremata in Mansi, XXXIA, 76C; and Eugenius in *RTA*, XV, 230; and Monte in Vat. lat. 4145, fo. 84r.

97

The authority of superiors is being overturned by discussion among the people; separate gatherings of the faithful, from the highest to the lowest, are being gravely inclined to separate tendencies by this schism... Confusion of rank is growing in the church... each day division creeps on more grievously; unless there is a speedy antidote... the church's unity, both among superior powers, and among the separate gatherings of the faithful, will be exiled from earth.[1]

An ecclesiastical prince, doubly threatened by the crisis, feared that 'criminal factions' would overthrow 'the ecclesiastical monarchy'.[2] The Emperor Albert II blamed Basle for disturbances;[3] when he died in the autumn, the electoral princes, fearing another imperial schism, pledged their support for the monarchical principles of authority and obedience, as the only remedy for an age of licence and disorder.[4]

The Council of Basle, well aware of sentiment in Germany, sought to placate the princes, by ensuring them of their support for the principles of law and order, and of hierarchical government.[5] To the Diet of Mainz, in June 1439, they once more protested against the attempt to compare them with a parliament. 'The church of God assembled in the Holy Spirit is not to be compared to a secular association, which the pope can dominate like a secular prince.'[6] This very distinction, however, between ecclesiastical and secular principles of government was perhaps hardly complimentary to the latter. The Council, they further argued, to the princes' Diet of August 1439, was itself the mainstay of ecclesiastical discipline.[7] In an address to the Imperial Diet of Mainz (June 1439), they again turned Eugenius's argument back onto himself; his disobedience to the Council was a threat to all ecclesiastical authority, and his contempt for law and judicial procedure (*sc.* his own trial) endangered the standing of secular authority as well.

We find this bringing disorder not only on all ecclesiastical ranks... but also on *all offices, all government, all authority*, in both spiritual and temporal

---

[1] Mansi, xxx, 1226B; cf. *ibid.* 1225B, 1228C, 1230A; *RTA*, xiv, 201.
[2] *RTA*, xiv, 315; cf. *ibid.* xv, 430. The Act of Neutrality had included the intention 'to uphold the government of the ecclesiastical polity': *MCG*, iii, 110.
[3] *RTA*, xiv, 205.   [4] *RTA*, xv, 183–4; above, p. 61.
[5] *MCG*, iii, 152, 521; Mansi, xxx, 1044D.
[6] *RTA*, xiv, 193, Cf. above, pp. 90, 93.   [7] *RTA*, xiv, 319.

spheres. Surely this is giving an *example and encouragement* to the subjects of any judicial authority to compel their own temporal and spiritual judges to refrain from passing judgment altogether?[1]

But even this argument was not an undisputed blessing for Basle; for, in repeating it the following year, they applied it to the disobedience not only of the pope, but of the neutral powers. Thus they assumed, perhaps more readily than the papacy, that the secular powers could be persuaded to accept ecclesiastical authority on a matter which, though itself concerned primarily with church affairs, touched their interests so closely; such an approach was not calculated to gain secular support.

Seeing ecclesiastical commands despised by their superiors...the people will, with little persuasion, aspire to the same freedom...they will directly claim that their burden is intolerable, their yoke will seem tyrannical and violent, and there will be a commotion among the people, who will furiously rise up, and shake this weight [*sc.* ecclesiastical authority] from their necks.[2]

This expresses the fear of anticlericalism, which had broken out fiercely in Germany about the time of the Hussite supremacy in the early 1430s. Another statement, also of autumn 1440, reiterated the threat to authority of every kind:

What destruction of Christendom...what an overthrow of commonweals, kingdoms and provinces!...Owing to this, ecclesiastical judgments will be wholly disregarded...all jurisdiction will be liable to perish, while they see the supreme authority of the church [*sc.* the Council] being opposed and rejected.[3]

Thus Basle tried to imitate a line of argument that had originated in, and was better attuned to, the papal ideology.

MONTE IN ENGLAND

The same papal arguments, meanwhile, were being employed in England by Eugenius's legate, Piero da Monte. Peculiarly conscious of the papacy's political impasse, he advocated concessions to royal demands for greater power in church government, as the only way

---

[1] *RTA*, xiv, 190; cf. *ibid.* 178, 182; Mansi, xxx, 1235; and above, p. 93.
[2] *RTA*, xv, 466.   [3] *MCG*, iii, 520, 524; cf. *RTA*, xvi, 123.

of taking the political force out of Conciliarism. Indeed, the whole policy of the concordats seems to be outlined in some of his letters from England. In 1438, for example, he wrote:

Such is the condition of the world and of our time, that it seems better to surrender a little than to expose everything to destruction...your behaviour towards these princes is harsher and more inflexible than the state of our affairs and the conditions of the time warrant...I advise you to seek a cure for this disease, not by knife and brand, but by gentle medicaments. We shall be doing all right, if we reconcile the minds of princes to the pope even with blandishment, persuasion and leniency.[1]

In 1440 he struck a more ominous note:

I see such great dangers arising for the Roman church every day, that, if the pope does not exercise this fullness of power, which the curial officials glory in so much, in a more moderate and temperate manner, then we must fear intervention by secular power.[2]

A trained lawyer hailing, like Roselli and Eugenius himself, from the imperialist environment of Venice, he had already advocated the conjunction of papal and imperial principles of authority.[3] He now applied this idea to the royal court of England, where recent events, particularly the Lollard risings, ensured him a receptive audience.

In a speech to the English court in 1436, soon after his arrival, he described the Council of Basle as a 'rebellion' and a 'subversion' by 'certain factions', a 'gathering' of 'conspirators', and 'a plebeian assembly bent on revolution'. Their activities were 'a kind of internal war' in the church, and they were involved in attacking 'the dignity and pre-eminence of their own head'.[4] He pressed the parallel between rebellion against ecclesiastical and rebellion against secular authority, in a reference to the rising of the Roman people against Eugenius in 1434, when the pope 'was expelled from his own see by force and the rebellion of subjects'.[5] He defended the papal case on the grounds of general monarchical principles, illustrated in paternal and military authority: there must be one leader 'who rules over all, keeping each in his place and rank'. Thus a threat to mon-

---

[1] Monte, ed. J. Haller, *Piero da Monte*, 73–4; cf. *ibid.* 21, 42, 50–1, 71, 89. For Monte's mission to England, cf. *ibid.* 40* ff.

[2] *Ibid.* 144.
[3] Cf. *ibid.* 31* f.; and above, p. 86.

[4] *Ibid.* 231, 234–5, 238–40.
[5] *Ibid.* 236.

4.0076

archical authority in the church is a threat to it in the state as well: 'What ruler's majesty and dignity will be maintained, if conspiracy against the papal primacy is allowed to go unpunished?'[1] In a speech to Henry VI in 1437, he added the legal argument: 'both canon and civil laws forbid appeal from the decision of the supreme prince'.[2] Before the Canterbury Convocation (April 1438), Monte again referred to Basle as a revolutionary populace, and this time actually accused them of having provoked the rising of Rome.[3] In private letters he continued the analogy, describing the Basleans as 'disturbers of the peace of the church...violators of the church's monarchical estate'.[4]

The English were in any case inclined to support Eugenius, both because of the French presence at Basle, and because of Henry's piety.[5] As early as 1433, Henry was regarding the Baslean affair in terms of a general attack on the principle of authority.[6] In letters to the emperor and Basle in 1437, Henry described the schism as an 'internal war in the kingdom of the militant church'; and its instigators at Basle were 'as it were seditious persons and manifest violators of both kinds of peace, ecclesiastical and civil'. He added a repetition of the papal warnings to rulers: 'This quarrel is a most harmful precedent, and seems liable to undermine all political authority'.[7] Archbishop Chichele of Canterbury took up the theme (May 1438), describing Basle as 'a sedition', which had 'invaded,... and shaken up not only the Roman Church, but all kingdoms, provinces...peoples and the whole world'.[8] Archbishop Kemp of York similarly, in a speech on behalf of the king in 1439, called the Basleans 'a conspiracy', which made them 'guilty of the worst

[1] *Ibid.* 240. [2] *Ibid.* 242, 247. [3] *Ibid.* 257–8.
[4] *Ibid.* 109, 110, 107; cf. *ibid.* 128, 137.
[5] Cf. E. F. Jacob, *The fifteenth century, 1399–1485*, 260 ff.; A. N. E. D. Schofield, 'England, the Pope and the Council of Basel, 1435–1449', in *Church History*, xxxiii (1964), 248 ff.; *id.* 'The second English delegation to the Council of Basel', in *Journal of Eccles. Hist.* xvii (1966), 29 ff. The Congress of Arras had helped to alienate England from the Council.
[6] Thomas Beckynton, *Official correspondence*, ed. G. Williams, ii, 65.
[7] *Ibid.* 39, 45; *RTA*, xiv, 310. The royal secretary from 1437 was the humanist scholar, and later bishop, Thomas Beckynton; cf. A. Judd, *The life of Thomas Beckynton*, 33 ff.
[8] Monte, ed. Haller, *Piero da Monte*, 66; cf. E. F. Jacob, *Archbishop Henry Chichele*, 56 ff.

crime', that is, treason.[1] These remarks suggest that the English court, which was alone in recognizing the Union of Florence in 1439, was to some degree influenced in its outlook by the propaganda of Eugenius and Monte.

THE COUNCIL OF FLORENCE (1439–1440)

By the middle of 1439 the political ideas of both sides were assuming their final form. Cusa's *Catholic concordance* and Roselli's *Monarchy*, both published in 1433, had started the process whereby the two ecclesiastical positions were defended in terms of general social and political argument. Escobar's *Government of councils* (1435) and Segovia's *Ten propositions* (1439) provided the link between earlier corporation theory (which was also being newly expounded by Panormitanus in his *Commentary on the decretals*), and Basle's doctrine of the absolute sovereignty of the corporate *universitas*. At the Council of Florence, Eugenius's supporters, having triumphantly celebrated reunion with the Greek church in July 1439, held disputations on the papal primacy in the light of the conciliar crisis. In these, the new elements in papal thought emerged with increasing clarity.

Turrecremata led the way in maintaining that papal sovereignty rested on generally valid principles of government, which could be gathered from Roman law, from those arguments of Aristotle which stated the advantages of monarchy, and from Pseudo-Denis' notion of an earthly hierarchy modelled on the heavenly. These themes from now on became the stock-in-trade of papal propaganda, and one suspects that Turrecremata's influence was widespread; he was certainly the most sophisticated exponent of the new ideology.[2] One speaker at Florence reiterated Eugenius's fear that Baslean doctrine, by 'reducing [the church], which was founded on a single ruler, to a popular confusion', would have the effect of 'giving rein to the fury of the ignorant populace'.[3]

Furthermore, after the reading of the rival decrees in May 1437,

---

[1] Monte, ed. Haller, *Piero da Monte*, 113.
[2] A formal debate was held, in which Turrecremata championed the papal position and Cesarini the conciliar: Valois, *Pape et Concile*, II, 203. See especially Turrecremata, *Oratio synodalis de primatu*, ed. E. Candal, 23–4; also Andreas de Santacroce, in *Concilium Florentinum*, VI, 3–7. Cf. J. Gill, *The Council of Florence*, 313.
[3] Santacroce, in *Concilium Florentinum*, VI, 6, 17–9.

numerous theologians had begun to trickle away from Basle to Eugenius's transferred Council of Ferrara–Florence. They maintained, with some justice, that Basle had put its own interests before reunion with the Eastern church, and that it was ceasing to be truly representative of the church. They did not altogether abandon the conciliar point of view, but wanted pope and council to work in harmony. Among these thinkers, Nicholas of Cusa was outstanding; he began to give an increasingly neoplatonic interpretation to his theory of consent through harmony, with power residing 'in essence' with the pope and being 'developed' by others. Consent, as he had always held, could be tacit as well as explicit, and here Florence had at least as good a case as Basle to represent the church.[1] John of Ragusio echoed the theme of the earthly following the heavenly hierarchy.[2] Versailles sought to harmonize the claims of pope and council by distinguishing between legal and moral sovereignty. The pope could not be overridden or judged by a council; but he ought to consult it, and decrees issuing from pope and council together carried greater weight than those issuing from the pope alone.[3] Similarly, Cusa and several of his colleagues continued to advocate reform, but from the top—and in vain.[4]

The papal viewpoint was to some extent echoed in 1440 by the ambassador of Castile, Sanchez de Arevalo, when Castile decided to support Eugenius in the summer of that year. Arevalo proceeded to lecture the newly-elected Emperor, Frederick III, on the political perils of the schism and of Baslean attitudes. He developed the view, previously expressed by Cesarini and Eugenius, that ecclesiastical schism was liable to escalate into political division, and added that the empire was particularly vulnerable in this respect:

[From recent annals] we will discover as an undisputed fact that schism in the empire and divisions in kingdoms have most often been produced by schism in the church. There are many records of this in the terrible schism not long ago, and now we shall witness the same with our own eyes...No-one can fail to see that various kinds of division have seriously

---

[1] Cf. P. Sigmund, *Nicholas of Cusa*, 228, 239, 259, 268 ff.
[2] *Tractatus de ecclesia*, fos 349v–350v. For details about him, see A. Krchnák, *De vita et operibus Ioannis de Ragusio*.
[3] Above, pp. 70; below, p. 113.
[4] Cf. Jedin, *History of the Council of Trent*, I, 117 ff.; FM, XIV, 885 ff.

increased among Christian people; every nation has witnesses to the appalling dissensions from which we are suffering. All this, if we investigate its origins, has obviously resulted from the division initiated in the church.[1]

Castile itself was in fact in the middle of a struggle between the nobles, championing the estates, and the king, whose minister, Alvaro de Luna, was accused of 'arbitrary government'.[2] Arevalo added that Conciliarism encouraged disrespect for authority and a 'confusion of all *status*'; in place of 'obedience, discipline and respect', it gave rise to 'self-will, rancour and ambition'.[3] Arevalo, to whom Cusa addressed a famous doctrinal letter (1440), later became a hysterical papalist, typifying the very attitudes that thwarted attempts to reform the Curia from within.

A doctrinal *memorandum*, composed at Florence in the summer of 1440 by Pierre de Versailles, a theologian and diplomat who worked both for the papacy and for the French court, combined the themes of Eugenius and Turrecremata. 'Reform' was but an excuse for disobedience, and Basle's sinister intention was 'to change the church's monarchy into its opposite'.[4] He answered the conciliarist claim that sovereignty necessarily resided with the community taken collectively, with the neoplatonic argument that society depended for its very existence upon a hierarchy headed by a monarch, to which it must therefore be subordinate.[5] He too warned that Basle's view, that only the community itself could hold supreme power, would undermine monarchical authority in any society:

This argument is absurd and seditious; and, if it were generally accepted, it would destroy all monarchs and princes for the same reason. For, it would be argued, if one man, the prince, has authority to kill a man for a just cause, he can also abuse this power, and kill a man without just cause: therefore, such power should never be given to a single individual. It is obvious that this argument is most seditious, and no attention should be given to it.[6]

[1] Mansi, xxxi, 15A–B. Cf. Valois, ii, 217 and n.
[2] J. Chartier, *Chronique de Charles VII*, ed. De Viriville, in *Bibl. elzévirienne*, ii, 18.
[3] Mansi, xxxi, 14C.
[4] Vat. lat. 4140, fo. 11r. Cf. Valois, ii, 207 f.; on Versailles, cf. above, p. 59, n. 1.
[5] *Ibid.* fo. 30v; cf. above, p. 61.   [6] *Ibid.* fo. 31v.

THE EUGENIAN OFFENSIVE: BOURGES (1440)

Turrecremata and Versailles were presented with an ideal opportunity for exercising the diplomatic potential of their arguments, when they were members of a papal delegation to the French court in August 1440. At Bourges, on 28–29 August, Charles VII held an ecclesiastical debate in the presence of the assembled clergy. The constitutional situation in France was at this moment particularly delicate. At the Estates General of autumn 1439, a decree had been passed enabling the king to raise taxes without the estates' consent, and placing the army under his control. This had the effect of making the estates more or less superfluous, and it also threatened the power of the nobility, some of whom, with the Dauphin's support, started a rebellion against this decree in the summer of 1440. This became known as 'The Praguerie' on analogy with the uprising in Prague in 1419, when the Hussites had successfully overthrown imperial— and papal—authority. During the nobles' rebellion, the Estates General was assembled, for what proved to be the last time in the reign, at Bourges; but, far from supporting the nobles, they wearied of waiting for the arrival of the king, who delayed until he had dispersed the insurgents, and when he came only the clergy remained.[1] It was then that the ecclesiastical debate took place.

Both the papal speakers seized this opportunity to appeal to the self-interest of a monarch who seemed to be in constitutional difficulties. Turrecremata, more bitingly than before, proclaimed monarchical sovereignty as a universal principle; the pope was simply the sovereign prince in the church.[2] He cited both Aristotle and Aquinas to argue that the best form of government was 'monarchical or royal sovereignty...[in which] power resides with a single person, the sovereign prince'. He argued against those who wished to assign power in different respects to both pope and council that sovereignty must reside with one man, *or* with a few, *or* with many; a theme, based on Aristotle, which he was to develop fully in his *Summa on the church*. Since the church was a *kingdom*, however, its sovereignty must reside with one man, the pope. He reaffirmed

---

[1] Valois, II, *Pape et Concile*, II, 226 ff.; cf. F. Lot and R. Fawtier, *Histoire des institutions françaises au moyen âge*, II, 572.

[2] Mansi, XXXIA, 75A, 93A.

that the pope was sovereign over his subjects, 'whether dispersed or collected in one place'.[1]

Now, Basle had recently been concentrating its attack on this very principle of pure monarchy, arguing that the ascription of all power to one man, since he might fall into sin, endangered the Christian commonwealth. 'What stability', Thomas Livingstone asked the princes assembled at Mainz (August 1439), 'could there be in the Christian polity, if it could all be overthrown by one sinner?'[2] In its reply to Eugenius's bull of condemnation, Basle stated (October 1439): 'It could clearly be envisaged what desolation would follow in the Church, if...one man could manage its affairs according to his own arbitrary whim.'[3] The same point had been put to the Diet of Mainz (June 1439) and to Charles VII himself (July 1439).[4] Aleman later (January 1443) warned that the pope might seek to extend over secular authorities too his principle of 'arbitrary domination...and bring everything under his own tyranny'.[5] These statements, as well as expressing Basle's insistence on the constitutional responsibility of the ruler, also seemed to echo the opinion current among Hussites, that 'sin' invalidated authority.[6] Turrecremata now described this Baslean view, in terms reminiscent of Hussitism: 'one sinful man' should not be permitted 'to dispose of all the affairs of the church at his own will', and above all had no power 'to transfer the council to any place or region he wished'. Having thus expressed Baslean doctrine in the form most calculated to provoke monarchical sentiment, particularly in France at this time, he explicitly compared it to Hussitism, as a 'seditious error', and went on:

What a seditious statement! Let sovereign princes pay attention and understand that this venomous Baslean tongue not only brings forth sedition against the pope...but also prepares *sedition and subversion for the rule of all sovereign princes.*[7]

---

[1] *Ibid.* 65D, 75A, 87–8, 93A; cf. above, pp. 67 ff.

[2] *RTA*, XIV, 336; cf. above, p. 98; on Livingstone, cf. D. Shaw, 'Thomas Livingstone, a conciliarist', in *Records of the Scottish Church History Society*, XII (1955), 120–35.

[3] *MCG*, III, 396; cf. *RTA*, XIV, 305.   [4] *MCG*, III, 329; *RTA*, XIV, 190.

[5] *RTA*, XVII, 85.   [6] Cf. above, pp. 3, 5.

[7] Mansi, XXXIA, 100B–C; cf. *ibid.* 69A, 107C.

Versailles also warned the French court of the danger of the subversive ideals of Basle:

If their ways prevailed,...no sovereign prince will ever be secure. For, if they are permitted to depose the pope, *it will be the same for the people against their king.*

Since Baslean doctrine 'subverts the monarchy of the church', it is 'filled with the crime of *lèse-majesté* and an examplar for rebellion'. Eugenius was in the same position as Charles VII, 'one king addressing another...a monarch, with a royal form of government'.[1]

Thomas Courcelles, replying to these points on behalf of Basle, said that they were merely intended 'to entice kings and princes'. He refuted the analogy with Hussitism by pointing out that it was the Council of Constance itself which had condemned the Hussite doctrine that people could judge their rulers at their own pleasure. He rejected the analogy between Baslean doctrine and secular constitutionalism, by reaffirming the distinction between the unique authority of the church's council, derived directly from God, and ordinary political authority, which was based on the principle of human domination: 'a secular assembly has no power from Christ to correct or punish its prince'.[2]

The effect of this whole debate appears to have been negative. Charles simply stuck to the *Pragmatic Sanction* and the Neutrality, continuing to demand 'a new, third council' to settle the disputed theological questions.[3] Nevertheless, one is struck by the fact that Conciliarism had many supporters in France, particularly at Paris University, and that when, in the autumn of that year, Charles demanded that the university should cease to support Basle, and be neutral like himself, it replied by defending its right to 'liberty of counsel', on the grounds that, without it, France would be a 'tyranny' instead of a royal monarchy.[4] Similarly, it was the supreme court of Parlement, with the status of which Gerson and D'Ailly had actually compared the general council of the church, which was

[1] *MCG*, III, 507; and J. Döllinger, *Beiträge z. polit., kirchl. und Cultur-Gesch. d. sechs letzten Jahrhunderte*, II, 426–7. The Bishop of Béziers also referred to 'sedition' in his speech: Valois, ii, 229 n.

[2] In *Preuves des libertez de l'Église Gallicane*, ed. P. Dupuy, in *Libertez de l'Église Gallicane*, ed. P. Pithou, II, 260.   [3] Valois, *Pape et Concile*, II, 234–5.

[4] Cited in Valois, *Pape et Concile*, II, 240; cf. above, p. 48.

responsible for foiling a ruse to get a spurious royal decree in favour of Eugenius promulgated as law.[1] It was also, surely, remarkable that the Estates General, which had met with unprecedented frequency during the 1420s and 1430s, was not convoked again, after this abortive meeting, until 1468. In fact, it was never to achieve political significance again until the very eve of the French Revolution of 1789.[2] But, while a second nobles' rising in 1442 caused some royal advisors to express fear of a constitutional revolution,[3] there is no evidence that Charles himself was in any way moved by the papal appeals to constitutional theory. It remains an illuminating coincidence that the French king listened to a tirade against the secular implications of Conciliarism at the very time when he was bringing to an end the political power of the Estates General. In general, we must conclude that the papal warnings, while they were wide of the mark in terms of contemporary political affairs, were based on a profound understanding of the real political significance of Baslean theory.

BASLE'S REPLY: MAINZ (1441)

Public, diplomatic discussion of the question of the political ideas implicit in Conciliarism reached its climax at the Diet of Mainz in March 1441. The doctrines of both sides were now fully developed, with an array of arguments taken from the sphere of ordinary government and society. A good deal of the argument at Mainz concerned the validity of Eugenius's transference of the Council and of Basle's deposition of the pope. In regard to the former, Segovia argued the validity of the majority principle in the Council —àpropos the rival decrees of 1437—on the precedent of the self-governing city-states; hardly an attractive example, so far as imperial sovereignty was concerned.[4] Cusa, in his case against the deposition,

---

[1] Valois, *Pape et Concile*, II, 235 ff. Cf. Gerson in *id. Opera*, ed. Du Pin, II, 279B; and D'Ailly, *ibid*. 957B.

[2] Cf. J. R. Major, *Representative institutions in Renaissance France, 1421–1559*, esp. 34; and P. S. Lewis, 'The Failure of the French medieval estates', in *Past and Present*, XXIII (1962), 3–24.

[3] *La Chronique d'Enguerran de Monstrelet*, ed. L. Douët D'Arcq, VI, 49. See also the remarks of Jean Juvenel, Archbishop of Rheims, in F. Maton, *La Souveraineté dans Jean Juvenel des Ursins*, 134 ff., 150.

[4] *RTA*, XV, 699; cf. *Ampl. disp.* in *MCG*, III, 844. For this Diet, cf. Valois, *Pape et Concile*, II, 244 ff.; FM, XIV, 283 f.

again referred to the Council's refusal to accept the advice of the secular powers; and he attacked the egalitarian implications of majority rule, complaining that 'one pope or one prince has no more authority in his vote than one servant'.[1] On this point he was strongly opposed by none other than the emperor's own representative, the Austrian theologian Thomas Ebendorfer, who poured contempt on 'this extraordinary and novel assertion, that kings and secular princes, being *the principal heads of the church*, represent it in a general council on behalf of themselves and their whole people'.[2] This drew attention to the basis of Cusa's contention, namely the hierarchical notion of representation itself. Nevertheless, Cusa was able to remark afterwards that 'this was the part [of his speech] best received by the Princes'.[3]

The highlight of this Diet was a magnificent exposition of conciliar doctrine by John of Segovia, which he later expanded into a long treatise and incorporated in his history of the Council. This *Expanded discourse* contained the most explicit universalization of corporation principles in government.[4] But its main purpose was to refute the allegations contained in Eugenius's 'letter directed to the Duke of Brittany' (*sc.* that of May 1439), which attempted 'to entice rulers away from the support of conciliar doctrine, on the grounds that respect paid to the authority of general councils detracts from the pre-eminence of secular princes'.[5] Segovia also referred explicitly to Eugenius's accusation that Basle was trying to change the church from a 'monarchy' into an 'aristocracy'.[6] He began his defence of Conciliarism against this charge, like others, by invalidating the parallel between the ecclesiastical and secular constitutions; the former was based on documents of revelation, particularly the decrees of Constance and Basle, the latter on reason and Aristotle.[7] He developed this by referring to the new principle of authority introduced by Christ for the church: 'he who wished to be greater among His people should be the servant and minister of all'. This meant that (as Courcelles had previously argued) the pope could not

---

[1] *RTA*, xv, 762.   [2] *Ibid.* 825. On Ebendorfer, cf. above, p. 71, n. 2.
[3] *Ibid.* 874. Cf. Sigmund, *Nicholas of Cusa*, 236.
[4] Cf. above, pp. 25 f. The original version of the speech is in *RTA*, xv, 649 ff.; the *Expanded discourse* (*Ampl. disp.*) is in *MCG*, iii, 695–941.
[5] *Ampl. disp.* in *MCG*, iii, 709: below, p. 145; above, p. 93.
[6] *Ibid.* 707–8: below, pp. 144 f.   [7] *Ibid.* 707–8: below, p. 144.

'dominate his subjects in the faith, nor behave as secular princes do'.[1] But Segovia based this on his own specific conception of the generically different type of authority obtaining in the church; the pope was set 'above' others, not in the ordinary sense of political sovereignty, but in a position incurring responsibility and service.[2] He further supported this differentiation between the mode of government in church and in state, by reference to the distinction between the church considered as a whole, in which sense it is 'a mystical body governed by Christ', and the church considered as a series of individuals, 'a political body...under a single president'. This twin conception of the church, which he had previously stated in 1439 and which the Cracow theologians were simultaneously elaborating, enabled him to say that the parallel with secular sovereignty applied to the pope as regards the church 'as a political body' —he could exercise full authority over its individual parts; and at the same time to deny that it applied to the church 'considered as a mystical body...that is in a general council'—the pope was subject to the authority of the church as a whole.[3]

But even this was only the beginning of his defence against Eugenius's accusations. He proceeded to enter the papal supporters' own territory of secular, and especially aristotelian, political theory. He maintained that Conciliarism was aimed, not at changing monarchy into aristocracy, but at perfecting monarchy itself, by making it include 'the sovereignty of the laws' and 'the use of consultation'.[4] He now added to the aristotelian argument past and present *practice* in the government of church and kingdom. It was 'observed' that rulers of all kinds consulted their chief subordinates in important decisions, and, what was more, that the more they did so the more weight their decrees had.[5] His conclusion was that:

The use of many wise men for counsel on difficult matters does not destroy, but rather glorifies, the monarchical form of government, both in secular and ecclesiastical rule.[6]

---

[1] *Ibid.* 724; cf. Courcelles and others, above, pp. 90, 93, 98.
[2] *Ibid.* 768; cf. above, pp. 33 f. Cf. an exchange between Segovia and Panormitanus in Piccolomini, *CBC*, 28.
[3] *RTA*, xv, 682, Cf. above, pp. 14 f.
[4] *Ampl. disp.* 709 ff: below, pp. 145 ff. Cf. above, pp. 45 ff.
[5] *Ibid.* 711, 894; cf. above, pp. 46 f.   [6] *Ibid.* 711–12: below, p. 147.

The holy Council of Basle, and the supporters of the conciliar doctrine
...that the pope is bound to obey the general council...profess beyond
doubt that the régime of the faithful people is the most orderly, and that
the holy church of God is and always should be ruled according to the
monarchical form of government.[1]

This line of argument, which Segovia was to repeat with still
more emphasis in his treatise of 1450, could certainly have appealed,
as it was designed to do, to the secular powers. The 'conciliar' form
of monarchy advocated by Segovia in this *Discourse* was by no
means inimical to their political interests; indeed, many of them were
to adopt it. It gave them the best of two systems; it provided them with
the moral support of a consultative assembly, without the legal
obligation of following it.[2] While Segovia condemned monarchy
as understood by Eugenius, as being 'arbitrary' and 'directed to the
private good' of the ruler, his work went far towards synthesizing
the conciliar and monarchical viewpoints. This was the solution
sought by many moderate papal supporters for the church; and it
was later adopted in several states, and endorsed by Bodin himself.
But there was also an underlying contradiction in Segovia's argument: while omitting legal sanctions in the case of secular monarchy,
he firmly maintained that the pope was 'bound' to obey the council.
This emerged quite clearly in other passages in the *Discourse* which
proclaimed the supremacy of the corporate community as a general
rule.[3] This, if part of the original speech, can only have left the
princes in doubt as to the real tenor of Conciliarism. Segovia further
contradicted himself by claiming a distinction between secular and
ecclesiastical principles, and then proceeding to argue from one to
the other.

But sympathy for the council was still strong in Germany, and
Ebendorfer himself, the Emperor's representative, defended Eugenius's deposition in general constitutional terms at this Diet:

In the case of any political ruler who acts against his own polity and
encompasses its destruction, it is permissible to resist him, bring him back
to better ways by various means, even by threats and penalties, and to
oppose him with, 'Why do you do this?'[4]

[1] *Ibid.* 708; below, p. 145.
[2] Cf. above, p. 95, n. 2.
[3] Cf. above, pp. 25 ff.
[4] *RTA*, xv, 842.

So far as the ecclesiastical policy of the secular powers was concerned, this Diet was again inconclusive; France and Germany upheld the Neutrality, and went on advocating a new council in their own lands.

THE RESPONSE OF THE SECULAR POWERS

But from now on the papal cause began to gather momentum among the neutral powers, most notably with the emperor himself. Young and idealistic, he was faced with the perennial problems of the late medieval empire: the ineffectiveness of imperial law and government, and the increasing independence of princes and cities. Many, including Nicholas of Cusa himself, ascribed the empire's disorder to the lack of a clear-cut constitution, which might make the emperor depend upon consultation with the princes, but would make their decrees effective throughout the empire.[1] Finally, the empire had proved vulnerable to the political consequences of ecclesiastical strife: Hussitism had robbed it of Bohemia, and threatened parts of central and southern Germany, where the demand for reform was strident.[2]

There are signs of a considerable change in the imperial attitude to authority in the church between the Diet of Mainz in March 1441 and the Diet of Frankfurt, held in the autumn of that year. Frederick wrote, asking the latter to 'drive forth the seditious errors of some people'.[3] Ebendorfer now related confusion in the empire to confusion in the church, as Arevalo had done in the previous year. The schism was dividing the people; because 'factious men' were tearing apart the church 'with popular fury', he feared also 'the destruction of the commonweal'.[4] He went on, like the princes at the imperial election of 1440, to apply monarchical ideology to the empire; only monarchy could bring peace, and nature and human society demonstrated the universal principle of 'one sovereign prince', as necessary to 'right order'. Quoting John of Salisbury, he

---

[1] *Conc. cath.* III, *passim.*

[2] Cf. *CMH*, VIII, 116 ff.; Barraclough, *Origins of modern Germany*, 320 ff.; H. S. Offler, 'Aspects of government in the late medieval empire', in *Europe in the late Middle Ages*, ed. Hale and others, 219 ff. For the ecclesiastical policy of the Empire in the 1440s, see J. Toews, 'Pope Eugenius IV and the Concordat of Vienna (1448)', in *Church History*, XXXIV (1965), 178 ff.

[3] *RTA*, XVI, 113.   [4] *Ibid.* 132; cf. Arevalo, above, p. 103.

said that royal authority should be revered as 'a corporal deity'.[1]

Meanwhile, at a meeting held at Florence in December 1441, the pro-papal theologian Pierre de Versailles, acting now as ambassador for Charles VII and urging the policy of a third Council, expressed almost entire agreement with the Eugenian conception of monarchy in the church. Basle, he said, was attempting 'to suppress this most beautiful monarchy of the church, degrading the noblest constitution to democracy or aristocracy'.[2] What was more, he agreed with his former colleagues that monarchy was the divinely-instituted form of government for secular as well as ecclesiastical affairs.[3] But the Council of Florence, on the other hand, had gone too far the other way; a new Council was required to balance the legal superiority of the pope over the council with 'some regulation' of papal power, to prevent its abuse. Further, as Segovia argued in a secular context, a council added moral lustre to papal authority.[4]

In rejecting the proposal for a new Council, on Eugenius's behalf, Turrecremata put forward a more uncompromising conception of monarchical sovereignty than before. He argued that the idea of a new Council was incompatible with papal sovereignty, because 'a popular assembly *by nature* hates the sovereignty of the monarch'; the two were irreconcilably opposed.[5] Turrecremata can hardly have meant this as more than a debating point, since the Council of Florence was itself still in session. His argument was similar to that contained in a treatise written by Arevalo in 1441, which ascribed the project of a new Council to a plot on the part of Basle and the Hussites, 'so that they can always have councils in session, set up a new constitution for the church...and be exempt from their superiors'. Arevalo propounded the view that monarchy and democracy were mutually exclusive, and that it was in the nature of things that monarch and people should hate one another. Any attempt, therefore, to combine the two in an assembly would be 'dangerous', and

[1] *Ibid.* 130, 133; cf. above, pp. 61 f.
[2] Rayn. xxviii, 362; Mansi, xxxv, 44D. Cf. Valois, *Pape et Concile*, 250 f.
[3] Rayn, xxviii, 361; cf. sup. pp. 72, 81.
[4] *Ibid.* 363-4. He had made a similar point in a letter of 1438: E. Cecconi, *Studi storici sul Concilio di Firenze*, DLXVIII.
[5] *Ibid.* 363; also in Vat. lat. 4039, fo. 13 ff.

would 'alter and overturn the Christian commonweal'.[1] Such ideas were to become more popular in papal circles as time went on.

The emperor held another Diet at Frankfurt in the summer of 1442. The debate once again centred on the legitimacy of Eugenius's transference of the Council in 1437, and once again political ideas were introduced into the discussion by both sides. Cusa argued that the pope, as 'sovereign prince', had the power to override laws, direct appointments, and overrule a council; otherwise, he maintained, the church would be lacking in 'sovereignty with fullness of power (*principatus cum plenitudine potestatis*)', which was requisite for the running of any society.[2] He thus followed Turrecremata in universalizing the principle of fullness of power.

Cusa was answered at great length by the formidable Panormitanus. In justification of the validity of the majority's decree, of May 1437, against the transference, he rehearsed exhaustively the civil- and canon-law texts and arguments for majority rule, mostly taken from laws referring to corporations and city-states, and including frequent citations from Bartolus. It was here that he reproduced, as an argument for the majority, Zabarella's view, based on Aristotle, that 'the government of a city belongs to the assembly of citizens, or to its weightier part (*valentior pars*)': but, while Zabarella meant status to be taken into account, Panormitanus used this as an argument for rule by a numerical majority.[3] He added his own observation on the Venetian constitution, where (he maintained) the doge, though first among individual citizens, might be overruled and deposed by the city as a whole, as a precedent for sovereignty residing fundamentally with the whole, and with the ruler as 'principal minister'.[4] This, of course, tended to substantiate earlier papal allegations about the secular import of conciliar supremacy; but Piccolomini's remark on this speech was of a different order:

> Only a fool thinks kings are influenced by tomes and treatises.[5]

Thus the diplomatic relevance of the secular implications of

---

[1] Barb. lat. 1487, fos 120v–122v. Cf. Jedin, *History of the Council of Trent*, I, 137 n.
[2] *RTA*, XVI, 421, 425, 431, Cf. Valois, *Pape et Concile*, II, 258. He produced similar statements in his speech at Mainz, 1441: *RTA*, XV, 642. He also reiterated, on the present occasion, the arguments based on the exclusion of secular influence by Basle: *RTA*, XVI, 428, 432.   [3] *RTA*, XVI, 456, 513; cf. above, p. 35.
[4] *Ibid.* 521; above, p. 11.   [5] Piccolomini, *De rebus Basileae gestis*, 82.

Conciliarism might have been on the wane, had it not been for a truly remarkable contribution from the English delegation. They first introduced the political analogy as an argument against the emperor's Neutrality. They argued, perhaps with a sidelong glance at English affairs, that the appearance of a rival claimant cannot justify suspending obedience to a reigning monarch. This would produce 'internal sedition', and would be 'clearly absurd in any human polity'.[1] But their most significant constitutional parallel was applied against Basle's claim that it could not be transferred or dissolved without its own consent, a claim which had already been heard from the English Parliament, and which was to become the focus of later controversy in England.

[The Basleans] decree that the Council can never be dissolved except with their consent; and so they have prolonged it for ten years, though the lords at Constance decreed that councils should be held every ten years, not for ten years. It is just as if a king summoned a parliament—which is seen as an act of great authority in kingdoms—and later, when the king himself also dissolved it, the parliament should on its own account decree that it must continue as long as it pleases. And this I say with confidence: *the council depends just as much on the pope, as the parliament does on the king.*[2]

They thus endorsed the papal claim as a general constitutional principle. They ended with a more opportunistic argument, suggesting that Basle itself might next claim the power to depose kings and princes; and they attacked it for admitting men of low status to full participation in its affairs.[3]

The neutral powers continued to press for a new Council, mainly no doubt as a way of promoting their private ecclesiastical interests. A weariness with the details of ecclesiastical theory was implicit in Charles VII's bland suggestion that 'the name "council" should be abandoned; it is best for the princes to assemble, to show themselves and to compose the affairs of the church; where the princes are, there is the church'.[4] Frederick III continued to press for a new Council with a strong representation of secular powers.[5] He reiterated the fear that the schism would add to the chaos within the Empire; it was already causing 'serious dissensions among the subjects of our

---

[1] *RTA*, XVI, 552–3.　　　[2] *Ibid.* 555–6.　　　[3] *Ibid.* 555–6.
[4] Piccolomini, *De rebus Basileae gestis*, 86–7; cf. *RTA*, XVII. 191; *CB*, VIII, 297. Cf. Valois, *Pape et Concile*, II, 256–7.　　　[5] *RTA*, XVII, 148.

empire, and disturbances of lands and churches'.[1] In a decree on benefices (July 1442), he reaffirmed the Neutrality, and forbade the condemnatory actions of either side from taking effect in the empire.[2] The Chancellor expressed his hope that 'the multitude of faithful peoples may find peace', and advocated the restoration of peace in both church and empire through the application of imperial authority, a view also taken by Ebendorfer in a letter to Savoy.[3] Above all, in a speech at Basle in September, Ebendorfer emphasized the sad secular effects of the schism, during which 'enormous ills are being produced in both spheres...the order of both secular and ecclesiastical affairs is collapsing from its former state'.[4] At a Diet held at Nuremberg in February 1443, the project of a new Council was again discussed inconclusively.

Events in Germany took a dramatic turn in the summer of 1443, when Frederick III became involved in war with the Swiss Confederation. There was a certain connection between this and the Council of Basle; the Swiss, as well as being in the Baslean allegiance, received active support from Duke Louis of Savoy, who was the son of Basle's antipope Felix V. (We may also note that the citizens of Basle itself showed sympathy for their fellow-countrymen during a decisive battle that took place nearby.)[5] Further, in September 1443 the nephew of Cardinal Aleman led an abortive coup in the town of Avignon on behalf of 'Savoy and Pope Felix', the only recorded example of a civic rising in support of Basle.[6] (The Viennese, in the revolt against Frederick in 1452, also included Nicholas V in their attack, and demanded a new Council.)[7]

Political ideology was introduced into the Swiss conflict by Frederick's newly appointed secretary, Aeneas Sylvius Piccolomini, who had only recently left Basle; it was he who had noted the use of political ideas in the Council's debates of May 1439.[8] Appealing to

---

[1] Chmel, *Regesta*, 23–4; cf. *RTA*, xvi, 574–5.   [2] Chmel, *Regesta*, 23–4.
[3] *RTA*, xvii, 37, 40, 47.   [4] *Ibid.* 23.
[5] T. Basin, *Histoire des regnes de Charles VII*, ed. Quicherat, i, 182. Cf. Valois, *Pape et Concile*, ii, 292 ff.; *CMH*, viii, 139 f.   [6] Valois, *Pape et Concile*, ii, 290.
[7] Piccolomini, *Historia rerum Frederici III*, in *Analecta mon. omnis aevi Vindobon.* ed. A. Kollar, ii, 356–7. Thus the ideological bond between Baslean Conciliarism and civic thought (above, pp. 10 f.) was not reflected in practice.
[8] On the development of Piccolomini's political and ecclesiastical views, see B. Widmer, *Enea Silvio Piccolomini*, esp. 130 ff. Cf. above, p. 12.

Charles VII, on behalf of Frederick III and Sigismund of Austria, for help against the Confederation, he argued the need for an alliance between monarchs against any rebels, on the grounds that they had a common interest in upholding monarchical authority, and in ensuring obedience to all forms of authority. He suggested that the Swiss (who on previous occasions had united with city-leagues of southern Germany) might extend their 'confederacy' to other 'subject' peoples, persuading them to follow their own 'bad example'.[1] As in Eugenius's warnings, the spread of the *idea* of rebellion received specific mention.

For subjects to be permitted to rise up against their lords is both indecent and dangerous for all kings. For everyone thinks he may perform what others do without being punished.[2]

This universal example, which concerns all princes, of servants rising up against their lords, of serfs humiliating nobles...which can spread with no small detriment to all kings.[3]

To this, Louis of Savoy replied in terms reminiscent of both Hussite and Baslean ideology:

If you consider our rights, you will not find any who gained dominion without virtue...Kings are made, not by wealth, the thundering attention of the people, or a noble house, but by outstanding virtue. On the other hand, foul and sordid men, without any virtue of their own, despite their resplendent ancestry, are lowered and besmirched by their filthy deeds, which overshadow the noble deeds of their forefathers. Who would deem that those who attack our public and human welfare, that public brigands...are uplifted by the prerogative of their *noblesse*? Certainly, no-one. That is why we maintain that our most blameless confederates, whom you call an uncivilized mob,...are friends and upholders of honesty and truth.[4]

This was just what Segovia, following Aristotle, said about the origin of monarchy and the transition to aristocracy; authority belonged by right to the best men.[5]

This similarity is brought out again in a letter from Eugenius to

---

[1] Piccolomini, ed. R. Wolkan, *Der Briefwechsel des Eneas Silvius Piccolomini*, part I, vol. II, 66, 68, 177–8.

[2] *Ibid.* 66. [3] *Ibid.* 68.

[4] *Ibid.* 175. [5] Above, pp. 44 ff.

Frederick in which he discounted the wisdom and justice of the latter's appeal for a new Council (August 1443). The Basleans, he said, were 'rebels', inspired by the 'ambition, greed, insubordination, conspiracy...new and insane doctrines', that were becoming everywhere prevalent. What both church and empire needed was peace. But, he went on, thanks to the Basleans, 'we are faced with impiety, ambition and tyranny; and we find many, whose dominions are far greater than Savoy, being attracted to the impiety of this idol'.[1]

In the autumn of 1443, Charles VII continued to urge the emperor to take the initiative in summoning a new Council, consisting 'of all the kings, princes and prelates, and the noble communities of the Christian world, for they too are concerned in this business'.[2] Eugenius's supporters among the secular powers meanwhile took up the papal warnings about the likely political consequences of Basle and also of Neutrality. Alfonso V of Aragon threw in his lot with Eugenius against Basle, as soon as the pope had recognized his claim to the Kingdom of Naples (April 1443), which he had conquered the previous year. This great renaissance monarch, in whose letters very soon appear traces of papal formulae, now expressed Eugenius's point of view in political terms. In the first place, he stated that the schism in the church was the cause of 'rebellion, disobedience and division in the Holy Roman Empire, in the kingdoms and dominions of Catholic princes, in every college, city and household'.[3] But he went further than this: by its very nature, the schism sets an example for rebellion against monarchy in every sphere:

No commonweal, no human society, no civil or political group can remain securely under a single head, so long as the division and schism in the highest monarchy of the church are displayed as an example.[4]

The Chancellor of Castile urged Frederick to regard the Baslean

---

[1] Braun, *Notitia hist.-lit.* 162–3. The Avignon rising occurred in September 1443 (above, p. 116).
[2] *RTA*, xvii, 191; Piccolomini, ed. Wolkan, *Der Briefwechsel*, vol. 1, 502.
[3] *RTA*, xvii, 182; cf. above, pp. 89 f. Cf. A. Ryder. 'The evolution of imperial government under Alfonso V of Aragon', in *Europe in the late Middle Ages*, ed. Hale and others, 332 ff.
[4] *RTA*, xvii, 182.

affair not simply as 'schism' but as 'rebellion'.[1] Finally, in September 1443, the papal legate Carvajal addressed a calculating speech to Frederick. He recommended for the emperor's consideration the hierarchical principle which operated in every part of the universe. He spoke in the same breath of 'the princes' and 'the church spread throughout the world', and referred to the former as 'the church's *honourable members*'. He declared Eugenius's readiness to hold an assembly of prelates 'from every nation...who will be conversant with the desires of the kings and princes', at Rome itself.[2] These arguments, coming from a hard-headed diplomat, reflect both his own intimacy with Cusa (with whom he had previously shared legations) and the ubiquity of the hierarchical argument in papal circles by this time. In the same year, Cusa's teacher, Heinrich Campo, wrote a remarkable and difficult treatise, teeming with the philosophical terminology of political neoplatonism, and in some ways suggestive of Hegel, to prove the compatibility of a new Council with the monarchical principles of the papacy.[3]

In the autumn of 1444, the Imperial Diet assembled again at Nuremberg, with the object of dealing with the two major issues confronting the empire: the schism between Eugenius and Basle, and the 'rebellion' of the Swiss cantons. So far as the Swiss affair was concerned, the emperor had at first suffered several defeats at the hands of the Confederates, who like the Hussites made up in skill and enthusiasm what they lacked in numbers. But his appeals of 1443 had succeeded in enlisting the aid of the French Dauphin, who, with some unemployed and ruthless soldiery, defeated the Swiss and pillaged their territory. A truce was arranged by the Council of Basle late in 1444. It was not to be long, however, before the Swiss succeeded in asserting their independence from the empire, and formed what was to become the Confederation of Switzerland.[4]

At this Diet, Panormitanus spoke for Basle; he had remained with the Council despite the changing policy of his king, Alfonso of Aragon. His speech, like the one he made at Frankfurt in 1442,

---

[1] *RTA*, xvii, 184.　　　　　　　　[2] *Ibid.* 144–5.

[3] Heimericus de Campo, *Tractatus de potestate papae et concilii generalis*. On him, cf. my forthcoming article, 'Heimericus de Campo: the council and history', in *Annuarium Historiae Conciliorum*.

[4] Cf. *CMH*, viii, 139 f., 289 f.; *The new Cambridge modern history*, i, ed. G. Potter, 204 f.

showed a more wholehearted espousal of conciliar sovereignty than appears in his more academic *Commentary on the decretals*. Following the logic of *universitas* theory, he gave the council unlimited scope, and made the role of the pope purely executive.[1] He reproduced the distinction, previously stated by Segovia and the Cracow theologians, between the church as a mystical body, 'according to which it is the whole church represented in the council', and as a political body. The political body is ruled by the pope, but the mystical body is ruled 'directly by the Holy Spirit'; so that the pope is 'head of all the members of the Church, but not of the whole church'. This, once again, implied that conciliar sovereignty was confined to the church, not a general political principle.[2]

Cusa, on behalf of Eugenius, once again played to the secular rulers' desire for more power in church affairs. Earlier that year, Vienna University had suggested that a council should take the form of 'a general parliament with the consent of the kings and princes';[3] this anticipated Podiebrad of Bohemia's idea of an international convention of secular powers. Cusa now asked the Diet what authority it thought Basle could have, 'to give commands to emperor, kings, cardinals...'? How could it claim to represent the universal church, when it clearly lacked 'the *consent of the emperor, kings and princes*, and especially of the cardinals...and bishops'?[4]

It was the ambassadors of the Duke of Burgundy who on this occasion, like the English at Frankfurt two years before, introduced the constitutional parallel and warned the emperor of the secular implications of the deposition. Burgundy, like England, had supported Eugenius all along, and had had its share of political disturbances at home in recent years.[5] They said that the Neutrality was like abandoning 'one who is in unquestioned possession of the principate'. They warned the emperor, probably with the Swiss conflict in mind, that it would be far easier for people to justify rebellion against him than against the pope:

Let Your Majesty's Highness consider whether it is permitted for subjects so easily to throw off the reins and rise up against their lords, and whether

---

[1] *RTA*, xvii, 351; above, pp. 41 f. [2] *RTA*, xvii, 351; cf. above, pp. 14 f.
[3] *RTA*, xvii, 268. [4] *Ibid.* 381, 384.
[5] Cf. J. Toussaint, *Les Rélations diplomatiques de Philippe le Bon avec le Concile de Bâle, 1431–1449*.

this befits the human monarchy. If your Serenity thinks this should be tolerated, who, I ask you, will have security in his presidency? If it is permitted for the prelates of the church to accuse the pope, who received power immediately from God, and whom God has reserved for his own judgment alone; why will it not be more easily permitted for the people to reprove Caesar, who first received his dominion and power from the people, and who is also subject to human judgment, namely the pope's.[1]

This argument was the same as that contained in Eugenius's *Tract of self-defence* (1436);[2] here too, it was argued that the secular monarch was more liable to suffer, because his power did not come directly from God. Exact parallelism was thus sacrificed for the sake of an *a fortiori* warning. The Burgundians went on to point out how 'much more terrible' it was for the pope to be challenged by his own ecclesiastical subordinates than by the secular power itself:

An eclipse, when the sun is obscured by the moon, is a scandal which brings terror to many. It would be much more terrible if the stars of heaven clouded over the rays of the sun! The sun is the pope, since he is the greater light; the moon is your Majesty, since it is the lesser light; the stars are the clerics or prelates of the church, or the other faithful.[3]

The parallel between this and the emperor's relation with the Swiss could hardly fail to be noticed.

At the end of 1444, Frederick himself decided to support Eugenius. Though he could not yet commit the empire in the face of the princes' continued opposition to Eugenius, his diplomatic activity was now aimed, not so much towards securing a new Council, but towards restoring allegiance to the reigning pope.[4] From now on, then, the project of the third neutral Council began to take second place to movements for the direct restoration of obedience to Eugenius. The papacy contributed to this process by showing itself more willing to discuss negotiated settlements with each secular power individually.

The emperor's new policy was accompanied by, and may have been directly related to, an increasingly conscious avowal of

---

[1] Cited in Toussaint, *Les Rélations diplomatiques*, 275. The phrase 'human monarchy' was sometimes a synonym for the empire.   [2] Above, p. 88.

[3] Cited in Toussaint, *Les Rélations diplomatiques*, 276.

[4] Cf. Valois, *Pape et Concile*, ii, 303 f.; Toews, 'Pope Eugenius IV', 182 f. For similar developments in France, cf. FM, xiv, 368.

monarchical ideology, for both church and state, in imperial circles. In a speech at Basle (autumn 1444), Ebendorfer now expressed both the fear of subversion and the general need for monarchical sovereignty, in ecclesiastical as well as in secular affairs. In order to achieve reunion in the church, he argued, there must be 'one ruler and prince', and he supported this on the grounds of the general principle of sovereign unity:

The instinct of physical nature, the voice of Seneca, the teaching of sacred Scripture, and daily experience, mistress of the world, all point to unity in the prince and reject plurality of princes.[1]

He now blamed the schism, not only for causing political dissension, but for 'the oppression of the clergy, and the vulgar common opinion of passionate men'. Above all, 'obedience in each sphere is being *subverted*'.[2] He was now, therefore, applying to the church the monarchical principle which he had advocated for the empire since 1441;[3] it is noticeable that both Ebendorfer and Piccolomini were strong imperialists a good while before they supported Eugenius IV.

The imperial court continued to amplify monarchical ideas in its own sphere. In a border dispute with Charles of France in the autumn of 1444, the imperial ambassadors defended the cause of the Emperor and princes in terms of their monarchical rights, based on Roman-law doctrine:

Every prince holds the position of the head, and plays the part of the soul, in the body of the commonweal; it is by him that the whole body of the commonweal or of his army is regulated and ruled. Since the prince is the people's foundation, and the justice of others must emanate from his justice, and since he is father of the fatherland—all other justice must be ruled and governed by him.[4]

Such a passage shows how the reception of Roman law could stimulate monarchical doctrine. The statement of papal sovereignty in general political terms could be used for the same purpose. Piccolomini, as imperial secretary to the emperor, even though himself by no means yet in favour of a return to papal monarchy, seems to

---

[1] *RTA*, xvii, 651; cf. above, pp. 67 f.   [2] *Ibid.* 647, 650.
[3] Cf. above, pp. 112 f.   [4] *RTA*, xvii, 453–4.

have been the first to realize that the emperor could borrow papal arguments. In a letter of 1443, he defended the emperor's power of taxation in Italy on papal precedent.[1] This parallelism was to be further exploited in his treatise *On the origin and authority of the Roman Empire*. In ecclesiastical affairs, meanwhile, he echoed Eugenius's warnings. In a treatise composed for Frederick in 1445, he urged him to call a new Council lest, if this question of *superioritas*, on which so much had been written, were to be left unresolved, 'they would stir up new factions each day, and there would be *many Bohemias*'.[2] In the autumn of 1445, he adopted the contrast between 'a popular and a royal régime' as an argument for the Hungarian nobles to accept Frederick's candidate as their king. He contrasted the 'utilitarian' outlook of the 'populace' and the 'merchants' with the nobility's code of 'honour'; he pointed out that where the former ruled, 'there are no nobles at court'.[3] Having recently read the *Politics*, he expounded the notion of 'natural' lordship and slavery; he extended the antagonism observed by Arevalo between monarchy and democracy to one between aristocracy and *plebs*.[4] In this way, the monarchical principle was naturally united, in secular circles, with hereditary status (a 'feudal' survival, one might say, in the 'new monarchies'). The papal propagandists appear to have glossed over this not inconsiderable difference between the papacy and most secular monarchies.

It was easy, moreover, to identify the Council of Basle with those without *status*, as did Poggio, Piccolomini (both intellectual aristocrats) and several others; for it demonstrated both 'ambition'—the class sin, in aristocratic eyes, of the bourgeoisie—and 'sedition', which was the political expression of the same desire.[5] Indeed, a

---

[1] Piccolomini, ed. Wolkan, *Der Briefwechsel*, II, 90; cf. above, p. 83. For the 'Herrschaftspropaganda' of this period, cf. H. Fichtenau, *Arenga*, 177, 182.

[2] Piccolomini, *Pentalogus*, in Pez, *Thes. anecd. noviss.* IV, iii, 662; cf. *id. De rebus Basileae gestis*, 114.

[3] Piccolomini, ed. Wolkan, *Der Briefwechsel*, I, 552, 554, 558–9; cf. *id. Historia rerum Friderici III*, 134, 204; and *id. Pentalogus*, 696. Piccolomini here anticipates the notion of 'ideology' in the sense of a set of ideas fitted to a certain social group; cf. A. Skinner, 'Economics and History—the Scottish Enlightenment', in *Scottish Journal of Polit. Econ.* XII (1965), 1 ff.

[4] Piccolomini, ed. Wolkan, *Der Briefwechsel*, II, 177–8; cf. above, pp. 112 f.

[5] *Ibid.* 178; cf. Cesarini in Braun, *Notitia*, VI, 134; Henry VI in Beckington, *Official correspondence*, II, 45, 91; and Arevalo, above, p. 104. For the attack on Basle as

modern writer has epitomized the Council of Basle, as comprising '*les ambitions des bourgeois*, toute la fermentation sociale du moyen âge finissant'.[1]

The convergence between the ideologies of papacy and empire was felicitously expressed when in Rome, with the verbal and visual pomp of a renaissance court, Nicholas crowned Frederick III as emperor (1452). It was a meaningful coincidence, as Pastor pointed out, that Frederick was at once the first of a continuous line of Habsburg emperors, and the last emperor ever to go to Rome for his crown.[2] This heralded the *Ancien Régime*, in which royal authority, while still leaning on religious sanctions for its own support, claimed autonomy from the church.

A DANGEROUS ALLIANCE

After negotiations lasting throughout the year 1445, Frederick and Eugenius reached agreement early in 1446. But Eugenius proceeded to prejudice his chances of securing the allegiance of the electoral princes, by deposing the Archbishops of Cologne and Trier for their neutrality. During the Diet of Frankfurt, which lasted from the spring well into the summer of 1446, the princes had cause to feel suspicious about the implications of the papal–imperial pact for their own territorial integrity.[3] Talk of the need to consult secular princes before calling a new Council, which was being used by some Eugenians as an excuse for shelving that issue, was attacked as contradictory to canon law.[4] Against attempts to bind the pope with conditions before submitting to him, the emperor argued that 'a law should not be laid down for the pope by his inferiors'.[5] By the end of the Diet, only three Electors had submitted to Eugenius.

Eugenius IV died in February 1447, after receiving the emperor's submission but without having reached a final agreement with the German princes. Negotiations between Nicholas V and the four reluctant princes, sponsored by Charles VII, continued during the

---

being a mere rabble, see Ourliac, 'La sociologie du Concile de Bâle', 13.
[1] Ourliac, 'La sociologie du Concile de Bâle', 32.
[2] L. Pastor, *History of the popes*, ed. Antrobus, II, 162.
[3] Valois, *Pape et Concile*, II, 303 ff.
[4] *Publicationen*, ed. Hansen, XXXIV, 227.
[5] Piccolomini, *De rebus Basileae gestis*, 99.

summer, and were successfully concluded in August. Archbishop Jouvenel, the French representative, remarked, perhaps jocularly, that 'the princes abhorred to hear (a new Council) mentioned, because of the evils done at Basle; if anyone spoke of a Council, they generally said that, even if it were held by children and old women, it would be for deposing a pope'.[1] He also reiterated the view that the princes more or less constituted the church in its *diffused* aspect.[2]

The controversy between pope and Council ended, not by agreement between the two warring parties, nor by the submission of one to the other, but by diplomatic negotiations issuing in ecclesiastical treaties, 'concordats', between the papacy under Eugenius IV and Nicholas V and a third party, the secular powers. Since the last effectively wielded the 'consensus of Christendom', their agreements with the papacy left the Council of Basle virtually without support. In April 1449, Felix V resigned: the Council elected Nicholas V in his place, and dissolved itself after reaffirming the supremacy of council over pope; its leaders agreed to retire with honour and an income.[3] Segovia was not the only one who noted that this was a victory of diplomacy, not of doctrine.[4]

The papal victory was indeed linked with the developing art of diplomacy. The controversy itself had assisted the growth of a class of professional ideologues, whose talents were highly valued by their ecclesiastical or royal patrons. Just as jurisprudence was yielding to metaphysics, so these new courtiers, of whom Piccolomini provided the most brilliant example, replaced the lawyers as the king's men. Oratory became the art form of the new political ideas. In flowery treatises they served their masters with the constitutional doctrines that fitted their policies, spiced with convenient quotations; their renaissance pens could make papal or royal documents glitter for a moment with classical rhetoric. To them, Aleman was 'a second Catiline'.[5] A Carthusian observed how Eugenius had seduced

[1] Cited in Valois, *Pape et Concile*, II, 362.
[2] *CB*, VIII, 277–8.
[3] Valois, *Pape et Concile*, II, 348 ff.; FM, XIV, 291–2. Cf. Toews, 'Pope Eugenius IV', 178 ff.
[4] *MCG*, III, 949; Vincent of Aggsbach, cited in Jedin, I, 37.
[5] *CBC*, 156; cf. above, p. 88. Visconti is said to have stated that a letter from Coluccio Salutati 'could do more damage than a thousand Florentine cavalry':

the *literati* with rewards.[1] The generation of the 1440s, it has been said, was less interested in reform, and more monarchical in spirit, than its predecessors; to this we may add that it was more inclined to neoplatonism which, with its notion of cosmic pattern and descending power, came increasingly to dominate in the arts, religion, and political thought.[2]

In this atmosphere, and with these agents, the controversy gradually turned into a series of negotiations, in which the chief aim became the achievement of peace. Under Nicholas V, a masterly diplomat, the papacy adopted as its slogans 'peace', 'order' and 'unity'.[3] This was particularly noticeable in the case of Poland where the interests of monarchy and national unity were closely intertwined. Eugenius IV had flattered Wladislas III with an observation as to 'how well you understand the advantage of that unity which... strengthens empires';[4] a theme which the Polish king himself stressed to the Hungarians during their succession crisis.[5] The restoration of Poland's obedience to Nicholas V in 1447 was motivated, according to King Casimir, by his desire to terminate 'these unseemly divisions and schisms, with their terrible consequences'.[6] As Cardinal Olesnicki pointed out, this meant that the pope too must make concessions in order to arrive at a peaceful settlement.[7]

Under Nicholas V, the papacy adopted, with far less reticence, the policy (advocated 10 years previously by Piero da Monte in England), of bargaining with the secular powers, in order to secure their allegiance. Thus, one of the main results of the Baslean controversy was a new series of concordats with the rulers of Germany, Poland, Burgundy and the Italian states. In these the papacy allowed

cited in J. Gill, *Eugenius IV*, 196. The importance of these years for the development of the practice and techniques of modern diplomacy is emphasized in G. Mattingley, *Renaissance diplomacy*, esp. 67 ff., 84 ff.

[1] Aggsbach: cited in Jedin, *History of the Council of Trent*, I, 37.
[2] FM, XIV, 285; cf. A. Dempf, *Sacrum Imperium*, 555, where he speaks of 'Monarchioptanten'. On Nicholas V and the Renaissance, cf. Vespasiano da Bisticci, *Lives*, 38; and Hay, *The Italian Renaissance*, 159 ff.
[3] See esp. the arengae of the Concordats: A. Mercati, *Raccolta dei Concordati*, I, 168, 170–7, 186, 194; also, Mansi, XXIX, 228A. Cf. Fichtenau, *Arenga*, 185.
[4] Rayn, XXVIII, 366.   [5] *Mon. Pol.* XII, part 2, 433.
[6] *Mon. Pol.* XIV, part 3, 17.
[7] *Mon. Pol.* II, part 2, 25. Cf. Valois, *Pape et Concile*, II, 260. On Olesnicki, cf. Ullmann, 'Eugenius IV', 380–2.

the secular power a greater say in appointments to ecclesiastical benefices, by specifically abrogating certain clauses of canon law.[1] In general, Nicholas allowed ecclesiastical appointments made during the Neutrality to remain in force, as the price for the restoration of obedience to himself. The papacy thus came to terms with the rationale behind royal and princely policy during the later 1440s, namely with the determination to maintain after the schism the degree of regional control over church affairs and finances which they had acquired during it.[2]

The concordats were contractual agreements between independent parties. Turrecremata's celebrated modification of papal temporal claims, to the effect that the pope's power over secular rulers in secular affairs was not, as earlier advocates of papal monarchy had been claiming, 'absolute and undifferentiated', but was 'a guiding and normative sovereignty', and his reduction of the sphere in which the pope could apply legal sanctions against the secular powers, may thus be viewed as an application, at the theoretical level, of Monte's urge to 'cede a little'.[3] It was an application of Roselli's programme, for a sharing of power between pope and emperor, to the relations between the pope and all secular authorities. The concordat policy and the advocacy of monarchical sovereignty thus pointed in the same direction: together, they formed the foundation for the royal and princely absolutism which was to be built up in the following century. National sentiment was used as a bait to foil demands for a new Council, and to obtain ratification of separate ecclesiastical treaties.[4]

Even so, the papacy's policy was not everywhere successful. In England, the Statutes of *Provisors* and *Praemunire* remained in force.[5] In France the *Pragmatic Sanction* of Bourges remained in force until the

---

[1] Mercati, *Raccolta*, I, 168 ff. Cf. FM, XIV, part 3, *passim*; and W. Bertams, *Der neuzeitliche Staatsgedanke und die Konkordate des ausg. Mittelalters*.

[2] See for example Mansi, XXXII, 51E–52A; and Toussaint, *Les Rélations diplomatiques*, 291. Cf. Piccolomini, 'nec Feliciani simus nec Eugeniani; sed *tantum ecclesiastici et regales*, Fridericoque nostro Imperatori rectum consilium demus': *Pentalogus*, 662.

[3] *SE*, II, c. 113–15, esp. fo. 265v; *Comm.* I, 637–47 on d. 96, c. 6 and c. 10, esp. 638. Cf. P. Theeuws, *Jean de Turrecremata. Les rélations entre l'Église et le pouvoir civil d'après un theol. du XVe siècle*. For Monte's expression, see above, p. 100.

[4] For example, Rayn. XXVIII, 242, 315, 366, 444; *RTA*, XV, 189, 480; and with reference to France particularly Rayn. XXVIII, 210, 306, 490.

[5] Cf. FM, XIV, 395; Jacob, *The fifteenth century*, 266 f.

Concordat of 1516.[1] Zwingli's disgust with that treaty signifies the close connection between these events and the Reformation. Piero da Monte, who had been papal legate in France since 1442, composed a treatise (*c.* 1450) attacking the *Pragmatic Sanction*, in which he reproduced his own earlier arguments, and added some of Turrecremata's.[2] The Council of Basle was a group of 'rebellious prelates . . .in synodal assembly'—one remembers the French nobles' rising of 1440 and 1442.[3] But the *Pragmatic Sanction*, by contradicting the pope's sovereign right to confer benefices and hear appeals, is also 'subversive' and 'seditious'.[4] At this point Monte re-formulated the papal warning on the spread of rebellious attitudes:

> Kings and princes who hold something back from the obedience they owe to the pope...should fear greatly lest the Lord...in just judgment should allow them to be betrayed by conspiracies of their own subjects. Someone who does not give the obedience due to the head of the church, makes himself unworthy of being obeyed by his own subjects.[5]

He re-stated, against the *Pragmatic Sanction*, Turrecremata's argument against Basle, that the church, being a 'kingdom', had the qualities described by Aristotle and Aquinas as proper to 'a monarchical régime'. He reiterated Turrecremata's analogy between the pope and the king who, according to Aquinas, possessed 'fullness of power'. The pope too, therefore, has the sovereign powers of a king; he can hear appeals, appoint to benefices, and he alone can make general laws.[6]

An incident in 1448 epitomizes the way the dispute had gone. Casimir of Poland had submitted to Pope Nicholas, and demanded that the University of Cracow follow suit. The university replied that the King ought first 'to consult other universities', and that they themselves 'wished to follow the other universities'. Refusing to submit to the threats of the papal legate, they proceeded to consult Paris University, 'as our prince and mother', and also various

---

[1] Cf. FM, XIV, 352 ff.
[2] Cf. J. Haller, *Piero da Monte*, 93* ff.; P. Ourliac, 'La Pragmatique Sanction et la légation en France du Cardinal d'Estouteville', in *Mélanges d'Arch. et d'Hist.* LIV (1938), 403–32.
[3] Vat. lat. 4145, fo. 88v; cf. above, pp. 105, 108.
[4] *Ibid.* fo. 10r, 34v; cf. *ibid.* fo. 110r.   [5] *Ibid.* fo. 107r–v.
[6] *Ibid.* fos 15v–23r, 36v–38v. Cf. above, pp. 62 f.

universities of central Europe: Vienna, Erfurt, Leipzig and Cologne.[1] The last two supported Cracow's refusal to acknowledge Nicholas and congratulated them for 'not fearing the countenance of an earthly prince'.[2] Cracow did not recognize Nicholas till Basle had dispersed, and the universities continued to be a stronghold of conciliar ideas.[3] This incident suggests the connection between Papalism and Conciliarism and court and university respectively.

With the Council of Basle disbanded, Conciliarism, though it formed a justification for the French-inspired Council of Pisa (1511–12), ceased to be the main channel of ecclesiastical dissent. After 1450, the medieval papacy enjoyed an Indian summer, symbolized by the Jubilee of that year. But Nicholas V and his colleagues might have listened with profit to advice once given by Pierre de Versailles, 'Princes, unless they are always getting something, are quick to change sides'.[4] The next century was to see princely and state interest capturing control of large sections of church life and organization; it was to see loyalty to the idea of the universal church punished as high treason. Both Reformation and Counter-Reformation relied heavily on royal power and patronage. In preferring royalism to Conciliarism, the fifteenth-century papacy contracted a dangerous alliance.

[1] *Mon. Pol.* II, part 2, 20; *Cod. dipl. Univ. Cracov.* part 2, 75–7. Cf. K. Morawski,
[2] *Histoire de l'université de Cracovie*, II, 87 ff.
  Cod. dipl. Univ. Cracov. part 2, 88.
[3] Jedin, *History of the Council of Trent*, I, 35–6; for the development of similar political ideas at Cracow university in the fifteenth century, see *Universitatis Iagelloniae, 1364–1764 Historia*, I, 139 ff. On Conciliarism and the universities, cf. above, pp. 23 f.
[4] Mansi Suppl. v, 235; Rayn. XXVIII, 364.

CONCLUSION

The issue which, during this ecclesiastical conflict, had split Europe into rival diplomatic camps was the question of the right form of government for the church, and this had been explicitly related to the question of the right form of government for any society. It was probably the first time in modern history that political ideas as such had played so significant a part in international conflict. At the same time, institutions such as papacy and council, kingship and city, were being championed no longer for their particular credentials in theology, law and custom, but rather for the political values they represented. Similarly, admirers of the ancient world were learning to associate certain values with republic and empire. It was no longer simply good laws, but a particular distribution of political, and above all legislative, power, that was being acclaimed as a means to human excellence.

But, as we have seen, this very form of argument went beyond the purposes for which it was originally developed. The focus was tending to shift away from papacy and council onto monarchy and democracy, away from particular institutions onto the general principles they exemplified. Explicit rationalization (for example, the defence of monarchical sovereignty as necessary for the unity of society) was beginning to replace local or national custom as a conclusive argument in politics. Aristotle's *Politics*, re-translated by L. Bruni in the 1430s, had been employed selectively to buttress this or that case; but his mode of thinking came to dominate those who sought to use him. Rationalization tends easily to lead to generalization. One important aspect of this dispute for the history of political thought was that it accelerated this tendency towards generalization (already inspired by the study of Aristotle). From now on, constitutional crises in one country after another were to lead political thinkers to ever higher flights of generality, a habit only cured by the return to the comparative method in some modern social thought.

What we have been witnessing is perhaps the birth of 'ideology' as such, the peculiarly modern habit of justifying political acts by reference to abstract, metaphysical ideals. Monarchy was presented as the form of government both doctrinally correct, and perfectly matched to rulers' interests. In the first instance, this was used to justify the temporary 'constellation of interests' between papacy and secular monarchy, enabling them to express as a norm what was in fact a convenient arrangement. The effect of this was shown both in the modification of papal temporal claims and in the appeal for voluntary co-operation against 'public enemies' (whether heretic or Turk).[1] But the underlying rationale, though doubtless largely *post factum*, was the monarchical ideology of the two partners.

Here, too, the side-effects were to prove more lasting than the original objective. The ideas furnished by the exponents of papal monarchy helped to provide kings and princes with the one quality they most of all lacked in their striving for the centralization of jurisdiction and other powers: theoretical ratification. From the point of view of the expanding monarchies, what was required was an idea, or perhaps more exactly an attitude, to justify their policies. So long as feudal rights and the normative supremacy of the church were accepted as the general rule, each royal intervention had to be squared with these factors—a tricky, and sometimes humiliating process. At the time when human qualities were being extolled, when rational procedures were everywhere demonstrating their efficacy, in art, law, trade and industry, architecture and town-planning, 'custom' still shackled the prince. Though even within the feudal-right system monarchical power could and did expand, it was hard going. The new doctrine, 'all power to the sovereign', cut the Gordian knot; it was a labour-saving device. Turrecremata's *Summa on the church* (1449), bristling with secular analogies, embodied a theory of sovereignty stated in such general terms that any 'sovereign' could make use of it. Hordes of scholars, courtiers, professional ideologues and renaissance *literati* were to help them to do so.

Partly thanks to the twilight ratiocinations of the medieval papacy, the new monarchies had the benefit of Minerva's owl from the start of their development. The doctrine of monarchical sovereignty issued as a clear and mature idea from the complexities of late medieval ecclesiastical thought, and was wholly in line with the interests and aspirations of national and territorial monarchy. It presented the

---

[1] Cf. Paul II, in Rayn. xxix, 432; and Pius II asking for peace, 'in huiusmodi rebus *non tam cogere quam rogare* possumus': R. Haubst, 'Die Reformentwurf Pius des Zweiten', in *Römische Quartalschrift*, xlix (1954), ch. 8.

formula that would become the basis of modern monarchy: the monarch epitomizes his whole people, represents their true interests, and so acquires a responsibility and power which, within his borders, are 'general' and 'absolute'.[1] The personal sovereignty of the hier-archical monarch fused the piecemeal actualities of royal power into the glorious ideal of monarchical unity, a single theoretical pattern, the monarchical good identified with the common good, the cor-poration sole governing for the welfare of (we may all but say) *the 'status'*—the only *status* worth mentioning in an otherwise 'classless' kingdom incorporated in the king. Just as this philosophy was a powerful consummation in theory of the monistic implications of the hierarchical cosmology; so it effected a felicitous conjunction in reality with the rising star of the sovereign monarchies, which identified the fortunes of national unity with their own.

At the same time this controversy, indirectly promoting the growth of diplomatic relations and international co-operation, helped to entrench monarchy as an international system. International relations meant relations between monarchical establishments; monarchs sometimes even recognized a vague common interest among themselves, particularly perhaps at the ideological level, in avoiding rebellion. The political norm of monarchy, the opposite of tyranny as well as of democracy, was becoming established as a common feature of Christendom, which—as the rulers of eastern Europe at least saw it—was a political as well as a spiritual entity, with an all too real enemy, the Turk, directed at its very existence as a single community of peoples.

The doctrines of sovereignty coincided for a while with the in-terests of hereditary monarchy. The doctrine that the prince was above the laws, and could himself make valid law, combining flexibility with stability, no doubt also helped to win them the support of the bourgeoisie, whose enterprises required a higher degree of rationalization, centralization and unification in the sphere of government. The advantage of monarchy here was that, while itself quasi-sacred and unchangeable, it could initiate changes any-where else in the political structure: here too the medieval papacy was an obvious forerunner. The monarch was acclaimed as the

[1] Cf. Hegel, *Philosophy of History*, 398–9; and for Weber on this, cf. R. Bendix, *Max Weber*, 405.

harbinger of 'liberty' and 'prosperity'; it will be noticed that private property was carefully excluded from his right of intervention.[1]

But absolute monarchy was in turn engulfed by the very ideas it fostered. Like a scientific invention, the doctrine that the sovereign was absolute because responsible for the common good became public property. In several ways, absolute monarchy was but giving shelter to the infant concept of the modern state. In the first place, the whole process we have been considering may be viewed as a transition from the primacy of the law to the primacy of the legislator.[2] Political acts tended to be justified less in legal and more in rational terms, less because they were in line with the existing laws, and more because they promoted the prosperity or security of the people. The power of legislation was, from this time onwards, increasingly appropriated by the sovereign himself, on grounds of efficiency and of Roman-law doctrine. The people, whose power had rested in their claim to be the mouthpiece of the law, found themselves temporarily without a title in government. We have seen how the argument for sovereignty progressed from the judicial to the legislative and administrative spheres: just as there must be a single supreme adjudicator, so there must be a single source of legislation and one chief bureaucrat. The increasing activity of government tended at first to play into the hands of monarchy.

But the very rationalization of the *raison d'être* of monarchy, that it existed not through ancient custom or biblical precept, but for public order and welfare, could not be contained, and overreached the target set for it. Monarchy itself was overwhelmed by the universal requirements of the common good, which it had unleashed. Notions which monarchy had culled from the papacy were now to serve yet another end. The idea that the monarch represented the general good, that his power was unlimited because so too was the public interest, led beyond monarchy itself. Hence, perhaps, some of the ambiguities of monarchical theory in this period: the application of the impersonal criteria of suitability and efficiency for

---

[1] Cf. H. Pirenne, *Histoire économique et sociale du moyen âge*, 171, 177–8; Jouvenel, *Sovereignty*, 181.

[2] This was consciously recognized by Segovia when he said: 'Editio legum, quibus politia quevis regulari debet, irrefragabile est testimonium de superioritate sistente in ipsarum legum conditore': cited in Haller, *CB*, I, 34 n. Cf. Turrecremata, *SE*, II, c. 4, fo. 119r.

tenure of office, which he supposed it to be his duty to apply to others, could not eventually stop short of the head official himself. The notion of the undying 'see', 'office', 'crown' or 'throne' was the predecessor of the modern notion of 'the state'; and Turrecremata himself had said (of doctrinal infallibility) that it applied 'not to the person, but to the office or the see of the pope'. However abstract, such terms signified that the sovereign had a function to fulfil. Monarchs borrowed techniques of account-keeping from the merchants,[1] and the bourgeoisie supported them insofar as they improved the conditions of commerce; but as the monarchs had turned their backs on the pope, so the bourgeoisie could abandon the monarch, on the grounds that accountability applied to him too.

Eventually the egalitarian, 'statist' elements inherent in rationalized monarchy came into the open; and the claim was once again heard, that 'what concerns all should be approved by all'. Laws concern the whole people; therefore, if the sovereign can make laws, his power must stem from and reside in the whole people, who could now return to their position of fundamental sovereignty.

The ideas of popular sovereignty, then, were revived in full force in the assertion that legislative authority resides ultimately only with the people as a whole, and in the application of majority rule. But it was surely Conciliarism that mediated between the medieval and the modern conceptions of popular government. For it took up the ideology of the commune and transplanted it onto the large scale. Though parliamentary movements had similar aspirations, these were hardly, at least until the English Revolution, so explicitly worked out, in theory or in practice. In the short-term, Conciliarism established within the church—for two decades—first the practice of constitutionalism, involving the full accountability of the ruler, and secondly the theory of popular sovereignty. In the long term, it anticipated, whatever its actual influence, the aspirations of later parliamentarianism, which followed a similar pattern, with the theory of democracy supporting constitutionalism in practice.

We may be permitted to speculate that the modern state is in fact composed of the union between 'the estate of the realm' and 'the king's estate', between the sovereignty of the people and the sovereignty of the monarch. All this means is that sovereignty and

[1] Cf. Ryder, 'Evolution of imperial government', 353–4.

responsibility reach a new equilibrium. The sovereign body is, broadly speaking, accountable to the people; but, otherwise, it is legally unfettered. The survival, in some countries, of old political customs, the independence of the legal system, and the permanent character of numerous offices and official bodies, renders the situation more complex, but also more stable. It is the one-party state which is probably the most logical heir of absolute monarchy; it too has the potential advantages of rapid action, official secrecy and the power to introduce sweeping innovations—in short, the very features of the military *imperator*, on which the monarchies of Europe, in the age we have been discussing, modelled themselves. Elsewhere, the introduction in modern times of regular elections is a further development of constitutionalism in the direction of popular sovereignty. The ideal of the commune is something to aim at, however imperfectly, remembering the moral values that are essential to it.

EPILOGUE

This book has concentrated, deliberately and exclusively, on the *political* ideas within conciliar and papal theory. This has led to a certain imbalance, since it was generally *ecclesiastical* ideas that were uppermost in the minds of the participants. It also meant emphasizing those elements in the two standpoints which were in most clear-cut opposition to one another; in general it seems that, the more they rationalized their differences in terms of political theory, the more they diverged. If we consider the two doctrines in their more theological and canonist aspects, we sometimes find them less diametrically opposed, and even in agreement on some points. There were, moreover, moderate thinkers on both sides, who wanted to devise a way for pope and council to work harmoniously together.

Looking very briefly at some specifically ecclesiological aspects of the two doctrines, we may note, first, that Turrecremata himself allowed certain restrictions on the absolute sovereignty of the pope when it came to questions of defining faith. For example, in strictly circumscribed cases, a council may be convened without the pope's consent, and may continue despite his opposition;[1] a pope may not

[1] *SE*, III, c. 8, fo. 281v, and c. 69, fos 356v–357r.

define a new doctrine in opposition to the council.[1] Infallibility belongs, not to the pope alone, but to the Roman see.[2] If the pope becomes heretical, he is 'self-deposed' *ipso iure* (i.e. without any judicial process or judge being invoked);[3] in this case, the infallibility of the Roman Church is preserved by the cardinals, without the pope.[4] In saying this, he was making more rigid the conditions for correction of a pope as envisaged by earlier canonists; but he still catered for the possibility of a heretical pope (though he also said that the view that Providence would prevent this miraculously might be correct). It was thus on the specifically theological question of the teaching authority on matters of divine revelation, that Turrecremata quietly abandoned some of his absolutism.

Turning to Segovia, we find that in his later works he emphasized the authority of pope and bishops within the council. In his *Discourse* of 1441 he said that a conciliar judgment came 'not so much from inferiors as from bishops and their superiors...more principally and intrinsically from the pope'.[5] His tract *On the great authority of bishops in a general council* (1450) was aimed above all at establishing that a council held authority direct from Christ, precisely because it comprised the assembled episcopate; it was they who constituted its authoritative element.[6] He maintained that the bishops held their authority direct from Christ, and were not dependent for it upon the pope;[7] thus perhaps anticipating the position held by some Spanish bishops at Trent. Again, it was apparently the introduction of the specifically theological concept of the episcopacy which led to a new outlook being adopted.

We can find a measure of agreement, also, on the question of the standing of the cardinalate. Panormitanus took a stage further the view of Johannes Monachus, that the cardinals had a *de iure* status 'by custom, being so to speak in possession'; he went further and maintained that their position was *iure divino*, and that therefore

---

[1] *SE*, III, c. 64, fo. 353r; *Comm.* I, 176a, on D. 19, c. 8.

[2] *SE*, II, c. 112, fos 259v–260r. On this question, cf. G. Massi, *Magistero infallibile del papa nella teologia di G. da Torquemada.*

[3] *SE*, II, c. 112, fo. 260r–v, and III, c. 46, fo. 332v.

[4] *Comm.* I, 176a, on D. 19, c. 8; and III, 270b–1b, on C. 24, q. 1, c. 14.

[5] *Ampl. disp.* 713–14; cf. *Auct. ep.* fos 87v–88r.

[6] *Auct. ep.* fos 87r, 97v, 192r, 201v, 202v.   [7] *Ampl. disp.* 778, 911.

the pope was bound to consult them.[1] Turrecremata, on the other hand, not only made the cardinals, as we have seen, an integral part of the Roman church, but also repeated D'Ailly's exaltation of their office: 'the rank of cardinals was originally and primordially founded by Christ alone...[they are] successors to the apostolic *status*'.[2]

Lastly, we must indicate a connection between these theological views and the theology of today. The notion of the church expressed by both sides in this controversy must seem to many, Catholic or not, strangely remote from modern theology. The change in circumstances, the renewal in thought have been almost complete. But the Catholic theologian of today might be able to see, in such men as Segovia and Turrecremata, some continuity with the living present. It might even be hazarded that the Second Vatican Council's decree 'On the church' embraces some of the interpretations of revealed truths, that were put forward on both sides in our dispute. This decree puts the bishops in the position allotted by D'Ailly and Turrecremata to the cardinals, as successors of 'the apostolic college'.[3] The medieval notion of the college as a real spiritual and jurisdictional entity is continued here;[4] but, instead of being applied to the council, it is applied to the episcopate, which by assembling forms a council. Segovia himself, in his later work *On the great authority of bishops in a general council*, provides a clear link between the application of the collegiate idea to the council and to the episcopate. For he maintains here that the bishops form the essential part of the council, and that 'in synodal assembly', though not 'singly', they possess 'fullness of apostolic power'.[5] Thus the distinction between the college collectively and separately continues to be important.

The Vatican decree seems to take this notion of 'collegiality', and to combine it with the inseparability of the college from its head (which was indeed the earlier doctrine which both parties in the fifteenth century expanded in opposite directions). The result, it

---

[1] *Comm.* VII, fo. 53r, on 4.17.13; cf. Tierney, *Conciliar theory*, 180; Ullmann, 'Eugenius IV', 365 ff. [2] *SE*, I, c. 80, fos 92–3.

[3] *The documents of Vatican II*, ed. J. Gallagher, 43. [4] Cf. above, pp. 13, 16.

[5] *Auct. ep.* fo. 192r: 'Quamvis non singillatim episcoporum cuilibet, tamen eis sinodaliter congregatis plenitudo apostolicae potestatis...'; cf. *ibid.* fo. 98v.: 'episcopis dum actu sedent in concilio generali communi invicem consensu pereunte ad tempus competit potestas regitiva populi fidelis'. He ascribes 'indeviabilitas' to the 'episcopalis status': *ibid.* fos. 200r, 203v; cf. *Ampl. disp.* 911.

would seem, is neither Conciliarism nor Papalism, but something which includes a good deal from each: 'Together with its head, the Roman Pontiff, and never without this head, the episcopal order is the subject of supreme and full power over the universal church'.[1] Indeed, the decree goes on to describe the significance of this college for the church as a whole, in words that strikingly unite the aspirations of both sides in the fifteenth-century dispute:

This college, insofar as it is composed of many, expresses the variety and universality of the People of God, but insofar as it is assembled under one head, it expresses the unity of the flock of Christ.[2]

Lastly, there is evidence of continuity between the idea of Gerson and others, that authority belonged primarily to the church as a whole, and the doctrine that the relation between teachers and taught is, under the inspiration of the Holy Spirit, so close as to be in a sense unbreakable:

(to a definition made by pope and bishops) the assent of the church can never be wanting, on account of the activity of that same Holy Spirit, whereby the whole flock of Christ is preserved and progresses in unity of faith.[3]

The story that has been told is one in which we are all participants.

[1] *Documents of Vatican II*, 43.   [2] *Ibid.* 43–4.
[3] *Ibid.* 49.

APPENDICES

EXCERPTS FROM
JOHN OF SEGOVIA AND
JOHN OF TURRECREMATA

The purpose of these excerpts is to present John of Segovia and John Turrecremata in a more coherent form, in the original. They may be used in conjunction with the exposition above, as indicated in footnotes. The punctuation, including italics, is my own throughout.

( ]   indicate editorial additions or interpolations.

[ )   indicate brackets used to punctuate the text itself.

. . . indicate an omission from the text.

JOHN OF SEGOVIA

1. *Decem Advisamenta* (1439). (Vat. Lat. 4039, fos 192r–231v)[1]
fo. 218v. [ON ARISTOCRACY AND MONARCHY IN THE CHURCH]

Que autem supradicta sunt—sc. quod generale concilium, in quo est congregatio episcoporum sive presbyterorum, doctorum, praedicatorum et pastorum plebis christianae, est regula et directorium omnium actionum et questionum que inter fideles contingunt; ac per hoc certum supremum tribunal in terris, iudicii cuius diffinitioni acquiescere tenetur universa communitas christianorum—[non solum] auctoribus sacre scripture, ut supradictum est, conforma sunt, sed etiam doctrine Philosophi et recte rationi. Aristoteles enim in 3 *Politicorum* dicit quod ubi sunt homines liberi pollentes ingenio et virtute, melius est regi communitatem a pluribus sapientibus virtuosis quam ab uno [he follows Aristotle's arguments, that many see better than one, and that they are more free from passion][2]... et hoc regimen aristocraticum, ut ipse Philosophus docet, in tantum est naturale quod necesse est quod hoc regimen concurrat, etiam ubi unus regnat.[3] Cum enim impossibile sit quod unus per se omnia videat, aviset, ordinet sive diffiniet et exequatur, oportet quod ille unus qui regnat assumat secum comprincipes laborum, et per consequens honorum socios...(fo. 219r) Itaque secundum doctrinam Philosophi regimen aristocraticum videtur consentaneum esse nature...fuit enim a principio introducta politia *regni*; que tunc erat conveniens, quia civitates erant parve, et quaelibet habebat unum regem qui poterat ad regendum sufficere; et quoniam omnes homines a principio non erant praecellentes ingenio et virtute.

Unde unus qui reperiebatur alios praecellere, merito constituebatur in regem...Sed quando regna ampliari coeperunt, et reges in libitum

---

[1] On the *Decem advisamenta*, cf. Haller, *CB*, I, 27, n. 3.

[2] Cf. Aristotle, *Politics*, III, vi, 1281b; x, 1286a; xi, 1287b.

[3] This might be deduced from *Politics*, III, xi, 1287b; it seems to anticipate D. Hume: 'The sultan of Egypt or the emperor of Rome might drive his harmless subjects, like brute beasts, against their sentiments and inclination; but he must, at least, have led his Mamelukes, or praetorian bands, like men, by their opinion': *Of the first principles of government*, in Hume, *Theory of politics*, ed. F. Watkin (Edinburgh, 1951), 148.

gubernare, homines vero effecti sunt intelligentes et virtuosi—quoniam, equaliter dispositis secundum naturam suam et virtutes, iniustum est quod inequaliter distribuantur honores et dignitates—hinc introducta est aristocratia, que est principatus plurium virtuosorum[1]...Et sicut in condendis legibus iudicia multorum sapientum praeferuntur iudicio unius, ita multo fortius ad discernendum et iudicandum de omni negotio dubio et arduo...[they have also the power of *diffinitio* and *executio*] Si ad multitudinem sapientum non pertineret auctoritas exequendi, sed ad alium, qui non prout ab illis diffinitum est, sed prout sibi videbitur exequetur, tunc frustra multitudo sapientum diceretur illi preferre... Mandare autem executioni fieri hii melius possunt qui habent notitiam legum[2]...[cuius] est supremum tribunal iudicii, concilii vel papae, et cuius iudicio sit potius acquiescendum, satis evidenter patet...Nam in concilio convenit magna multitudo sapientum... Et sic potius ex hac ratione standum est iudicio concilii quam papae... (fo. 219v) Nam cum summi pontifices sepe in regimine subditorum tantum excedant quod ordinationes sanctorum patrum...observare redignantur...hinc merito oportuit ordinari hoc aristocraticum regimen, videlicet plurium virtuosorum et sapientum convenientium in generali concilio...notificetur deprivatio mali regiminis cuiuslibet ministri ecclesie, ut, si exposcant demerita sua, possint deponi; sicut de iniquo rege, qui assisteret tyrannisare. Item quoniam, prout apparet ex dicta doctrina Aristotelis, hec politia aristocratica rationabiliter potuit et debuit introduci at correctionem alterius, [sc.] regni, quando tyrannisaret[3]...Nec, si contingat quod papa [propter] demerita sua deponatur, ab hoc supprimitur excellentia summi pontificatus, sic nec quando summus pontifex moritur naturaliter[4]... iudicium concilii, *ad exemplum prefati regiminis aristocratici incorrupti*[5]... est institutum ad reformandum potentium ministrorum ecclesie et aliorum quorumcunque fidelium, specialiter summi pontificis, qui aliquando abutitur vel abuti potest maxima, qua fulget, potestate ad modum tyranni...

fo. 224r. [ON THE RELATIONSHIP BETWEEN RULER AND PEOPLE, AND THE NATURE OF AUTHORITY][6]

Verum si quis debite consideret naturam universitatis et singulorum,

---

[1] *Politics*, III, x, 1286b; cf. Cicero, *De officiis*, II, xii; a speaker at Basle, *CBC*, 28 ff. and Segovia again, below, p. 152.

[2] Cf. *Ampl. Disp.* 710–11: below, pp. 146 f.   [3] *Politics*, III, x, 1286b.

[4] For the pope's deposition as *mors civilis*, cf. above, p. 47; and Segovia again, in *Auct. ep.* fo. 174r: below, p. 158.

[5] Contrast *Ampl. disp.* 708, 712: below, p. 145; and *Auct. Ep.* fo. 174r: below, p. 158.

[6] Cf. *Ampl. disp.* 720–1: below, pp. 148–50.

non absurdum, sed quod dictum est iudicabit [es]se nature et consonum rationi...Qui enim praeest multitudini in virtute...licet singulos, non tamen excedit universos,[1] quando videlicet ad eamdem actionem simul concurrerent. Unde, licet cum favore unius partis adversus aliam possit, [si] velit se toti multitudini comparare, superatur indubie. Patet in duce exercitus militaris, vel in praesidente cuiuslibet alterius multitudinis. Ratio autem huius est, quoniam qui praeest multorum regimini, si debite habet praeesse, desinit esse privata, et efficitur persona publica, et perdit quodammodo solitariam unitatem, et induit unitam multitudinem; ut non iam unius, sed dicatur gestare sive representare personam multorum.[2] Et intantum agit vicem boni rectoris, quamdiu publicam utilitatem multorum intendit;[3] quando vero, contempto publico, procurat studiose privatum bonum, iam desinit esse idoneus talis multitudinis rector. Et ex hoc, quod censetur gestare personam idoneam omnium, sicque intendere ad bonum publicum, quando comparatur ad personas singulares sive particulares congregationes illius multitudinis,[4] quia ipse presidens dicitur habere vices omnium—huiusmodi autem persone aut particulares congregationes sunt non tota multitudo, sed aliquid illius, et sic se habent tamquam pars ad totum—hinc est quod ipse presidens excedere dicitur. Sed, si contingat totam illam multitudinem in unum congregari et asserere vel optare aliquid, econtra autem ipse presidens dicat—quia ipsa veritas praefertur fictioni—ipsa multitudo merito superabit.

Veritas enim hanc multitudinem esse multas personas, fictio autem quod ipse presidens, qui unicam personam vere, multas autem esse dicitur representative. Namvero qui dicitur habere auctoritatem, ex eo quod dumtaxat alterius vel multorum representat personam, eo ipso quo adest presentia representatorum, illorum auctoritas, non huius, attenditur. Quare auctoritas presidentis in presentia totius multitudinis, [si] se prefert illi, (fo. 224v) non sicut primo censetur habere vigorem; propterea quod presumitur iudicium suum esse conforme intentioni omnium quibus presidet, ad reipublicae et ipsorum utilitatem. Et hec est summa potestas concessa cuilibet presidenti, videlicet [quod] id quod sibi videtur debere, omnibus credi quod sit de intentione omnium, qui pro tunc in diversis locis separatim existunt. Verum cum ipsa tota multitudo principaliter adest et iudicat aliquid sibi esse utile, presidens autem econtra dicit, intelligitur manifeste iam cessare causam quare plus sibi quam illis assentiri

---

[1] Cf. Aristotle, *Politics*, III, x, 1286b.
[2] Cf. St Thomas Aquinas, *Summa theologiae*, I^{a}2^{ae}, q. 90, a. 3, resp.; q. 97, a. 3, ad 3; and T. Gilby in his ed. of *St Thomas Aquinas, Summa Theologiae*, XXVIII (I^{a}2^{ae}), *Law and political theory* (London, 1966), 173–4.
[3] Cf. Aristotle, *Politics*, III, v, 1279a–b.   [4] Cf. Aristotle, *Politics*, III, x, 1286b.

debebat; videlicet quod credebatur iudicium suum esse conforme ad intentionem omnium. Equidem, cum ipse demonstrat se contrariam fovere sententiam, evidenter cognoscitur iudicium suum non esse conforme intentioni omnium aliorum, qui tunc expresse proferunt quale sit iudicium suum. Quare merito non videtur eo casu standum esse ipsius solius iudicio, nisi forte iudicatur ipsum solum videntem, omnes autem alios caecos esse. Sed positum est, multos et unum adinvicem referri similitudinem ac alias preter respectum presidentie paritas comparationem[1]... [the passage continues as in *MCG*, III, 721–2].[2]

2. *Amplificatio Disputationis* (1441) (*MCG*, III, 695–941)[3]

[ON THE MONARCHICAL AND ARISTOCRATIC ELEMENTS IN CHURCH GOVERNMENT]

(P. 707)... Quia igitur inter aristocratiam et monarchiam illa precipue differentia est, ut altera principem habeat unum, velut dominans principaliter, altera vero plures virtute pollentes, sub nullo constituti principe, sed summa gaudentes libertate—christiana vero religio in eo gloriatur, quod Christo sub principe pollet, qui rex regum... et ob eius reverentiam summum pontificem, eius vicarium, magnopere veneratur—hinc igitur regimen eius nullatenus aristocraticum est dicendum. Est enim christianus populus permaxime regnabilis, huius conditionis nota veritate non solum intellectu, sed et *palpabili experimento*, quia non solum in maiori parte, sed fere ubique per reges et principes gubernatur. Et quando ecclesia congregata est in generali concilio, propterea gaudet, quia credit Christum in medio esse congregatorum in nomine suo,[4] et quia presidet in eo per se aut suos papa, vicarius eius. Quocirca, non mediocrem iniuriam ei facere videtur affirmans, politiam ecclesiastici regiminis in aristocratiam alterari, tempore quo sedet generale concilium... (p. 708) Amplius, cum omnis politia aristocratica potestatem suam habet ex hominibus, sancta synodus predicat potestatem se habere immediate a Christo;[5] itaque, premissis aliis multis differentiis ex doctrina Aristotelis annotatis, nullatenus generali synodo attribui proprie potest aristocraticum regimen,[6] nisi sub

---

[1] Cf. *Ampl. disp.* 721: below, p. 149.   [2] Below, pp. 149 f.

[3] This was originally delivered as a speech to the Diet of Mainz (March 1441); it was later 'enlarged' and incorporated in Segovia's history of the Council of Basle. This 'edition' is severely and justly criticized by Haller (CB. 1, 43, n. 4; *Historisches Jahrbuch*, xv (1894), 464); its 'punctuation' has here been completely altered. Cf. Fromherz, *Johannes von Segovia*, 131–44.

[4] Cf. Matt. xviii:20.

[5] Cf. *Auct. ep. fo.* 174r: below, p. 158.

[6] Cf. *ibid.*, and contrast *Dec. advis.* fos 218v–219v: above, pp. 141 f.

hypothesi, propterea quod plures virtuosi et sapientes viri in eo conveniunt...

Aliud nempe est secundum aristocratiam se habere in regimine, aliud esse aristocraticum principatum.[1] Disserit namque Aristoteles, quanto melius una politia aliis miscetur, tanto magis mansivam esse;[2] praveque esse politiae, nolle omnino partem politiae alterius; ac securiores aristocraticos ad politiam declinantes, propterea quod quanto pauciores sunt domini principantes, ampliori tempore necessarium est manere eiusmodi principatum.[3] Utcumque autem de hiis philosophus senserit, sancta synodus Basiliensis, prosecutoresque synodalis doctrine declarate per Constantiense concilium, quod papa tenetur obedire generali concilio, illorumque minimus, harum scriptor allegationum, haudubio profitetur ordinatissimam esse politiam populi fidelis, sanctamque Dei ecclesiam regi, semperque regi debere, monarchici forma regiminis; quemadmodum ab initio sui rectus gubernatusque semper fuit populus fidelis; in lege quidem nature per patres, filiis totique familiae principantes[4]...
(p. 709) Quia vero lex gratiae naturam perficit, legemque adimplet, utique in ea monarchici est forma regiminis, mansura certissime usque ad mundi consumationem, quoniam *regni* Christi non erit finis,[5] cum sit regnum omnium seculorum. De hac igitur excellentia, quod summi pontificis principatus non aristocraticus sed monarchicus est esseque debet inter concilium Basiliense et papam olim Eugenium questio numquam fuit...

At vero, quoniam fautores adversae positionis arbitrantur papam, si non pro libito suo agat, sed conformat se ordinationi synodali, derogare excellentiae sui monarchici principatus—fortassis eo fine, prout littere eius pretendunt directe duci Britanniae, ut principes retrahantur a favore synodalis doctrine, tanquam generalium auctoritas conciliorum venerationi habita detrahat secularium principum exellentie—ideo, pro declaranda significatione terminorum, id dicitur: quod, attendens doctrinam Aristotelis, manifeste agnoscit illam non esse precipuam excellentiam, quin fortassis nullam, monarchici principatus, ut, reiectis legibus ad commune conferens pertinentibus, subditos regat pro sue libito voluntatis; quoniam, ut inquit, in legibus est salus civitatis; ubi vero non principantur

---

[1] Cf. *Auct. ep.* fo. 175v: below, p. 159; and J. Bodin, *Commonwealth*, II, ii.

[2] *Politics*, II, iii, 1266a; IV, x, 1297a.

[3] This could conceivably refer to *Politics*, IV, xi, 1298b; but in *Politics*, IV, x, 1297a, Aristotle says that such a régime is stabler because it *widens* the sphere of participation (cf. *Politics*, V, vi, 1307a).

[4] Cf. *Auct. ep.* fos 97v, 104v and 105v, where these points are expanded: below, p. 156.

[5] Cf. *Auct. ep.* fo. 105v and 97v: below, p. 156; cf. Luke i:33.

leges non esse politiam; sed quod oportet legem principari omni, politiam autem et principatum de singulis iudicare...Adicit autem monarchiam que existit omnimode regnum, talem necessarium esse tyrannidem, quoniam oportet leges recte positas dominas esse, principem autem, sive unus sive plures, de hiis esse dominos, de quibus non possunt leges dicere certitudinaliter; quos oportet secundum leges principari et observare transgredientes[1]... (p. 710) Magis autem ille convenit sensus, ut [papa] eum, cuius est vicarius, sequatur; qui non venit ministrari, sed ministrare[2]...Alterum vero irrefragabile presuppositum est, ab initio novi testamenti summos pontifices, quanto doctiores et sanctiores, tanto magis usos fuisse aliorum consilio in rebus arduis,[3] propterea quod salus est ubi multa consilia, et integrum est iudicium quod plurimorum sententiis confirmatur; et quod sapientia profiteatur habitare se in consilio, eruditis interessens cogitationibus; et quod sapientia fulgens non spernit sed audit consilia...Consiliis utique non interpolatim, pote anno isto aut mense non verum illo, sed continuo; nec solum pro libito voluntatis sed ex regiminis necessitate.[4]

Etenim, quamvis tam in statu seculari quam ecclesiastico ut communiter consiliis utantur omnes principantes, vix aut nullum tam fixum reperitur consilium sicut et pape cardinalium respectu; nec enim, ut ceteri sive reges sive prelati, novos sibi eligit consiliarios, sed cardinales recipit eosdem qui suorum predecessorum consiliarii fuerunt. Postremo autem presupponitur quod nullatenus obviat monarchico regimini secularis aut ecclesiastici principatus, nec eius diminuit excellentiam, sapientum uti consiliis. Additur autem quod nec dignitatem obscurat principatus, sed magno illustrat splendore, plenoque robore confortat,[5] (p. 711) gloriosum efficiens eo ipso ministerium eius. Ut namque iusta esse iudicia, necessaria vel expedientia esse mandata, subditi percipiant illisque pareant, permaxime est et omnino confert quando notitiam habent, presidentem suum consiliis usum fuisse sapientum[6]...quoniam ferrum ferro acuatur,

---

[1] Aristotle, *Politics*, III, vi, 1282b; x, 1286a; xi, 1287a. This passage is virtually repeated in *Auct. ep.* fo. 176r: below, p. 159. The language shows he is using Moerbeke's old translation of the *Politics*, not the recent one by Leonardo Bruni.

[2] Cf. below, pp. 156, 159: *Auct. ep.* fos 105v, 176r.

[3] For an antecedent, Joannes Monachus, cf. Tierney, *Foundations*, 180–91. Cf. *Auct. ep.* fo. 176–rv: below, p. 159.

[4] Cf. *Auct. ep.* fo. 182r: below, p. 161.

[5] Cf. *Auct. ep.* fos 174v–175r, 176v, 178r, 180r: below, pp. 158 ff.

[6] For a strikingly similar sentiment, cf. Macchiavelli, *The Prince*, ch. 22: transl. G. Bull (London, 1961), 124: 'The first opinion that is formed of a ruler's intelligence is based on the quality of the men he has around him. When they are competent and loyal he can always be considered wise...'

audiens sapiens efficitur sapientior. Ubi autem multi multa scientes invicem conferunt, quid sit iustum vel expediens melius decernitur... plus vident oculi quam oculus...[1] Et consequenter ipsa diffinitio seu sententia, quando eorum consiliis ac deliberationi est conformis, eo ipso recta iustaque presumitur, et abinde liberius executioni traditur; nemine audente affirmare iniustum quod de plurimorum consilio processit sapientum; quantoque maior eorum multitudo concurrit, tanto in maiori habetur veneratione. Etenim cum, docente Philosopho, omne virtutis opus recta determinatum sit ratione prout sapiens determinabit, illud profecto iustum regimen reputatur, quod deliberatum est multitudine sapientum.

Quorum uti consiliis, sicut principatum monarchicum illustrat magno splendore, ita et singulari robore confortat, ut maxima cum fiducia consumandi illud omnis presidens aggrediatur prosequaturque opus arduum, quando, ut sic fiat, accessit maiorum sui principatus assensus,[2] velut si comes, generali previa convocatione aliquid faciat de consensu militum et seniorum civitatis sue, dux autem comitum et baronum, rex vero de consensu predictorum omniumque procerum et civitatum regni atque dominiorum suorum. Illustrat utique nimio splendore dignitatem imperii, siquando circumsedentibus regibus atque principibus leges fiant nomine suo de predictorum consensu. Tunc etenim, velut legibus armisque decorata imperiali maiestate, leges sue paratam habent executionem, nemine audente illis resistere. Quod sepe non contingit legibus illis, que fierent pro suo placito, vel paucis consultis. In ecclesiastico preterea regimine, preferuntur synodales constitutiones, facte per episcopum de unanimo consensu abbatum, decanorum, prepositorum, aliarumque dignitatum, canonicorum et plebanorum diocesis illius; simili quoque modo statuta metropolitana de consensu facta omnium suffraganeorum, ita et que primas aut patriarcha de predictorum consensu. Si igitur, tam in seculari quam ecclesiastico principatu, nihil deperit monarchici forme regiminis, quinimmo eandem illustrat, in arduis rebus consilio uti multitudinis sapientum...(p. 712) Quocirca, premissis attentis, palam fieri potest intuentibus cunctis, an celebratio generalis synodi alteratio sit ecclesiastice politie;[3] ut, cum papa regit per se solum aut consilio cardinalium, dicatur quod monarchicum—quando vero in concilio presidet, quod aristocraticum sit ecclesie regimen...Potius autem dicendum videtur, ordinationem synodalem maioris esse roboris atque virtutis, quodque dignitas summi pontificatus celebratione concilii generalis non

---

[1] Cf. Aristotle, *Politics*, III, vi, 1281b; x, 1286a; xi, 1287b. Cf. above, p. 37.
[2] Cf. *Auct. ep.* fos 176v–177r: below, pp. 159 f.
[3] Cf. *Auct. ep.* fo. 174v: below, p. 158; and contrast *Dec. advis.* fos 218v–219v: above, pp. 141 f.

diminuta vel obscura, sed aucta sit, splendore fulgens singulari et magno confortata robore.[1]

[ON THE RELATIONSHIP BETWEEN RULER AND PEOPLE, AND THE NATURE OF AUTHORITY][2]

(p. 720)...Sed et altera sumpta consideratione speculandum est: an papae liceat synodali contravenire iudicio, seipsumque anteponere auctoritati concilii generalis. Plane, quicumque ille sit, dummodo eiusdem nature, sapientie et virtutis, quamvis singulos subditorum quadam excellat comparatione, non videtur agere vicem boni presidentis, quando se ipsum prefert toti multitudini cui principatur, vel ipsius generali et supreme congregationi. Etenim, licet cum una partium adversus alteram possit, quod tamen omnes universaliter presumat subicere, ratio principandi ad hoc non se extendit, ut solus ipse pugnare debeat contra totam multitudinem.[3] Factus quippe est presidens, ut defendat foveatque, non vero ut destruat vel pugnet.

Rector namque aut presidens, quisquis efficitur multitudinis alicuius, privatam deponit et publicam induit personam—tanquam non, ut primo, quod sibi utile, sed quod omnibus utile est, querere debeat.[4] Quia igitur duas gerit [sc. personas]—fere persona privata est, sed publica iuris fictione, siquidem presumitur, ut bonum publicum dumtaxat procurare debeat; et propter hanc iuris fictionem creditur eius mandatis ac iudiciis, quod sint pro bono communi, obediturque illis—unde ipsius iudicium prefertur iudicio quarumlibet singularum personarum, vel societatum multitudinis illius, nulla earum representante totam multitudinem principatus sicut ipse.[5] At vero, quando comparat se toti multitudini, quia tunc comparatio est inter veritatem et fictionem—veritas autem fictioni prefertur; hinc iudicium suum non prefertur iudicio totius multitudinis. Et rursus iudicium presidentis ideo prefertur aliorum iudiciis particularibus, quoniam presumitur conforme esse intentioni omnium, quibus presidet, seu maioris multitudinis eorum. Et hic est summus apex excellentie principantis, ut quod ipse iudicat, subditi arbitrentur esse de intentione totius multitudinis vel maioris partis. Quando vero tota multitudo congregata iudicat illud non sibi esse conveniens aut utile—causa cessante (p. 721) quare plus sibi quam aliis assentire debeat, ex eo quia presume-

---

[1] Cf. above, p. 146, n. 5.
[2] Cf. *Dec. advis.* fo. 224r–v: above, pp. 142–4.
[2] Cf. Aristotle, *Politics*, III, x, 1286b.
[4] Cf. Aristotle, *Politics*, III, iv, 1297a. For the same idea, quite independent of Aristotle, in Carolingian times, cf. W. Ullmann, *The Carolingian renaissance* (London, 1969), 122 f., 177 f.   [5] Cf. Aristotle, *Politics*, III, x, 1286b.

batur iudicium suum esse conforme intentioni omnium, constat autem de contrario—propterea illi non prefertur. Nec enim, quando in unum convenit multitudo eiusdem generis, tollerari potest reputari omnes simul tam gravi percussos cecitate, ut quid eis conveniat non possint discernere vel iudicare;[1] secus autem non convenientibus, quorum vix aut nunquam est conforme iudicium.

Preterea, cum aliquis iudex vel rector multitudinis constituitur, quoniam iudex idem est quod custos, equitatis velut mediator efficitur...habet rationem medii inter ipsos custoditurus, videlicet quod suum est unicuique ministrando. Quando vero in aliqua causa habet rationem partis, ratio iudicantis sibi iam non competit, quia nemo debet esse iudex in causa sua. Dato igitur casu presidentem aliquid affirmare esse iustum aut conveniens, contrarium vero affirmat tota, cui presidet, multitudo—quia iam non mediatoris, sed vicem habet partis—presidentie ratio, ut primo, sibi non videtur competere. Aliud quippe esset, si pro causa tangente bonum communitatis adversus aliquem vel aliquos iudicium agitaretur. Etenim, quia non tota communitas se opponit, sed pars eius, adhuc retinet rationem publice persone, tanquam solus ipse pro illis intendat ad bonum commune. Ceterum, in quocumque iudicio, ut iudici credatur, alterius quam sui ipsius requiritur testiomonium; iure communi circa hoc providente contra eam, que posset frequenter contingere, falsam assertionem iniqui iudicis. Quando igitur papa solus quicquam vellet asserere iustum et verum, nullo preter se de hoc testimonium perhibente, quinimmo tota multitudine Christianorum contrarium attestante—quoniam se habet tanquam extremorum alterum—non iudicis, sed potius diceretur habere rationem partis; dimissa publica, privata indutus persona.

Considerandum preterea, qualiter quicumque presidens supremus (pote papa, imperator aut rex) sententiam ferre posset contra totam sibi subditam multitudinem, hiis (videlicet imperatore ac rege) decernentibus subditos eorum omnes esse reos criminis lese maiestatis; et papa heretica infectos labe omnes Christianos—quorum utique vel papa hic aut illi remanerent principes, omnibus declaratis non-civibus aut non-catholicis? Inintelligible haudubio hoc diceretur esse. Nam et tunc iuxta ypothesim, nullo nisi unico dato fideli, ecclesia non esset neque regnum aut imperium, quando ex una dumtaxat persona constare diceretur.[2] Omnibus autem hiis demonstrantibus multitudini presidentem toti se non debere aut preferre posse, scripture divine exempla non desunt... (p. 722) Distat namque a

---

[1] Cf. *Dec. advis.* fo. 224v: above, p. 144.
[2] Cf. the canonists' dictum, 'non potest collegium constitui in uno': e.g. in Panorm., *Comm.* I, 138v, on 1.6.1; also *ibid.* I, 129v, n. II on 1.5.2.

Appendix A

dispotico polliticus principatus; domino potente vendere quos habet servos; non vero imperium aut regnum qui illi principatur. Servus quidem domini est gratia...Politicus vero principatus illorum est gratia, quibus prefertur;[1] ut tam voluntate quam ratione a suo presidente regantur,[2] nolente se illi preferre, velut contendente parte, aut suarum magnitudinem virium in totum populum sibi subditum exercere volente.

[THE COMMUNAL THEORY OF SOVEREIGNTY]

(p. 802)...Sicut identitas potestatis manifesta fuit, septemplici considerato respectu; ita disserendum est quod, non obstante septemplici differentia modi inexistendi, adhuc intelligere possumus unam eandemque esse trium, [sc.] ecclesie, concilii et summi pontificis, potestatem. Prima differentia est subiecti, respectu pape: etenim competens suprema ecclesie potestas sic respicit unitatem personae pro subiecto, quod repugnat eidem in pluribus esse personis. Sed, cum ecclesie vel concilii potestas suprema competere intelligitur, *multitudo personarum est subiectum potestatis ipsius, ita quod in unica esse non potest:* ecclesia autem quod multitudo personarum sit, iam ratio evidentissima plenifari[e] demonstravit, (pro eo quod ecclesia 'domus' est, 'civitas Dei', 'Christi regnum' et 'imperium')—: de concilio autem patet, quacumque data eius descriptione (sive dicatur 'ecclesia legitime congregata', sive 'episcoporum congregatio', sive 'multitudo personarum ex omni statu ecclesie catholice congregatio, virtualiter continens omnes eius status'). Iste profecto, sive alie quecumque descriptiones, ex ratione sua, multitudinem personarum denotant.[3] Quamvis tamen tam varie sumatur potestatis ecclesie subiectum (quia vel una, multe aut omnes persone fidelium), non propterea ratio sive essentia potestatis huius multiplicatur; sed una indivisibilisque manet in eis.

Exemplum accomodum est in aliqua magna communitate, superiorem in temporalibus non recognoscente. Etenim suprema potestas ipsius ad se tuendum regendumque se ipsam sibique subditos, *primo* consistit *in ipsa communitate; abinde* in rectoribus et magistratibus sive consulatu aut senatu (quocumque nomine appelletur); et *consequenter* in executore sive potestate, dictatore aut gubernatore; cui commissum est de omnibus disponere, consulatu in adversum non disponente, et executioni tradere ea, que consulatus diffinivit.[4] *Primo* vero inexistere huiusmodi potestatem supremam communitati, patet ex eo quod illi competere videtur tanquam propria passio sive innata virtus, ab ea inseperabilis, ut in ea sit tanquam in *primo* et, quamvis non solum, sed per se adequato ac *principali subiecto.*

[1] Cf. Aristotle, *Politics*, I, ii, 1255b.   [2] Cf. *MCG*, III, 844–5: below, pp. 152 f.
[3] Cf. Turrecremata: below, pp. 165, 169 ff.
[4] Cf. Zabarella and Panormitanus, above, pp. 10 f.

Data quippe communitate, *eo ipso potestas eidem inesse* intelligitur; nulla vero communitate sistente, quomodo nec in ipsa ita nec in magistratibus aut gubernatore sive executore manet. Hii namque, nomine et in vigore communitatis, suorum officiorum exercent operationes; et, quia deficiente subiecto omnis eius deficit virtus, omnis potestas hiis abesse intelligitur, nulla sistente communitate. Que, dum est in suo esse, potestatem *sibi intrinsecus competentem per semetipsam exercere potest*;[1] vel se ab hostibus defendens, vel iudicium faciens de sibi subditis malefactoribus, benefactoribus gratiam recognoscens, vel leges statuens (quibus (p. 803) subditi vivere debeant), vel ministros instituens rempublicam gubernaturos, aut eius officia particularia. Ceterum, quomodo *per se ipsam exercere potest* supremam potestatem regendi, ita eandem potestatem in alios transferre seu transfundere potest; quando agnoscit quod, si per se ipsam exerceret omni die et hora universaliter, [in]conveniens, irreparabile damnum subditis proveniret. Porro, quantumcumque aliis suam potestatem communicet, *numquam sibi abdicat*, propterea quod inseparabilis est ab ea.[2] Per quam, si contra adversarios et hostem se ipsam defendere potest, utique et contra domesticos inimicos, sive unus aut plures illi sint—leges suas custodire nolentes, vel alias quomodocumque eius idemnitati contravenientes et procurantes destructionem—quamdiu in esse permanet, eiusmodi potestate se ipsam tuendi inamissibiliter sibi competente. Dum vero aliis committit sive tuendi aut potestatem regendi, illis dumtaxat supremam suam communicat potestatem, quibus competit eius nomine ac de omnibus disponere universaliter...

Quibus patet quod tribus simul competere potest una eademque potestas—una, inquam, ab unitate finis unitateque forme subiecti et obiecti.[3] Namque bene ac tranquille vivere finis est cuiuslibet potestatis supreme ad regendam communitatem. Que, propterea quod unicum subiectum est ac immediatum potestatis ipsius, quamvis communicetur consulatui et rectori, non variatur; communicatione huiusmodi vim habente potius transfusionis sive extensionis cuiusdam, quam nove generationis (ut, ratione dependentie, intelligatur differentia essentialis). Quamdiu namque manet communitas, quamvis modo sic modo aliter variari contingat regimen magistratus, nusquam tamen diu communitas existere potest absque simili congregatione, similiter et absque potestate vel gubernatore. Propter quod, non delegata, sicut delegatis pape aut vicariis episcopi ad nutum removibilibus; magis autem et consulatui et

---

[1] Cf. Panorm., above, pp. 18, 42.
[2] Cf. Rousseau, *Du Contrat social*, II, i.
[3] Cf. D'Ailly and Gerson, cited in Lewis, *Medieval political ideas*, 375: attacked by Turrecremata, *SE*, II, c. 71: below, p. 169.

Appendix A

gubernatori ordinaria videtur potestas competere. Cumque, omni habenti notitiam regiminis quarumlibet communitatum, ista notissima sint, utique ex ipsis intelligere possumus de identitate supreme potestatis in ecclesia, concilio et papa—ordine tamen quodam, ut primo ecclesie inexistat, in ipsaque maneat continue, tam mortuo quam vivente pontifice summo, et tam dissoluta quam sedente synodo generali.

[ON TRUST IN AUTHORITY]

[Segovia illustrates his notion of theological trust by drawing analogies with the trust given to poetic and philosophical 'authorities'. He argues, on the basis of St Augustine, that 'auctoritas est dignitas pre-eminentie, cuius preceptis fides exhibetur tanquam potentis illa patefacere vera iustaque esse'; thus reverence is paid to the name and doctrine of scriptural authors, 'tanquam potenti[bus] rationem reddere de hiis, que affirmabant esse vera'.[1] Next, he proceeds to the analogy with political authority.]

(p. 844)...Rursus, Aristotele libro 3 *Politicorum* testante,[2] quod ab initio dignitas cepit regie potestatis, propterea quia parum erat in quovis populo invenire viros multum differentes ab illis secundum virtutem; ideoque in regem assumebant unum excellentem alios; huic autem regi per eos assumpto et sic appellato, quia sua prudentia et sapientia regebat populum, in tantum attributa est auctoritas, ut eius verbo simplici crederent; populo in hoc se habente conformiter ad auctoritatem doctrine attributam philosophis. Nam quemadmodum philosophorum dictis crediderunt quia intellexerunt que dicebant ratione constare; ita et regum illorum mandatis, regiminis eorum prudentiam experti. Cum autem regni potestas non tam sapientia, sed violentia sepe aliisque causis ad multos pervenit, hii etiam voluerunt auctoritatem sibi tribui, ut eorum preceptis atque dictis omnis reverentia exhiberetur, quomodo hiis, qui ratione sapientie et virtutis a populo fuerant accepti. Et hec fuit altera impositio nominis, ut hiis, qui in fastibus agerent sive in principatu quovis constituti essent, auctoritatis nomen tribueretur, eorum mandatis, priusquam id constaret ratione, tanquam vera iustaque essent et credendo et obediendo. At quia, dum venerunt seculi tempora erudita, iam rarum non fuit invenire homines virtuosos, sed quam multi floruerunt, sapientia et virtutibus prestantes regibus ipsis (sicut de Tarquinio contigit Superbo);

[1] Cf. St Augustine, *De vera religione*, c. 24, in *Corpus Christianorum ser. lat.* (Turnholt, 1962), 215; and *Epistola ad Dioscorum*, ep. 118 in his *Opera omnia*, II, pt. i, ed. Monachi ordinis sancti Benedicti (Paris, 1836), 510–12, esp.: 'Itaque totum culmen auctoritatis *in illo uno* salutari nomine *ac in una eius ecclesia* recreando et reformando humano generi constitutum est' (p. 512).
[2] Cf. *Dec. advis.* fo. 219r: above, p. 141 and n. 2.

[sc. regibus illis] pro libito voluntatis imperare volentibus, et propterea eorum multis in tyrannidem versis, alterata persepe fuit politia a monarchico in aristocraticum principatum. Et tunc antiqua rediit auctoritas, qua virtuosis, per sapientiam legesque iustas regentibus populum, sicut et regibus, reverentia exhibita est venerationis; in eorum legibus et mandatis exposita ratione, quemadmodum probavit experientia, cum a Romanis, tempore iurisconsultorum, condite sunt leges ipsarummet explicantes rationem in eodem contextu legis. Quocirca, verificatum est commune illud dictum, Romanos plus sapientia quam armis subiugasse orbem... Quando autem postea vigorem obtinuit, 'quod principi placuit legis' habere 'vigorem', itaque, preterita ratione, dispositio voluntatis principum, in scriptis redacta, pro lege habita est—non vero, ut leges priores, rationis evidentia, sed (p. 845) vigorem accipiens potentia conditoris: quia nullum violentum perpetuum, utique quomodo accepit, ita et perdidit, eiusmodi legibus principum uti nolentibus, quicumque non recognoscebant eorum dominium.

Unde apparet manifestissima differentia auctoritatis illius, que est doctrine ratione, et illius, que est principatus sive potestatis imperio, ista requirente subiectionem venerantium, illa minime.[1] Propter quod, sicut auctoritas philosophorum naturalium et moralium sive poetarum et aliorum auctorum in quibuslibet scientiis cepit, ita et continuata est, nomina eorum venerantibus, qui numquam illorum dominio subiecti fuerunt, sed propter manifestationem veritatis doctrine, quam in suis reliquerunt scriptis. Et ita doctrine ratione leges civiles locum obtinent, in quibus eisdem non contraveniunt municipales...

Ex premissis igitur, declarantibus quid proprie sit auctoritas, perspicuum est agnoscere, quod tanto maior est auctoritas, hoc est, magis fit exhibitio reverentie dictis cuiusque, *quanto plus creditur minime aberrare posse eum a veritate.*

[Segovia goes on to assert that absolute trust is due only to God, and to His word directly revealed in Scripture. Segovia's chief purpose is to emphasize the distinction between such absolute trust and the merely relative trust due to all other 'authors' and 'authorities'.]

...(p. 846) Profecto eorum [sc. those others] auctoritas non est illa, cui omnimoda absque alia examinatione reverentia firmaque debeatur. Sed illa [sc. absolute trust], ut Augustinus inquit, debetur *Christo et ecclesie in Christo*;[2] namque plenissime reperitur competere totum, quod est de ratione auctoritatis, quoniam in ipso est dignitas praeminentie, *cuius*

---

[1] Cf. Aquinas, *Summa theologiae*, 1ª2ᵃᵉ, q. 90, a. 1: 'utrum lex sit aliquid rationis'.
[2] *Epistola ad Dioscorum*, ep. 118 in *Opera omnia*, II, pt. i, 510–12.

*preceptis fides exhibenda est, tanquam potentis illa patefacere vera iustaque esse...*Magna profecto differentia est inter auctoritatem Christi, et aliorum omnium, quibus auctoritas competere dicitur: in eo persone nomine dante doctrine auctoritatem; in aliis autem preeminentia doctrine dante auctoritatem eorum nomini.

[ON THE NATURE OF LEGAL AND POLITICAL ENTITIES]

...(p. 851) aliter assignatur causa efficiens effectusque eius in naturalibus, aliter in artificialibus, aliter in civilibus seu politicis, aliter in hierarchicis seu ecclesiasticis atque divinis...[In nature and artifice, first, both cause and effect consist in external real objects. But a 'political cause' consists in one abstract, namely a human rule or plan, having an effect on another abstract, namely subsequent human attitudes]...(p. 852) si lex sit, fugientem de bello occidi propterea debere, lex est causa mortis, non quia mortem efficit, sed quia illam per fugam [aliquis] meruit; reatum incurrens per hoc, quod non implevit casum legis—que profecto *non est causa instrumentalis et naturalis* mortis, sed dumtaxat *politica vel civilis*...[Thus a 'political cause' is 'ens rationis', and takes its effect 'ex precedenti actu voluntatis' working through other (natural or artificial) causes. Thus Segovia also says that its action is not 'determined' or 'necessary', as is the action of a natural cause (e.g. the sun) or an artificial cause (e.g. a paintbrush). These points are further illustrated by another example.]

...(p. 853) Si vero lex ordinaretur ut sumens toxicum moriatur; quia, nulla lege stante, id certe proveniret, mors utique contingeret in sumente toxicum, non ex legis ordinatione sed ex natura actus; et, sicut toxicum est realis causa, ita et mors, effectus eius, natura rei eveniret: propter hoc mortis huius causa non esset politica, tali lege de nihilo serviente; quia, etiam si non fuisset illud lege insinuatum, mors nihilominus sequeretur...

[Segovia now proceeds to explain what kind of causality operates in politics and law.][1] Politica igitur causa, sicut ens rationis dicitur, ita et

---

[1] We may perhaps summarize this passage as follows. Political 'causes' are acts both of will and of reason. They are thus not inherent in the nature of the objects, nor are they the automatic consequences of objects being in a certain mutual relation; they arise from the deliberate implementation of mental constructs. This applies to all aspects of politics, to the offices themselves as well as to official acts; and it applies whether these are just or unjust. Being acts of a human, not a divine, mind, they achieve their effects, not *ipso facto* and immediately, but through the mediation of subsequent human activity, which takes them from the realm of mental 'fabrication' into the realm of the real world. Similarly, being neither natural nor divine, they may vary. Government, as well as its acts, is thus placed implicitly in the sphere of positive law and of deliberate, 'artificial' construction. One is strongly tempted to see in all this a stark anticipation of the views of H. Kelsen, when he affirms that

effectus ipsius...Sub hoc genere cause politice se habent omnes, fere leges iudiciales Exodi civilesque ac municipales et statuta quorumcumque principatuum; omnes item gradus qui in universitatibus generalium studiorum propter studium in scientiis conferuntur; omnia quoque officia regiminis in populo. Sicut namque lex sive ordinatio, per quam ista conferuntur, ens rationis est; ita et sunt entia rationis officia ipsius gradus vel dignitates etiam ecclesiastice, que positivi iuris sunt aut per consuetudinem, causa et effectu huiusmodi non natura sed voluntate constantibus ordinatoris. Et propterea utrumque non res nature sed ens dicitur rationis causatum per intellectum, sicut est fabricare seu fingere per imaginationem castra aurea in Africa supra mare, et argentea in Austria supra Danubium. Intellectus namque non est causa productiva alicuius rei ad extra, nisi forte dicatur sermonis, qui potius dependet a voluntate. Ipsa autem voluntas, quamvis non sit potens res producere in esse reale seu nature, producit tamen in esse rationis, effectu eius constante, quomodo constat lex sive ordinatio aut mandatum...Itaque tria ista (p. 854) habentia se consequenter, quamvis eorum subiecta realia sint, ipsa tamen entia sunt rationis; videlicet, dignitas principatus...item lex sive ordinatio vel statutum promulgatum a principante; effectus quoque legis, pote reatus supplicii vel meritum premii. Et *per* hec tria entia rationis pervenitur ad [ens] reale, [sc.] supplicii; videlicet, pene inflictionem in eo qui deliquit, vel adeptionem premii in eo qui recte agit...Et quantumcunque rationi et iustitie contrarieretur sive dignitas principatus sive lex, mandatum quoque et legalis sive legittimus effectus eius, omnia tamen dicuntur entia rationis quoniam a voluntate procedunt, rationis participe; utique, si et iniqua sunt a voluntate ration[i] obviante, quando autem iusta a voluntate rationem sequente...(p. 855) Causa igitur politica seu civilis, sicut ipsa *non reale sed est ens rationis*, ita etiam *effectum, qui est ens non reale sed rationis*, producit; communi loquendi usu distinguente inter *mortem civilem et naturalem* sive realem, quam nulla lex sui conditione facit, sed bene civilem in casibus multis. ['Hierarchical causes', lastly, by which he means acts of divine intervention, that is of grace, such as miracles and the sacraments, are similar to political ones, in that they are willed, but, coming from God, they can produce as results either 'ens rationis' or 'ens reale'.]

'the state as an acting person is not a reality but an auxiliary construction of legal thinking' (*Pure theory of law*, trans. M. Knight (Berkeley, 1967), 292); cf. also his *General theory of law and state*, trans. A. Wedberg (repr. New York, 1961), 182 ff., where, attacking the view that the state is a natural-social reality, he asserts that it is rather a 'political fiction' (*ibid.* 184).

Appendix A

3. De magna auctoritate episcoporum in generali concilio (1450)
(MS. Universitätsbibliothek, Basle, Cod. B. V. 15)[1]

[ON THE NATURE OF THE MONARCHICAL FORM OF GOVERNMENT IN THE CHURCH]

fo. 97v, proposition 10, chapter 1. *De forma monarchici regiminis ab initio et usque in finem seculi in ecclesia duraturi*[2]

[He re-opens the discussion undertaken in *MCG*, III, 707 ff] (fo. 98r)...
Unde quod in ecclesia esse debeat monarchica forma satis esset allegare Philosophi testimonium, docentis quod entia mundi huius nolunt male disponi, et quod pluralitas principatuum non bona, unus igitur princeps[3] ...Imperator unus mundi huius, unius provincie iudex unus...ita unius ecclesie catholice non plures sed unus est episcopus primus, actu habens potestatem regendi omnes fideles...

fo. 104v, chapter 7. *Tempore legis nature et scripture in populo fideli viguit semper monarchici forma regiminis*[4]
...ordinatissima semper fuit politia populi fidelis, cum omnis ordo ab uno incipiat, utique politia monarchici regiminis, cui proprium est in unum respicere, ceteris celsiorem esse intelligi oportet...

fo. 105v, chapter 8. *In lege gratiae forma monarchici regiminis fuit a Christo instituta, ordinata, perfecta atque firmata.*[5]
...Item in lege nature et in lege scripture presidentes populi Dei non erant ad proprium intendentes, sed ad multorum bonum commune... quomodo patres ad filios[6]...Sed [forma monarchica regiminis] non perfecta erat, donec Christus eius monstravit perfectionem (fo. 106r) cum ad apostolos, quos gregis sui constituit rectores, ait, 'Vos autem non sic, sed qui maior est in vobis, fiat sicut minister, et qui precessor est sicut ministrator...sicut minister et servus'.[7] Quocirca videtur non satis esse ad

---

[1] Cf. Haller in *CB*, i, 40 ff. While accepting the events of 1449, the election of Nicholas V by the Council and its self-dissolution, Segovia did not so much alter his views, as seek to develop them further in one more effort to reconcile the principle of Conciliar with that of papal authority: the result was extremely illuminating.

[2] Cf. *Ampl. disp.* 708–9: above, p. 145.

[3] *Metaphysics*, XII, x, 1076a; cf. Homer, *Iliad*, II, 204–5. See furthermore St Jerome in Gratian, VII, i, 51; Dio Chrysostom, *On kingship*, III, 50. Cf. below, p. 165.

[4] Cf. *Ampl. disp.* 708: above, p. 145. The preceding chapter discusses Mohammedanism; he remarks, 'Sarraceni...dominantur ut communiter principaliter *despotico*': fo. 99r. Cf. C. Rodriguez, *Juan de Segovia y el problema islamico* (Madrid, 1944).   [5] Cf. *Ampl. disp.* 709: above, p. 145.

[6] Cf. *Ampl. disp.* 708: above, p. 145.

[7] Matt. xx:25–8; cf. *Ampl. disp.* 710: above, p. 146.

perfectionem regiminis in populo Dei, presidentem beneficum esse et reputatum ut talem. Nam et 'reges gentium' erant benefici...sed 'forma facti gregis ex animo',[1] potiusque gererent se ut ministri et servi...Dans ...consumatam perfectionem monarchico principatui, voluit Christus ut qui preest fideli populo tamquam precessor, tanquam primus et tanquam maior, quod se habeat sicut minor et sicut ministrator, quodque fortius astringitur ut omnium sit minister et servus...Propter quod summus pontifex, quicumque sit, hanc monarchici regiminis perfectionem profitetur, illamque fatetur publice...omnibus suis litteris auctenticis vocat se servum servorum Dei.[2] Nec id satis esse ad consumatam perfectionem monarchici principatus ecclesiastici, sed etiam adicit Christus boni esse pastoris dare animam suam pro ovibus suis.[3] Hec certe est forma perfecta (fo. 106v) monarchici regiminis quam Salvator docuit...

fo. 107r, chapter 9. *Quod ab apostolis et cunctis fidelibus tamquam monarcha fuit Petrus recognitus et veneratus*

[He argues that from the very beginning the church was, in this sense, a monarchy.]

fo. 172v, proposition 11, chapter 26. *Incipit pertractari utrum celebratio sinodi generalis adversetur monarchico principatui papae, et intimetur que politie sunt invicem compatibiles.*

[He discusses once more the apparent contradiction between the 'aristocratic' form of the council and the statement of Scripture that the church is a 'kingdom']...Satis erit compendio demonstrare, quod monarchico regimini ecclesie minime repugnat, (fo. 173r) summum pontificem attendere debere sinodales diffinitiones, earum iudicia exequi, et aliter se conformare, ab aliisque observari facere. Id autem ostenditur, exposito primum quod uti consiliis sapientum non adversatur regio sive monarchico principatui, nec illud obscurum reddit, sed magno clarificat splendore...Rursus exponetur tertio quod sic agendo nihil deperit sue monarchice potestati, quinimmo quod ex celebratione generalis concilii splendorem maximam atque speciale robur suscipit et incrementum[4]... Posset igitur dici quod non repugnat unam eandemque communitatem illis duabus [*sc.* the monarchical and aristocratic forms] contemperatis dirigi politiis. Etenim Aristoteles videtur in secundo *Politicorum* Lacedae-moniorum civitatem, praeter tyrannicam, habuisse in se omnes politias[5]

---

[1] I Peter v:4.
[2] For the origin of this in Gregory I, cf. Ullmann, *Growth*, 37, n. 5.
[3] Cf. John x:11.
[4] Cf. *Ampl. disp.* 710–12: above, pp. 146 ff.   [5] *Politics*, II, iii, 1265a.

...Sola vero tyrannis deerat, que recte politie, immo et omni politie incompatibilis est...[he proceeds to summarize Aristotle's views on oligarchy and democracy]¹ (fo. 173v)...Si igitur non repugnat unam eamdemque communitatem differentibus regi politiis, ecclesia profecto nomine regni non amittat, actu sedente generali concilio...

Chapter 27. *Quod directio sinodalis assimilatur monarchico principatui, non vero alteri ex quinque politiis designatis ab Aristotele*

...(fo. 174r) Quamvis plurimum Aristotelis proficiat doctrina ad elucidandam ecclesie politiam, nulli tamen politiarum prout ipse pertractat esse comparandum simpliciter concilium generale...[he discusses the three perverse régimes, tyranny, oligarchy and democracy, and establishes their dissimilarity to the council] (fo. 174v)...Sed quoniam in hoc convenit synodus rectis politiis—quomodo illae non ad proprium sed ad commune intendant conferens—cui illarum trium [sc. which of the good forms of government: monarchy, aristocracy and polity]² assimilatur concilium, intuendum est. Et certe facile intelligere possumus quod soli monarchie, quia dicitur 'regnum'...Ratio huius existit quoniam celebratio synodi generalis...non est alteratio politie ecclesiastice, quin potius, monarchici forma regiminis, papali conveniens dignitati, tunc roboratur et confirmatur, resplendetque (fo. 175r) multo quam prime clarius et eminentius.³ Si nam concilio intererit pontifex summus, in medio sedet patrum ut princeps, monarcha populi christiani...convenit ad sinodum...proponit materias...concludit. Eius quoque nomine promulgantur sententie sinodales, statuta fiunt atque mandantur canones ...Nec, prout in aristocratia, eliguntur qui secundum virtutem praesident sed quos papa instituit, nisi iam personis quid grave obicitur, admittit sinodus...[it is therefore neither an oligarchy, nor a democracy] Sed est ut simpliciter est dicere mixtio oligarchiae et democratiae.⁴ Et consue-

---

¹ Aristotle, *Politics*, IV, vi, 1293b ff.; x, 1297a ff.; VI, i, 1317a–b. Segovia's main purpose is to show that, since Aristotle envisages a mixture of oligarchy and democracy, there is nothing contradictory in saying that monarchy and aristocracy can operate side by side in the church. In his insight into, and use of, Aristotle, he surely excels over his opponents; he seems to grasp that Aristotle's types of government are partly intended as concepts and definitions by means of which to dissect existing constitutions, and not as necessarily existing in 'pure' form.

² Aristotle, *Politics*, III, v, 1279a–b.

³ Cf. *Ampl. disp.* 712: above, p. 147; and contrast *Dec. advis.* fos 218v–219v: above, pp. 141 f.

⁴ Aristotle, *Politics*, IV, vi, 1293b, a definition of 'polity'. Segovia presumably sees this as a definition of the conciliar element in church government; for he clearly also envisages a further 'mixture' of this with (papal) monarchy.

verunt declinantes ad democratiam politiam vocare, ad oligarchiam vero declinantes aristocratiam[1]...[he goes on to point out that, furthermore, the council differs from each of Aristotle's good types, in that it is not permanent, and is not composed of citizens—as remarked on fo. 174r, 'synodus constituitur ex hiis qui populis multis principari consueverunt'] Nec unquam synodus convenit ad transmutationem monarchici ecclesie principatus in aristocraticum, etiam si intenderet ad depositionem summi pontificis et alterius electionem, sicut nec alteratur politia ecclesie per mortem naturalem unius et creationem alterius...(fo. 175v) Deus ipse instituit politiam ecclesie esse monarchici principatus[2]...Aliud profecto est monarchiam secundum aristocratiam esse, aliud principatum esse aristocraticum[3]...Si quis autem diceret regimen concilii esse aristocraticum, quia studiose et secundum virtutem disponat de regimine ecclesie, opportuno diceret.

fo. 175v, chapter 28. *De maxima differentia politie Aristotelis et evangelii, quodque non obviat monarchico principatui conformare se consiliis sapientum* ...(fo. 176r) Salvator...in ecclesia voluit ut discipulorum suorum, qui erat maior esset sicut iunior, et qui precessor sicut ministrator, quinimmo ut qui maior esse vellet omnium servus[4]...ubi non principantur leges non est politia, sed oportet legem principari omnium; de singulis autem principatus et politiam iudicare...Quinimmo diffinit monarchiam quae existit omnino de regno, talem necessarium esse tyrannidem, quia oportet leges recte positas esse dominas, principatus autem, sive unus sive plures sint, de hiis esse dominos de quibuscunque non possunt leges dicere certitudinaliter. Sed secundum leges oportet principes principari[5]...Illud propterea absonum est, quod summi pontificis principatus despoticus sit tamquam solius sui gratia; quoniam regimen summi pontificis ad christifideles non est velut domini ad servos, semetipso publice profitente se servum esse servorum Dei...quanto doctiores et sanctiores [sc. summos pontifices], tanto usi sunt aliorum consiliis...[he continues in similar vein to *MCG*, III, 710 f.]...(fo. 176v) Nulla igitur facta mentione sinodalis iudicii in ista prima expositione, ex commemoratis clarescere potest, utrum rex (quicumque sit ille) aut supremus monarcha amittat vel potius custodiet formam monarchici regiminis, suaque dignitas obscura fiat vel splendida, quando in arduis operatur consilia sequens suorum procerum et sapientum, qui tale *creditum* in regno illo atque principatu

---

[1] *Politics*, IV, vi, 1293b; vii, 1294b; v, vi, 1307a.   [2] Cf. above, p. 145.
[3] Cf. *Ampl. disp.* 708: above, p. 145.
[4] Cf. fo. 106r: above, pp. 146, 156.
[5] Cf. *Ampl. disp.* 709: above, p. 146.

habent, si eorum consiliis utatur princeps, negotia regni bene disponi[1]...
Habet autem se consequentia operatio quarta, eiusmodi sententiae executionem fore tradendam de qua homines *creditum* habent, quod multorum
sapientum iudiciis fuisse examinata mature...Quinimmo hic rex aut
quivis monarcha permaxime principari intelligitur, quando iudicia sua
nullo resistente executioni traduntur. Et hoc contingit quando subditis
constat illa processisse de consilio sapientum; et ultra hoc, quia quanto
constat maiorem multitudinem sapientum intervenisse, tanto diffinita
maiori habentur veneratione et facilius executioni demandantur.[2] Hinc
certe monarchico regimini non obviat in arduis rebus bonum concernenti-
bus commune sapientum multorum uti consiliis...

fo. 177r, chapter 29. *Radicalis ostensio quando monarchico principatui facile
obediatur*
    ...Presidens quippe monarchico regimine ideo *creditum*[3] habet ut eius
accepta[ntur] mandata tradunturque executioni, quoniam subditi arbitrantur eundem non proprium sed commune intendere bonum. Et
quanto in ea re validius atque plurimorum habet testimonium, facilius ei
creditur...(fo. 177v) Vere igitur monarchico regimini nihil obest etiam
si aliorum consiliis princeps utatur ...ex tot adiuvat ut subditi agnoscunt
monarchice principantem illorum commune bonum, non vero proprium,
intendere...

fo. 178r, chapter 30. *Quod habet auctentica ecclesie doctrina papam conformiter
esse acturum ad iudicia sinodi generalis*
    ...(fo. 178v) Attentis igitur professionibus hiis, in Dei ecclesia ab
initio ordinatis et continue approbatis, nostris quoque diebus ampliatis,
indubie dicendum erit monarchico regimini papae obviare minime, ut
sinodales exequantur diffinitiones, illis suas actiones confirmans...(fo.
179r) Hoc enim nomen primus ipse in ecclesia possidet, quia executor sit
canonum sinodi generalis. Et quanto maior convenit multitudo sapientum
uniformiter determinans verius pontifici attribuitur nomen virtuosi
regiminis in populo Dei, virtuosi inquantum quia recta ratione deter-
minati prout sapiens, magis autem prout sapientum multitudo, deter-
minavit...
    [There follows a lengthy exposition of the doctrine contained in *Ampl.
Disp.* 710–12,[4] as the following chapter-headings indicate.]

---

[1] Cf. *Ampl. disp.* 710–11: above, pp. 146 f. and esp. p. 146, n. 4.
[2] Cf. *Ampl. disp.* 711: above, p. 147.
[3] For a different use of this term some years after, cf. Macchiavelli, *The Prince*, ch. iv,
   vii, xi: trans. G. Bull (London, 1961), 46, 57, 76.   [4] Cf. above, pp. 146 ff.

fo. 179r, chapter 31. *Ex celebratione generalis sinodi nihil papae deperit de forma sui regiminis monarchici, sed magno illustratur splendore...*

fo. 180r, chapter 32. *Quod principalium accedente consensu maxime roboratur monarchicus principatus, et quod papa uti debet consiliis cardinalium...*

fo. 182r, chapter 34. *Explicantur modi quatuor demonstrantes incrementum papalis auctoritatis ex sinodi generalis congregationis...*

Appendix B

JOHN OF TURRECREMATA

1. *Summa de ecclesia* (Venice, 1561)

John of Turrecremata's *Summa de ecclesia* (1449) is generally acknowledged to be the most full-scale and systematic treatment of ecclesiology in the Middle Ages and is perhaps the first complete theological discussion of its kind. Bristling with citations, from friends and opponents alike, it is also a very competent summary of medieval doctrine. The following excerpts, giving Turrecremata's views on the constitution of the church insofar as they bear on political theory are, therefore, a minute selection; they should be seen as giving his views on political theory rather than on ecclesiology, for elsewhere in his work he modifies some of the statements made here, for theological reasons.[1]

Book 2

Chapter 1. [*On hierarchical order in the church*]

(fo. 116r...hanc legem naturalem [Deus] posuit omnibus ut ultima per media perficerentur et media per prima, ut dicit beatus Dionysius[2]... Aeque vel magis debet esse regulatus processus ecclesiae quam processus naturae...sed in processu naturae est ordo quo quidam aliis sunt superiores officio et habent aliis influere; ergo et in ecclesia debet esse ordo quo quidam aliis sunt superiores potestate et officio et habent aliis influere... Ecclesia militans exemplata est a triumphante sive celesti; secundum illud Exodi. 24: 'Inspice, et fac secundum exemplar tibi monstratum in monte'. Unde beatus Dionysius in c.6. *Ecclesiasticae hierarchiae* dicit ita: 'nostra enim hierarchia, a Deo traditis ordinibus sancte disposita, sanctis et coelestibus hierarchiis conformis est'[3]... (fo. 116v) Ecclesia militans est instituta ad formam hierarchiae. Unde de ecclesiastica hierarchia beatus Dionysius

---

[1] Some snippets from Book II, ch. 41, pp. 70, 71, are translated in Lewis, *Medieval political ideas*, 239–40, 422–9.

[2] Cf. *De ecclesiastica hierarchia*, I, ii; Aquinas, *Commentum in librum Sententiarum*, d. 24, q. 1, a. 1, q. 5, sol. For a summary of Pseudo-Denis and the influence of this work, cf. Ullmann, *Principles*, 46 ff.

[3] *Ibid*, VI, v; cf. Aquinas, *Summa contra Gentiles*, IV, 76, 4.

librum illustrem fecit, qui ita *De ecclesiastica hierarchia* intitulatur. Sed ratio hierarchiae in ordine potestatis consistit. Dicitur enim hierarchia a 'hieros' quod est 'sacrum', et 'archos' quod est 'princeps', quasi sacer principatus[1]...Ecclesia constituitur ex duplici pariete...sc. laicali et clericali;[2] sed in pariete laicali est ordo, utpote imperator, rex, dux, comes, tribunus, ballius, centurio, decurio; omnia haec ordinem dicunt. Ergo videtur quod in pariete clericali, qui spirituali militia Deo militat, debeat esse huiusmodi ordo...secundum illud beati Gregorii, in [d. 89, c. 7] ita dicentis: 'Ad hoc dispensationis provisio gradus diversos, et ordines constituit esse distinctos, ut dum reverentiam minores exhiberent potioribus, et potiores minoribus dilectionem impenderent, vera concordia fieret, et ex diversitate contextio, et recte officiorum gereretur administratio singulorum. Nec enim universitas alia poterat ratione consistere, nisi huiusmodi eam magnus ordo differentiae servaret'[3]...

Chapter 2. *Ostendens quod talis ordo sit et debeat esse in ecclesia ut unus in ea superior sit princeps ac rector existat*

Ordo autem, qui in ecclesia est et esse debuit, ita accipiendus est, ut unus in tota universitate reipublicae christiane summus princeps, rector ac gubernator esse credatur...ordo iste intelligitur secundum praelationem et subiectionem. Praelatio autem attenditur secundum ascensum et descensum, non secundum aequalitatem; et ascendendo superius necesse est status, et reductio ad unum, cum 'non sit processus in infinitum',[4] et econverso descendendo multiplicatio. Ergo secundum rectum ecclesie ordinem oportuit aliquem esse praelatum et supremum, *in quo totius potestatis ecclesiastice esset status*, qui omnium aliorum esset rector et pastor...(117r) sic iuxta sanctum Thomam in 4 *contra Gentiles*: 'nulli dubium esse debet quin ecclesiae regimen sit optime ordinatum, utpote per eum dispositum per quem "reges regnant et legum conditores iusta decernunt". Optimum autem regimen multitudinis est quod regatur per unum, quod patet tum auctoritate Aristotelis 11 *Metaphysicae*, et 3 *Politicorum*, tum ex fine regiminis. Pax autem et unitas subditorum est finis regentis...Unitatis autem causa congruentior est unus quam multi.'[5] Ergo regimen ecclesiae Dei sic a Deo esse dispositum creditur, ut unus in eo toti ecclesiae praesit...in triumphante ecclesia unus presidet qui etiam

---

[1] *Ibid.* i, iii.
[2] On the antecedent of this in Hugh of St Victor, cf. Ullmann, *Growth*, 428.
[3] *Regestum*, v. 59, p. 371: cited in Ullmann, *Growth*, 41; repeated by Gregory VII: Ullmann, *Growth*, 289.
[4] On the antecedents, cf. Grabmann, 'Studien über den Einfluss der aristotelischen Philosophie', 106 f.   [5] Aquinas, *Summa contra Gentiles*, iv, 76, 3.

presidet toti universo, sc. Deus. Ergo in militante ecclesia etiam debet esse unus praesidens etiam universis...

Iuxta sanctum Thomam in 4: 'Ubicunque sunt multa ordinata in unum, oportet esse aliquod universale regitivum super particularia regitiva...ideo supra potestatem regitivam quae (fo. 117v) communicat bonum speciale, oportet esse potestatem regitivam respectu boni communis',[1] alias non potest esse colligatio ad unum; ergo cum tota ecclesia sit unum corpus, oportet, si ista unitas debeat conservari, quod sit aliqua potestas regitiva respectu totius ecclesiae...et haec est potestas papae... tota machina universi est unum celeste corpus...est unus supremus, sc. Deus...ergo pariter in regimine ecclesiae oportet quod sit unus qui toti christianae universitati praesideat...ergo necessario in tota ecclesia est dandus unus supremus praesidens et rector, unum caput totius corporis, unus princeps totius civitatis, unus hierarcha totius hierarchiae, unus pastor totius ovilis sive gregis dominici...Ecclesia est regnum, sive ecclesiae principatus est monarchicus sive regalis. Hoc patet tum ex multis sacrae scripturae locis ubi ecclesia 'regnum coelorum' nominatur...Tum etiam quia optimum genus politiae est monarchicum sive regale, cum iuxta sententiam Aristotelis 3 *Politicorum*: 'omnium urbanitatum perfectissima sit regnum quod consistit ex omni ordine ad unum'.[2] Dionysius [in] libro *De divinis nominibus*, c. ii dicit: 'Quod regnum est omnis finis legis et ordinis distributio';[3] sed regnum est in quo potestas regiminis residet apud unum toti multitudini praesidentem, ut tam ex 8 *Ethicorum* quam ex 3 *Politicorum* aperte colligitur.[4] Ergo talis a Deo ecclesiae principatus constitutus est ut unus in eo superior potestate praesideat et principetur. Hoc enim est de ratione regalis sive monarchici principatus ut dictum est. Dicitur enim monarchicus a 'monos' quod est 'unum', et 'archos', quod est princeps, quasi unus princeps toti multitudini praesidens ...(fo. 118r) Principatus ille videtur omnibus aliis praestantior...quo inter subditos charitas et pax ac concordia maxime nutritur...et quo seditio et discordia, quae est cuiuslibet communis corruptio praecipua, devitatur...sed hoc magis et congruentius sit, si principatus fuerit apud unum sicut est in regno, quam si fuerit apud plures, sicut in aristocratia sive in politia; unitatis enim et pacis congruentior causa est unus quam plures.

---

[1] Aquinas, *Comm. in quartum Sent.* d. 24, q. 3, a. 2, q. 3, sol. 3: verbatim, except he has 'communicat' for 'conjectat'.

[2] But cf. Aristotle himself, in *Politics*, III, xi, 1287b–1288a; cf. *ibid.* viii, 1284b, and v, viii, 1310b; Turrecremata may be thinking of *Ethics*, VIII, x, 1160a, cited by Aquinas, *Comm. in quartum Sent.* d. 24, q. 1, a. 3, q. 2, a. 1, 3.

[3] *De divinis nominibus*, XII, ii.

[4] Aristotle, *Ethics*, VIII, x, 1160a; *Politics*, III, v. 1279a.

Ergo sequitur quod talis ecclesiae principatus, sc. monarchicus sive regalis, in quo omnium ordinatorum reductio ac adunatio est, redigatur ad unum principem, potestate et auctoritate omnibus praesidentem...

Chapter 4. [*Replying to the objection that Christ alone is head of the church*]
    (fo. 119v)...eadem species politiae manet in principatu respectu principalis et respectu vicarii instituti a principali cum plenitudine potestatis; unde idem consistorium reputatur episcopi et vicarii, ut in [VI:2.15.3]... Aristoteles, probans unitatem primi principii, 12 *Metaphisicae*, ait: 'Entia nolunt male disponi, neque bona pluralitas principatuum; unus ergo princeps'.¹ 'In apibus etiam unus est princeps et grues unam sequuntur ordine litterato', ait beatus Hieronymus in [C. VII, q. I, c. 41]. Secundo quia inter species regiminis humanarum civilitatum nobilior et praestantior est species regalis regiminis, in quo summa potestas et principatus [et] auctoritas est apud unum, ut 3 *Politicorum* Aristoteles docet²...Non sic autem est de aliqua alia unitate in quacumque politia inter fideles observanda, cum non sit necesse omnes eos convenire in politia communi, sed possunt secundum diversitatem climatum et linguarum et conditionum hominum esse diversi modi vivendi et diversae politiae...[he continues to cite at length John of Paris, *De potestate regia et papali*, c. 3.]³

Chapter 25 [*In answer to the argument that the pope is head of the church 'distributive' but not 'collective'*]
    ...Vana quidem praefata responsio est; quia, licet signum universale cum cadit supra nomen commune non collectivum possit fieri ista distinctio (verbi gratia: distinguitur apud logicos ista, 'Omnes apostoli Christi sunt duodecim'—quia collective est vera, distributive sumpto signo universali est falsa. Et econverso illa, 'Socrates est fortior omnibus hominibus', quia distributive potest esse vera, collective est falsa); tamen, quando signum universale cadit super nomen collectivum, cuiusmodi est 'ecclesia', 'plebs', 'populus', 'familia', 'grex', 'collegium', 'concilium', 'synodus' et huiusmodi, non videtur habere locum ista distinctio, quia contra naturam nominis collectivi est quod teneatur distributive et non collective...quod papa dicatur caput singulorum membrorum corporis ecclesiae, et non ipsius corporis quod ex ipsorum membrorum resultat multitudine, videtur nobis stultum, sicut quod rex sit caput omnium regnicolarum, et non regni.⁴

¹ *Metaphysics*, XII, x, 1076a; cf. Homer, *Iliad*, II, 204–5. Cf. above, p. 156.
² Above, p. 164, n. 2.
³ Ed. and trans. R. Lerner and M. Mahdi, in *Medieval political philosophy* (New York, 1963), 411.   ⁴ Cf. above, pp. 150 f.

Chapter 26 (fo. 139v)

[The term 'body' may be used either to describe the whole body, including the head, or to describe the rest of the body apart from the head.]

Et similis distinctio fit de regno et de omni principatu; quandoque enim nominat simul principem et subditos, aliquando regnicolas tantum subditos alicui principi; sicut dicimus, 'istud regnum est illius', 'ille dominatur huic regno'...[in] corpore mystico...possunt plura capita subordinata esse, sc. unum principale, et aliud secundarium principali subordinatum. Sicut in uno corpore civitatis est caput rector eiusdem, et cum hoc rex, qui totius regni caput est...papa non est omnino aliud caput distinctum a capite quod est Christus, sed est vicarius eius et vicem eius et personam, potestatem et auctoritatem representans in terris...

Chapter 52 *Quod Romanus pontifex habeat plenitudinem potestatis in ecclesia Dei*

(fo. 166r) In omni communitate bene recta oportet apud supremum residere plenam potestatem se extendentem ad omnia necessaria, et evidenter expedientia bono reipublicae illius communitatis. Cum ergo papa sit supremus in communitate totius christianitatis, utpote caput et rector omnium fidelium, sequitur quod apud illum plenitudo resideat potestatis, extendens se ad omnia necessaria et expedientia saluti reipublicae christianae...(fo. 167r) Cum enim Romanus pontifex caput totius christianae communitatis et princeps existat, eius non tantum est promovere ea et ordinare quae ad bonum reipublicae et consecutionem supernae beatitudinis [spectant]...sed ea tollere et submovere, prohibendo et corrigendo, quae ad motionem ad talem finem fideles impediunt... (fo. 167v) non arctatur eius potestas ad hoc, ut semper servato ordine inferiorum potestatum operetur, sed potest—mediantibus illis, vel illis intermissis—immediate in quemcumque christianum operari, ut immediatus ordinarius, pastor et praelatus, quando viderit expederi...

Chapter 53. *Quod solus Romanus pontifex in ecclesia Dei habeat plenitudinem potestatis*

(fo. 169v)...Necesse erit, secundum ordinem rectum ecclesiae, quod suprema potestas regiminis et plenitudo iurisdictionis stet in uno primo, et [quod] in simplicissimo in illo genere *est status omnis praelationis ecclesiasticae*. Ultimo sic: Principatus est quoddam *totum potestativum* cuius haec est natura, quod secundum completam rationem perfectionis sit in uno solo, sc. in principe; in aliis vero in quos distributum est per gradum diversarum dignitatum ac officiorum, est aliqua participatio ipsius; sicut principatus regni est in uno, videlicet rege, in aliis vero secundum participationem quandam, videlicit secundum potestatem praesidis...Exemplum etiam huius totius potestativi apparet in sacramento ordinis, cuius 'plenitudo in uno ordine, sc. sacerdotio; in aliis vero est quaedam participatio ordinis', ut dicit sanctus Thomas in 4 *Dist.* 24[1]...Ex quibus manifeste confunditur error et stultitia Marsilii de Padua...

Chapter 55. [Continuing from chapter 54: *Quod potestas iurisdictionis omnium praelatorum ecclesiae derivetur a papa sive apostolica sede mediate vel immediate*]

(fo. 171r)...In omni principatu potestas iurisdictionis derivatur ad quamcumque personam illius principatus a (fo. 171v) monarcha sive principe illius principatus; sed papa est princeps sive monarcha in sacro ecclesie principatu; ergo sequitur quod potestas iurisdictionis omnium praelatorum derivetur a papa...patet ex sententia Dionysii, qui tam in *De ecclesiastica* quam *coelesti hierarchia* docet ab ipso hierarcha in omnes hierarchiae personas lumen irradiationis perfluere[2]...In unoquoque ordine, ab eo in quo maxime residet plenitudo virtutis sive potestatis originaliter, dependet virtus omnium sequentium in illo ordine...ex sententia Aristotelis 2 *Metaphisicorum*[3]...Inter habentia ordinem secundum influentiam, omnia quae aliis influunt, virtutem influendi recipiunt a primo illius ordinis; sed ordo qui est inter Romanum pontificem et alios praelatos est secundum influentiam, prout unus movet alium ad actus hierarchicos. Ergo potestas iurisdictionis omnium praelatorum ecclesiae derivatur a Romano pontifice...Omnia membra a capite recipiunt immediate derivationem virtutis, sensus et motus sive regiminis... (fo. 172r) in ordine autem politicorum regimen administrantium omnes particulares potestates auctoritatem iurisdictionis suscipiunt a suprema potestate...Ergo sic erit in hierarchia ecclesiastica, quod potestas iurisdictionis, secundum quam attenditur ordo superioritatis et inferioritatis inter praelatos ecclesiae, primum a Deo immediate in papam descendat, et per eum in sequentes derivetur...

---

[1] *Comm. in quartum Sent.* d. 24, q. 2, a. 1, ad 2: 'Distinctio ordinis non est totius integralis in partes, neque totius universalis, sed totius potestativi; cuius haec est natura, quod totum secundum completam rationem est in uno, in aliis autem est aliqua participatio ipsius...tota enim plenitudo huius sacramenti (*sc.* ordinis) est in uno ordine, sc. sacerdotis; sed in aliis est quaedam participatio ordinis.' Cf. Turrecremata, *SE*, ɪɪ, c. 83, fo. 216r: below, p. 171; and Aquinas, *ibid.* ad 3, cited below, p. 171, n. 3.

[2] Cf. *De ecclesiastica hierarchia*, vɪ, vi. This 'descending' notion of hierarchical authority had previously been stated by Robert Grosseteste (cf. Ullmann, *Growth*, 443, n. 4), and by Augustinus Triumphus (cf. Wilks, *Sovereignty*, 9, 48, 163). On the idea of 'derivation', cf. Ullmann, *Principles*, 48, n. 1.   [3] Cf. *Metaphysics*, ɪɪ, ii, 994a.

Appendix B

Chapter 61. [*The successors of the apostles derive their power through the pope*]

(fo. 179r)...Poterunt enim esse instituti a suo vicario generali, cui totius regni sui curam et regimen [Christus] committit; sicut contingit in politiis secularibus, et etiam spiritualibus, quod cum principalis dominus longo tempore disponit se absentare se, committit suo generali vicario, ut si interim vacare contingit officia aut loca aliqua, provideat de idoneis ministris...

Chapter 64

(fo. 187v)...potestas papae se habet ad potestates episcoporum...non sicut potestas regis ad potestates principum habentium potestatem iure hereditario; nec etiam sicut potestatem regis ad potestates iudicum habentium potestatem delegatam vel commissariam; sed sicut potestas imperatoris vel regis se habet ad potestates iudicum in aliquo gradu regiminis regni vel imperii simpliciter institutorum ad regendum populum per se vel per alium. Ista est sententia sancti Thomae, unde in 4 *dist.* 19 dicit quod, 'potestas papae se habet ad potestates episcoporum sicut potestas regis ad potestates iudicum constitutorum per singulas civitates'.[1] Et in fine 2 *Sententiarum* dicit quod, 'Ita se habet potestas papae ad potestates inferiorum, sicut potestas imperatoris se habet ad potestatem proconsulis'.[2]

Chapter 65. *Quod papa est immediatus praelatus et iudex omnium fidelium ac in toto orbe terrarum facere possit quicquid inferiores praelati facere possunt*

(fo. 188v) In quocunque ordine quando tota potestas inferiorum dependet et originatur a potestate superioris, ad quaecunque se potest extendere potestas inferiorum, ad omnia illa se potest extendere immediate potestas superioris...ut dicit sanctus Thomas 2 *Sententiarum dist.* 9, quod 'divisio hierarchiae in ordines est totius potestativi in partes potentiales, cuius tota conditio est quod secundum completam virtutem est in parte suprema; et quod talis potentia sive potestas superior habet in se completius ea quae sunt inferioris ordinis'.[3] In ordine hierarchico quicquid potest inferior virtus sive potestas, potest superior...

---

[1] Something close to this appears in *Comm. in secundum Sent.* d. 44, expos. textus, resp.; but not in *Comm. in quartum Sent*, d. 19, q. 4.

[2] *Comm. in secundum Sent.* d. 44, expos. textus, resp.

[3] *Comm. in secundum Sent.* d. 9, q. 1, a. 3, ad 1: 'divisio hierarchiae in ordines est totius potestativi in partes potentiales...(whereas a universal whole is predicated equally of all the parts, and an integral whole cannot be predicated of the parts at all) totum potentiale adest quidem secundum essentiam cuilibet partis, sed secundum completam virtutem est in parte suprema, quia semper superior potentia habet in se completius ea quae sunt inferioris'. Cf. Turrecremata, *SE*, II, c. 83, fo. 216r: below, p. 171; also Aquinas, cited above, p. 167, n. 1.

[*Chapter 70 gives an admirable summary of the Baslean conciliarist arguments against papal plenitude of power*][1]

Chapter 71. [*Reply to the Baslean argument based on the organic analogy*]

(fo. 195v) Licet aliqua similitudo sit corporis mystici ecclesiae ad corpus naturalis hominis, videlicet in multitudine membrorum...nihilominus multiplex est differentia...membra corporis humani constituunt aliquod unum numero reale totum, quod subiective in se toto capax est alicuius formae aut qualitatis sive influxus realis, quod est ipsum corpus humanum; non autem sic membra quae dicuntur corporis mystici...cum distinguuntur personis et locis, non dicuntur constituere aliquod reale unum numero totum quod subiective in se toto capax alicuius formae...Unde etiam iuriste dicunt quod universitas 'non habet animam'[2]...(fo. 196r) Per hanc plane considerationem evanescunt multae fantasiae adversariorum novellorum magistrorum atque doctorum canonistarum...Communitas ecclesiae non consecratur, nec insignatur sacerdotio...Nulla universitas potest dici cum veritate habere perfecte aut plene aliquam potestatem in cuius exercitium numquam per se potest exire...Sed tota communitas ecclesiae non potest exire in actum potestatis ligandi et solvendi a peccatis. (fo. 196v)...Potestas clavium nec subiective nec formaliter nec radicaliter nec fundamentaliter (ut omnibus verbis adversariorum uteremur) potest esse in ecclesia universalis, nec in universitati clericorum, aut collegio sacerdotum, [aut] in quodam subiecto communi[3]...(197v) quoniam hoc regimen est nobilius reputatum tam a philosophis...quam a theologis, et credendum est quod Deus instituerit regimen ecclesiae suae in nobiliori specie regiminis; sed in principatu monarchico plenitudo potestatis non est apud omnes, sive apud communitatem, sicut est in regimine politico, sed solum apud unum, sc. apud principem, qui solus principatur...Si apud totam multitudinem populi christiani...resideat, sequitur quod principatus ecclesiae sit politicus, et non monarchicus, et per consequens in nullo [alio] quam in ipsa tota communitate est ponenda potestatis plenitudo. Haec autem differentia ponitur ab Aristotele, 8 *Ethicorum* et 3 *Politicorum*, inter tres species principatus quas ponit, vid. monarchicam... in quo solo residet plenitudo potestatis. Secundo dicitur aristocratia, quasi potestas sive principatus plurium secundum virtutem imperantium, ita quod nullius. Tertia species communi nomine dicta politia, in qua multi, ut populus, principantur, ita quod apud nullum residet plenitudo potestatis, sed apud omnes[4]... (fo. 198r) Impossible est quod in aliqua una

---

[1] Cf. above, p. 54.   [2] Cf. Gierke, *Political theories*, trans. by Maitland, 70.
[3] Cf. Segovia, above, pp. 150 f.
[4] Cf. *Ethics*, VIII, x, 1160a; *Politics*, III, v. 1279a. Cf. Aquinas, *Comm. in quartum Sent.*

universitate praelatus et subditi habeant eandem plentitudinem potestatis. Patet; quoniam non capit ratio, quod illud, per quod quis constituitur superior et praelatus aliorum, sit commune praelato et subditis in eadem plenitudine; sed in tota universitate christiana, Romanus pontifex est praelatus, et ceteri omnes alii fideles sunt subditi...Plenitudo potestatis quae ponitur in ecclesia aut est una et eadem numero cum ea quae ponitur in papa, aut est alia; sed non potest dici quod sit alia, quia sic duae supremae potestates, sive plenitudines potestatis, quod esse non potest... quia 'pluralitas principatuum non est bona' (12 *Metaphysicorum*).[1] Tum quia duas supremas potestates non patitur unitas ecclesiae. Non potest dici una et eadem numero plenitudo potestatis, quia si sic tunc neque papa esset superior et praelatus, nec ecclesia posset dici superior potestate ipso Romano pontifice...quia si 'par in parem imperium non habet', multominus ubi est identitas potestatis...

Chapter 78

(fo. 210v)...Praetendunt enim...quod ecclesiae in omnibus suis membris data sit potestas spiritualis gubernandi et regendi, more quo dicimus quod in principatu politiae potestas gubernationis est apud populum, et non apud aliquem unum qui toti populo praesideat[2]... Potestas regendi et gubernandi dicitur...potestas publice administrationis ...Talis autem potestas non est data cuilibet indifferenter nec cuilibet convenit, sed his tantum qui in communitate publicam habent administrationem regiminis secundum diversas species politie sive principatus. Sane sine huius ordinis differentia nulla universitas subsistere posset... (fo. 211v) potestas conservandi se in esse inest cuilibet creaturae rationali ...sed huiusmodi potestas non potest dici potestas clavium...

Chapter 82. [*Reply to the argument that the pope, as a member, is less than the church as a whole*]

(fo. 214v)...Sed dicimus quod in gratia iurisdictionis, in qua unus peccator potest esse maior quam multi iusti, papa sit maior toto residuo corpore ecclesiae...in virtute aut gratia quam unum membrum recipit, potest ita excellere omnia alia membra; ut, licet non simpliciter potest dici maius toto residuo corpore, possit tamen in tali gratia dici maius...hoc patet in quolibet principe, respectu multitudinis cui praesidet; non est dubium quin princeps sit membrum universitatis reipublicae (quam Policraticus instar corporis dicit esse formatum),[3] et tamen, licet non

---

d. 24, q. 2, a. 1, ad 3: 'In aristocratia autem apud nullum residet plenitudo potestatis, sed apud omnes.'   [1] *Metaphysics*, XII, x, 1076a; cf. Homer, *Iliad*, II, 204–5.
[2] Cf. above, p. 10.   [3] Cf. John of Salisbury, *Policraticus*, Book v, c. i.

possideat omnes virtutes et gratias quae possidentur ab omnibus aliis universitatis ...nihilominus potestate iurisdictionis superior universis aliis sive tota illa universitate est...(fo. 215r) in donatione sibi specialiter prae aliis facta huius particularis gratiae gratisdatae, videlicet potestatis iurisdictionis, ipse [papa] est maior toto residuo corporis ecclesiae...potestas in eo non sit particularizata, sed sit plena et integra...

Chapter 83. [*Reply to the argument 'ecclesia quoddam totum, papa autem non est tota ecclesia sed pars eius'*]

[This argument, he says, which 'apud eos Achilles reputatur', is true 'de toto integrali' or 'de totalitate quantitatis dimensive', but not 'de toto potentiali' or 'de totalitate quantitatis virtualis'.]

(fo. 216r)...in ratione potestatis est magis dicendus papa [esse] tota ecclesia virtualiter, cum in eo solo sit totalitas et plenitudo totius potestatis ecclesiastice...Ordo namque inter potentias hoc habet (ut dicit Boethius) quod quicquid virtutis potestative sit in inferioribus, est in superiori.[1] Unde in suprema potentia quantitas omnium aliarum inferiorum potentiarum includitur; et ita, cum potestas papalis sit suprema, in ea continentur virtute omnes aliae potestates ecclesiae; et ita ipsa, in ratione potestatis, non habet rationem partis, sed totius. Unde beatus Dionysius, in 6 *Ecclesiasticae hierarchiae*, dicit: 'Ipsa autem hierarchica ordinis dispositio in omnibus locatur sanctis totalitatibus'[2]...Potestas enim ecclesiae non est arbitranda...quasi sit aliquod totum integratum ex particularibus potestatibus...sed adinstar totius potestativi...(fo. 216v) sanctus Thomas in 4 *dist.* 24: 'Tota plenitudo huius sacramenti [sc. ordinis] est in uno, sc. sacerdotio, sed in aliis est quaedam participatio ordinis...in regno, quamvis tota plenitudo potestatis resideat penes regem, non tamen excluduntur ministrorum potestates, quae sunt participationes quaedam regiae potestatis'[3]...

Chapter 84. [*Reply to the argument that the pope is under the church because he exists 'propter ecclesiam'*]

(fo. 217r) Cuius exemplum possumus dare in potestatibus secularibus,

---

[1] Cf. Boethius, *Philosophiae consolatio*, ed. L. Bieler, in *Corpus Christianorum, ser. lat.* (Turnholt, 1957), 53, 79.

[2] This does not appear in *De ecclesiastica hierarchia*, VI.

[3] *Comm. in quartum Sent.* d. 24, q. 2, a. 1, ad 3: 'In regno, quamvis tota potestatis plenitudo resideat penes regem, non tamen excludunter ministrorum potestates, quae sunt participationes quaedam regie potestatis...' This refutation of the Baslean doctrine contained in the Cracow *memorandum* of 1442 (sup. p. 14) derives from Aquinas, *Comm. in secundum Sent.* d. 9, q. 1, a. 3, ad 1; and *Comm. in quartum Sent.* d. 24, q. 2, a. 1, ad 2: cited above, p. 167, n. 1 and p. 168, n. 3.

in quibus finis ad quem tendit regimen praesidentis et gubernantis est ipsa pax et tranquillitas universitatis, sive felicitas politica...ipse vero universitas dicitur finis regiminis sicut ad cuius utilitatem est ordinatum universum opus praesidentis...princeps enim, tam secularis quam ecclesiasticus, dicitur esse propter universitates sibi commissas et non econverso; nihilominus non sunt inferiores, sed maiores auctoritate subiectis sibi populis...

Chapter 101. [*Reply to the analogy between the pope and a secular tyrant*]

(fo. 241r)...non enim loquitur ibi sanctus Thomas nisi de communitate quae ius habet providendi sibi de rege per institutionem sive donationem iurisdictionis; sicut est communiter in institutione regum et principum secularium.[1] Secus est de principe ecclesiae, cuius auctoritas pendet ab ipso Deo immediate et non a communitate ecclesiae...Praeterea hoc etiam patet ex eo quod licet aliquod collegium canonicorum et alicuius ecclesiae cathedralis expectet provideri sibi per electionem de episcopo, nihilominus, quantumcunque conversus [est] ad tyrannum... non pertinet ad eum deponere illum, sed oportet recurrere ad superiorem. Ex his patet deceptio eorum adversariorum qui, ex conditione communitatis mundanae, ad quam spectat ut dicunt principis correctio vel totalis destructio si inemendabilis perseveret, arguunt de communitate ecclesiae, quod ita sit aut debeat esse in ea respectu ipsius principis ecclesiae; decipiuntur autem turpe, cum nullo modo sit simile hic et illic, ut dictum est.[2]

Chapter 107. *Quod ad Romanum pontificem pertineat determinare ea quae fidei sunt*

(Fo. 248r)...quemadmodum in omni republica bene ordinata dandus erat unus praesidens in ea, qui totam rempublicam posset auctoritate sua movere ad omnia, maxime sine quibus salus reipublicae stare non posset; ita etiam in communitate ecclesiae necessario erat dandus unus princeps, qui ad ea quae maxime conferunt ad salutem fidelium...sua auctoritate et magisterio totam ipsam christianam rempublicam moveret et dirigeret, cum Romanus pontifex sit huiusmodi presidens super totam rempublicam christianam...

[1] Cf. *Summa Theologiae*, 2ª2ᵃᵉ, q. 42, a. 2; and *Comm. in secundum Sent.* d. 44, q. 2, a. 2, sol.

[2] Turrecremata cannot miss an opportunity for a good argument; he thus overlooks the fact that throughout has been relying on this very analogy.

BIBLIOGRAPHY

ORIGINAL SOURCES

MANUSCRIPTS

Arevalo, Rodrigo Sanchez de. *De appellationibus*, Barb. lat. 1487, fos 79–88.

Circa convocationem...generalis synodi, Barb. lat. 1487, fos 89–115.

De remediis afflictae ecclesiae, Barb. lat. 1487, fos 120 ff.

Campo, Heimericus de. *Tractatus de potestate papae et concilii generalis*, Biblioteket, Kungliga Universitetet, Upsala, Cod. C. 160.

Forojulio (or Strasoldo, or Cividale), Ludovicus. *Dialogus de papali potestate*, Vat. lat. 4143, fos 1–27; and ed. B. Ziliotti, In *Memorie storiche forogiuliese*, XXXIII (1938), 151–91.

Galganus. *De potestate summi pontificis*, Vat. lat. 4129, fos 1–35.

Leonis (or de Urbe), Joannes. *De synodis et ecclesiastica potestate*, Barb. lat. 1487, fos 1 ff.

Monte, Piero da. *Contra impugnantes sedis apostolicae auctoritatem liber*, Vat. lat. 4145 and 4279.

Ragusio, Johannes Stojkovic. *Tractatus de ecclesia*, Universitätsbibliothek, Basle, A. 1.29.

Segovia, Joannes de. *Decem advisamenta*, Vat. lat. 4039, fos 192r–231v.

De magna auctoritate episcoporum in generali concilio, Universitätsbibliothek, Basle, B. V. 15.

Versailles, Pierre de. (Memorandum) Vat. lat. 4140, fos 11–12, 30–3.

PRINTED WORKS

Authors

Aquinas, Thomas (St). *Commentum in libros IV sententiarum, Opera Omnia*, ed. S. Fretté, XXX (Paris, 1878).

De regimine principum, ed. A. P. D'Entrèves, in *Aquinas: selected political writings* (Oxford, 1954).

Aristotle. *Politics*, ed. and trans. H. Rackham, Loeb edition (London, 1950).

Basin, Thomas. *Histoire des regnes de Charles VII et de Louis XI*, ed. J. Quicherat, I, *Société de l'Histoire de la France*, LXXXI (Paris, 1855).

Beckynton (or Beckington), Thomas. *Official correspondence*, ed. G. Williams, 2 vols (London, 1872).

Bisticci, Vespasiano da. *Lives of illustrious men of the fifteenth century*, trans. W. George and E. Walters (New York, 1963).

Bodin, Jean. *Six books of the commonwealth*, ed. and trans. M. Tooley (Oxford, n.d.).

Boyer, Nicholas. *De ordine et precedentia graduum, Tractatus Universi Iuris*, XIV (Lyons, 1549), 300–7.

De custodia clavium, Tractatus Universi Iuris, XII (Lyons, 1549), 118–23.

Bibliography

Capistrano, Joannes de (St). *De papae et concilii sive ecclesiae auctoritate* (Venice, 1580).

Chartier, J. *Chronique de Charles VII*, ed. V. de Viriville, in *Bibliothèque elzévirienne*, I (Paris, 1858).

Corseto, Antonio. *De potestate regia, Tractatus Illustrium Iurisconsultorum*, XVI, 130–45.

Cusa (or Cues) Nicholas Khryppfs de. *De concordantia catholica*, ed. G. Kallen (Hamburg, 1959–65).

Epistola ad Rodericum (sc. Arevalo), Opera (Basle, 1565), 825–9.

Escobar, Andreas. *Gubernaculum conciliorum*, H. v. d. Hardt, *Magnum Oecumenicum Constantiense Concilium*, VI (Leipzig, 1700), 139–333.

Gerson, J. *Opera*, ed. L. Dupin, 5 vols (Antwerp, 1706).

Hooker, Richard. *Of the laws of ecclesiastical polity* (London, 1958).

Locke, John. *Two treatises of government*, ed. P. Laslett (Cambridge, 1960).

Monstrelet, D'Enguerran de. *La Chronique*, ed. L. Douët-D'Arcq, V, *Société l'Histoire de la France*, CVIII (Paris, 1861).

Monte, Piero da. *Monarchia, sive De primatu papae et maiestate imperatoris, Tractatus Illustrium Iurisconsultorum*, XIII, part 1 (Venice, 1584), 144–53.

    ed. J. Haller, *Piero da Monte, ein Gelehrter und päpstlicher Beamter des 15. Jahrhunderts. Seine Briefsammlung. Bibliothek der deutschen Institut in Rom*, XIX (Rome, 1941).

Mornay, P. de. *Vindiciae contra tyrannos* (London, 1689).

Panormitanus (or Tudeschis), Nicholas de. *Commentarium in primum-quintum Decretalium librum*, 7 vols (Venice, 1571). Also as *Super primo-quinto Decretalium*, 4 vols (Lyons, 1534). Unless otherwise stated, the ed. of Venice, 1571 is used; the Lyons, 1534 ed. is used only for passages omitted from the former.

Consilia, tractatus, quaestiones et practica (Venice, 1571).

Piccolomini, Aeneas Sylvius (Pius II). *De gestis Concilii Basiliensis commentariorum libri II*, ed. and trans. D. Hay and W. Smith, Oxford Medieval Texts (Oxford, 1967). Written *c.* 1440, when he supported Basle and the conciliar position.

De rebus Basileae gestis stante vel dissoluto concilio, ed. C. Fea, in *Pius II...a calumniis vindicatus* (Rome, 1823), 31–115. Written *c.* 1450, when he supported the papal position.

Pentalogus de rebus ecclesiae et imperii, ed. B. Pez in *Thesaurus anecdotorum novissimus*, IV, part 3 (Augustae Vindelicorum, 1723), 639–744.

Historia rerum Friderici III, ed. A. Kollar in *Analecta monumentalia omnis aevi Vindobonensia*, II, 1–475.

    ed. R. Wolkan, *Der Briefwechsel des Eneas Silvius Piccolomini*, part 1, I–II, in *Fontes rerum Austriacarum*, LXI–LXII (Wien, 1909).

Poggio, Bracciolini. *De potestate papae et concilii liber* (Rome, 1510–20).

Prior of Dijon (anon.). ed. G. Kallen, *Sitzungsberichte der Heidelberger Akademie des Wissenschaften phil-hist. Klasse*, 1935–6, no. 3: *Cusanus-Texte II, Traktate*, 92–103.

Rickel, Denis. *De auctoritate summi pontificis et generalis concilii, Opera Omnia*, XXXVI (Tornaci, 1908), pp. 525–674.

Roselli, Antonio de. *Monarchia*, ed. M. Goldast in *Monarchia*, I (Hanover, 1612), 252–556.

Rousseau, J. J. *Contrat social*, ed. C. Vaughan in *The political writings of J. J. Rousseau*, 2 vols (Oxford, 1962).

Segovia, Joannes de. *Amplificatio disputationis*, in *id. Historia gestorum generalis synodi Basiliensis*, XVII, 25–60; ed. C. Stehlin in *MCG*, III, 695–941.

174

Bibliography

Turrecremata (or Torquemada), Joannes de. *Summa de ecclesia* (Venice, 1561).
Commentarium super toto Decreto (Venice, 1578).
Oratio synodalis de primatu, ed. E. Candal (Rome, 1954).

Collections

Baronius, C., O. Raynaldus and A. Theiner. (edd.) *Annales ecclesiastici*, XXVIII–XXIX (Barri-Ducis, 1874–6).

Boulay, C. Égasse du. *Historia Universitatis Parisiensis*, V (Paris, 1670).

Braun, P. *Notitia historico-litteraria de codicibus manuscriptis in bibliotheca monasterii ad SS. Udalricum et Afram Augustam extantibus*, VI (*Augustae Vindelicorum*, 1796).

Bullarium Romanum magnum, I (Luxemburg, 1727).

Bullarium Romanum Taurinense, V (Augustae Taurinensis, 1870).

Chmel, J. (ed.). *Regesta chronologico-diplomatica Friderici III* (Wien, 1859).

Codex Diplomaticus Universitatis Cracoviensis, Part 2 (Cracow, 1873).

Conciliorum oecumenicorum decreta, ed. Centro di documentazione, Bologna, 2nd ed. (Basle–Freiburg–Rome, 1962).

Concilium Florentinum, documenta et scriptores, ed. Pontifical institute of oriental studies. I. *Epistolae pontificiae*, ed. G. Hofmann, parts 1–3 (Rome, 1940–6). VI. Andreas de Santacroce, *Acta Latina Concilii Florentini*, ed. G. Hofmann (Rome, 1955).

Dupuy, P. (ed.). *Preuves des libertez de l'église Gallicane*, in *Libertez de l'église Gallicane*, ed. P. Pithou, II (Paris, 1639).

Freiburg, A. (ed.). *Corpus iuris canonici*, 2 vols (Leipzig, 1879–81).

Gallagher, J. (ed.). *The documents of Vatican II* (London–Dublin, 1962).

Haller, J. and others (edd.). *Concilium Basiliense, Studien und Quellen zur Geschichte des Conzils von Basel*, 8 vols (Basle, 1896–1936).

Hansen, J. (ed.). *Publicationen aus den königlichen preussischen Staatsarchiven*, XXXIV (Leipzig, 1888).

Koller, H. (ed.). *Das Reichsregister König Albrechts* II (Vienna, 1955).

Mansi, J. D. (ed.). *Sacrorum Conciliorum nova et amplissima collectio*, XXIX–XXXIA (Venice, 1788–98); XXXIB–XXXII (Paris–Leipzig, 1901); Suppl., IV–V (Lucca, 1750–1).

Martène, E. and Durand, U. (edd.). *Thesaurus novus anecdotorum*, I (Paris, 1717). *Veterum scriptorum amplissima collectio*, VIII (Paris, 1723).

Mercati, A. (ed.). *Raccolta dei Concordati*, I (Vatican City, 1954).

Monumenta medii aevi res gestas Polonias illustrantia, II (Cracow, 1876), XII (Cracow, 1891), XIV (Cracow, 1894).

Ordonnances des rois de la IIIe race, XIII (Paris, 1782).

Palacky, F. and others (edd.). *Monumenta Conciliorum generalium seculi decimi quinti, Concilium Basiliense, scriptorum*, 4 vols (Vienna–Basle, 1857–1935).

Pez, B. *Thesaurus anecdotorum novissimus*, 6 vols (Augustae Vindelicorum, 1721–9).

Rogadeo, E. *Diplomatico Aragonese, Re Alfonso V* (1435–58), *Codice diplomatico barese*, XI (Bari, 1931).

Rymer, T. (ed.). *Foedera, conventiones, literae*, X–XI (London, 1710).

Theiner, A. (ed.). *Codex diplomaticus dominii temporalis sanctae sedis*, III (Rome, 1862). *Vetera monumenta Hibernorum et Scotorum historiam illustrantia* (Rome, 1864). *Vetera monumenta historica Hungariam sacram illustrantia*, II (Rome, 1860). *Vetera monumenta Poloniae et Lithuaniae historiam illustrantia*, II (Rome, 1861). *Vetera monumenta Slavorum Meridionalium historiam illustrantia*, I (Rome, 1863).

Bibliography

Weigel, H. and others (edd.). *Deutsche Reichtagsakten*, XIV–XVII (Stuttgart–Göttingen, 1935–63).

Würdtwein, S. (ed.). *Subsidia diplomatica*, VII (Heidelberg, 1776).

SECONDARY WORKS

Allen, J. *History of political thought in the sixteenth century* (London, 1960).

Andreas, W. *Deutschland vor der Reformation; eine Zeitenwende* (Stuttgart, 1932).

Bachmann, A. *Die deutsche Könige und die kürfurstliche Neutralität, Archiv für oesterreichische Geschichte*, LXXV (Vienna, 1889,) 1–236.

Baron, H. *The crisis of the early Italian Renaissance*, 2 vols (Princeton, 1955).

Barraclough, G. *Origins of modern Germany* (Oxford, 1947).

Bäumer, R. 'Eugen IV und der Plan eines "Dritten Konzils" zur Beilegung des Basler Schismas', in *Reformata Reformanda, Festschrift für H. Jedin*, ed. E. Iserloh, and K. Repgen (Münster, 1965), 87 ff.

Beer, R. *Urkundliche Beiträge zu Johannes de Segovia's Geschichte des Basler Conzils* (Vienna, 1897).

Bertrams, W. *Der neuzeitliche Staatsgedanke und die Konkordate des ausgehenden Mittelalters, Analecta Gregoriana*, XXX, Series facultatis iuris canonici, B. II (Rome, 1950).

Binder, K. *Wesen und Eigenschaften der Kirche bei Kardinal J. de Torquemada, O.P.* (Innsbruck, 1955).

Bloch, M. *Les Rois Thaumaturges. Étude sur le caractère surnaturel attribué à la puissance royale particulièrement en France et en Angleterre* (Strasbourg, 1924).

Brunner, O. 'Vom Gottesgnadentum zum monarchischen Prinzip', in *Vorträge und Forschungen*, ed. T. Mayer, III (Lindau–Konstanz, 1956), 279–305.

Buisson, L. *Potestas und Caritas; die päpstliche Gewalt im Spätmittelalter, Forschungen zur kirchlichen Rechtsgeschichte und zum Kirchenrecht*, II (Cologne–Graz, 1958).

Burckhardt, J. *The civilization of the Renaissance in Italy*, trans. S. Middlemore (London, 1955).

Burns, J. *Scottish churchmen and the Council of Basle* (Glasgow, 1962).

Cam, H. and others. 'Recent work and present views on the origins and development of representative assemblies', *Relazioni del X Congresso internaz. di Scienze storiche*, I (Florence, 1955), 3–101.

Cambridge Medieval History, VIII: *The close of the Middle Ages*, edd. C. Previté-Orton and Z. N. Brooke (Cambridge, 1936).

Canedo, L. G. 'Juan de Carvajal y el cisma de Basilea', in *Archivo Ibero-americano*, I (1941), 29 ff., 209 ff., 369 ff.

Carsten, F. L. *Princes and parliaments in Germany from the fifteenth to the eighteenth centuries* (Oxford, 1959).

Cecconi, E. *Studi storici sul Concilio di Firenze* (Florence, 1869).

Chrimes, S. *English constitutional ideas in the fifteenth century* (Cambridge, 1936).

Church, W. *Constitutional theory in sixteenth century France; a study in the evolution of ideas, Harvard historical Studies*, XLVII (Cambridge, Mass., 1941).

Cognasso, F. *Amedeo VIII, 1385–1451*, 2 vols, *Coll. storica sabauda* (Torino, 1930).

Cohn, N. *The pursuit of the millennium* (London, 1957).

Coville, A. 'Pierre de Versailles (1380?–1446)', in *Bibliothèque de l'école des Chartes*, XCIII (1932), 208–66.

Bibliography

De Vooght, P. 'Le Conciliarisme à Constance et à Basle' in *Le Concile et les Conciles* (Paris, 1960), 143–80.

Dempf, A. *Sacrum imperium* (repr. Munich, 1962).

Döllinger, J. J. von. *Beiträge zur politischen, kirchlichen und Cultur–Geschichte der sechs letzten Jahrhunderte*, II (Regensburg, 1863).

Eckermann, K. *Studien zur Geschichte des monarchischen Gedankens im 15. Jahrhundert., Abhandlungen zur mittleren und neueren Geschichte*, LXXIII (Berlin, 1933).

Fabricius, J. *Bibliotheca Latina medii aevi*, 6 vols (Florence, 1858–9).

Fichtenau, H. *Arenga: Spätantike und Mittelalter im Spiegel von Urkundenformeln, Mitteilungen des Instituts für oesterreichische Geschichtsforschung*, Suppl. vol. XVIII (Graz–Cologne, 1957).

Figgis, J. *Studies in political thought from Gerson to Grotius, 1414–1625* (Cambridge, 1916).
  The divine right of kings, ed. G. R. Elton (New York, 1965).

Fijalek, J. *Mistrz Jakob za Paradyza i Uniwersytet Krakowski u okreie soboru bazylejskiego*, 2 vols (Cracow, 1900).

Fink, K. 'Papsttum und Kirchenreform nach dem grossen Schisma', in *Theol. Quartalschrift*, CXXVI (1946), 110–22.
  'Zur Beurteilung des grossen abendlandischen Schismas', in *Zeitschrift für Kirchengeschichte*, LXXIII (1962), 335–43.

Fliche, A. and V. Martin (edd.). *Histoire de l'église depuis les origines jusqu'à nos jours*, XIV: *L'Église au temps du grand schisme et de la crise conciliaire (1378–1449)*, by E. Delaruelle, E-R. Labande and P. Ourliac, 2 vols (Paris, 1962–4).

Fromherz, U. *Johannes von Segovia als Geschichtsschreiber des Konzils von Basel, Basler Beiträge zum Geschichtswissenschaft*, LXXXI (Basle, 1960).

Gierke, O. von. *Political theories of the Middle Age*, trans. F. Maitland (Cambridge, 1900).
  Natural law and the theory of society, trans. E. Barker (Cambridge, 1958).

Gill, J. *The Council of Florence* (Cambridge, 1959).
  Eugenius IV, Pope of Christian union, The popes through history, I (Westminster, Maryland, 1961).

Gilmore, M. *Argument from Roman law in political thought, 1200–1600* (Cambridge, Mass., 1941).

Gilson, E. *History of Christian philosophy in the Middle Ages* (London, 1955).

Gonzalez, J. *El maestro Juan de Segovia y su biblioteca* (Madrid, 1944).

Grabmann, M. 'Studien über den Einfluss der aristotelischen Philosophie auf die mittelalterlichen Theorien über das Verhältnis von Kirche und Staat', *Sitzungsberichte der Bayerische Akademie der Wissenschaften*, phil.-hist. Klasse, part 2 (Munich, 1934).

Hale, J. and others (edd.). *Europe in the late Middle Ages* (London, 1965).

Hallam, H. *View of the state of Europe in the Middle Ages* (London, 1818).

Hay, D. *The Italian Renaissance in its historical background* (Cambridge, 1961).

Héfèle, C-J. and H. Leclerq. *Histoire des conciles d'après les documents originaux*, VII, part 2 (Paris, 1916).

Hegel, G. *The philosophy of history*, trans. J. Sibree (New York, 1956).
  The philosophy of right, trans. M. Knox (Oxford, 1942).

Heredia, B. de. 'Colleccion de documentos ineditos para illustrar la vida del Card. J. de Turrecremata', in *Archivum fratrum praedicatorum*, VII (1937), 210–45.

Bibliography

Hödl, G. 'Zur Reichspolitik des Basler Konzils. Bischof Johannes Schele von Lübeck (1420–1439)', in *Mitteilungen des Instituts für oesterreichische Geschichtsforschung*, LXXV (1967), 46–65.

Hofmann, G. *Papato, conciliarismo, patriarcato, 1438–9, Miscellanea historica pontificiae*, II, no. 2 (Rome, 1940).

Hove, A. van. *Prolegomena (ad codicem iuris canonici)*, 2nd. ed. (Mechelen–Rome, 1945).

Imbart de la Tour, P. *Les Origines de la réforme*, vols I–II (Paris, 1905–9).

Institut d'histoire de Genève. (ed.) *Les Universités européens du xive au xviie siècles* (Geneva, 1967).

Jacob, E. F. *Essays in the conciliar epoch*, 3rd ed. (Manchester, 1963).

The fifteenth century, Oxford history of England (Oxford, 1961).

Archbishop Henry Chichele (London, 1967).

'The Bohemians at the council of Basel, 1433', in *Prague essays*, ed. R. Seton-Watson (Oxford, 1949), 81–123.

'The conciliar movement in recent study', in *Bulletin of the John Rylands Library*, XLI (1958), 26–53.

'Giuliano Cesarini', in *Bulletin of the John Rylands Library*, LI (1968), 104 ff.

Jaroschka, W. 'Thomas Ebendorfer als Theoretiker des Konziliarismus', in *Mitteilungen des Instituts für oesterreichische Geschichtsforschung*, LXII (1963), 87 ff.

Jedin, H. *A history of the Council of Trent*, trans. E. Graf, I (London, 1957).

'Juan de Torquemada und das Imperium Romanum', in *Archivum fratrum praedicatorum*, XII (1942), 247–78.

Jöcher, C. *Allgemeines Gelehrten-Lexicon*, 4 vols (Leipzig, 1750–1). *Supplement*, ed. J. Adelung, 7 vols (Leipzig, 1784–1897).

Jouvenel, B. de. *Sovereignty* (Cambridge, 1957).

Judd, A. *The life of Thomas Beckynton* (Chichester, 1961).

Kaminsky, H. *A history of the Hussite revolution* (Berkeley, Cal., 1967).

Kantorowicz, E. *The king's two bodies: a study in medieval political theology* (Princeton, 1957).

Kern, F. *Kingship and law in the Middle Ages*, trans. S. Chrimes, *Studies in Medieval History*, IV (Oxford, 1948).

Kisch, G. *Enea Silvio Piccolomini und die Jurisprudenz* (Basle, 1967).

Krchnak, A. *De vita et operibus Ioannis de Ragusio, Lateranum*, n.s., XXVI, 3–4 (Rome, 1960).

Lagarde, G. de. *La Naissance de l'esprit laïque au declin du moyen âge*, V, new ed. (Paris, 1963).

Recherches sur l'esprit politique de la Réforme (Paris, 1926).

'Les Théories représentatives des xive–xve siècles et l'Église', in *Studies Presented to the International Committee for the History of Representative and Parliamentary Institutions*, XVIII (Louvain, 1958), 63–76.

Lazarus, P. *Das Basler Konzil, seine Berufung und Leitung, seine Gliederung und seine Behordenorganisation* (Berlin, 1912).

Leclerq, J. 'L'Idée de royauté du Christ pendant le Grand Schisme et la crise Conciliaire', in *Archives d'Histoire Doctrinale et Litteraire du Moyen Âge*, XXVII (1949), 249–65.

Lecoy de la Marche, A. *Le Roi René* (Paris, 1875).

Léderer, S. *Der spanische Cardinal J. von Torquemada, sein Leben und seine Schriften* (Freiburg-i-Br., 1879).

Bibliography

Lefèbvre, C. 'L'Enseignement de Nicolas de Tudeschis et l'autorité pontificale', in *Ephemerides Iuris Canononici*, XIV (1958), 312–39.

Leff, G. *Heresy in the later Middle Ages: the relation of heterodoxy to dissent, c. 1250–1450*, 2 vols (Manchester, 1967).

Lepszy, K. ed. *Universatis Iagelloniae, 1364–1764 Historia*, I (Cracow, 1964).

Lewis, E. *Medieval political ideas*, 2 vols (London, 1954).

Lewis, P. S. 'The failure of the French medieval estates', in *Past and Present*, XXIII (1962), 3–24.

Lhotsky, A. *Thomas Ebendorfer, ein oesterreichischer Geschichtsschreiber, Theologe und Diplomat des 15. Jahrhunderts, Deutsches Institut für Erforschung des Mittelalters, Schriften der Monumenta Germaniae Historica*, XV (Stuttgart, 1957).

Lovejoy, A. *The great chain of being; a study of the history of an idea* (Cambridge, Mass., repr. 1961).

Major, J. R. *Representative institutions in renaissance France, Studies Presented to the International Committee for the History of Representative and Parliamentary Institutions*, XXII (Madison, 1960).

Martin, V. *Les Origines du Gallicanisme*, II (Paris, 1939).

Massi, G. *Magistero infallibile del papa nella teologia di G. da Torquemada, Scrinium theologiae*, VIII (Turin, 1957).

Maton, F. *La Souveraineté dans Jean Juvenel des Ursins* (Paris, 1917).

Mattingley, G. *Renaissance diplomacy* (London, 1955).

McIlwain, C. *The growth of political thought in the West* (London, 1932). *Constitutionalism: ancient and modern*, rev. ed. (Ithaca, 1947).

Morawski, K. *Histoire de l'Université de Cracovie*, trans. P. Rongier, II (Paris–Cracow, 1903).

New Cambridge Modern History, I, ed. G. Potter (Cambridge, 1957).

Nörr, K. *Kirche und Konzil bei Nicolaus de Tudeschis (Panormitanus), Forschungen zur kirchlichen Rechtsgeschichte und zum Kirchenrecht*, IV (Cologne–Graz, 1964).

Oakley, F. *The political thought of Pierre D'Ailly; the voluntarist tradition* (Yale, 1964). 'On the road from Constance to 1688', in *Journal of British Studies*, I (1962), 1–32.

Ourliac, P. 'La sociologie du Concile de Bâle', in *Revue d'Histoire ecclésiastique*, LVI (1961), 2–32. 'La Pragmatique Sanction et la légation en France du cardinal d'Estouteville', in *Mélanges d'Archéologie et d'Histoire*, LIV (1938), 403–32.

Pastor, L. *History of the popes*, ed. F. Antrobus, I–II (London, 1891).

Pérouse, G. *Le Cardinal Aleman, Président du Concile de Bâle, et la fin du Grand Schisme* (Paris, 1905).

Pirenne, H. *Histoire économique et sociale du moyen âge*, rev. ed. (Paris, 1963).

Pleyer, K. *Die Politik Nikolaus V* (Stuttgart, 1927).

Plöchl. W. *Geschichte des Kirchenrechts*, I–II (Munich–Vienna, 1953–5).

Pocqet du Haut-Jusset, B. *Les Papes et les ducs de Bretagne; essai sur les rapports du saint siège avec un état, Bibliothèque des écoles françaises d'Athènes et de Rome*, CXXXIII, 2 vols (Paris, 1928).

Post, G. *Studies in medieval legal thought: public law and the state, 1100–1322* (Princeton, 1964).

Preiswerk, E. *Der Einfluss Aragons auf dem Prozess des Basler Konzils gegen Papst Eugen IV* (Basel, 1902).

Rashdall, H. *The universities of Europe in the Middle Ages*, eds F. Powicke and A. Emden, 3 vols (Oxford, 1936).

Bibliography

Robertson, W. *A history of the reign of the Emperor Charles V*, I (London, 1818).

Ryder, A. 'The evolution of imperial government under Alfonso V of Aragon', in *Europe in the late Middle Ages*, ed. J. Hale and others, 332 ff.

Sägmuller, J-B. 'Der Verfasser der Traktates De modis uniendi ac reformandi Ecclesiam in Concilio universali vom J. 1410', in *Historisches Jahrbuch*, XIV (1893), 562–82.

Savigny, F. *Geschichte des römischen Rechts im Mittelalter*, 7 vols (Heidelberg, 1834–51).

Savio, C. *Il cardinale d'Arles, beato Lud. Alemandi (1382–1450)* (Alba, 1935).

Schmitz-Kallenberg, L. 'Die Lehre von den Papsturkunden' in A. Meister's *Grundriss der Geschichtswissenschaften*, I, part I (Leipzig, 1906), 172–230; and *ibid.* part 2 (Leipzig, 1913), 56–116.

Schofield, A. 'The first English delegation to the Council of Basel', in *Journal of Ecclesiastical History*, XII (1961), 167–96.

'The second English delegation to the Council of Basel', in *Journal of Ecclesiastical History*, XVII (1966), 29 ff.

'England, the Pope and the Council of Basel, 1435–1449', in *Church History*, XXXIII (1964), 248 ff.

Schramm, P. *Der König von Frankreich; das Wesen der Monarchie von 9. zum 16. Jahrhundert. Ein Kapitel aus der Geschichte des abendländischen Staates*, 2 vols (Weimar, 1960).

Schulte, J. *Die Geschichte der Quellen und Literatur des canonischen Rechts von Gratian bis auf die Gegenwart*, II (Stuttgart, 1877).

Schweizer, J. *Nicolaus de Tudeschi, seine Tätigkeit am Basler Konzil* (Strasbourg, 1924).

Sigmund, P. *Nicholas of Cusa and medieval political thought* (Harvard, 1963).

'Cusanus' Concordantia, a re-interpretation', in *Political Studies*, X (1962), 180–97.

'The influence of Marsilius on fifteenth-century conciliarism', in *Journal of the History of Ideas*, XXIII (1962), 392–402.

Stadelmann, R. *Vom Geist des ausgehenden Mittelalters. Studien zur Geschichte der Weltanschauung von Nicolaus Cusanus bis Sebastian Franck* (Halle–Saale, 1917).

Stockmann, J. *Joannis de Turrecremata, O.P., Vita eiusque doctrina de corpore Christi mystico* (Bologna, 1951).

Theeuws, P. *Jean de Turrecremata. Les relations entre l'Église et le pouvoir civil d'après un théologien du XVe siècle, Université de Louvain, Receuil de travaux d'histoire et de philologie*, 3, XVIII (Louvain, 1943), 138–78.

Thommen, R. 'Die Lehre von den Königs- und Kaiserurkunden', in A. Meister's *Grundriss der Geschichtswissenschaften*, I, part I (Leipzig, 1906), 131–71; and *ibid.* part 2 (Leipzig, 1913), 21–55.

Tierney, B. *Foundations of Conciliar theory: the contribution of the medieval canonists from Gratian to the Great Schism, Cambridge studies in medieval life and thought*, n.s., IV (Cambridge, 1955).

'Hermeneutics and history: the problem of *Haec sancta*', in *Essays in honor of Bertie Wilkinson* (Toronto, 1969), 354–70.

Toews, J. 'Pope Eugenius IV and the Concordat of Vienna (1448), an interpretation', in *Church History*, XXXIV (1965), 178 ff.

Toni, T. *Don Rodrigo Sanchez de Arevalo* (Madrid, 1935).

Toussaint, J. *Les Relations diplomatiques de Philippe le Bon avec le Concile de Bâle, 1431–1449, Université de Louvain, Receuil de travaux d'histoire et de philologie*, 3, IX (Louvain, 1942).

Bibliography

Trame, R. *Rodrigo Sanchez de Arevalo (1404–1470)*, *Spanish diplomat and champion of the papacy* (Washington, 1958).

Ullmann, W. *Origins of the Great Schism: a study in fourteenth-century ecclesiastical history* (London, repr. 1967).

Medieval Papalism: the political theories of the medieval canonists (London, 1949).

The growth of papal government in the Middle Ages: a study in the ideological relation of clerical to lay power, 3rd ed. (London, 1965).

Principles of government and politics in the Middle Ages, 2nd ed. (London, 1966).

'De Bartoli sententia: concilium representat mentem populi', in *Bartolus de Sassoferrato, studi et documenta*, II (Perugia, 1961), 703–33.

'The legal validity of the papal electoral pacts', in *Ephemerides iuris canonici*, XII (1956), 246–78.

'Eugenius IV, Cardinal Kemp and Archbishop Chichele', in *Medieval studies presented to A. Gwynn*, edd. J. Watt and others (Dublin, 1961), 359 ff.

Vacant, A. and others (edd.). *Dictionnaire de théologie catholique*, 15 vols (Paris, 1915–50).

Valois, N. *Le Pape et le Concile (1480–1450). La crise religieuse du XVe siècle*, 2 vols (Paris, 1909).

Histoire de la Pragmatique Sanction de Bourges sous Charles VII, Archives de l'histoire religieuse de France (Paris, 1906).

Vansteenberghe, E. *Le Cardinal Nicolas de Cues (1401–1464)* (Lille, 1920).

Villien, A. and others (edd.). *Dictionnaire de droit canonique* (Paris, 1924–).

Vinogradoff, P. *Roman law in medieval Europe* (Oxford, 1929).

Voigt, G. *Enea Silvio Piccolomini als Papst Pius der Zweite und sein Zeitalter*, 3 vols (Berlin, 1856–63).

Walters, L. *Andreas von Escobar, ein Vertreter der konziliaren Theorie am Anfange des 15. Jahrhunderts*. Inaugural dissertation (Munster, 1901).

Weber, M. *The City*, trans. D. Martindale and G. Neuwirth (New York, 1958).

The theory of social and economic organization, trans. T. Parsons (New York, 1947).

Werminghoff, A. *Nationalkirchliche Bestrebungen im deutschen Mittelalter, Kirchenrechtliche Abhandlungen*, LXI (Stuttgart, 1910).

Widmer, B. *Enea Silvio Piccolomini in der sittlichen und politischen Entscheidung, Basler Beiträge zur Geschichtswissenschaft*, LXXXVIII (Basle, 1963).

Wilks, M. *The problem of sovereignty in the later Middle Ages: the papal monarchy with Augustinus Triumphus and the publicists, Cambridge studies in medieval life and thought*, n.s., IX (Cambridge, 1963).

Woolf, C. *Bartolus of Sassoferrato* (Cambridge, 1913).

ADDENDUM TO BIBLIOGRAPHY

ORIGINAL SOURCES

PRINTED WORKS

Authors

Aquinas, Thomas (St.) *Commentary on the Ethics of Aristotle*, trans. C. Litzinger in *Medieval political philosophy*, ed. R. Lerner end M. Mahdi (Toronto, 1963).
Commentary on the Politics of Aristotle, trans. E. Fortin and P. O'Neill, in *Medieval political philosophy*, ed. Lerner and Mahdi.
Summa Theologiae, 1^a2^{ae}, q. 90–7, ed. T. Gilby in *St Thomas Aquinas, Summa theologiae*, vol. XXVIII, *Law and political theory* (London, 1966).
Summa contra gentiles (Turin–Rome, 1934).
Aristotle, *Metaphysics*, ed. and trans. H. Tredennick, Loeb edition (London, 1962).
Nicomachaean Ethics, ed. and trans. H. Rackham, Loed edition (London, 1962).
Augustine (St) *De vera religione*, in Corpus Christianorum series latina (Turnholt, 1962).
Epistola ad Dioscorum, in *Opera omnia*, II, part 1, ed Monachi ordinis sancti Benedicti (Paris, 1836).
Cicero, *De officiis*, ed. and trans. W. Miller, Loeb edition (London, 1913).
Macchiavelli, N. *The Prince*, trans. G. Bull (London, 1961).
Paris, J. of *On kingly and papal power*, trans. E. Fortin, in *Medieval political philosophy*, ed. Lerner and Mahdi.
Pseudo-Denis. *De ecclesiastica hierarchia*, in J-P Migne, *Patrologia Graeca* (Paris, 1857–66), III.
De divinis nominibus, in J-P. Migne, *op. cit.*, III.

SECONDARY WORKS

Rodriguez, C. *Juan de Segovia y el problema islamico* (Madrid, 1944).
Ullmann, W. *The Carolingian renaissance and the idea of kingship* (London, 1969).

INDEX

(Appendices and quotation are refered to in italic)

Index

Cardinals, status of, 40, 50, 136 f, *146*, *161*

Carvajal, 58, 88, 119

Casimir, King of Poland, 126, 128

Castile, 53, 92 f, 103 f, 118

Centralization, 1 f, 73, 80, 131 f

Cesarini, J., 85, 89, 102 n, 103, 123 n

Charles VII, King of France, 90, 93 ff, 96 f, 105 ff, 113, 115, 118, 123 f

Chichele, Archbishop of Canterbury, 101

Christ: as source of power, 8, *17*, 21, 65, *83*, 136 f, *144*, *165*, *168*; presence of, 22, 34 n, 38, *144*; teaching of, 38, 90, 109, *156* f

Church: as sovereign, 8 ff, 14, 21 f, 138, *150* ff; as collective whole, 17 f, 54 ff, 138; assembled as council, 16 ff; as *universitas*, 9 ff, 15 ff, 35, 39 ff; compared to secular state, 1, 55, 58, 60. *See also* Body, City-state, Corporation, Kingdom, Person

Church, W., 84 n

Cicero, 41

City-state: church compared to, 8 ff, 10 ff, 16, 22 ff, 34 ff, 39, 49 ff, 114, *150* ff; church compared to assembly of, 17, 20, 34 ff; contemporary examples of, 9, 23, 32 n, 36, 41, 46 n

Civil lawyers, influence of, 10, 54, 58, *169*

Collective–dispersive distinction, 12 ff, 17, 21 ff, 27, 37, 43, 50 f, 54, 81 f, 95 f, 110, 120, 125, 137, *142* ff, *148* ff, *165*

College, 13, 16, 95, 137 f, *169*, *172*. *See also* Corporation, *Universitas*

Cologne: Archbishop of, 124; University of, 129

Commerce, 26, 69, 134

Common good: ruler as servant of, 25 ff, 33, 38, 45, *143*, *148* f, *156*, *160*; in monarchical doctrine, 75 ff, 81, 133

Common Life, Brethren of, 23

Commune, idea of, 22 f, 36 f, 47, 51 f, 135, *150* ff

Community: as collective whole, 9 ff, 15, 54 f; as sovereign over ruler, 9 ff, 15 ff, 39, 25 ff, *142* ff, *148* ff, *169*; assembly of, 16 ff, 27, 37, *143*, *148* f; will of, 25 ff, 29, *144*, *148* f. *See also*

Person, Representation, Responsibility, *Universitas*

Concession theory, 63

Conciliarism, 1 ff, 6, 129; doctrine of, Part I *passim*, 60, 94, 108 ff, 138; seen as threat, 87 f, 96, 110 f; and parliamentary theory, 8, 12 f, 15, 20, 28, 35, 44, 47, 49 f, *51*, 98, 107 f, 115; Baslean c., doctrine of, ix, Part I *passim*, 91 f; arguments against Baslean c., 55 f, 65; Baslean c. compared with that of Constance, 13, 16, 21, 39

Concordats, 2, 125 ff

Consent, notion of, 34, 37, 64, 66, 97 n, 103, 115, 120, 125, *147*, *161*

Conspiracy, notion of, 90, 100 f, 128

Constance, Council of, 2 f, 7, 13, 21, 39, 96, 107. *See also* Conciliarism

Constitutional monarchy, 44 ff, 50; Constitutional rules, 35 ff, 42 f; Constitutional sanctions 34, 47 f, 49 f, 111

Constitutionalism, 1 f, 8, 32 ff, 39, 41 ff, 47, 107, 134

Consultation, 33, 43, 45 ff, 110 f, *146*, *157* ff

Corporation: ecclesiastical, church compared to, 9 f, 20, 25 n, 42, 50, 55 f, *169*, *172*; council as a c. 35 ff, 39; c. theory, 9 ff, 28, 50, 55, 89, 109. *See also Universitas*

Corseto, A., 82

Council: as *universitas*, 35 f, 39 ff; as assembled church, 15 ff; autonomons, 34, 91; self-assembly of, 35 f; self-dissolution of, 35 f; regular assembly of, 42 f, 47, 49; deputation-system in, 16, 35 f, 91; legislative power of, 40, 42; sovereign over pope, 11, 22, 39 ff; power direct from Christ, 7 f, 21, *144*; 'new third', 5, 94, 97, 112 f, 117. *See also* Basle, Church, City-state, Constance, Corporation, Florence, Parliaments, Pisa, Siena

Courcelles, Thomas, 94 f, 107

Cracow University, 24, 128 f; *memorandum* (1442), 14, 20 n, 29 n, 38 n, 78, 79 n, 110, 119

Credibility, 30, 32

Credit, 32, 46, *153*, *150* f

Index

Index

Universitas: concept of, 9 ff, 15 ff, 24, 29, 34 ff, 44, 50 ff, 54 f, 62, 102, 120; as sovereign, 9 ff, 34 ff, 39 ff; *u.-rector* model, 9, 25 ff, 39 ff, 44, 114, 120. *See also* Church, College, Community, Corporation, Person

Universities: role of, 23 f, 128 f; analogy with, 23 f

Vatican Council, Second, 137 f

Venice, 100, 114; constitution of, as cited, 11, 41

Versailles, Pierre de; as thinker, 48, 59 n, 60 n, 61 n, 63 n, 66, 67 n, 68 n, 70, 72 n, 77 n, 81 n, 103 f; diplomatic presentation of ideas by, 94, 105 ff, 113, 129

Vienna: City of, 116; University of, 120, 129

Vindiciae contra tyrannos, 50

Virtue (*virtus*) and governmental power, 20 f, 37 f, 44, 59, 62 f, 65, 71, 78 f, 117, 152, 158. *See also* Legal and moral power, Representation, virtual

Weber, Max, 36 n, 132 n

Whole, concept of community as. *See* Body, Church, *Collective–dispersive* distinction, Community

Wilks, M., 53 n

Wladislas III, King of Poland, 86, 126

Zabarella, Cardinal F. de, influence of, 9 f, 13, 22 n, 33, 35, 39, 50, 64 n, 114

Zwingli, 127

189

in the middle of a class period. What is the teacher to do but believe a child, even one she cannot trust as far as she can toss him, who looks terribly pained of bladder? To Spud's great fortune, he entered the boys' room at the precise time the kindergartners were taking their bathroom break. Four little boys were lined up at the urinals when Spud was inspired to turn the light off, leaving the room pitch-black, causing them to lose concentration and panic, thereby hosing one another down.

I listened and nodded. It was a terrible thing he'd done. The boys didn't have a change of clothes. Some of them cried. Spud and I walked straight to the car without exchanging a single word. And this once—just this once—I set my head down on the steering wheel and burst out laughing. The two of us laughed until our sides screamed. I knew then that boy was bright. I'd not know what to do with him. I wouldn't be a great success with him. I wouldn't be able to love him to wholeness. But I knew he was bright. And, my, that boy was beautiful.

CHAPTER FIFTEEN

WITH SPUD IN SCHOOL, my study life ramped up. I could study from school bell to school bell if I wanted, and much of the time, I wanted. The more I studied, the more I wanted to teach what I learned. I'd added on a Thursday morning class at a Baptist church closer to my home in hopes of taking a group deeper in the Scriptures than Sunday school accommodated. Bible Study Fellowship and Kay Arthur's Precept Upon Precept Bible studies were stirring up ravenous appetites in Christian women for homework in addition to weekly Bible study lectures. My class began harassing me—in the holiest way—to write segments of homework for them to complete between Thursdays. I taught a series on a collection of Psalms the next semester and threw together some very basic assignments. They weren't great, but they invited the women into the experience as full participants rather than passive recipients. The difference would prove life changing for all of us.

Shortly before the next semester, I stumbled onto something in a daily Bible reading plan that, seemed to me, appeared on the pages out of nowhere. After the Lord rescued his people from their slavery in Egypt, he led them into the wilderness—that much I knew—and told them through his servant Moses to build a mobile structure for him according to his exact instructions, and there he would meet with them. The detail alone was astounding. Chapter after chapter followed, documenting precise measurements, colors, textures, furnishings, embroidery, and lighting. Who knew God had such a flair for architecture and interior design? One golden calf, two broken tablets, a plague, a cleft of the rock, and two new tablets later, the people of God followed the pattern of God. And sure enough, when the structure was accomplished to the minutest detail, God kept his promise. A cloud settled over the Tabernacle, and his glory filled the house. As long as the cloud was directly over it, the Israelites knew to stay put. When the cloud lifted, they knew to pick up and move with it. I'd never seen anything more fascinating.

With the kind of naiveté only a first-timer could possess, I got a bright idea. *My class wants homework. I'll do a series and write them homework on this!* Mind you, I had exactly zero training in writing curriculum. My attempt was to take them on the same journey in Exodus—*turn here, now turn to the book of Hebrews and watch this come together*—that had, at times, moved me facedown to the floor. I got in so far over my head, I was buried alive. I wrote a ten-week Bible study in real time for several hundred women *as we went.* Through most of the course, the class was only one week behind me. I finished it not because I ever figured out what I was doing, but because I'd made a commitment to my class members.

While the clock counted down every second of my children's school hours, I studied and wrote maniacally. Every Tuesday afternoon, I turned in five new days of extensive homework to my dear friend Johnnie, who oversaw women's ministry at the church where we met. All day each Wednesday, she ran off copies by hand on an old-school mimeograph machine for our class members. On Wednesday nights, she collated and three-hole-punched them, and on Thursdays at the beginning of each class, she handed them out. Johnnie and I kept up this pace for two and a half months, fifty days of homework in all, a minimum of four pages for each day. She could have strangled me. I could have strangled myself.

Except for one thing.

Jesus met me there in the small dining room of our home where I'd set up my first word processor. I'd either bought, borrowed, or checked out so many books and commentaries from the First Baptist Church library that my rectangular table looked like a model of a city skyline. Papers were everywhere in the form of stapled articles, rough drafts, or wads of lessons I'd printed out, proofread, and trashed. It was a mash-up. A disaster area. But it was the most intense time I'd ever spent with God.

I moved into that Tabernacle in the wilderness for weeks on end and fed on the Bread of the Presence. I bathed in the bronze basin. I was as high as a kite from sniffing incense from the altar in the Holy Place. I'd awakened to a startling awareness that Jesus was more real, more vivid and alive, more utterly conscious, engaged, and energized right here among mortals in the briars and thorns than anyone we could see.

I worked so hard during those months of research and writing, I didn't know what to do with myself when the course was over. The crash was violent. Breakers of fear began to hit me at the first stoplight on my way home that final Thursday. I drove headlong into an emptiness, a void, that was instantaneous and unexpected, entering me whole and hollowing me out. I still find the haste with which it hit me to be curious. I was no weakling. I was a survivor. Headstrong, self-disciplined. I'd learned to run my race of faith weighted down and against heavy winds. But I'd never run into this wall of nothingness, and now I'd run into it going ninety-nine miles per hour.

Writing a second study of equal volume hadn't seriously occurred to me and, had it, I would have known instinctively the first experience couldn't be replicated. Some things can't be mimeographed. Five years earlier in my Bible doctrine class, I'd shaken awake to a world of study I knew I never wanted to leave. I'd been climbing that mountain ever since, and the last several months, I'd made it to the top, to the tip of my mortal experience with the divine. I'd get to stick a flag in the treeless, sun-scorched ground, but I would not get to stay.

● ● ●

Thirty years have blown off the calendar since that season of my life, and while I've climbed many a mountain and beheld vistas that took my breath away, that was my Everest. My thin air, my once-in-a-lifetime climb. I would not hike back down to sea level. I'd jump from the cliff.

I received a phone call from my beloved pastor within twenty-four hours. "Beth, I need you to do me a favor."

"Of course! What is it?"

"A missionary couple we love very much are back in the States staying at our house for a couple of days and in need of some help and healing. The wife is struggling with abuse in her childhood, and I'd like for you to spend some time with her."

I was taken aback. I'd only recently referenced my own background of abuse and done so in very general terms. I'd made no big boasts of healing, nor had I received a moment's counseling. Quite appropriately, my pastor wanted to make sure she was in the safe company of a woman and one who understood and could empathize and encourage, but I wasn't sure I was the one. I was young. Ill-equipped and early-in.

"I just don't know, Pastor. I just—"

"Would you pray about it and let me know tomorrow? They are only in Houston for a few days. I told her I was almost sure you'd be willing to minister to her."

"Oh, I'm so willing to minister to her, but I just . . . well, yes, I will pray about it."

And I did. And the next day I told him I didn't have peace about it.

My pastor was a very persuasive man, but by no stretch of the imagination was he forcefully authoritarian. For him to come across as a bully would be a severe misrepresentation. The fact was, he believed in me and believed with all his heart I could help her. These were days when women rarely came forward to say they'd been abused. He knew I wasn't a counselor. He just wanted me to hear this woman out, and he assumed the only thing holding me back was a lack of confidence in myself.

Driving to his house, I knew I was making a mistake. A terrible foreboding flipped my stomach. As promised, they left the two of us alone. We sat at a table and she, a woman beautiful and incalculably dear to God and worthy to be heard, began to tell me her story. Best I can recollect, she'd talked about fifteen minutes when I could see her lips moving but no longer make out what she was saying. My ears started ringing. Perspiration beaded on my upper lip and the blood seemed to rush to my head as if I were swinging upside down again from the monkey bars on the school ground across from my childhood home.

I tried to shake out of it. *Listen to her. This is important to her. Pay attention!* I couldn't focus to save my life. I could barely make out the features on her face. I was engulfed in the blurry edges of a dream scene, the table where we were sitting, now some thirty feet long, the two of us on opposite ends. Mouths moving but no sounds. I shivered. *It's too hot in here. No, it's too cold. Pull yourself together. What is wrong with you?*

I can't recall a single word I said to her. I have no idea if I acted as bizarre as I felt. I don't have a notion whether I prayed with her as I normally would pray with any woman in turmoil. I'd give anything if this dear woman had been in better hands than mine that day. Two drowning people cannot save each other. I was too vulnerable, caught in midair, free-falling from a mountaintop into a dark abyss. I don't know if I behaved normally when my pastor and his wife returned or if I muttered unintelligibly. I don't know how I got to the car or drove home.

What I do know is that scenes from my childhood and adolescence began playing in front of me, like on a silver screen, one right after another. I viewed them like a one-person audience. Like an outside party, a voyeur in the back of the theater. The scenes, situations, and players varied. Some were scenes of sins against me. Others, scenes of my own sins. Others, no one's sins but Adam's. Just the scathing, scorching-hot, flailing reality of being alive on this fearsome, fallen soil. I'd known most of those experiences occurred. I hadn't forgotten them. But I'd shut myself off from them.

The Lord alone knows why this missionary's story swung the door so wide open on my youth. She certainly bore no responsibility for my baffling reaction. She was brave, and what she did was good and right and vital. Her story was known and heard and esteemed by heaven. She mattered. Her experiences mattered. God help me, I don't even know what happened to her after that. I've been on the receiving end of innumerable accounts from the mouths of women and girls since then, no few of them graphic, and yet never been triggered to such a degree.

The door that swung wide on my past was bound to open at some point. It was begging to be opened, the knob throbbing. I would not be able to seek any measure of authentic wholeness until everything behind it spilled out into the light.

What happened at the table during the missionary's account kept happening almost every time I shut my eyes for several months. My mind turned into a circus, clever clowns with melting faces playing tricks on me. I couldn't tell reality from fantasy. Worst of all, I couldn't tell what was God and what was the devil.

I did my best to function as normally as possible for my children, but they knew I was out of character. If my instability was as obvious to them as it was to me, I'd say I can't imagine how frightening it must have been. But unfortunately, I can. I knew well what it was like to think your mother is losing her mind. I didn't crawl into bed because, unlike my mother, I was terrified of closing my eyes. I managed to live by rote, doing mechanical things like straightening up the house, cooking supper, checking to see if homework was done, taking them here and there. We went to church throughout. Foolish woman that I was, I kept teaching Sunday school. God knows what I taught. Then night would fall, and I'd whirl into a black hole.

Keith was having problems of his own and had withdrawn into his own world, but not far enough removed to miss my compromised condition. He recounts times he awakened during the night and found me curled up behind a chair, disoriented and talking in half-realities. These days we'd know to go to a hospital. Those days were not these days. *What hospital? And where? And with what money?* The person in the mirror became unrecognizable and loathe-worthy to me. I couldn't trust my judgment or my perceptions. My brain felt like it had jarred loose from the skull, floating now in a laboratory jar. "Dissect this one. She was crazy, you know. Disturbed. This will be interesting."

Three hours of sleep. Get up, Beth. Read your Bible. Pray. Confess your sins. Your awful sins. Get the kids up. Do the things. Iron, iron, iron. Play the music. Don't let them see the wreckage behind your eyes. Don't let them figure it out. Get them off to school. Wash the dishes, Beth. Jesus, Jesus, Jesus, what has become of me? What will become of us? Do you still love me? Do you still love me? Do you still love me?

Tormenting thoughts engulfed me, and guilt for what I interpreted solely as a grotesque and ruinous estate slid me shoulder-deep into the mud of despair. I reached a point where I believed my mind would snap and I'd lose my children.

Don't let go. Don't let go. Whatever you do, don't let go.

I was thirty-four, a mother of three with a fulfilling ministry, getting to do what I loved to do, on the verge of total self-destruction. In my life story, this was my perfect storm. The best I can calculate, this season was the violent collision of three forces, unequal in strength but all stronger than I and each nearly impossible to distinguish from the other. Dividing them was sorting the wind.

One force was my troubled past. I'd kept that broken person crouched down as long as she was willing, and the moment I became too vulnerable to cover for her, she stretched her folded legs and stood to her feet, the size of Goliath. Some of the guilt and self-hatred that plagued me in the midst and aftermath of this season came from the absolute certainty that others had suffered far worse and handled it far better. How pathetic could I be?

Another force in this perfect storm came from the domain of darkness above and below, from the haunts of demons tormenting bearers of the divine image, where unseeable wolves are unleashed to steal, kill, and destroy. A darkness descended on me during those months that wasn't simply the absence of light. It was the presence of evil. Intelligent, cogent evil with a frighteningly uncanny knack for timing and the wherewithal to cause complete havoc. It surrounded my home and closed in on it and, had God not given it a boundary it could not pass, would have consumed us to dust. It came for my mind, my heart, my body, my husband, my marriage, my children, my home, my relationships, my fruitfulness, my hope, my joy, my ministry, my faith, and my future. The old flashbacks from my youth have faded now, dissipating into the light. Any flashbacks that make me shudder these days are of this season.

The third force, preeminent over all persons, principalities, and powers, was God himself. He was at hand in the fury, hidden and unhidden, revealing—not himself so much, but the pact I'd make with self-destruction. It was a time of divine testing, of tearing down and clearing out. The first months of my perfect storm, the worst part, when my mind was the least coherent, lasted the better part of a year. I'd spend the rest of my thirties in the wake of it, sorting through the rubble, trying to understand and recover from the trauma and navigate how to go forward.

Part of me would not survive this season. I'd experienced a killing. God had come with sword and shield to kill what was killing me. Destructive patterns I'd fallen into all my life would ultimately be broken. I'd stared into the surfaced face of the victim lurking within who kept falling for lies, falling prey to poisonous relationships. I'd ultimately get the help I needed to keep from self-destructing, and my victim mentality would gradually be starved of oxygen.

• • •

In the fresh wake of this awful season—timing I see as no coincidence—the publishing arm of the Southern Baptist Convention came calling for the Tabernacle study I'd written. They'd pick it up, clean it up, and publish it. It would be their first official women's Bible study. Their edited version would still be hefty, but I smile thinking of the enduring, hardworking women who humored me, working through every line of the voluminous original version. They and I joined those Israelites in the wilderness, and though we could not see the cloud nor the fire, we felt the heat. We moved with Jesus that semester, and for many of us, there was no going back.

I would write four more Bible studies in my thirties in happy partnership with Lifeway Christian Resources, with numerous others to follow in the decades to come. Though every cover bore the same author's name, I was not the same woman. Despite the title of the Bible study closest to my life message, I didn't break free from the bondage built into my past. I was *broken* free. Over and over I'd plead to the Lord the words of the psalmist David: "Make me to hear joy and gladness; that the bones which thou hast broken may rejoice" (Psalm 51:8, KJV).

Once you've broken to pieces, the luxury of imagining yourself unbreakable evaporates. Your outlook changes, not for the better in every way but in most ways, I think. Does compassion ever come easy? Where are those with no need of mercy to find it within themselves when someone desperately needs it? I still bear scars sustained in the casting-about of a perfect storm, but the hit to my pride, having believed myself whole and above certain lows, has never scarred over or scabbed. I figure it never will. I hope it never will. It's not a bad idea for wounded pride to bleed for a lifetime. Let that self-righteous fool in me hemorrhage.

Much of my mid-to-late thirties was spent in my parental happy place: on the bleachers at legions of volleyball games and basketball games, hollering and carrying on, consuming fistfuls of popcorn, containers of concession-stand nachos, cokes, and Snickers bars. The parents of our children's teammates comprised the near entirety of our social circle. We knew little to nothing about one another's personal lives. We loved each other's kids. We knew when they were having off days on the court and on days. We cheered them on and, when they'd let us, cheered them up.

I was still wet behind the ears and under the arms from my perfect storm in those days. I can't recall a time I sat flat-bottomed on a set of bleachers that I did not have thoughts like this go through my head: *I'm here. I'm sane. Shaken but sane. And there—right there before my eyes—there are my beautiful children. God, thank you, God, thank you.*

I was as good as done, sinking to the ocean floor, and he who walked on water plunged his hand beneath the churning brine and brought me forth from the belly of the sea.

CHAPTER SIXTEEN

"Bethie?"

The hour was unusually early for my brother Wayne to call. He worked live-theater hours, getting home past midnight, rarely to glimpse the sunrise. His soft-spoken voice carried an intensity even in the one-word endearment, instantly causing my throat to clench.

"I think you better come on out here. I think she probably won't make it through today."

"You calling the rest of them, Bro?"

"Yeah, I just called Sandra. I'll call Gay and Tony next."

"I'll change clothes and be in the car in ten minutes. I love you, Wayne." Oh, mercy, I did. Mercy, I do.

Our mother was dying. I was forty-one. It was early August,

and in two short weeks, I'd move Amanda into the freshman dorm at Texas A&M. Melissa was entering her junior year of high school.

We were already waist-deep in a season of loss. Spud had been back with his biological mother, Keith's cousin, for many months. She'd met a decent guy, she said, and had given birth to a second son and wanted her firstborn back. She was clean and holding down a job. Spud was eleven years old by then, and wounds of parental abandonment gaped wider with age and grew increasingly infected and angry. We could have refused to let Keith's cousin have her son and perhaps taken her to court, but right or wrong, we didn't resist.

Spud had been with us seven years by then, and we, a family gulping and treading water to stay afloat, had given him what we had. In our eyes, we'd failed abysmally. Keith had mostly withdrawn from him. Their challenges were similar enough that every flame near our home lit both fuses. I'd seen all the specialists, exhausted all the resources, and tried all the methods and come up ridiculously short—not just on answers for Spud, but also in successfully mothering the boy, the one gift I had been most confident and enthusiastic I could offer him. You haven't drunk deep from the cup of unfiltered failure until you've failed at what you were best at. No chaser on earth rids the tongue entirely of such an acrid taste.

My marriage needed attention. My daughters needed attention. I was determined for them to get it. It was time. It was also devastating and guilt-inducing. The second-guessing still haunts me. I didn't know if Spud would do well with his biological mom, but I'd grown certain by this point that he wouldn't do well without her.

I didn't know what I was going to do without mine. I had been filling the dishwasher with supper plates two years earlier when she phoned to tell me about an upcoming biopsy. I wiped off my hands, pitched the dishrag, and backed up against the refrigerator. Butterflies migrated into my stomach.

"Hopefully, it's just benign tissue. You know, fibrocystic disease. They've told you before you had that. Was it a little mushy and indistinct?"

"No."

"Sore like before a cycle?"

"No."

"Still, Mom, it could be anything. I mean, has the breast dimpled or anything like that?"

"Yes," she said weakly, almost defeatedly, like she already knew exactly how all of it would go. My back slid against the stainless-steel door as I sank to the floor. I sat cross-legged on the tile for the rest of our conversation and tried to control the shakiness of my voice.

One breast was removed, then a similar lump developed in the other, metastasizing rapidly. We really never did get ahead of it. Dad took her for radiation treatments, and Gay and I tagged along to rounds of chemo and doctors' appointments. Cancer is vicious. Ravenous. Hers was not satisfied to merely eat her alive on the inside, consuming muscle and fat like schools of microscopic piranhas, leaving nothing but flesh on her bones. It also externalized in large, gruesome sores on the skin surrounding the two horizontal scars where breasts had once been.

We'd have given her anything she wanted just to soothe her pain and fears. Mom wanted then what she'd wanted all along: her children and Campho-Phenique. We'd been slathered down with the latter our entire lives for every conceivable malady: chiggers, mosquito bites, fleabites, tick bites, cat scratches, warts, blisters, hives, wasp stings, fever blisters, burns. In our family, it was the cure-all, the one dependable remedy in a spitefully uncooperative

world. Who could think the Lord unkind to Mom when countless tubes of prescription cream failed to do for her chest sores
what one bottle of Campho-Phenique accomplished? I took it as
a sign—of what, I cannot clearly say. A sign, I suppose, that God
knew his patient. To be a stranger to God in sickness and death is
an incurable blow.

• • •

Wayne called my other siblings and me from the cordless phone
in Mom and Dad's kitchen that morning. Soon after her doctor
indicated her cancer had advanced to a terminal stage, Wayne
had wrapped up a contract on the latest show he'd conducted in
Vegas, arranged for temporary work at Theatre Under the Stars in
Houston, and driven his wife, Lisa, and their toddler, Ben, all the
way from the Nevada desert to our parents' home in Sugar Land,
Texas.

They'd lived with my parents for the past nine months, Lisa
caring for Mom around the clock like a combination nurse-cook-
housekeeper-cleaner and Wayne tending to her as best he could
while still earning a necessary paycheck. Weakened beyond the
rallying point, Mom spent most of her days on the couch, cat-
napping and watching her youngest grandbaby, curly-headed and
beautiful, play with blocks and toys teethed and well-seasoned
with the sweet slobber of a passel of older cousins. Having watched
her progress for months on end, Wayne and Lisa perceived from
her condition that morning that she'd not likely make it till sun-
down. They'd prove right.

All of us, children and grandchildren alike, made it to Mom's
side with long, hard hours to spare. The whole lot of us crowded
around her twin bed for much of the time, then we'd take turns,

a few in, a few out, never leaving her alone. She tried to talk to us and with urgency, but her words were hieroglyphic. I'm only a little ashamed to say this was lucky for her five adult children because it afforded ample license to exercise our own creative interpretations. Conveniently, she said to each of us in her unknown tongues all the things we most wanted to hear from her. Among those things were how much she loved us, how proud she was of us, how she probably shouldn't have said this or that and how each of us were her favorite. We knew she felt all these things and, hallelujah, we'd finally deciphered them.

My daughters, much like their cousins, were devastated. The downside of human closeness is that, to the degree you have loved their presence, you grieve their loss. Amanda, the tenderest of empaths, couldn't bear to see her nanny dying. Melissa couldn't bear to leave the room. They loved their grandmother equally and processed her suffering distinctly. As shadows from the afternoon sun crept across the carpet, dimming the light to mark the inevitability of night, Melissa came into the den and held her hand out to her big sister and said, "Come in with me."

"I can't," Amanda insisted, shaking her head, the rims of her eyelids bright red.

"Yes, you can."

"No, I can't!"

"Why?" Melissa asked.

"Because I'll cry!"

"So, cry! She knows we're sad. She's sad, too."

Amanda hesitated a moment, then took Melissa's hand, and the two girls disappeared into the small bedroom and had their nanny all to themselves for a little while. They knelt right by her side, held her limp hand and talked to her through their tears. She talked back to them, too.

"Nanny," Melissa said, "guess what. I just got my driver's license. I drove all the way over here on the freeway and everything."

Mom dramatically gasped.

"Like she was hollering, 'Somebody call the police!'" Melissa interpreted.

This was how I knew Mom was still in there. Still coherent. Aware we were near. Still witty and mischievous, even there on the brink of death. There with her organs giving out. There with her cheeks caving in. Nothing delighted her more than making those kids laugh. She'd dreaded Melissa getting her driver's license from the first moment she saw her haul like a wild goat with its tail afire down the driveway on a Big Wheel.

Mom talked to those two girls with all the oxygen and feeling she had left in her lungs. She told them she loved them like there was no tomorrow.

It didn't matter that they couldn't make out the words. They knew what she was saying. *"You are my best friends. You all are."*

Sensing the swelling weariness and angst in a small house full of grieving people, the hospice nurse asked to see us in the den.

"You've each asked me how much longer I think it will be, and I can't answer that. But what I can tell you, if you're longing for your mother's suffering to end, is that if I were her, looking into the faces of all the people I loved most, I wouldn't want to let go either. I'm not telling you what to do, but if I were you, I'd give her a little space."

We'd given her everything *but* space. She'd wanted us to entertain her in her dying months just like her living months, and that's what we'd done. Nothing was sacred. A month earlier, we'd dragged out all her turbans and worn them tight like we were bald as onions, too, and she'd laughed and coughed and laughed and coughed. And smoked. Doctor told her not to. Way she saw it, she'd given up enough. Hers wasn't going to be death by cigarette anyway. But she hadn't smoked today. She was never going to smoke again unless the Lord saw fit to have a pack in one hand and a lighter in the other when he met her at the pearlies.

Now it was just the waiting. We did what hospice said. We let the house get quiet and the floors creak. We were still near but not making a big racket, breathing right in her face and trying to get a response from her. We knew by the slowing rise and fall of her chest when the time was drawing near. We stepped back and let Dad move up close to her head. One of us said to Dad, "Tell her we release her." I think it was me. The hospice nurse had said it might help, but I regretted it the moment I said it. He cradled her face in his hands and whispered something in her ear.

Our mom, Esther Aletha Rountree Green, opened her mouth wide to catch one last breath from the thinning air but it would not come. There would be no waking her. No more Gay, Tony, and me, tiptoeing into her bedroom in our tiny three-person train, whispering, "Mom?" No more scaring us half to death with a sudden loud awakening of, "What? What? What is it?"

Our own nanny, Minnie Ola, spent torturous moments hovering outside Mom's bedroom door in the days on Twelfth Street in Arkadelphia when Mom would sink into the mattress, swallowed up in a shroud of sheets, and go someplace we could not reach. So, maybe Jesus let Nanny stand with him at the door on this day, when her daughter shook awake to bliss, and flash an eternal smile with no false teeth and the glistening tears on her face evaporated. Maybe right then Esna Irene, Prentis, and Anthony Dalton, her three tiny siblings tucked in the ground before she was born, ran out from under their mother's apron laughing and playing. Maybe Mom tumbled to the ground, to the greenest and cleanest of grass, tackled by gleeful, childlike affections of the Kingdom of Heaven.

Maybe that's when she heard a fiddle playing and she knew without looking that her daddy, Micajah, was the one playing it. She'd know the sound of his bow sliding across those strings anywhere. Maybe it was foot-tapping Saturday night on the Rountree porch in the sweet by-and-by.

Maybe.

But what I know for certain—as certain as a mortal mind can be—is that my mother finally knew she was loved by Jesus. Loved completely. Loved all along. She'd believed to her bones Jesus was partial and certainly not to her. I'd talked my face blue trying to reason with her. But now she knew. Now she knew that, if Jesus was partial, he was partial to all his own, just like she'd been to all her own. Jesus had never lost interest in her. Never replaced her with another. He'd never lied to her. Never cheated on her. He never even thought she was crazy.

The floor came out from under our Green family. We knew it would. Dad remarried in six months. We knew he would. And it was just as well. He'd done his time. God knows, she'd done hers. But we would never not miss her. Never stop aching for her. Never stop wondering if she was happy and laughing. Never stop hoping she'd forgotten the hard parts. We five, who never agree on much of anything else, agreed unanimously on what we'd have chiseled into the granite beneath her name: "Queen of Everything."

She was safe near the water now, eternal Sunday mornings now, her momma in her pillbox hat, singing, "Shall We Gather at the River?"

Yes, we'll gather at the river, she'll croon. *The beautiful, the beautiful river. Gather with the saints at the river that flows by the throne of God.*

CHAPTER SEVENTEEN

IT'S A PECULIAR THING, this living long enough to take a good look back. We reflect on moments that seemed ordinary enough at the time, when an idea germinated that turned out to be enormously consequential. Then there's the opposite experience: the stumbling and fumbling into something that sticks. You're a barely passable farmer on your way to a particular field with a carton of seed, and you accidentally trip and spill it onto soil you'd never choose, and a few seasons later, you're staring at acres of cornstalks, scratching your head, wondering where they came from. My nanny would say, "Some things don't make a lick'a sense."

If we're people of faith, we chalk it up to God's sovereignty, and if we do perchance have a lick of sense, we refrain from making a formula of it. God appears to be robustly committed to disproving human formulas. I believe in vision casting. But I believe in it only to the degree we accept that mortals, by and large, have distorted vision. We have a nearly immutable tendency to see things either bigger or smaller than they really are. And truth be told, we're poor prophets, squinting to see what's only a few inches in front of us.

The same year my mom's soul vacated her sick body for heaven and my firstborn vacated her bedroom at home for a dorm room at college, I was asked to lunch by a couple of colleagues from Lifeway Christian Resources in Nashville. They said I could choose the place. I loved these people by now. I also feel sorry for folks who live outside our state line and have to deal with wretched attempts at Tex-Mex, so I took them to Pappasito's Cantina as a mercy.

We chitchatted through the first wicker basket of tortilla chips, hot from the fryer. Novices don't know that every Mexican restaurant can be judged by its salsa. If it's poor, don't order. Simply leave a tip for the waiter's trouble and proceed directly to your car and put on your sunglasses so no one will see you crying.

Pappasito's can make salsa like wizards stirring up magic potions, and their confidence in their enchantments is displayed in liberality. Each person at the table gets his or her own little bowl. This is as it should be. Stay out of my salsa and I'll stay out of yours. This is key to long-lasting relationships in Texas. I was on my second bowl when my guests said, "We'll get right on to why we're here. We were wondering, since God has been so gracious to bless our partnership in Bible studies, if we might think about putting on some events together."

I'd gotten a bit of a heads-up this question was coming, so I'd been thinking about it for a couple of days. I was already doing all the events I could handle, so these couldn't be additions. They would have to be substitutes, trade-ins of a wide variety of events and conferences for something more uniform, and I'm resistant to an overabundance of sameness. These were creative people at my table, though, and not the type who wasted your time, and anyway, I'd not gotten my enchiladas yet.

"What would that look like?" I fear overcontrol in the same way a sane person fears stepping barefooted into a nest of rattle-snakes. I'm not proud of it. It's just a fact. So, the first thing I needed to know was this. "Would I have to speak on something we're publishing—like the latest Bible studies—or would I have the freedom to develop the material from scratch?"

"No, no, we wouldn't expect you to speak on the Bible studies, unless you thought that was what the Lord wanted you to do. We'd have in mind for you to teach however he led."

"Could it be intentionally interdenominational?" Mind you, I couldn't have been more denominational in my own church attendance if my life depended on it, but from the earliest days of my calling, I'd wanted to serve beyond Southern Baptist walls. That vision was already in drive—not exactly speeding, but not meandering either—and my heart would sink to put it in reverse.

"We'd work extremely hard at it." I knew they meant it. These were not showmen. These were some of the best people I knew.

Right about now, the server approached our table with a giant tray of plates balanced on his left palm. Once my colleagues were appropriately impressed with their fare, I beheld my own. The enchiladas were just the way I like them: two corn tortillas rolled into perfect cylinders, melted yellow cheese oozing from the ends, tucked under a generous blanket of chili gravy—not too thick, not too thin—topped with shredded cheddar cheese and bordered by flaky Spanish rice and soupy refried beans. Lord, hear my plea: let my final meal be this.

We asked God to bless the food, the conversation, our friend-ship, and our families. These were my people. I understood how they talked and prayed and thought and ate. Southern Baptists don't pick at their food. What we don't drink, we eat. About the time I was thinking how to bluntly ask the benefit of doing joint events, they got right to it.

"We'd choose the number of events you'd be interested in doing a year, then we'd take care of everything but the teaching and the music. We'd do all the scheduling, setup, preparation, and managing. We'd book your flights and hotel. Your part would be to show up and do what you love most. *Teach.*"

The thought of another office taking care of all the logistics was rapturous. I had exactly two employees, one full-time, the other part-time, and we were way over our heads. "How many teaching sessions?"

"We're thinking, what, *three*?"

I nodded my head. Flying in here and there to give a twenty-minute message was fine, but what I loved most was to actually get somewhere with a group: to move from A to B, then from B to C. So far we were on the same page. "Just one night away from home?"

"Yes. We figure we'd go Friday evening and Saturday till noon. The schedule would leave sufficient time to fly home that evening and still be able to go to our churches on Sunday."

Lifeway's first priority was the local church. It was mine, too. Coming home on Saturday nights would be a must because of my Sunday school class. I could miss a handful of Sundays a year but no more than that. "What would we call it?"

"What would you *want* to call it?"

"Well, you know, the name of my ministry is Living Proof. Could we call it that?"

"Sure! We could call it Living Proof Seminar."

I carry an offense against certain words for no reason at all except the sound of them, and *seminar* is one of them. But since I loved everything else my guests from Lifeway put on the table, I figured I could live with it.

I had one last question, and it wasn't small. This aspect of the event would be as crucial as the teaching. "Who'd lead worship?"

"We're praying that through. We're trusting God knows exactly who it needs to be. Beth, honestly, we don't even know if churches will respond to an outside event coming in, but we're willing to give it our best shot if you are."

I was every bit willing. A few weeks later, they let me know they'd found a great pick for worship leader. I couldn't wait to hear.

"It's a young guy in his twenties. Married, brand-new daddy. Name is Travis Cottrell. Seems to be a really good leader in the making, and we feel like he'll put together a solid team." I rubbed my head, wishing I had an ice pack. A man? Seriously? For a women's event?

Travis turned out to be one of the most astonishingly gifted individuals I've ever encountered. And he was uncannily humble, hilarious, and just plain likable. I tend to be a fan of likable. After my first Living Proof Seminar with Travis, I fed a piece of paper through the fax machine to Lifeway with three words on it: *It's a match*.

Travis would become like a son to me; his wife, Angela, like a daughter-in-law. They'd add two more children to their brood, and I'd get to watch all three of them grow up.

The caliber of singers and musicians God sent our way was an embarrassment of riches. Each of them, true worshipers. We'd have new ones come and others go, and yet the generous and humorous culture never changed. No big conflicts. No big dramas. No split-ups. No sketchy relationships between members.

Jealousies and rivalries never raised their heads either, unless we were playing Fishbowl during flight delays.

Not many things in my life have neared ideal. I knew life was hard by the time I was six years old. But the idea borne over bowls of salsa, over chips, queso, and jalapeños, over enchiladas and chili gravy, over handmade tortillas and garlic butter that ordinary day in Houston, Texas, by God's kindness, came mighty close.

That said, no amount of training could have prepared us for what was ahead, and had it been prophesied with any accuracy, I'd have been the first one to tuck tail and run. I handed Lifeway about half of my travel schedule, partnering in a dozen events a year. The Bible studies were picking up momentum, and we'd just published *Breaking Free*, the series I'd written after emerging from the abyss where I'd faced down my past.

Let me rephrase that: where my past had faced me down. I'd been sure at times that I'd either die in the process of healing up or lose my marriage, family, or mental faculties. Instead I came out of those months and years with a liberation in Christ that changed my insides—the ways I thought and felt and the ways I viewed life—dramatically enough that, for a while, it seemed to me like I was wearing someone else's body and thinking with someone else's brain. I wasn't fixed—I'm still not fixed—but I was free in a way that striving alone could not possibly have won me. I'd been on the receiving end of a miracle Jesus can do with a handful of fragments offered to him by individuals at the end of themselves.

All the studies were better received than we could have predicted on our best day, but *Breaking Free* hit a nerve. Our part of the evangelical world didn't talk much about topics like strongholds, spiritual warfare, freedom from bondage, and breaking yokes of addiction or oppression. I probably wouldn't have talked about them either had the harrowing ride I'd taken in my thirties not wrecked me to the point where I knew that if God wasn't bigger and abler than I'd been raised to believe, I was ruined. It turned out that he was indeed bigger.

What happened next indicated I might not have been the only one who needed hope that, if you trusted Jesus and really sought to know him, you didn't have to stay the way you'd been. Didn't have to live your life beaten down or up, or with a victim mentality, or as a lifelong addict. Didn't have to stay in a maddening spiral. You didn't have to turn out like your parents or their parents, not if you didn't want to.

Breaking Free skyrocketed, and instead of leaving the other studies in a cloud of dust, it caught them up in the vortex. The more women took the video-driven Bible studies, the more they sought out a similar experience live. In order to make the distinction clear, the name of our events transitioned, thank God, from Living Proof Seminar to Living Proof Live.

•　•　•

By my midforties our Living Proof Live events had outgrown church sanctuaries, and we were heading into arenas. Then the arenas started selling out. Our first ten-thousand-person event was in Pensacola, Florida. Despite every butterfly in Escambia County fluttering in my stomach, I tried to keep my head down and stay focused on preparation for the three messages. But when I stood up from the desk to get dressed for the Friday night session, I made the mistake of glancing out the hotel room window. The tenth floor captured a panoramic view of the grounds surrounding the arena. Throngs of women were lined up outside, waiting for the doors to open. We wouldn't begin for two hours.

My stomach lurched into my throat. I went facedown on the brown tweed carpet. *Dear God, dear God, dear God, dear God. Help me, help me, help me.*

I'm not opposed to well-placed hyperbole to make a point, but I'd have a hard time overdramatizing the effect this season in large arenas had on my insides. There were times I wondered if that feeling in my stomach, all that churning and burning, was the lining peeling off. I pictured an autopsy being performed on my body someday and the medical examiner saying to Keith, "Did you know your wife did not have a single inch of intestines?"

How in the world does anyone live up to arena-size expectations? What even makes it worth trying to find your car in the parking lot when it's over? This would be the cue for a smug saint to say, "It wasn't about you, Beth." I knew that. All of us on the team knew why we were there. We never once lost sight of it. We wanted to exalt Christ and please him more than anything in the world. But the sheer task of preparing and posturing ourselves before God, trying to be crucified to our own flesh and filled with the Spirit, enduring the relentless spiritual warfare, and praying feverishly for his presence to be among us to save, rescue, deliver, and satisfy was monumental. There's a reverence for the enormity of divine trust and the recognition you won't prove worthy of it.

Those arena events marked the wildest, most surreal experiences of our ministry. We saw God move—*felt* God move—in ways we lacked the vocabulary to describe. We saw marvels of God, beautiful and mystifying. Yet no matter how celebratory an environment, there is no such thing as a crowd lightly populated by affliction. We saw people in gut-wrenching pain, soaked in what seemed unrelievable suffering, some who'd been suffering so long they could no longer weep. We heard endless stories, held people in our arms who'd gone through catastrophic losses, and prayed for people in circumstances we had no idea if we ourselves could withstand.

And we endured a thousand mishaps in a world where the quirks exceeded the perks. The bowels of an arena serve as backstage, and since they're windowless by design, they're usually poorly lit. They also tend to be a bit dank and sometimes a little spooky. Once, when observing a moment's privacy in a toilet stall, a mouse ran out from behind the bowl and scurried right between my feet. Birds, on the other hand, loose and flying around in the arena, were not nearly as startling, but they could be distracting during a teaching session. Once we had a bat. Sometimes I'd have a bee buzzing around my head while I was trying to read a Bible passage. I blame hair spray. Another time I swallowed a fly. The wardrobe mishaps were innumerable, and after a while, it was hard not to think God was causing them for his own amusement.

During the segment when people could come forward for prayer, anything at all could happen. Once when I was praying over a woman, she fell completely out in the Spirit. Now, we were interdenominational and we dearly loved and cherished our many Pentecostal attendees, but this was early on, and I already knew the fastest way to get shut down by the Baptists was for people to start falling out. I bent over, grabbed sister by the waist on her way down, slung her deadweight up like a sack of flour, hooked her chin onto my shoulder, and whispered with no small measure of authority, "With everything in me, I ask God to bless you and grant your petitions, but I'm gonna need you to wake up in Jesus' name or I'm gonna get fired." She came to a few seconds later. I never did figure out what happened to make her drop the way she did, but it was months before I got guts enough to lay hands on someone again.

Another time we had an accidental exorcism. Having no clue under God's blue heaven what we were dealing with, the way the woman was writhing on the floor, we called the paramedics. But before they could get to her, she'd slithered up like a snake, hissed, and tried to bite my coworker. Because the Lord is merciful, a woman standing nearby recognized the signs and leapt into action, calling forth every unseemly thing a soul could possibly possess from that devil-beleaguered woman in Jesus' name, and in a minute flat, she was calm as a lamb. It was a bit too much for us. We hadn't signed up for demons.

On occasion, we'd have individuals attend, inexplicably, in full costume. The most memorable one was a clown, dead center on the fourth row. Between the enormous orange wig, the red-ball nose, the thick, full-face makeup, gloves, and long, cartoonish shoes, it was hard to tell if it was a man or a woman. My guess was that it was a woman, only because the clown raised its hands during the praise portion and I've found women to be, by and large, more demonstrative in worship.

There were also the glorious parts, sacred and holy. Going to sound check midafternoon on Friday and prayer-walking an enormous room of empty seats moved me nearly to tears every time, thinking how Jesus knew precisely who'd occupy each one and how he wanted to reveal himself to her. Then, come 7:00 p.m., the sounds of ten to twenty thousand voices under one roof ascending to the throne of heaven in worship and the palpable sense of God's delight in it were otherworldly. We tried to take in every minute, knowing it was exceedingly temporary and rare. And we knew it was extraordinary grace. Not one person on our team believed he or she deserved to be there. I knew my being there was the scandalous work of the Cross of Christ.

The vast majority of individuals in the arenas for Living Proof

Live events were women who'd come to worship Jesus and study Scripture together in an atmosphere wholly given to those two things. They wanted to be faithful to God through successes and sicknesses, sorrows, disappointments and discouragements. They were single women wanting to follow hard after Jesus. They were wives trying to hang on to their marriages. They were teenage girls who'd already sensed a calling to ministry or to the missions field. They were moms parenting alone, trying to make ends meet and raise their kids to love Jesus, as well as widows longing to find purpose in unsolicited solo journeys. They were women who'd met Jesus but wanted to get to know him and to come to love him and find that ever-elusive satisfaction in someone safe. Altogether, they were sisters in Jesus, many to whom I felt a deep connection from hours and hours we'd spent together on the pages of Bible studies. I loved them so. I love them still. And there were seekers in those audiences, those who'd come along with a friend or chanced a ticket and had no idea what they'd gotten themselves into.

Some people, of course, came with different agendas, different expectations, and ones we couldn't have met had our lives depended on it. Among those were individuals who reportedly had been sent by God to deliver me a message and intended to get to me if they had to long-jump over twenty rows of people to do it.

Or lie.

One evening I was in my hotel room preparing for an event. My assistant had given me a folder with letters and emails from women who'd written our ministry, saying they'd be attending, and I came across one of the worst stories I'd ever heard. A woman who'd be in attendance that evening had been shunned for standing up for what she believed by every person in her life: her husband, family members, friends, and fellow church members. She'd managed to scrape together the money for the event and was hoping to gain courage to keep going. Well, I called her immediately on my cell phone and told her that she could sit with me.

When I told Ron, my colleague in charge of security, to make room for her, he sighed. "I wish you'd run that by me first."

I loved and respected Ron tremendously and was normally compliant. But as I said, I don't tend to thrive with overcontrol, and I sometimes kick against restraints for the pure freedom of it. I shrugged my shoulders dismissively and said it would be fine.

When he picked me up several hours later for the event, he said matter-of-factly, "Well, at least this one turned out better than a few others. This one has only been arrested three times, and you should know that's not her real name or her real story." Obviously, the arrests were not the objection. It was our privilege to serve former or current inmates, either one. All under the roof of a Living Proof Live event had fallen short of the glory of God. Offenses weren't the issue. Deception was.

All told, we served in all fifty states, some of them many times over, and at any given time, in a room of two generations of women from at least fifteen denominations. We had the ride of a lifetime—seats toward the front of a mighty move of God in discipleship.

●　●　●

But with visibility comes scrutiny.

Once upon a time, we Christians in the world's West mostly kept to our separate compartments. The scholars and academics stayed over there in their universities, seminaries, and graduate schools. Pastors and their staff members were primarily preoccupied with their churches and, if required or desired, their denominations. Lay leaders—by that I mean volunteer servants of influence within a church body—focused largely on the individuals entrusted to them, the fellow lay leaders within their departments and staff members overseeing their departments. Christian speakers knew other Christian speakers. Sunday school teachers looked to other Sunday school teachers. Writers were concerned with readers and knew by heart the names and styles of other authors within their fields. The lives of singers and songwriters were composed by the daily rhythms of a world of music. We all knew our places.

It was within these compartments that most of our camaraderie, encouragement, enjoyment, competition, critique, ranking, bashing, making, breaking, rivalry, gossip, appropriateness, inappropriateness, inspiration, restoration, despair, and repair took place. We were a mansion of many rooms but, generally speaking, on separate floors.

Then out of practically nowhere came the World Wide Web, and birthed from its dystopian womb, social media marched on the scene like so many Joshuas, its armies circling, shouting, and blasting horns around our compartmentalized Jerichos, and the walls came tumbling down. And outside our compartments, some of us were exceedingly, abundantly weirder than you could ask or imagine. Namely me.

My path, for instance, would hardly have crossed with a whole host of seminary presidents and professors and, God help me, seminary students. Let it be nailed on some sacred door that there is no scrutiny on earth like that which proceedeth from the mouth of a first-year seminary student. What, after all, did we who were Sunday school–taught have to do with we who were seminary taught? We were neither one pretending to be the other. We'd have simply minded our own business, judged and made fun of one another behind each other's backs, and been foils for one another's narratives. Suddenly, we were all in the same big yard—where nobody wanted to be—with the rest of the world watching.

I'd seen many a purebred theologian—by this I mean formally educated and holding fast to a well-established system by which they organize, exegete, and interpret Scripture—have their tails set on fire for this heresy or that on social media platforms, and by their own camps. The competition was fierce, and for some, the only way to get on top was to discredit those above them. All to say, if the purebreds couldn't pass the tests of public scrutiny, mongrels like me were stuck at the barbecue.

I knew early on I was over my head and in serious need of education. In my twenties, I applied to and was accepted at Southwestern Baptist Theological Seminary, but the distance of the Houston branch from my home made it impossible to go a second semester because the schedule didn't coincide with my children's school hours. I continued being tutored by my Bible doctrine teacher until he moved out of state, and then I sought out tutoring in Greek. To supplement the few formal classes I could take, I began building a library of Bible resources so I could study on my own. Every extra dime I got from speaking or writing, I spent on Bible commentaries. Their writers became my professors. I saw no problem with this approach. The way I looked at it, I was learning from the purebreds. What could possibly go wrong?

I ordered every set of commentaries I could get my hands on, tore through them voraciously, and flourished with them. With a little more money and a little more training in technical terms and Hebrew and Greek words, I moved up to bigger leagues: multiple-volume sets that had a separate volume for virtually every book of the Bible. I had two basic standards for the resources I studied: shared belief that the Scriptures were God-breathed, complete, true, and authoritative for life and godliness, and that Jesus Christ is the Son of God and very God who came in the flesh and, though he knew no sin, was crucified for our sins, raised from the dead, ascended to God's right hand, and will one day return. I believed to my bones those two guideposts would keep me between the ditches and on orthodox ground. I didn't realize until years into my study life that my thinking was being shaped by schools of Christian thought as wide on the denominational spectrum as they could be deep.

I cycled through countless phases of religious readings. I went through a phase of reading works of renowned rabbis, one right after another. I read every book the late Abraham Joshua Heschel ever wrote and shook my head over his sheer mastery with words. I went through a phase of reading works of monks, mystics, and early church fathers and desert mothers. Then there were the reformers, of course. Oh, and the English Bible translators. I came just short of developing a crush on William Tyndale.

At least every five or six years I'd go through a Pentecostal phase. I'm not talking about the prosperity gospel variety. That's never made a speck of New Testament sense to me nor to any Pentecostal I know who takes the Gospels seriously. But I'd still check to see what their theologians and writers were saying when I was running low on faith that God still moved in miraculous ways because I knew good and well that he did. And, of course, everybody I knew either went through multiple phases with Anglican writers like C. S. Lewis, John Stott, and J. I. Packer—or they entered one once and never came out.

Perhaps some of these phases were little more than a search for my own identity, but it was the hunt for Christ himself that consciously fueled them. I'd spend my entire adult life looking for someone I'd already found. Looking for something else about him. For what his face looked like in this light or that. For what his profile looked like in this relationship or that. Spent decades looking up and down the lives of those who'd also searched for him and found him to see if they'd stumbled onto something I'd missed.

Every phase was in pursuit of some little something I might glean about walking with Jesus. Yes, even from the rabbis. Jesus was a rabbi, for starters. Further, Jesus said to know him was to know the Father. So it was no waste of time to learn from those who wrote on the Father that I might gain some riches of understanding about the Son in whom "are hidden all the treasures of wisdom and knowledge" (Colossians 2:3). While my shelves would have undoubtedly furrowed the brows of a committed denominationalist, I was nonetheless underwhelmed by any library filled with ink drawn from one slender stream. But these curiosities produced a mongrel, and a mongrel is a mess waiting to happen.

Now, God cannot be blamed for all the twists and turns my path has taken, but I do believe he charted my hike through hills and dales that had me wading in multiple streams of Christianity. To be sure, I got in too far and lost my balance at times and had to grab on to a branch to pull myself out, but mostly I was the happier for having splashed and sloshed around in them.

I praise-danced myself dizzy in front of the sanctuary with children in charismatic churches and spoke at more of them than I can remember. I served in Methodist churches, Lutheran churches, Nazarene churches, Assembly of God churches, Bible churches, Friends churches, Presbyterian churches, and all kinds of non-denominational churches. I walked through the doors of marvelous Black churches, not only to serve, but also on occasion to simply attend, taking full part, often thinking to myself, *This is the way I was born to do church.* God allowed me to serve more Catholic women in my Tuesday night interdenominational Bible study than I could possibly count. They tended to be among the most insatiable students in our classes.

I loved this part of ministry, finding something of value to take home with me nearly everywhere I went. I wanted to be spared nothing God was willing to give. I should qualify that by saying nothing *wonderful*. I wanted, after all, to be spared skin diseases, boils, and the like, and the kinds of instructions Isaiah received. Prophesying naked does not appeal to me. I'm not even all that comfortable reading the Bible in my swimsuit. And if I hide my underwear under a rock like Jeremiah did, I'm hoping my daughters will sweetly but swiftly catch me in the act and confiscate my phone before I post a picture of it on social media.

Now, I can't say I ever asked God to speak to me from a burning bush, but one time I thought I was on the cusp of a visitation from within the holly bush by my front door. I'd ended my devotions that morning before dawn by going out on the front porch, thrusting out my arms and praying over our property and that of our neighbors. We were in a terrible drought and at high risk of fire, the nearest one a mere county over. All of a sudden, the bush three feet from where I was standing started shaking wildly and making an awful racket. Wide-eyed, I dropped my arms and steadied myself to behold what manner of greeting this was, and before I could say, "Speak, Lord, your servant is listening," out from under the holly bush came the biggest armadillo I've ever seen in my life. Nothing more ubiquitously Texan had ever happened to me in prayer.

The thing is, I've had a good time with the Lord, and I hope he's had a good time with me. I've also had terribly hard times. My friend Bill reminds me that critics are the guardians of our souls. In this case, I'm as blessed as anyone I know. Critics, too, have been my teachers. I needed to know where I'd spoken out of turn, taught wrongly, or been misunderstood. As humiliating as it could be, I also needed to see at times how others saw me or hear at times how they heard me. Those in the public eye will never be relieved of criticism. It's baked in and probably should be. The trick to dealing with criticism is letting it do its good work but forbidding it to demoralize and destroy or to embitter.

What was so complex to me was how I could be so bold as to live, read, serve, speak, pray, and interact with God well beyond the norms of my lifelong and dearly loved denomination and yet be, at the same time, so thoroughly contained within it. So deeply indoctrinated by it. I suppose I felt venturing out was fine as long as I knew where I belonged. As long as I knew which way was home. As long as I knew how I identified as a follower of Jesus.

And, make no mistake, I knew. At the end of the day, at the end of *every* day, mongrel or not, I was a Southern Baptist, and I was certain it would, in all ways, keep me.

CHAPTER EIGHTEEN

My coming of age coincided with two simultaneous movements within the evangelical world that marked my life indelibly: Jerry Falwell's Moral Majority and the Southern Baptist Convention's Conservative Resurgence. Falwell, a Baptist minister, founded the Moral Majority in 1979, the year after Keith and I married, in order to mobilize Christian conservatives to take political action on issues they deemed of chief concern. Though the organization would remain intact for only a decade, it normalized a way of talking, thinking, and politicizing in my part of the evangelical world that became almost synonymous with godliness. The message could not have been clearer in the white evangelical church world: if you're a good Christian, you think this way. If you're a bad Christian—or more likely no Christian at all—you think another way.

I wanted to be a good Christian. I wanted to think all the right ways. I wanted to be on all the right sides. The issues weren't the problem. I shared similar enough convictions. I was pro-life, though I lacked the guts to be overtly pious about it because it was a wonder I hadn't ended up with an unwanted pregnancy. I certainly believed in religious liberty. To the extent I understood the concepts in early adulthood, I believed in fair capitalism and preferred smaller government. I should have qualified for the Moral Majority in every way.

Most of my friends who were serious about their faith were all in. They listened regularly to radio programs espousing the same basic idea: Christians should rally and use what power God has given us to see to it that America—a Christian nation, after all—is led by Christian principles and morals. But I couldn't listen to *Focus on the Family* without feeling guilty. The pitch in the voices of spokespeople for the Christian Right triggered my shame and shut me down. I didn't want it to. I wanted to be one of them. But I qualified for the Moral Majority about as much as I qualified for head of brain surgery at the medical center. My kind belonged to the immoral minority and, boy, was it lonely.

My parents were Democrats. As far as I know, neither of them ever voted for a Republican presidential candidate. I couldn't imagine being anything different. I helped distribute yard signs during Jimmy Carter's presidential campaign. Then came Bill Clinton. For the life of me, I could not pull that lever in the voting booth. I was an Arkansan, for crying out loud. Where was my Razorback spirit? But something about him seemed smarmy to me. I watched television until every vote was in and the winner of the election was announced. Tears streamed down my cheeks. *Dear Lord, here we go.*

Clinton was my induction to the world of Republicanism. I

was a reluctant Republican all along. But I'd have been a reluctant Democrat, too. Understand, I could not possibly have believed more strongly in democracy. The right to cast a vote according to personal conviction is, to me, the pulsating heart of American liberty, but I always thought diehard party loyalties and predetermined straight tickets were a bit fraught for Jesus followers. Handshaking and back-scratching could be hard to tell apart.

The Conservative Resurgence, underway at the same time, hit much closer to home. It didn't involve the larger landscape of conservative evangelicals. These were Southern Baptist concerns. Anyone paying attention to SBC matters by the mid-eighties clearly got the message that the entire denomination was in danger from godless liberals who did not believe the Bible was the Word of God. Glory to God, we'd been saved from the catastrophic demise of the entire Southern Baptist Convention. I had not even known to be worried, but what a relief others had.

I do not say this mockingly. We'd dodged a bullet, but more bullets were coming. This was war. We'd have to be continually proactive against Southern Baptist liberals and drive them out or they'd take us over.

Of course, my idea of Baptist conservatism was that of my own home church. Jesus was preeminent in all things, the Bible was unmistakably revered as God-breathed and authoritative, and sanctification was taught without apology. Our church was welcoming, generous, and warm, and its sheer size offered ample opportunity for both men and women to serve and reasonable space for leaders to see a few things differently, at least on secondary matters.

Generally speaking, I concurred with our church's climate in regard to men's and women's roles. Ours was a patriarchal world. To be anything different wouldn't have been Southern Baptist. The dual concepts of wives respecting and submitting to their husbands and husbands loving and caring for their wives as Christ loved the church were as familiar to me as my own hands. I taught some version of the same concepts in my classes and in my materials any time the subjects were relevant to the message.

My pastor and his wife, a brilliant force in her own right, modeled a healthy dynamic of mutual esteem and tremendous affection. I was around them too often for too long and under too many circumstances for it to have all been a show. During any given sermon series on the family, my pastor taught that wives were to be submissive to their husbands, but he didn't pound on it.

In our church, submission would not have included accepting physical abuse. I don't say this as rationalization but as a fact as far as I knew it. I was neck-deep in women's ministry and occasionally called into meetings between my pastor and a woman in a bad marriage. I never heard him counsel a wife to stay in an environment where she was unsafe. If she wasn't in danger of getting hurt, I'd heard him say several times, "Leave him and force a crisis. If he's willing to get help, your marriage has a chance. If he's not, it likely doesn't." Today I'd know a recommendation like this was woefully insufficient for the woman's well-being, but back then he was ahead of his time.

In the larger denominational landscape, generally speaking, women's well-being wasn't the priority. Our husband's was. We catered to them. This was part of submission. This notion did not only come from the men. I was taught in so many words by women mentors that if I treated my husband as if he already were everything I wanted him to be, he would become that. Also, if we women would do our part, God would see to it that the men would be won over and do their part. We took these to be guarantees. I would not recognize for years that my devotion was, in part, dealmaking with God.

I was never blind to varying degrees of sexism in our church culture, but I accepted it. It was affirmed and reaffirmed and, in case anyone missed it, reaffirmed again as scriptural. Here were the verses. Tap, tap, tap, tap, tap. Right here. Over and over and over again. If we didn't like it, we could take it up with God. "He wrote it."

That was that.

Never mind all the Scriptures in Matthew, Mark, Luke, and John where Jesus pushed back hard against cultural norms, affirmed the dignity of women, and gave them revolutionary places in the gospel story. Never mind that Luke reported women followers of Jesus in the eighth chapter of his Gospel. Never mind that, according to Peter's sermon on Pentecost in Acts 2, what was happening before the very eyes of the crowd was the fulfillment of Joel's prophecy: God pouring out his Spirit on his sons and daughters and promising they'd prophesy. Never mind how many women Paul named among his co-laborers.

Women like me played by the rules or we were off the court.

I couldn't afford to think in any other way, even if I was tempted to. I'd be finished as a teacher in my denomination.

As long as I stayed under the radar, serving at my own church and traveling here and there to speak and teach at small-scale women's events, I got minimal pushback. It was not until the invitations and opportunities grew and the first Bible studies were embraced by growing numbers of women in Southern Baptist churches that I was exposed to disdain and palpable disapproval.

I have this crystallized memory of a moment in time when it first hit me that I was unaccepted—and *unacceptable*, no matter how I'd try—to some of the main movers and shakers in our denomination. I was attending my first Southern Baptist convention, having been asked to speak to a small gathering of women.

My room was on the ninth floor of the Marriott. I'd been looking out the window at all the moving bodies on the sidewalk, marveling at how many of them had the exact same hairstyle. This was almost as true of the women. I checked the time, grabbed my Bible and purse, and headed to the elevators to catch a ride to the lobby. After a minute or two of waiting, the red down-arrow lit up with a ding.

I stepped toward the door, and it opened like the stage curtain of a musical theater on some of the most familiar players in my denominational world. I couldn't believe my good fortune. My eyes bounced from lanyard to lanyard while the elevator door bounced against my palm. It was them all right and, next to them, their wives, as lovely as I'd pictured them. Elated, I commenced greeting them by their first names and hugging them like we were kinfolk at a family reunion. I could build a compelling case that nothing says awkward like being fully committed to a hug—gravity forcefully, unstoppably throwing your body forward—and realizing the sentiment is unrequited. They didn't want to hug.

A sick feeling went through me that I wouldn't shake for decades. They didn't like me. Not together they didn't. They might have liked me two on one, but all huddled up, it was clear they didn't think we were one big happy family like I did.

• • •

In the years that followed, I frequently spoke at a variety of conferences for men and women where I was the only woman on the program. I'd meet with the same elevator air of disapproval on virtually every occasion. The host, having issued the invitation, was gracious and, at times, so was this man or that. A little hostility, however, can go a long way in a hospitality room. It wasn't always blatant. The social temperature in the room might just be a little frosty, or I might be invisible even in close proximity, like the car ride from the hotel over to the venue.

At some point in the conference, disapproval would almost inevitably take the form of ridicule. I've lost count of the times a fellow plenary speaker would ignore me in the hospitality room but bring me up in the introduction of his message. It might go something like this:

"We're just glad we get to be on the same platform as Beth Moore. Sure hope we get some of that anointing."

Uproarious laughter would follow. Sometimes the guy would do a little imitation of me speaking, going heavy on the drawl and big with the mannerisms, prancing on the platform just short of airborne, waving his arms gratuitously and hollering as thick and countrified as possible, "GLO-REE TO GAWD!"

The face of my real self would burn red with embarrassment at the dramatization of my easy caricature. I was supposed to take these things like a good sport, and I tried to. I recognized good-spirited humor. But if the guy hadn't said a word to me when we were three feet apart for half an hour backstage, I had a hard time thinking these things were meant well. The biggest offense I brought into these environments was my gender, but my personality and lack of academic training were also factors.

The challenge became doing what I felt God was calling me to do without making trouble or posing any threat. For example, if I knew I'd be serving or standing alongside a man on the platform who was short of stature, I'd wear flats. Once I was in Sydney for a conference with a couple of hours to kill between sessions, so I dressed down to a T-shirt and yoga pants and took a walk with my dear friend Christine Caine. I had a terrible craving for a chocolate malt, so we stopped at a popular burger joint to partake. As we wove our way through the restaurant to leave, a small group of people entered the establishment. Christine motioned toward an elderly gentleman at its hub and whispered to me, "That is *So-and-So*. He is one of the most highly esteemed men of God in this city. I would love for you to meet him."

He was also one of the shortest men of God in the city. A full head shorter than me. This was not my fault, but it was my responsibility. Christine introduced us, and the man's graciousness and soft-spokenness disarmed me. I don't know if it was his age, humility, or custom, but the longer he talked, the further over he bowed.

This presented no small challenge for me. I felt the need to bend over even further so I could somehow show deference, placing my head beneath his while also tugging at my T-shirt to keep it over my hind end. Before our conversation was over, I was nearly twisted into a pretzel.

When we walked out the door, Christine looked at me aghast and said, "What was that?"

"I don't know!" I said. "I couldn't help myself. It was involuntary!"

"I don't ever want to see that again."

We laughed until we nearly collapsed on the sidewalk.

Meanwhile, back in the States, I'd address men even in casual conversation by their titles when we were part of the same gatherings or meetings. If they had a doctorate, I called them *Dr. So-and-So* even if they were fifteen years my junior. I was more than happy to show respect, but this wasn't about respect. This was about rank. I responded according to the cues, showing inordinate deference.

"I could learn so much from you, and goodness knows I need to."

"You're so much better at message delivery. I mostly blurt stuff out."

"You know better than I that [insert anything at all about theology, the Bible, the church, or Christian spirituality in general]."

"I'm anxious to study under you."

And over and over, "I'm just a layperson."

I didn't do this to flatter. I did it because I believed it to be true.

When I got up to speak, if there were even a dozen men in eyeshot in a room full of women, somewhere in my introduction or opening prayer, I made clear I was "coming under authority" and did not "wish to lord authority" over anyone. And I meant it. I found some way to apologize for being there. These kinds of practices were not actions I took here and there. They constituted an attitude I carried continually. *Men are the boss. Make sure they know you know that.*

Once I nearly gave myself an ulcer over a large Sunday school class I taught that had both women and men in it. We'd intended for it to be women only. My classes had always been women only. But the men kept coming and kept coming.

"They're going to need to sit in the back," I said early on.

"How are we going to facilitate that?" my greeters asked.

"We're just going to have to say it to them like this: 'Could you kindly sit in the back?'"

The guys sat in back at first, and then they didn't. They plainly sat where they wanted, and no one in the class seemed particularly bothered but me.

"If this keeps up," I said to one of the leaders at my church, "I'm going to need a male Sunday school director. That's the only way we can do this. I'll have to have a male covering."

"As long as you have a male covering," were words I'd heard over and over again, and I believed them to my bones. A male covering was the key to a woman being blessed by God in ministry.

I rationalized that God brought a male worship leader to

Living Proof Live not only because he was tremendously gifted and well suited for the environment but also to provide the event with—you guessed it—a male covering.

● ● ●

Every time something hard or bad happened in ministry, I automatically assumed that either I was failing to remain under Keith's covering or Keith was failing to provide good covering. I'd say stuff like, "I think there's a tear in my covering" or "I must be out from under my covering."

And the more visible I became, the more those who objected to a woman at that level of leadership brought my marriage into question. One of the key concerns was that Keith didn't attend church regularly and was clearly not the spiritual leader of our home. I heard it over and over: God was not pleased with my marriage. I got it in my head that, though my calling was sure, God's blessing and approval on it hinged directly on what kind of wife I was. I grew increasingly terrified of losing the favor of God, and I had gotten the message loud and clear that the fastest, surest way to lose it was by turning into Jezebel and taking over the throne of my home.

I'd frequently read or hear of men saying, "Can you imagine what it would be like to be her husband?" as if Keith were meek and I were hairy-chested. A man's boldness with the gospel was seen as godly passion. A woman's boldness with the very same gospel was ungodly impertinence. It was *masculine*. And what you knew in my world without a shred of doubt was that nothing was more off-putting to the men at the helm than a masculine woman.

I was deeply disturbed by the entire legitimacy of my ministry being conflated with my marriage. I was around my pastor and my mentor often enough to mention here and there some of the insults I received.

"They don't know what they're talking about. Ignore it."

But I couldn't, so I'd overcompensate. I'd pray harder and try harder to be a godly wife. I'd make our roles clearer in the illustrations I used in my teaching.

"You just keep being a sweet wife," my pastor and my mentor would say.

It wasn't their fault I'd then compulsively overthink what qualified as *sweet*.

A lot of men in my world loved referring to their spouse as "my sweet wife." What was sweet exactly? If sweet was unopinionated, I was a lemon. If sweet was being cheerful about Keith going hunting and fishing any time he pleased, I was honey on the comb. If sweet was passive, I was a chili pepper, but if sweet was affectionate, well then, I was Keith Moore's sweet wife.

My man may not have felt particularly obligated to be at church every Sunday—"Lizabeth," he would say to me, after all, "Jesus loves a fisherman"—but he always prayed for me before I spoke. If I was out of town, he did this by phone. He was so committed to making sure I knew he had my blessing, he'd take his phone into the deer blind in order to stay reachable. If you're not properly impressed with this self-sacrificing act, you're not a hunter. I can't count the times he prayed for me in a whisper so as not to compromise his hunt.

But amid all the bowing, deferring, objections, and accusations, Keith and I were dealing with issues far exceeding one-size-fits-all formulas.

CHAPTER NINETEEN

OUR NIGHTMARE BEGAN without much fanfare in 2014, ironically in Keith's happiest place. Of a myriad of ways to describe my husband, nothing sums him up more aptly than a saltwater fisherman, salty as the sea. When I close my eyes and imagine him most content and at peace with his life, it is always there in the water, by himself, waist-deep, fishing rod in hand. There where the only sounds are croons of seagulls and the whirring of a fishing line whipping a lure toward yonder top water. I am bound and determined to have the words "Beth's Man of the Sea" etched in the granite on Keith's half of our double marker.

He was fishing one of his favorite spots: Sabine Pass at the border between Texas and Louisiana, where a river by the same name spills into the gulf. Knows the area like the back of his hand. He'd taken his boat out to shallow water and looked for slicks. After anchoring, he jumped overboard, grabbed his rod and reel, and, holding it over his head, trudged the current to what looked like a sweet spot. Said he was catching reds right and left, standing amid a school. He hooked a ten-pound thirty-incher, and instead of letting it fight long enough to expend some energy as he normally would, he drew it in at its full vigor and went to grab it around the gills.

"I was greedy, wanting to get it on the stringer fast so I could catch the next one."

As he cupped his right hand around its gills, the red shot straight up with a splash, piercing the inside of his middle finger with the spine of its dorsal.

"Felt like a sharp nail. Hurt like a son of a gun. I felt it hit bone."

Now, you'd have to know Keith or an equally devout saltwater fisherman to understand that a minor wound in no way impairs or abbreviates a trip. The lone exception for Keith was the time a barb of a lure sunk into the soft center of his palm, making it most inconvenient to keep casting. He has small hair-thin scars like geometric shapes all over his sunbrowned hands, signatures of a lifelong fisherman. His kind of casters don't quit. He shook the blood off and kept fishing. When he got home, what he showed me was the stringer in the cooler, not the wound on the finger.

Some days later, "Look at this, Lizabeth."

"Is that where that redfish nicked you last weekend?"

"Yep. Blasted thing."

"Huh." I held his open hand in mine, studied the wound, and kissed it gently. "Looks to me like it's getting infected. Better get some antibiotic cream on it."

This seemed nothing but a nuisance to us at the time. Over the coming weeks, the wound—no bigger than a pinhead—got angrier and angrier, and the skin on the inside of his finger darkened to a fiery red, like he'd clutched a flat iron. When his finger nearly doubled in size, he headed to the doctor and got a prescription-strength antibiotic. Still no alarm. More of an inconvenience really.

At the end of fourteen days of antibiotics, it still hadn't improved, annoying Keith considerably since fishing season had passed and deer season was beginning. The last thing he wanted was to waste the winter in a doctor's office whining over a sore finger. While he was hunting, the wounded finger all of a sudden stiffened straight as a board, and within hours, the surrounding fingers froze, too.

Keith headed with haste back to the doctor who, thinking the tip of the fish's spine must have lodged in the bone, referred him to a hand surgeon. Soon Keith was in day surgery and I, in the waiting room, pecking away at my laptop, praying all would be well and believing fully that it would. We were alert and anxious for the issue to be over but not worried. The surgeon failed to find a foreign object, a fact we found disappointing, but he assured Keith he'd cleaned the wound and the bone and it should be fine. "Here's a prescription for a better antibiotic."

It wasn't better. Weeks passed and Keith's hand worsened.

"Mom, what on earth?" our girls protested.

"No clue, but I'm going to tell you right now that your Dad's hand looks like it belongs to a bloated dead body that washed up on the seashore. It's like this sick combination of yellow and gray."

"Mom, gross! Somebody's got to do something!"

"We've been referred to an infectious disease doctor downtown at the medical center, and we'll make a beeline that direction as soon as they'll give us an appointment."

Heading an hour downtown to Houston's renowned medical center would be the beginning of finally getting some answers. It would also be the beginning of the end of life as we knew it. After extensive testing, Keith learned that his condition was caused by *Mycobacterium marinum*. It was a rare, serious, and enthusiastic bacterial infection transferred from marine life of some kind into the human body through a wound.

"I can tell you what it is, and that's a win," the physician said. "But I'm not familiar enough with it to treat it. I'm referring you to the only one I know who is."

Off Keith and I went to a second infectious disease doctor, reputed to be the best of the best. We will both say to our dying breaths we've never met a more peculiar individual than the physician who'd oversee Keith's care for the next several months. We'd look around the examining room sometimes, wondering if we were being recorded for a spoof. I suppose an echelon of brilliance exists, an Everest-high IQ, that gives a person a certain singularity. If so, this was as smart a man as either of us had ever met. There was no beating around the bush or lagging confidence. Scratching a pen across a pad of paper, his eyes disappearing beneath haphazardly forested brows, the doctor said without looking up, "I can get you over this."

"You can?" This was the best news we'd heard in months.

"Yes. Settle in. It'll take about six months and require a cocktail of antibiotics that aren't easy on the body. But this is the way to the other side."

●　●　●

We left the office with prescriptions in hand—and, prescriptions soon in body, Keith left us.

The specialist was right. The bacteria in Keith's finger, which had spread to his hand and threatened his arm, was not going to heal without the treatment. We had no choice but to take this route, but it wreaked havoc on Keith's system at every level, leaving nothing unscathed. His blood pressure shot up and stayed nearly stroke-high. His pulse raced. His body could not slow down. He could not sleep. He could hardly eat. He paced like a lion.

The drugs were so strong, they nullified every other medication he took, including the protocol for bipolar disorder and severe PTSD that had been a heaven-sent reprieve and joyously successful. The antibiotics would indeed eventually heal him from *Mycobacterium marinum* and keep him from losing his arm, hand, or finger. But the treatment set in motion an unforeseen and—who knows—perhaps unavoidable domino effect that would last several long years, escalate to a breaking point that nearly killed Keith literally, nearly destroyed us, and threatened to wipe out our family closeness.

I don't know much about physiology, but I know a little about computer technology. To make sense of what happened to Keith, I think in terms of my laptop contracting a virus. The virus caused the computer to start overheating. It grew increasingly hot until the software collapsed. It continued to intensify until the computer was revving and roaring inside and out. Picture me running to every IT tech I could find because this laptop no longer seemed to be mine. My fingerprints on it were unidentifiable. I couldn't recover documents. I couldn't update it. I couldn't restart it. I couldn't even turn it off. I sounded alarm after alarm, and specialists tried to help, but nothing worked. And finally, one night, the hard drive crashed.

We sent Keith by ambulance to a hospital, and before dawn, he was admitted to the ICU, his kidneys failing. Over the next several years he'd spend over thirty-two days in hospitals. I brought a man home from the final hospital stay who was nearly catatonic. He talked very little and mostly wanted to sleep. When he was awake, his frame of mind was dark and his disposition toward me was uncharacteristically heartless. His contempt toward me wasn't personal, though I'd not believe that for many months or ever successfully sift the emotions out of it. For a while, he couldn't have told me the date if his life depended on it. He couldn't concentrate to read. He couldn't stay awake through a half-hour sitcom. He didn't want me to talk to him. He didn't want to talk to me. He just wanted to be left alone. Left to sleep.

It was a gradual thing, both coming and going. There wasn't a day I could mark on the calendar when Keith left me, nor a day I could mark when he returned. But there was a day I remember in shivering, Technicolor detail when my daughters and I wept openly on a three-way call and finally admitted to one another what we'd each been afraid to say.

I remember the precise time of day, the pattern of the clouds in the sky, the white dashes between lanes on the dark-gray pavement of the freeway, the temperature in the car, the pitch of my voice, the pitch of theirs.

I'm the mom. It was up to me to say it. "He's gone. And the infernal thing is, we never even knew the day he died so we could grieve."

I regularly pass the exit where I spoke the words we'd each been thinking and still have to remind myself to breathe. Oh, we cried until our ribs felt bruised. We believed to our inmost beings he'd never be back. We hadn't jumped to that conclusion. We'd been sloth-slow to say it out loud. We'd done everything we knew to do to bring him back.

We're faulty for a thousand reasons, but we aren't people of low tolerance. We're hardy in this family, hard to run off and not hard to please. We're too flawed and too challenged by history, circumstance, and chemistry to hoard grace for long. So when I say we came to a place where we believed my husband and their father was gone forever, I'm not writing for dramatic effect.

I slept in the house with a stranger. A stranger slept in the house with me. A man I didn't like. A man who didn't like me. My life, his life, our girls' lives, became unrecognizable, and as is often the case, especially for people in ministry, we were trapped in a secret, unsure who we could trust with the truth.

I did my best to advocate, keeping daily records of his condition, administering and overseeing all his prescriptions, writing down the precise times and milligrams. He was under the constant care of a whole handful of physicians. And they cared. They did. I'm satisfied that most of them did everything they knew to do. They just couldn't fix it. Not at that point, anyway. I couldn't fix it. Keith couldn't fix it. Though I believe costly mistakes and miscalculations were made along the way, the heart-scorching days of overheating followed by our long dark months of cold, contemptuous silence were no one's fault and least of all Keith's. He doesn't remember most of it. A whole handful of years are a blur to him, and it's no wonder. His nervous system had nearly fried. Amanda, Melissa, and I had to process much of our trauma together because no one else, including Keith, knows what life was like inside our home in those brutal days. We'll get tempted to think maybe we overdramatized the situation, then we'll stumble on pictures from those years. Keith looked like a completely different man, not just twenty years older, but, as I live and breathe, a different face.

• • •

I've rarely been mad at God. He's baptized me in such sparkling brooks of mercy that, even when I couldn't for the life of me understand his decisions, I was continually aware of how good and kind he'd been to me. But one day about three years ago I stormed through the woods around my home, mad, miserable, and screaming, "How long, O Lord? How long?? What do you want from us? How long will you punish us?"

That may be one of the worst parts of being a religious person with a dark past. The temptation to view persistent hardship as punishment is almost too much to resist.

Regardless of what the naysayers said, I needed to work. My income and insurance were essential. I'd also been told by one of Keith's specialists, who could see the heavy toll it was taking on me, that I'd be unwise to remove all my distractions. I did my best to operate normally and diligently at work, but one day in the thick of it, I couldn't hold back the tears at lunch. My beloved coworker, Susan, with compassion coursing in streams down her own face, said, "Beth, God loves you so much."

I looked at my dear friend and finally voiced the horror that had started stalking my soul day and night.

"I know he does, Susan. But does he love Keith? Does he care that he has never had a day of rest from his pain? Does he care at all? Does he just like some of us and to heck with the rest of us?"

My insides broke wide open. I'd said it. Said in the light of day what dogged me in the dark. And somehow it was good to have it out in the air. Out in the atmosphere. Out where angels could hear it. Out where demons could hear it. Out where my workmates could hear it. My heart was so battered by that time, I couldn't discern a flicker of marital affection in my chest. I would have told you commitment was all I had left. And then I heard myself. Heard myself clearly enough to get wind of the emotion pumping the words with air and sound.

"GOD, WHY DON'T YOU LOVE MY HUSBAND?"

Fact is, you don't carry a fury, a deep offense, over a person being unloved that you don't love. I loved Keith Moore. I wanted him back. God, forgive me, right then, I felt like I loved him more than God did. And I wanted God to answer for what he'd put that man through all his life. And what he'd put us both through for decades.

God didn't answer. Not out in the open, he didn't. But he also didn't stop talking to me through the Scriptures. Didn't stop meeting with me in my prayer time. Didn't stop filling me to teach and write. I can't even say he really pushed me to repent. He just endured with me. Endured with us. Endured with Keith.

CHAPTER TWENTY

D<small>URING THESE YEARS</small> when Keith and I were dealing with mental health dynamics that made our home life particularly complex, a fear of ruling over my husband and the guilt of having to go around him at times made my life ten times harder than it had to be. There were countless occasions when I had to take charge because Keith needed me to. My daughters needed me to. This I'd finally sort out with the help of medical professionals, but it would be a long, arduous journey and would include profuse tears in prayer.

Eventually I'd grasp how tender were the mercies of God toward Keith's and my humble estate. The voice of Christ on the God-breathed page would become distinct enough to hear over the others. "Come to me, all of you who are weary and burdened, and I will give you rest" (Matthew 11:28).

We were so weary and burdened. The last thing we needed was the pressure to conform. Couples dealing with complex mental illnesses rarely have the luxury of conforming. We'd give anything to.

The fears and fixations I developed in an effort to be pleasing to both man and God also seem incongruent with my personality, which is neither weak by nature, nor meek. I'm determined to a fault, have an independent streak a mile deep, and in situations and against obstacles many people would find terrifying, I don't have an ounce of fear. I can kill a water moccasin wrapped around the paw of my dog in sixty seconds flat and sling it limp and dangling on the branch of a tree. This incongruence, to me, is part of what makes the story particularly worth telling.

I've done significant soul-searching and self-examination about how much of this bondage to male approval and acceptance I brought on myself and how much of it was imposed on me. I've heard from no few women who ran into similar dynamics and also performed all sorts of mental gymnastics to be able to use their God-given gifts in a man's world, even to teach other women. We knew instinctively that we could either find someplace else to go or turn into pretzels. So I turned into the Auntie Anne's of pretzels.

Then came the autumn of 2016.

●　●　●

The date was October 8, 2016. I'd just boarded a plane to begin my trek back to Houston after a four-day stay in Chinle, Arizona. We'd held a Living Proof Live event that weekend in response to an invitation from a small group of women who'd done several of the Bible studies and prayed for a couple of years that God would make a way for us to come. Their invitation came to me by way of a deeply touching video in which they shared their vision for an event not only for Navajo women but for Native American women from any tribe, any reservation, any state.

I didn't want to go in like an idiot, presumptuous and insulting, like I knew their world and how to speak to challenges I'd never faced. I flew in several days early to meet as many women as I could ahead of time. I was invited to several different homes in and around the city, toured canyons where ancient drawings were visible from a distance, got some history lessons from a Navajo guide, and spent hours in the car with a couple of local women, hanging on every word they said. I mostly listened those first several days, mesmerized by the land, spellbound by the strength and pure tenacity of the women, and won over by their pursuit of Jesus.

By the time Travis and the worship team hit the first chord at our event, the women had already marked me permanently. Several had shared with me their stories of sexual abuse because, through the Bible studies, I'd shared mine with them. There is often a sacred trust between women who have been sexually abused. A certain amount of understanding. A certain acceptance that we feel few other places. No one on earth is glad to have been victimized, but I count it a privilege to stand alongside those who have.

Now that the event was over, I grabbed a newspaper before my flight in order to catch up on whatever had set social media on fire. I'd gotten online the day before just long enough to see a barrage of references to some random *Access Hollywood* tape. I'd jumped off quickly because, whatever it was, I could tell it was big enough to steal my focus. I hadn't come to Chinle three days early to lose my focus.

By the time I got home and crawled into bed that night, I'd not only read the full transcript of Donald Trump's off-the-air comments, I'd also read the rationalizations of multiple evangelical leaders who'd been fawning over him like he was God's gift to American Christianity. *It was just locker room talk. He's a baby Christian. He's not the same man. He made mistakes. He was just big talking like men do sometimes. Boys will be boys.*

In my admittedly limited understanding, boys being boys who grab girls by their genitals are boys being boys committing acts that are criminal. Sexual immorality is one thing. I'm not naive about such things. This kind of thing was different. This kind of thing moved into the realm of sexual criminality.

You think this kind of talk is okay? That's what I wanted to ask. *Do you happen to know women who have had hands forced on them? Because I do. I know more of them than you can count. I can say many of their first names to you. And I can tell you this is no small matter. What he said, at the very least, calls for public shock and deep dismay among evangelicals across the board.*

A few voiced disgust, and I was grateful for those, but most either remained silent or actually offered excuses. Their support for Trump's candidacy didn't appear to waver. My own brothers in the faith, who'd been easily scandalized by others, had developed a sudden and protracted case of uncharacteristic tolerance.

I thought back over all the years of dealing with the grabbing. I thought about my story and hundreds of others I'd heard, some as recently as the previous three days. I thought about how maddeningly difficult it is to get people who haven't been victimized to care. To comprehend the reverberating repercussions of the actions of those who think they have the right to force themselves on another. The audacity it takes to joke about it like it's nothing. Like we're nothing.

I was no longer that terrified child who'd been pulled by her own father into the middle of the car seat, then, in the wake of the attack, clung to the door handle on the passenger side, shaking uncontrollably, forehead bouncing against the window with every bump on Highway 67.

I was no longer that adolescent girl who, for the life of her, could not draw a boundary and simply say no. I was even a long, long way from the young woman who couldn't listen to a missionary's story of abuse without dropping into a dark and deep downward spiral, reliving her own.

And, as much as any of those things, I'd lived too long now to buy the lie that keeping your mouth shut protects the family's interests. No, it doesn't. A family that provides a safe space for abusive people to remain unrepentant and unchanged and unaccountable is already shattered.

The next morning, I awakened dead calm, had prayer time, opened up Twitter, and posted a series of tweets:

Wake up, Sleepers, to what women have dealt with all along in environments of gross entitlement & power. Are we sickened? Yes. Surprised? NO.

Try to absorb how acceptable the disesteem and objectifying of women has been when some Christian leaders don't think it's that big a deal.

I'm one among many women sexually abused, misused, stared down, heckled, talked naughty to. Like we liked it. We didn't. We're tired of it.

"Keep your mouth shut or something worse will happen." Yes. I'm familiar with the concept. Sometimes it's terrifyingly true. Still, we speak.

Something happened, all right. The punishment was swift and severe. A friend tried to save me from some of it by calling me a day later. Said it was circulating on some pretty legit websites that I'd "joined Hillary's campaign." Said he knew it wasn't true, but others didn't know me as well and they'd believe it. Said several leaders, knowing we were friends, asked him to call me. He suggested ways I could—in my words, not his—walk back the cat.

No.

He put his wife, whom I loved dearly, on the phone.

"I know, Beth. But all the babies."

All the babies. She, like so many of my evangelical friends, believed that reversing Roe v. Wade was the most important thing to God, perhaps the only thing that mattered, and they believed in all sincerity that Donald Trump in the White House could make that happen.

I am pro-life as well. Not just antiabortion, but pro-life, across the board from conception to coffin or cremation and for people of every kind and creed and every shade of skin. I believe that is the only Christian response. But when pro-Christian starts to look less and less like Christ, something's gone off the rails. It was, to me, like they were under a spell. Like someone spiked their iced tea. I knew many of these people and no longer recognized them nor them me.

What happened immediately following those tweets was the psychological equivalent of standing in front of a firing squad bereft of the benefit of dying. The trolling on social media was scathing and unrelenting. Over and over: "Baby killer!" Hundreds and hundreds of emails.

It brought a firestorm unlike anything we'd ever experienced to my coworkers, women I dearly love, at Living Proof. The phones never stopped. They'd put the receiver down only to pick it back up. The switchboard blinked bright red for days. My coworkers, some of them staunch Republicans and some of them Trump supporters, were left answering for something none of them would have said. Let me rephrase that. They were left answering when they actually got the chance to speak. Many callers screamed and cursed, demanding answers but not taking breath enough to get one. My coworkers would say to the railers, "I'm going to have to hang up now," and they'd call right back for rounds two, three, four, five, and six.

There was no avoiding the bonfire at the ministry. There was no putting the matter on the back burner. We'd meet around our table—fifteen people no demon in hell had been able to divide—and I could see the demoralization on their faces. Living Proof had been a place teeming with joy, and literally overnight, it turned into a house of dread. We did our best. These were women of character who deeply loved God and were committed to loving one another. They tried to reassure me. I tried to reassure them. But the hate and malevolence invading our space pounded every aphorism into powder. At the end of each day, we dragged ourselves to our cars weary, sometimes in tears, and only for the war to follow us all home, where families and friends wanted answers.

These were brutal days at Living Proof and, as hard as we all tried to work together, fracturing days. That we survived it and found our way to the other side is a testimony to my coworkers' character and the grace of God.

Daily, I received word that my Bible studies were being pulled out of more churches. Some were boxed up and sent back to us. I was told some of them were burned. I expected reactions from men to the thread I'd published on social media, but I didn't see the women coming. Some of them posted pictures on social media of stacks of studies they'd thrown in the garbage, the wavy, weathered edges of the workbooks testifying to the weeks they'd spent in those pages.

Why would you throw them away?

The men mostly called me names. The women went for the jugular. These words played on a continual loop: "I am so disappointed in you. I trusted you!"

I'd known my comments would cause a backlash, but I couldn't wrap my mind around the enormity, the pure thoroughness, of it. For a stunning number of people, that one set of comments rendered years of ministry null and void. I couldn't make sense of it.

I'd spent untold energy trying to be obedient to what I felt God had called me to do and not cross the line by getting into the men's lane. I'd done everything I could think of to make clear I had no feminist agenda. I'd gone out of my way to make sure they knew I was neither trying to seduce them nor reduce them.

Oh, let there be no mistaking, I esteemed the men. Out from under their authority, I could hardly be trusted, let alone be blessed and used as an instrument for the gospel. The system wasn't the men's fault. They were just serving according to the Bible. I believed this wholeheartedly. I'd chalked up some of the most bizarre, socially awkward situations imaginable with male leaders to their rendition of obedience to Scripture.

All this time, I'd accepted the rampant sexism because I thought it was about Scripture. What I was watching in the wake of the *Access Hollywood* report, however, did not appear to be a whit about Scripture, nor did it evidence fruit of the Holy Spirit, as far as I could discern. In my estimation, this thing playing out in front of the world was about power. This was about control. This was about the boys' club.

You lied.

I bit those two words on my tongue until it nearly bled.

I believed you and you lied. I thought this was all about Scripture. All about pleasing God. This does not look God-pleasing to me.

I couldn't get these thoughts out of my head. I became increasingly vocal about it, until the words I'd bitten down were finally blatantly spoken. I also began to voice my alarm about the racism and white nationalism (not love of country, mind you, but idolatry of country) that seemed to me were intensifying under Trump's influence. It has been my observation that racism and sexism have an uncanny way of showing up together, like two fists on one body. The common denominator was clear as a bell from where I sat. It was superiority.

I spoke out specifically to my own Southern Baptist world because I believed we'd been party to things that were wrong, and I wanted to use what God-given influence I had to come alongside others in making them right. Part of a shift—not toward liberalism, for crying out loud. Toward Christlikeness.

I wanted us to be Jesus-loving, Jesus-like people of the great commission, following him wherever he led, serving people, meeting needs, sharing the gospel, laying down our lives for his name's sake. This is what I wanted for myself. This is what I wanted for my children and grandchildren, and it's what I wanted for our denomination.

The Baptist church had been my safe place. My sanctuary. These were my people. I loved them. But something was happening to us. Something bad. Maybe it had been happening all along and I was too blind to see it. Too busy in my own world. Too privileged. Too partial. Too immersed.

• • • •

In April 2018, the *Houston Chronicle* reported on two separate court affidavits accusing one of the primary architects of the Conservative Resurgence of sexual misconduct. Additional lawsuits would be filed. One month later, the other primary architect of the Conservative Resurgence was removed from his position for grossly mishandling an allegation of sexual abuse that occurred at his previous post at Southeastern Baptist Theological Seminary.

In February 2019, the news broke in the *Houston Chronicle* and the *San Antonio Express-News* of sexual abuse of scandalous proportions in SBC churches. Journalists had been doing their homework for six months, poring over records, documents, and court cases from the previous two decades. By the time they went to press, they'd tallied over seven hundred victims.

The article was the first of numerous installments shining a flashlight not only on abuse cases, but also on multiple cover-ups. The most prominent commonality was that the predatory wolves were sheltered, and the victimized sheep were left wounded and wandering. The news was devastating, sending shock waves all over the Christian world. Many Southern Baptist leaders were deeply grieved and determined to do everything possible to hold churches accountable. Their efforts met with tremendous opposition. Ultimately, those fighting on behalf of abuse victims would win some key battles and start a long journey forward, but it would take several years and bitter disputes.

Three months after the news broke on the biggest sexual abuse crisis in the history of the Southern Baptist Convention, there was a new crisis. After my ill-advised tweet about speaking in my church on Mother's Day, suddenly the biggest threat to the denomination was publicly portrayed as women trying to get to the pulpit and supplant their pastors. I did not know one. Permit me to say that again, I did not know a single one. But whether or not a woman could stand at the pulpit of a Southern Baptist church and give a message somehow became all we could talk about.

I knew what gaslighting looked like long before I knew what it was called. It thrived under our roof on Twelfth Street. It buttered our bread and paid our light bill. It deflected blame and shifted responsibility. My mother was the cause of my dad's problems. She'd drummed up those accusations in her own unstable mind. It was Mom's own sick suspicions tearing the family apart. It couldn't have been further from the truth, but it also could not have been more effective.

I can't imagine that a solitary pastor, seminary president, or leader in the SBC really believed I had an inkling of interest in taking over a pulpit, nor leading the charge for female takeover of the denomination. They had four decades of history as proof to the contrary. All that time I'd obsessed over having a male covering, a mind-boggling number of male leaders were providing a covering, all right. They were covering up sexual abuse. But because I'd been so outspoken and had already annoyed them, a horde of Southern Baptist brethren came for me like I'd burned down churches.

This one got me. I'd survived the 2016 firestorm, but I wouldn't survive this one. These dogs got through the fence. These dogs hit home and knocked me down in my own yard. These dogs bit.

I might have survived it, had it not been so personal. This mob wasn't from the broader social-media spectrum I'd worked up three years earlier. Not this time. These were Southern Baptists, many of them pastors, and not only from the fringes. I could not imagine my life outside my denomination. I didn't want to imagine it. Didn't even know who I was aside from them. I'd been disgusted with them, disappointed with them, frustrated with them, and baffled by them any number of times in six decades, but that's how it goes with family, isn't it? And make no mistake, this was my family. I didn't want to leave the house. I wanted the Holy Spirit to come in the house.

Don't let go. Don't let go. I'd said it to myself over and over. *Don't let those people push you out. Stay and watch what God will do. Hold on, old girl. Hold on.*

So much life lived there . . .

Butter cookies and baby bear chairs.

Tiny white choir robes with big red bows.

Running up and down the halls with my childhood friends.

Walking the aisle and extending endless right hands of fellowship.

The waters of baptism.

Ten thousand hymns.

My grandmother, her hats, and all her friends.

Handbell choir.

Regular choir.

Wadded-up dollar bills in gold offering plates.

A lifetime of Sunday school classes.

Too many Wednesday night suppers to count.

Missions classes.

Vacation Bible School.

Moving to Texas.

All the First Baptists.

Summer camps.

Sixth graders.

Young women.

Middle-aged women.

Older women.

Bible studies: one, two, three, four . . . fifteen, sixteen, seventeen . . .

All my friends at Lifeway, the publishing arm of the Southern Baptist Convention.

My event team at Lifeway.

My curriculum team at Lifeway.

All my friends at Lifeway.

Don't let go. Don't let go.

I loved these Lifeway people like flesh and blood. I loved so many Southern Baptist women. So many Southern Baptist men, many of them pastors. To leave the SBC would mean leaving them.

No. Don't let go. Don't let go.

That undertow pulled hard, but I held on harder, fingers laced, swinging around with the tide, saltwater rushing through my head.

And then it was simply, horribly, plainly, unmistakably, *Let go.*

And the current sucked me under and into the dark water and out to the middle of the sea.

CHAPTER TWENTY-ONE

My dad died.

Albert lived just shy of nine years longer than Aletha. To the closest of observers, these appeared to be the happiest years of his life, and despite my cynicism, I don't believe they were his best years simply because my mother had vanished from the scene. I believe they were his best years because he got a fresh start. He married a good friend of Mom's from church, a widow about the same age. She was marvelous, warm and lovely with five grown kids of her own and a litter of grandkids. Dad had a brand-new family with no history. This is not to say he dispensed of the old family. He would've relished us all being one big happy family. These were gracious and likable people, and the few times we occupied the same space, we had ease and enjoyment in one another's company as far as I could tell. It's just that we were all too far along in life and, as for the Greens, too bogged down by decades of mire—and still missing the one who'd made it bearable.

Only eight weeks had passed when Dad announced to my sister and me that they were going to "throw their lot together."

"Come again?" we asked.

"Throw our lot together!"

"What does that mean?" Gay asked. She was always the one to ask on behalf of both of us. She absorbed what Dad was saying faster than I did. "You're getting married?"

Affirmative. Could somebody drop a thermometer six feet under and check Mom's temperature? Is she even cold yet?

"There are worse things," my brother Wayne said to me on the phone a few hours later. "He's an old man and he's lonely, Bethie. Mom's gone. She's not coming back. Do you want him to live with you?"

Point taken.

The happy couple asked Gay and me, the only two who lived in the Houston area, to meet them for lunch at Joe's Crab Shack soon after they made the announcement, and we complied. Right there in the booth with brown vinyl benches, they flirted with one another like fourteen-year-olds. I have nothing against old love. I'm, in fact, in favor of it. I just don't want to see it get handsy.

Finding the scene somewhat surreal, Gay and I turned to two extra orders of hush puppies. They were gumball small and decidedly overcooked—more on the blackened side than golden brown—and could have used more onion, but they were not entirely inedible and were easy to pitch in our mouths. God knows we needed something to keep our mouths full. We wouldn't have said anything awful. We could clearly see how happy they were. But I think we'd have each liked to say stuff like, "Stop that. Keep your hands to yourself right now."

Gay and I carried each other to our cars the way sisters do, ping-ponging between shock and hysteria.

"What just happened?"

The wedding came with considerable haste, but then again, these weren't spring chickens. By the big day, all of Dad's children but one had adapted to the idea as much as we were able and could be found among the attendees. Now, I've never once been at a Baptist wedding reception with spiked punch, but I feel it might've been a mercy in this case. The way Jesus loves weddings, I'm making the lone observation he missed a fine opportunity to show up and mess with the ginger ale.

Off the smiling couple went on their honeymoon, a thought which kept me from getting a wink of sleep all night. After they returned, the two of them bought a house together, traveled all over creation together, bought a time-share on a lake together, played card games together, gardened together, went to church together, and lived happily ever after together for nearly nine years. They'd found the love of their lives. I was in their company multiple times through those years, and they were always as giddy and glad-spirited with one another as they'd been at Joe's Crab Shack. Less handsy, thank God, but giddy. Every day of their married life, Dad clipped a flower from their yard if one was in bloom and presented it to her.

I never knew what to do with any of this. I still don't know what to do with it. I was happy for them. I really was. I was happy to the fullest possible extent I was ever going to be happy with anything wonderful happening to Dad, without him ever fully owning the scars he'd left on us.

I believe in the grace of God. I breathe by the grace of God. I have needed the floodgates of forgiveness opened wide all my life. I believe in nothing more passionately than I believe in the power of repentance and the completeness of forgiveness in Christ. But I believe the wheel of repentance cranks by our coming nose to nose with the wrong and owning responsibility and confessing and coming into agreement with God's opinion on it.

I could never tell that Dad ever understood what pain, insecurity, and instability he'd brought to us. To me. I do not speak for my siblings here or for our late mother. I speak for myself alone. I never knew if my father comprehended the catastrophic consequences of the inability to draw relational boundaries and attract emotionally healthy people that dogged me throughout my adolescence and young adulthood. He said he was sorry, but in what seemed to me a rush to move on and forget it. But that's just it. I'd never have the luxury of forgetting it. It would take years to, in some biblical way, forgive it.

Father, forgive them, for they know not what they do.

Dad claimed to have changed. And here's where it gets, by far, the most convoluted: I never saw a shred of evidence to the contrary. He served his neighbors. He served his church. He served his wife. He served the poor every week at a local soup kitchen. No one ever surfaced with allegations against him or, really, a bad thing to say about him. The whole lot of it was maddening because I wanted to believe and yet struggled laboriously to do so. I struggled with guilt, but the moment I'd try to accept the change to drain the guilt, I'd struggle with disbelief.

I've spent an entire lifetime trying to figure out whether I could trust my gut. I'm convinced, this late in the game, that I should have trusted it exceedingly more than I did. But the question remains, was my gut so scarred where my dad was concerned that it couldn't be trusted? So scarred where he was concerned that I'd just have to go with the facts? If so, the facts were in his favor. He seemed to grow old in peace.

Would I? That was the question.

● ● ●

My cell phone rang around eight o'clock that morning. My stepmother's voice was trembling and weak.

"Beth?"

"Yes, ma'am?" I responded right away. She was a love. I never labored to show her kindness and affection.

"Beth, something's wrong with your father!"

"What happened?" My pulse quickened and the blood thickened in my veins.

"He got out of the bed just a few moments ago and started for the bathroom and fell to the floor. He's breathing but not responding to me at all!"

I met her urgency with my own. "Have you called 911?"

"An ambulance is on the way. I don't know if he will be okay!" She was crying now, devastated.

"Is he trying to communicate at all?" I asked. She'd already told me he was unresponsive, but my mind couldn't absorb the information.

"He was at first. Not now. Oh, no. Oh no, no, no."

I cried with her and tried to keep from asking her all the same questions. There was nothing else to be done.

"Beth, I think I hear the ambulance!"

Relief. "Call me the second they tell you where they're headed with him, okay?"

"Yes, yes, okay!"

Twenty long minutes later she called me back and told me where the EMT driver was taking Dad.

"I'm getting in the car this instant and heading that way," I assured her. "I'll meet you there!"

I called a couple of my siblings on the way. "It doesn't sound good."

"No, it doesn't," they agreed.

My stepmother looked so frail, so small and pale, when I reached her in the waiting area outside the emergency room. Dad had suffered a massive stroke. Gay knew by this time and was on her way across town. I held my stepmother in my arms while she wept, my hard heart cracking like a windshield in a collision, caving in, shards cascading to the floor.

In a few minutes an emergency room nurse summoned my dad's wife to fill out paperwork. Glancing my way, she said, "You an immediate family member?"

"Yes, that's my father."

"You want to go in with him while I borrow your mother?"

"My stepmother," a correction I made with affection, nodding my head toward the gracious woman in her mid-eighties, the love of my father's life. "Yes, I would very much like to go in."

God has given me grace for the dead and dying. I've had it as long as I can remember. I'm not scared or put off by the atmosphere. It feels holy to me. I go in as a woman anointing a body for burial but with the anointing oil of prayer, the spice and fragrance of soft touch and quiet worship. I guess God knew I'd need this grace for all the years of teaching Sunday school and doing ministry. I've sat beside many a still body, a cooling body, and often by myself. Sometimes I didn't know the person. I'd simply be there for someone who couldn't. This wasn't one of those times.

This was my father. And there he was, motionless, and there we were, alone.

"Hey, Dad," I whispered. "It's Beth. I'm right here. Gay is on her way. We've called the others. Everyone sends so much love and concern."

I looked at his hand, my insides wrenched and wrestling with wanting and not wanting to hold it. I'd held the dying hands of perfect strangers. But only strangers are perfect. It's the known ones that muddle.

I pulled up a chair, sat down beside him, and wrapped my fingers around his palm. His hand was limp. I pictured a scene from a movie: he squeezes my hand ever so slightly to let me know he hears me. He knows me. No, not so much as a twitch. Flaccid nothingness. A void. It's just me alone holding on.

I feel awkward but awake. Determined. I know that I love him. To the capacity my maimed heart is able, I know in that moment that I love him. I lean over and whisper in his left ear. "I forgive you, Dad. I forgive you. All is well. Be at peace."

Nothing. Nothing at all. But *nothing* is better than "Forgive me for what?"

Maybe somewhere deep in the cavern of his consciousness, he was saying, "Thank you, honey. Thank you. I'm so sorry." Maybe he just couldn't get his body to register a response. I don't know. I never did know. That's just it. I never will know.

All I could do was hope. Hope he was truly sorry. Hope he'd completely changed. I'd lied for him, after all. Lied for my mother, really.

When I was in my early thirties, I ached to get some of my story off my chest, so I wrote and self-published a poetry book. It was my first publication and embarrassingly poorly done, but an earnest attempt to even out my story with the broken side.

I left no doubt in those pages that dark things had happened in my childhood. I originally wrote that my perpetrator had "betrayed my parent's trust," intending, in a slightly veiled way, to absolve my mother. Then just before it went to print, panic set in, and knowing what was at stake, I moved the apostrophe one tiny space. It became "my parents' trust." The shame I'd have brought my mother in implicating my father would have upended our relationship. As it was, she hardly spoke to me for the better part of two weeks. I'd dedicated the book to her to soften the blow. It didn't.

It's a peculiar thing, isn't it, how we feel at times we have to lie to tell the truth? Victims of childhood sexual abuse who tell their stories often tell the first version with a mixture of honesty and dishonesty. It's our job, we feel, to protect people from the truth. Our job to protect people from the burden or disappointment of knowing the real us.

As I held Dad's motionless hand, I said to him silently, where God alone could eavesdrop, *I don't know you. I wish I did, but I don't. Who are you, really? Which one of these men was the real you? I bet you were interesting. I bet you had such stories to tell. True stories to tell.* And he did. He'd typed out an informal autobiography to all five of us kids and presented it to us several years earlier. Pages and pages that few of us could read for years.

The terrific, inescapable irony was that I felt no less connection with him in that emergency room, him in a coma, than I'd felt every time he'd answered the phone all those years of my young adulthood. After a lightning-quick, happy-go-lucky, disengaged "How are you?" that slid straight into "So glad you called!" like a pro baseball player stealing home plate, he'd say, "Let me put your mother on!"

Dad's chirpiness on the phone got on every last nerve I had.

If he'd ever once taken a breath between "How are you?" and "So glad you called," I'd have experimented with something like, "Well, I've been arrested for robbing the 7-Eleven at gunpoint for three Salisbury-steak frozen dinners. I shaved my head to get rid of the lice I caught my first night in jail, and would you believe my cellmate is a tattoo artist whose common-law wife smuggled his ink jets through security in a birthday cake and now I have a bright-red heart on the back of my head with a banner that says 'I Love Thugs'?"

For once I had the glaring chance, but there he was, an old man. Helpless. Defenseless. Small somehow, like someone was deflating an Army-green air mattress.

I called my Uncle Roy, Dad's only sibling, from my cell phone. He was tender and sweet like always. Listened to every word. How two people from the same parentage can be so different is a mystery as old as Cain and Abel. Uncle Roy believes it was the war. Dad had too much trauma. Too much death. He was in it too long. It was all too dark. He feels Dad learned to dissociate to survive. I've come to believe he's likely right. Such a truth would neither excuse nor absolve the man. It's just a wooden spoon in a shaky hand to stir up bits and pieces of compassion stuck to the bottom of a pan of thick stew.

"Honey, can you put the phone up to his ear for me?" Uncle Roy requested.

"Yes." And I did so. I have no idea what my dad's younger brother said to him, but tears dripped from my jaw to my lap.

Gay arrived soon after that, and I have never been gladder to see her. Orderlies moved Dad to a hospital room, but we were told he'd never wake up. His skull was a wading pool.

"How long?"

"Who can say? Could be hours. Could be days."

My stepmother, my sister, and I knelt around his bed, joined hands at his feet and across his legs, committed his spirit to his Maker and asked the Lord to take him gently and let him not linger long.

Soon the waiting room nearest Dad's room was humming with people. Melissa was neck-deep in grad school exams at Wheaton College in Illinois, scrambling toward the first opportunity to fly home. Amanda and her husband, Curtis, were living in the Dallas area and packed their Jeep Cherokee and headed four hours south to Houston soon after they received the news. My grandson, fifteen months old at the time, lunged for me the moment he saw me and wrapped his arms tightly around my neck, hiding his face under my hair. He was a long way from reading a book but even a toddler can read a room. He was the happiest little fellow in the world, but he knew something bad had happened and he loved his grandmother, who conveniently had the heaviest hair in the room to hide under. When his parents needed to leave and head to my house to settle in for an inevitable funeral, he did not want to let go. Amanda had to unwind his arms from my neck with him screaming bloody murder until all three of us—Amanda, my grandson, and me—were sobbing.

When Dad's condition remained unchanged for several hours and I couldn't get my little guy off my mind, I asked Gay and our stepmother if it would be all right for me to go home for a little while and rock him. Of course, it was.

I had that plump and beautiful blue-eyed toddler with the world's longest lashes in my arms, rocking him and singing to him and smooching his sweet head, when Gay called.

"Dad's gone, Beth."

She'd been the only one with him when he breathed his last. Our stepmother had slipped out of the room for the merest moment. But it felt right. My sister was the one to get to walk him home. I believe God calendars those kinds of appointments, and I'm as certain as I know to be that the man went to Jesus.

●　●　●

From where I sit, my father was loads of trouble in his living, but he was the least trouble in his dying of anyone I ever knew. He lived actively, healthily until he fell to the floor that morning in his eighty-seventh year. Volunteered. Served. Socialized. Like overstuffing a suitcase, he packed the last eight years of his life to broken zippers with good memories and lighthearted fun and games with his second wife. You know the one. The love of his life. Who can understand these things?

The Scrabble board was still set up on their kitchen table from a hot competition the night before; some *Q*s and *Z*s and other abominably difficult letters to play were perched on their wooden stands. They'd decided to finish the game the next day. A yellow ledger was close by with their scores, in my father's penmanship, from recent rounds of Scrabble and dominoes. A travel atlas was wide open right beside it with a green highlighter in the crease, plotting the next road trip.

We steadied ourselves and prepared to meet with the funeral director to see to Dad's final needs. But in iconic Albert B. Green fashion, he'd already planned his going-out to the minutest detail, and to his substantial credit, his casket and funeral and burial expenses were paid in full. We had his handwritten instructions of his wishes, numbered one through fourteen.

Thirteen of them were easily implemented. We'd have given up on the fourteenth except for Keith. He was adamant the old man had earned the twenty-one-gun salute and had half a dozen medals to prove it. He'd fought in two wars, done four tours, taken a bullet in the face and shrapnel in the back. His hands helped shove the gates of Dachau open in April of 1945, and his eyes saw sights of living ghosts in clattering bones stumbling toward the realization of their liberation, black eyes widening in the deep hollows of skeletal faces. His ears heard their weak wails of relief and gratitude. His skin felt their desperate pawing.

Keith was bound and determined to see to his father-in-law's wishes of a full military burial if it was the last thing he did. He contacted the VA and chased down every possible lead, refusing to take no for an answer. All this left me with a sizable crush on Keith because I knew like I knew my own name why he was doing it. He liked Dad well enough, but this wasn't about Dad. This was about Keith Moore's wife. He wanted to help me see a different side of my dad, an honorable side of my dad, here at the end. Though I'd still have to sort out all the complexities for years to come, my husband's good intentions were not wasted.

Keith didn't get to meet the veterans beforehand. He was simply assured they'd show up at the burial site and would he have a cash donation in hand.

All this was over the phone. Keith would have preferred names and a printout of concretized plans, but none were forthcoming, and he had no choice but to take them at their word. "Just tell us the time and place."

And they were good for it. We were already sitting under the awning, Dad right there in the open casket, awkward as usual but, also as usual, oblivious to it, when several cars pulled up to the nearest curb with bumps and screeches. There were seven of them, all right around Dad's age, so it understandably took them a while to get out of their vehicles, tuck their shirts back in, get their rifles out of the trunk, and make their way over to us. They'd not taken quite the care of themselves that Dad had, and though this did nothing to diminish their due honor for service to their country, it appeared to me that several of them had not tried on their uniforms in roughly twenty pounds.

I looked at Wayne and he at me with no uncertain expression. "I hope," I whispered to my big brother, "one of them doesn't trip over a grave marker getting over here and the gun go off."

We would all live through this event and find it varying degrees of meaningful, as Keith had hoped, even if he was let down somewhat by the disheveled condition of a couple of the veterans. Anyway, only a fool could remain unmoved by taps. The twenty-one-gun salute—which on this occasion was seven guns, three shots each—was also effective. And loud. I knew Dad really was dead when he didn't wake up. The man deserved to be honored by his country for his service. He was a good soldier, whether or not he'd always been a particularly good dad.

I'm ashamed to say the whole affair was also a bit theatrically comedic. Skit-like, if I may. We are terrible people, my siblings and me. I blame Wayne for our inappropriate laughter. He blames me. And there we were in folding chairs, the right legs of mine digging into soft ground beneath the fake grass rug, and me wondering if we were about to topple on our mother.

• • •

I saw Mom and Dad about a year later. Well, not really. What I mean is, I imagined them. I was minding my own business, thinking about a dozen other things, when a live picture like we can take nowadays with our cell phones sprang into my mind's eye out of seemingly nowhere. They looked to be in their late twenties or early thirties. Dad was dapper in a perfectly ironed and creased gray-green uniform and a garrison cap, and Mom was in a white short-sleeved dress with a fitted bodice cinched at the waist by a crisp white belt. Her flared skirt just below the knee was whipping in the breeze like a freshly bleached sheet on a clothesline. They were both smiling wide, maybe laughing, and the beams of an unseen sun were picking up the gold strands of Mom's pecan-brown hair. The sky in the backdrop was as blue as my grandson's eyes. Mom and Dad weren't holding hands or gazing at one another. Nothing like that. Just there in the scene together, happy as larks.

I know it wasn't real. I don't claim a vision of any kind. But it was a most unexpected picture to pop into my head and one that brought me considerable comfort. I so hoped, somewhere beyond the veil, my parents were each exactly that gleeful and were at complete peace with one another, fully liberated, the gates of pain pushed open by the hand of God.

CHAPTER TWENTY-TWO

The happiest year of my married life converged with the saddest year of my church life. As much as I hate to admit it, the two might not be entirely unrelated.

Keith had been too sick to feel the earth shake beneath me in October 2016 or to fully register the unabating aftershocks in 2017–2019. But he'd started coming awake to the broader world in late 2020 and was wide-eyed and fully cognizant in March 2021, when I made public my departure from the SBC, the denomination I'd loved all my life and served since I was twelve.

His return from the abyss was slow, two steps forward and one step back, but once he was back, I had the happiest year of my married life, bar none. Easy? No. Flawless? Heavens, no. That's not our vibe. *Happiest.* Lest you be thinking God gave me a brand-new man and that's why I was happy, nope, I mostly just got back the same ornery one I married and with the same mouth that needed washing.

And I needed Keith like a calla needs rain. He knew better than anyone but my Maker how much this decision meant to me. Knew I wouldn't know what to do with myself. Knew I wouldn't even know myself. He knew letting go of my long and happy partnership with Lifeway was a dagger to my heart. Many of my dearest relationships were tied to the SBC, and though most of them would survive the shift at least to some degree, we no longer shared the same bond. The leaving had come with a dying. Keith showed up for it and mourned with me. Mourned for me. Wept for me. Cussed for me.

For the first time in my life, I didn't have a home church. Didn't have a clue where to go. To Keith, this meant we were footloose, and what could be better than footloose? To me, this meant we were legless. Harborless. Detached. No place nor people of faith we could call our own. The yearning to belong is woven into the human fabric. We had nowhere we belonged.

We'd been watching online services for a year, but I was starving half to death for corporate worship and the corporate reading of Scripture. As multiple churches reopened their doors following the worst of the Covid-19 pandemic, we visited several denominations closest to our tradition—and some great congregations—but each time we were faced with an undeniable reality: our presence was loaded. That's not to say we weren't welcome. It's to say we came with baggage and triggered reactions and opinions. Sometimes we humans are simply too known in a particular environment to have the luxury of starting over. And make no mistake, we were starting over.

During this season, Saturday evenings meant one thing for

me: anxiety about where we would go to church the next morning. Keith would've been content to keep watching online where he could stay in his blue-checkered pajama pants, eat scrambled eggs and toast, and steer clear of an offering plate. But we don't sing that well. I found online praise and worship to be unbearably awkward, us sitting there smelling like Jimmy Dean sausage, with unbrushed teeth, uncombed hair, one dog sprawled over us and another dropping a slimy ball in our laps. Sometimes Keith would bust out laughing at the way we sounded, and by that time, false piety beaten to smithereens, I'd have to bust out with him. It wasn't working. Neither, so far, was finding a church.

One Saturday evening, me sitting on the couch, down in the mouth again, Keith said out of a concoction of compassion and frustration, "Elizabeth Moore, pick up your cell phone right now."

"Why?"

"God, help me, woman, you'd exasperate the pope. Would you just pick the thing up?"

So I did—but in a huff.

"Google *Anglican churches in Houston*," he said, bossy-like.

"What?"

"You heard me."

Our daughter, son-in-law, and their three children had moved to Missouri the previous summer, and in need of a breather from our tradition, they'd attended an Anglican church for a while and found considerable consolation in it. By this time, Keith was at his wit's end with me and my church drama and knew we were going to have to get off the beaten path to find a place we were less controversial.

So I did what he said. I sat right there on the couch and dictated into the tiny microphone of my phone, "Anglican churches in Houston, Texas."

Keith looked over my shoulder while my phone proceeded to search. When a half dozen red locator pins popped up on the screen, he circled around the couch and sat down next to me.

"Let's see," he said, leaning in close.

"None of them are anywhere near us," I quipped.

"Well, which is the closest?" His tone was a tad put out, but his posture was love through and through, sitting thigh to thigh with me, his arm tight around my shoulders.

He'd left this decision up to me for the previous forty-two years because, frankly, he didn't care. I don't mean he didn't want to go to church. I mean he didn't care where we went. The way he saw it, he wasn't going to get involved anyway. If I was happy at a church, he was fine with it. Right now, however, I was anything but happy in a church, having grown increasingly self-conscious and imagining we were too radioactive to be welcome anywhere. We'd just be tolerated, the way I saw it, and a headache to whatever poor pastor ended up with us. Keith faced the fact on his own that he was going to have to step up.

"This one right here." I tapped the screen with my fingernail. "About a half hour away."

"Good," Keith said. "That's where we're going tomorrow."

I was mostly quiet on the drive except to parrot every direction the voice assistant on my iPhone gave us. Siri would say, *Take a left at the stoplight in nine hundred feet.*

And I'd say, "Take a left at the stoplight in nine hundred feet, babe."

"I heard it."

"Okay. Just making sure." *At the four-way stop, continue straight ahead.* "Babe, at the four-way stop, continue—"

"I heard it."

"Okay."

This for thirty minutes. We pulled into the parking lot at five minutes till. I reached for my purse and Bible on the floorboard, crunching butterfly wings in my stomach. Keith walked around the car and held his hand out to me. I grabbed it and we started for the entryway. As I replay the scene in my imagination, I'm all but wearing a white stick-on name tag with red letters: *Hello, I'm a Southern Baptist.*

A man wearing a real clip-on name tag with his picture and the church logo on it—the kind that says you really, really belong—greeted us at the door.

"Mornin', folks!"

"Morning," I said, avoiding eye contact, my volume trailing off with a mumble. "We're vis'tors."

"They know," Keith said under his breath, reading the room, and perhaps reveling a bit in my rare onset of social awkwardness.

To a couple who'd come of age during the peak years of evangelicalism's megachurch, the building seemed small. I'd loved the loudness of three-thousand-seat worship centers. The energy of it. I'd long appreciated the ministry of the man or woman sitting at the control center of a large sanctuary with enough sensitivity to know when to dim or brighten the lights. *Take them down during praise and worship so people aren't distracted. Take them up for the sermon so people can read their Bibles.* I loved it. I still love it. But we knew this time around, the last thing we were looking for was big.

When we entered the foyer, the double doors to the sanctuary were twenty feet ahead of us and wide open. A few dudes were standing at the doors handing out bulletins. Hardly a sound was coming from inside. We were looking to slip subtly into a pew, but a whole handful of people were huddled at the door, each in some kind of robe. Now, I'd worn a choir robe at church no telling how many times, but this did not appear to be the choir. For one thing, a couple of kids were in the huddle. Most everybody was holding something. Keith assumed the gentlemanly role, motioning me to go first, then pressed my back between my shoulder blades like a cattle prod for me to get going.

"Right through them?" I whispered.

"Yes, Lizabeth, *go*."

Okay, I was thinking, *but this is awkward*. Seemed obvious to me they were about to have a ceremony. We must have inadvertently visited on a special Sunday. I stepped through the huddle, weaving my head around the candlesticks and trying to avoid hitting my forehead on a cross a man was holding on the end of a wooden cane. I smiled at a small girl, maybe seven years old, holding another cross. Several men in various robes and stoles were standing nearby. Instead of being annoyed by us, each of them smiled at us warmly, motioning us forward and whispering various renditions of "Come right in," and "Welcome" and, to my profuse repetitions of "I'm so sorry, excuse us please," saying, "No, no, no, we're glad you're here."

A man around our age with a gentle face and warm, genuine smile was among them. He had on a white robe overlaid with a green stole bearing a grapevine pattern. He reached out his hand to me and, in a louder whisper, introduced himself as the rector. "Welcome to our church. And you are?"

"Beth—" I hesitated for half a second—"Moore."

"Oh!" he said, tilting his head back with surprise and an infectious, harmless chuckle. "Like *Beth Moore*."

"Unfortunately, yes." The verger who'd worked with him for decades would inform me later with a wide grin that the rector was simply amused I had the same name as the infamous Beth Moore. Nothing further occurred to him.

"Come right on in," he said in the dearest way. "We're glad to have you."

Somewhere around 120 people were seated in the pews of the sanctuary, and a small worship band with two singers at standing mics was poised to the left of an otherwise empty stage. We'd hardly sat down when a bell rang.

The band commenced immediately, the congregation stood and Keith with them, and I scrambled to my feet. Lo and behold, here they came, right down the center aisle, that huddle of people, smiling and singing.

Keith leaned his head toward me and whispered, "Get your bulletin."

Now, I didn't know when Keith thought he'd become such an expert, but I could see he was already holding his. I perused the room and saw that most of the other attendees were holding theirs. I grabbed mine just in time for the main guy, the man who had welcomed us at the door, to start saying phrases and the congregation hearkening back.

This included Keith, who'd never darkened the doors of this church. He acted just like he'd come into a sudden storehouse of knowledge. He pointed to the top of the right-hand column of my bulletin. "We're right here."

Anybody paying attention in the sanctuary could hear the sound of inexperience in the rattling of my bulletin. My hands were shaking uncontrollably with nerves.

And Keith? Well, let me ask you a few questions. Did your family ever have an aquarium when you were growing up? Did your mom or dad or aunt or older sibling ever take you to the pet store and buy you a goldfish of your very own to add to it? Remember how the employee submerged a dipper into the large fish tank and drew out a cup or so of water into a clear plastic bag, then grabbed a small net with a handle on it, scooped up a goldfish, dropped it in, and secured the bag with a twist tie? Remember how that fish would get all wild-eyed and anxious in that small bag on the way home in the car? Then, how you'd get it home to an aquarium your new goldfish had never seen, filled with fish it had never met, and you'd untwist the tie and pour the water and the new goldfish into the tank and it would just swim right in, smooth as warm butter, like it was home? Like it knew just what to do?

That was Keith. He took to it literally like a fish to water. He knew just where we were at all times in the order of service on the bulletin. When he read responsively, nothing about his voice was thin or throaty. He called it forth from his gut, bold-like. A few minutes in, he reached down and lowered the kneeling bench like he'd built it. He dropped to his knees on that fixture like he knew precisely what to anticipate . . . and began to weep. And he wept and he wept. Wept for most of the service. Unhidden, unashamed. He'd wipe his face with both his hands, stare up at the ceiling a few seconds, then drop his face to his forearms, balanced on the back of the pew in front of us.

When we stood to say the Nicene Creed, he hardly glanced at the paper. I was trying to catch up with the words, wishing they'd slow down. The phrases were so beautiful. Rhythmic. Potent. True. Transforming. I'd heard them before, of course, and said them here and there in various services, but not like this. Not the way people say them who've built their entire faith lives upon them. I was still on "He ascended into heaven" when Keith and the rest of the congregation were declaring, "And we believe in the Holy Spirit."

One reason I couldn't keep up with the reading is that I couldn't keep my eyes off Keith.

Who even are you? I asked silently.

I was lost through much of the service, with one exception. I could tell we were proceeding toward the Lord's Supper, and I intended to receive it. And I intended to receive it, not just with hand and mouth, but with my whole soul. I'd have thrown my body on the table if they'd let me. In fact, the closer we got to the Eucharist section of the bulletin, the more I felt like I couldn't live without it another second.

I was so worn out, beaten down, and lost, that by the time the usher reached our row and motioned for us to proceed to the center aisle, I lunged toward it, Keith right on my heels. We stood in line behind other congregants moving forward and dividing right and left at the altar. Keith's hands were on my shoulders, my heart pounding in my chest. It was everything we could do not to break out of line and run to the altar. We dove for those kneeling cushions with our whole weight, set our elbows on the wooden rail, and cupped our hands for the wafer like starving people begging for bread. I dipped the wafer into the wine, set it on my tongue, and just held it there. Held it there until it softened and blanketed my tongue. I felt it fit. Felt it fold over me.

I finally swallowed and opened my eyes to see Keith in my peripheral vision, already on his feet, extending his right hand to help me up. We returned to our row. He went right back to the kneeling bench, so I followed suit until the Eucharist was complete and Keith climbed back in his seat.

I loved the things we said toward the end. I didn't know how badly I needed to say them.

All our problems,
We send to the cross of Christ!

On that second line, the whole congregation, old and young, thrust their hands up and out vigorously. Now, I love nothing better than hand motions. I caught right on to this one.

All our difficulties,
We send to the cross of Christ!

Oh, heck, yeah, this was right up my alley.

All the devil's works,
We send to the cross of Christ!

I came just short of throwing my back out with enthusiasm on that part.

All our hopes,
We set on the risen Christ!

Yes. We do. You're all we've got, Jesus. Yes, we do.
That same wad of robed people who were at the back of the sanctuary when we came in gathered up their sacred paraphernalia and processed out, just like they'd processed in, but with double joy. "Celebrate, one and all! By the power of the cross, Jesus welcomed us to his table!" Little girls in white robes snuffed the candles on the tables of the platform and filed out.

A loud voice came from the back. "Let us go forth into the world, knowing Christ and making him known!"

The congregants, who'd been quiet as church mice at the beginning of the service, shouted, "Thanks be to God!"

And it was over. I wasn't sure what just happened, but I wasn't opposed to it. A man got Keith's attention immediately, and I gathered up my Bible, purse, and bulletin. When I stood up and turned to leave the pew, several women were gathered there. In just seconds, a few more joined them.

I'll replay this scene in my head for the rest of my days, and Keith declares he will, too, but my words will fail to do it justice. It was something felt more than seen. About five women circled around me, the closest ones setting their hands on my forearms. It couldn't have been planned. No one knew we were coming. And we had no thought whatsoever that anyone there would know who we were.

"Beth," one of them voiced with palpable tenderness, "we don't know what brought you and your husband here today, but we want you to know—"

All of them nodded their heads like they knew exactly what she was about to say.

"We're so glad you came. You are welcome here, Beth."

God smote the rock, and water gushed forth from my eyes like waterfalls. I can't think of a time I've ever cried with less restraint in a public place. I couldn't stop. Couldn't get ahold of myself. Couldn't say a syllable. I just sobbed.

One of the women touching my arm said, "Can I simply ask you if you're okay?"

I nodded.

"Those are just tears of tenderness, right?" she followed up.

Nodded again.

"Okay, then. Those are allowed." And they gently laughed, and I smiled, and, one by one, they embraced me. Keith and I drove home mostly in silence, his arm across the console and his hand stretched over mine.

Drained, I took a nap when we got home. Several hours later I sat down next to him in our den. "How'd you know to do all that?"

"What do you mean?"

"At church today."

"You mean the liturgy?" He seemed surprised I was asking.

"Yes."

"Lizabeth, we did those things at my Catholic church and Catholic school throughout my whole childhood."

"Babe, why didn't you ever tell me you wanted to go back?"

"I didn't want to go back. Don't want to now."

"But, Keith, I've never once seen you enjoy a service like that. Never ever seen you participate like that. What on earth?"

"Those were the parts I loved back then. I didn't love all of it. But I loved those parts. I loved saying and praying those words. I was such a hyperactive kid that all the sitting and the kneeling and the standing and walking—constantly changing positions— worked for me. I hadn't expected that today. I hadn't expected it all to hit me that way. I had no idea I'd missed it. It was surreal having you with me. Surreal to have you not object to it."

"They read a lot of Scripture," I said. "Nearly three full chapters."

"Yeah, they did." He grinned, knowing full well I'd calculated how much Bible was used.

I continued on. "I thought the sermon was good. It wasn't loud and flashy, but it was good. It was solid."

"Agree with that."

"A lot was said about the gospel in the service, and I guess you heard at the end how we were supposed to go out and make Jesus known. I mean, Keith, that was tonic for this old evangelist's bones."

"Yep," he laughed, "I guess it was."

We sat silently awhile.

"I want to go back next Sunday," I said.

"Okay. We'll take it a week at a time. Deal?"

"Deal."

We stumbled accidentally, woundedly, wearily onto the Via Media. A middle road. It would take us a while to recognize the scenery.

• • •

I was nearly as terrible the second time as I was the first. I stayed a phrase behind the congregation with every sentence, and half the time, I was too face-planted in the bulletin to make it to my feet before it was time to sit down. I tried to keep an eye on Keith and do what he did.

I wasn't quite as out of sync the third week. It felt good to begin to anticipate a thing or two rather than constantly chase the liturgy. I could settle in for a couple of minutes while the offering plate was passed and review my bulletin and see what we were doing next. I was going to be ready for it this time.

What I wasn't ready for, however, was the offertory music that day. It was instrumental, keyboard only, in the hands of a silver-haired, sweet-smiling gentleman about my age, wearing a suit and tie. I recognized the song four notes in. *Middle C, F, A, treble C.*

My hope is built on nothing less
than Jesus' blood and righteousness;
I dare not trust the sweetest frame,
but wholly lean on Jesus' name.

I closed my eyes and mouthed the words. The wind of the Spirit picked up in my imagination and blew year after year from old wall calendars, ink-smeared pages tearing, whipping, and tumbling from the scene, the breeze dying down right around June 1966.

There we were again in my imagination, all of us on our feet in the sanctuary of First Baptist Church, Arkadelphia, Arkansas: Nanny and her friends in their pillbox hats, Mom and Dad, my brothers and sisters and me, nine years old. My Sunday school teacher yonder to the right, my choir teacher, front-center in the loft, Brother Reeves standing in front of his fancy tall chair with the red velvet cushioned inserts, Elwyn Raymer, our minister of music, holding a hymnal in his right hand and keeping the tempo with his left. We were all singing with our hymnals wide open, but who needed them anyway?

> When darkness veils his lovely face,
> I rest on his unchanging grace;
> in every high and stormy gale,
> my anchor holds within the veil.

Swept back vividly in my memories to First Baptist Church, sitting squarely and consciously on the pew of this Anglican church, it occurred to me how firmly I'd been held and how fittingly maneuvered. Through a chain of endless storms, pocked by furious tornadoes, my sanity mocked in the darkest of nights, Jesus had held. I knew no truer truth in all of life than the profession of faith I'd made public at nine years old. I kept mouthing the words while the organist played on.

> His oath, his covenant, his blood,
> support me in the whelming flood;
> when all around my soul gives way,
> he then is all my hope and stay.

I hadn't drowned. Even when I let go and gave myself wholly to the undertow and was swept into the heart of the sea, his hand was wrapped round me. Though the waves roared and tempest raged, at no time was I adrift from his presence.

When he shall come with trumpet sound,
O may I then in him be found:
dressed in his righteousness alone,
faultless to stand before the throne.

All that shame I'd felt. All that time I was so sure everyone could see all that had been done to me and all that I had done, the God Who Sees, who really sees, saw a beloved child, not an outcast laid bare in condemnation, but a daughter draped sublimely, safely in Christ's righteousness.

On Christ, the solid Rock, I stand:
all other ground is sinking sand;
all other ground is sinking sand.

I'd track down the organist after the service and thank him for such an act of service, playing that Baptist hymn for this old Baptist girl, and he said how glad he was that I enjoyed it. Said he keeps the hymnals of other denominations and chooses from one every week in case a wanderer is in the house pining for home.

I walked to the car nearly stumbling with wonder. With every step I took, it occurred to me with more startling clarity, that somewhere beyond the clouds all was calendared. Neither my pain nor my path could be reduced to mere consequences. Even the detours on this road were marked by Providence. The travel atlas was out on my Father's table up north; a route I could not see was highlighted in green. In the words of the great apostle, God was, all along, *finishing what was lacking in my faith*. Such will be the course for the rest of my days, come what may.

My heritage, so precious to me, could not be stripped from me any more than my future could be stolen. God would see to his good pleasure. No trading in. No trading out. No such scarcity can be found in the Spirit. I could hold on to all of it. Every last bit of it. For he who called me was holding on to me.

EPILOGUE

TEN YEARS AGO my man built me a house in the woods where, God willing, we intend to live out the rest of our days. By *built*, I don't mean he took hand to brick or hung the doors, but as surely as our metal roof is spring-grass green, he took a pen to paper and drew it right before my eyes.

"What would you think about living in something like that?"

Keith is a bit of an anomaly. He's a grimy outdoorsman with a fine eye for design, but he's never claimed to possess a fleck of drawing prowess. It didn't matter. I got the picture.

"Yes," I replied.

"Really?"

"Baby, absolutely, yes. That's the house I want to grow old in."

His face lit up with delight. "You mean it?"

"Honey, *yes*." And I did. "Where'd you get that idea?"

"I've pictured it for years."

"Why didn't you ever tell me?"

"I thought I'd sooner bury you than blow you out of this house where we raised the kids."

I'd sworn and declared I'd never leave it. Sworn and declared when I breathed my last, he could hurl my cold, stiff body into one of a dozen holes the dogs had dug in the backyard.

We'd bought the blue Victorian in a greater Houston neighborhood at a foreclosure rate when our girls were five and two. I loved every square inch of it. Amanda had learned to ride a two-wheeler and Melissa, a Big Wheel, in that driveway. They'd learned to shoot hoops in it. I'd waited at the curb of that house for the bus to come get each of them for their first days of school. I'd taken pictures of my girls in their prom dresses in that house. My first grandchildren crawled and toddled and ate off the floor in that house. Eight pets—dogs and cats both—had been raised and spoiled rotten within those walls. For the love of God, I'd gotten "yard of the month" once at that house.

I'd risen up before dawn more mornings than I have math skills to count over the course of twenty-seven years to meet with Jesus in its small dining room. I'd prepared a jillion Sunday school lessons and conference messages and written fourteen Bible studies there. I'd rolled out butcher paper on the den floor and drawn a timeline of the seventy weeks of Daniel for Bible study in permanent marker. And when I rolled it back up, the black ink had bled through to the hardwood. Now, who's going to buy that house? Nobody, and not just because I'd ruined the floor. I wasn't budging.

A couple of developments weakened my firm resolve. We'd made the ghastly mistake of getting two puppies at the same time. I needn't explain to anyone with similar regrets what that decision did to my "yard of the month." Between the landscaping, furniture, rugs, book spines, stair rails, cabinet knobs, and every pair of shoes we owned, those two gremlins managed to do thousands of dollars' worth of damage in two years' time. The fields nearby where we'd run these dogs and their predecessors, letting them chase rabbits till their paws were nubs, were now covered with storage-unit eyesores. I ask you, how many storage units does one neighborhood need? If it sounds like I decided to leave the home in which I'd sworn to live out my days and uproot to the country over a pair of dogs, then you've got the picture.

I'd just said it once. And I said it no louder than a whisper— and with a disclaimer. "Don't even think of reminding me that I said this. Don't even pay attention to it. But I might one day consider moving."

Keith called a Realtor the next day. She and Keith searched for a piece of land first. After several weeks of exploration, they discovered acres down a one-way dirt road behind a few farms on the outskirts of Houston. The land was so dense with trees, brush, vines, and thorns, they had to hack their way in to see if adequate space for two houses was above the floodplain. We weren't moving without Keith's parents. They lived one minute from us in town, and we weren't giving that up even for dogs. We'd build their house first since, in their late seventies, bar a tragedy, they had less time left to enjoy it.

Keith drove me out to see the property and walked me down the spider-webbed path he'd hacked, and it was love at first sight. I'd ached for a fresh-air, moving mural over my head, painted with long, leafy arms of pines, oaks, and sycamores, ever since my family moved away from the hill in Arkadelphia.

We dove into our savings and made an offer nearly overnight. Keith and his dad began the monumental task of clearing enough land for our houses, digging a well, and putting in electrical lines and butane and septic tanks. My in-laws settled on a house plan quickly, but no matter what Keith put in front of me, nothing made my eyes sparkle.

"Babe, I'm telling you," I said over and over, "any one of them is fine. I don't care. You know I'm not a house snob. I'm in it for the trees. I don't care what house you put in the middle of that little forest, I'll be blissful."

"But I want you to care."

"Well, honey," I said, "I'm sorry. I don't care. You pick. I'll be so happy."

And all that was true until the day at our breakfast table when Keith sketched an image on a piece of 8½-by-11-inch printer paper and asked, "What would you think about living in something like that?"

"It's a church!" I exclaimed, taken aback.

"Well, yeah, but we'd design it into a home."

"Keith, where did you even come up with this idea?"

"You know I'll take a country road over a freeway any day, and driving between here and San Antonio or Dallas, either one, I've seen some rendition of this style church several times and had to stop and stare. They're almost always a basic, no-frills chapel, the roof a twelve/twelve pitch like this, and a couple of Sunday school rooms on each side in the back. I've dreamed of it for years. Seems like, as much as your faith has shaped our lives up to now, it would make a fitting shape for the rest of them. The way I'm picturing it, a combination den, dining area, and kitchen would go in the chapel part of it, then bedrooms to each side of the rear. It wouldn't be ornate, but that's not us anyway. I think it could work."

He had me, hook, line, and sinker. Keith started poring over online catalogs of local architects and driving by examples of their handiwork. He found an architect whose drawings showed imagination and asked him if he'd meet us for dinner. After we'd small-talked a few minutes, Keith took a folded piece of paper out of his shirt pocket with the same drawing, unfolded it, pressed out the creases with his fingertips, turned it 180 degrees, and slid it across the table. "Have you ever designed a house like this?"

The tall, slender, gray-haired gentleman looked like a character from a movie. He was perfectly put together from head to toe with a mesmerizing South African accent, a trimmed goatee with a meticulously spun handlebar mustache, and a crimson bow tie at the neck of a shirt sufficiently starched to stand alone. He picked up the paper, lifted his chin, squinted through his bifocal lenses, then raised his brows and grinned. "Like an old church?"

"Yessir," Keith said. "My wife has a calling, and all these years she's—"

"No," he interrupted, "I can't say I've ever created a blueprint for a home like this. But I also can't say I haven't wished to."

He just didn't seem like the lying type. We hired him on the spot. Pleased to euphoria with the resulting blueprints, Keith met with a custom builder right away and oversaw every square inch of construction. He found five pieces of unmatched stained glass and had windows cut to fit them.

Bereft of a gifting for interiors, I left everything entirely to Keith. He chose all the flooring, countertops, cabinets, and appliances with the easy agreement that the insides would be homey, not fancy. We were moving to the woods so two gnarly dogs would have space to romp. We're the opposite of the sort of people who don't let their pets on their couch. One sleeps with us, for pity's sake.

We'd move into that brand-new old-country church a year later. I'd once again swear and declare I'd never move.

● ● ●

We're all we have out in these woods. We can either find a way to be happy out here together or be miserable out here together, but the unchanging fact is, we're out here alone together. Our kids grew up. Keith's daddy died. His mother moved into assisted living. A pandemic hit and pinned us in these acres alone for months. Our daughters—Sunshine and Moonshine—and our darling, hilarious, and endlessly energetic grandchildren all live many miles away.

We're still thick as thieves, those girls and I. Not a day goes by without us talking, stalking, commiserating, laughing, deliberating, planning, scheming, or crying. We text, we call, we video and Zoom. We're together in person as often as possible, and when we're not, we pine for one another. They're the best friends and confidantes I have. My closest advisers. My favorite humans. My funniest comediennes. They're beautiful and brilliant, witty and deep, bold and full of grace, and I miss them every dang day. Those gorgeous creatures are doing exactly what they should be doing. Doing exactly what I want them to be doing. They're living their grown-up lives. They love Jesus. They love their parents. They're never out of touch nor out of reach. But here's the God's honest truth of our everyday lives: their dad's all I've got left of them in these woods.

Not too long ago, Keith came in the house looking like he'd seen a ghost.

"Lizabeth," he said, "I'm gonna need you to get in the truck and right now and I don't want to hear any arguing. I've got somewhere I've gotta take you."

"Where on earth?" I asked.

"You'll see."

We drove for half an hour, Keith winding this way and that, and finally pulled into the gravel parking lot of a church near Waller, Texas.

"This was my grandparents' church, Lizabeth. This was the

place I went with them when I was a kid and spent all those weekends in the country. Hadn't been back in all these years."

He'd gotten a serious case of nostalgia earlier in the day. The kind that gets in your lungs and makes you pant for something—*anything*—meaningful, purposeful from your past. He'd driven out to those country roads in Waller, aching for his grandparents who had given themselves to a little lost boy with scars on his legs and scars on his heart, remembering how they'd saved his life. Their ninety acres had long since been halved and sold and locked behind gates. He sat on the shoulder of the road, reliving memories. He remembered how he felt when he'd sit between them in the pickup truck. He hadn't even minded going to church with them every Sunday, as long as he was snug and secure between that old woman and that old man.

Where was that church, anyway? he'd asked himself on the earlier drive. *It couldn't be too far from here.*

He knew it wasn't in town back then. It had been somewhere out in the country, nothing but pastures around it. He drove all over those country roads, and just about the time he was ready to give up, he finally spied it. He read the sign on it over and over to make sure he wasn't imagining things. A new building had gone up since the last time he'd been there, but they'd seen fit to keep the old one and mark its history with a placard just for remembrance's sake. It was the one, all right. The one where he'd squirmed in the pew between his grandpa and grandma, them saying what seemed a thousand Our Fathers.

I got out of the truck and stared, my hand slowly rising to cover my gaping mouth.

It was my house. Size, shape, the roof pitch, the white paint.

The very house Keith had drawn on a scratch sheet of paper and built for me was the spitting image of his grandparents' church.

The memory of its appearance had been buried alive beneath the charred wood and gray ash of his childhood, a pulse of faith too faint for Keith to perceive and too loud for God to forget.

All this time, Keith thought the chapel he'd built as a home for us was a matter of his taste in design and, in his words, a monument of sorts to my faith. The connection between the two places had never occurred to Keith. But it had never stopped occurring to Christ.

As I stood in front of the old church, seeing in my mind's eye the squirrels skittering up and over that same roofline on my house in the pines, I knew I'd been wrong about God, thinking that day I stormed through the woods, wet-faced with boiling, angry tears that Keith never got a break and, therefore, neither did we. Copious questions remained unanswered. But one answer alone caught the clear glimmer of the setting sun on the stained glass of Keith's grandparents' old church. God loved my husband. He'd loved him all along. Of course, I knew it inside, but I'd needed in the worst way for God to show it. And he'd chosen a way I could not possibly miss. Could not possibly forget. I'd awaken to it every morning and drive up to it every evening after work.

God was the unseen architect of our chapel in the woods. Keith had built it for me, but God had built it for us.

• • •

I saw this life of mine going differently than it has. I saw myself turning out better than I have. Surer about how things go. I expected to have more riddles solved. More people sorted out. More grays dissolved to black-and-white.

I never was able to divide up the room into the good and the bad the way I'd wanted. I couldn't even unmix my own feelings, let alone those of others. I needed neatness from God. What I got was a tangled-up knot.

Funny thing is, not once had it occurred to me how little difference exists between a tight knot and a firm tie. Somewhere inside the balled-up, walled-up mass of tangled strands in the life of faith, the inscrutable God of heaven and earth has the loose ends tied. The ones that mean anything, anyway. Tied securely. Tied sturdily. Tied in such a way that all the human tugging, doubting, and fretting in the world can't loose them. Tied in such a way no mortal mind could calculate. What God is this who can keep a secret so long? What God is this, so unhurried to prove himself? So confident of his own spotless character that he is unpressured by all the second-guessing of his own children?

I'm growing old now, quickly, the clock ticking, the days flying. I'm not very sure of myself anymore, if I ever truly was. But I am utterly sure of one thing about my turn on this whirling earth. A thing I've never seen. A thing I cannot prove. A thing I cannot always sense. Every inch of this harrowing journey, in all the bruising and bleeding and sobbing and pleading, my hand has been tightly knotted, safe and warm, with the hand of Jesus. In all the letting go, he has held me fast. He will hold me still. And he will lead me home. Blest be the tie that binds.

ACKNOWLEDGMENTS

Lord-a-mercy, this would go a heap faster if I could just mention the people I *don't* need to thank. Alas, I'm having trouble coming up with enough of their names to fill a page, so I'll attempt to do this the customary way, but I will inevitably overlook people to whom I owe so much gratitude.

I'm deeply grateful to Ron Beers, senior vice president at Tyndale House, for entrusting me with another project. I don't take it lightly. I always fear being more of a liability to my publishers than a blessing. Karen Watson has been my closest compadre at Tyndale for as many as ten years, one of my most powerful draws to Tyndale and the one with whom I feel safest to try new things and speak my mind. She is more valuable to me than gold. I'm so grateful for the care and excellence of editor Kathryn Olson and copy editor Danika Kelly. You are both fabulous. I'm wild about the whole Tyndale crew, among them Maria Eriksen, Kristen Magnesen, and publicist Katie Dodillet. I can't wait to be on the road with you again. Huge thanks to Jackie Nuñez and Dean Renninger for your work on the cover. It delighted me to no end. I knew what I was getting into with these individuals on my Tyndale team when I partnered with them on this work. Knew I wouldn't regret it.

The gift I didn't know to anticipate was Carol Traver. I'm going to need a minute here. Carol's niche at Tyndale is memoir, so our paths hadn't crossed. Once I settled in my mind that this was the direction God meant for me to go with the next Tyndale book, Karen Watson quipped, "Oh, I know exactly who we need to assign to you. You will love her." Oh, man, was she right. Let me say with tears in my eyes and a wide grin across my face, no therapist on earth knows as much about my personal life as Carol Traver. God bless her. A memoir is uniquely difficult to write because a life is immensely hard to honestly face. Mine has been anyway. Every draft hit her desk first, raw and unfiltered.

Carol helped me navigate what was too much to tell and what was too little. I came to one part that messed with me so much, she checked on me every day for a week. I had such difficulty with another chunk of my story, one far more recent, that I finally said, "I'm just going to write it all to you, exactly how I perceived it, exactly how I felt it, saw it, and get it all off my chest, and let you decide what to keep, what is of actual benefit to the reader, and what needs to go." She did exactly what I asked, and a three-chapter segment of the book turned into a two-chapter segment. Those deleted portions will rightly never see the light of day. By the time all was said and done, Carol walked with me through every chapter, every page and paragraph of this book. She's read this manuscript more times than any human ought to have to and far more times than I. I can't imagine this would be the same book with a different editor. Carol, I'm so glad I took this ride with you, and I forgive you for cutting my marvelous Pony Bee story. The reader has no idea what you put out to pasture.

I'll never live long enough nor have vocabulary enough to adequately thank my coworkers at Living Proof Ministries for their constant support, camaraderie, prayers, laughter, grace, patience, hilarity, and affection. They are my closest fellow sojourners in the faith, and they continually increase my love for Jesus. No margin exists for me to write a trade book without them picking up the slack. Kimberly McMahon (K-Mac to me) deserves a double portion of gratitude as she serves alongside this Enneagram 7 as my personal assistant while I bounce like a Ping-Pong ball all over the place. When I can't remember my last name, she can.

I loved every second of reliving with Helen Maerz that momentous week of missions camp when I was eighteen and she was one of my sixth graders.

I'm so thankful for close and unreplaceable friends in the faith like Travis and Angela Cottrell, whom I love like my own flesh and blood, my whole Living Proof worship team, Keith's and my double-dating friends Danny and Charmaine Mitcham, our beloved Steven, Amy, and Ainsley Purcell, Johnnie Haines, Priscilla Shirer, Lisa Weir, Steve Bezner, Derwin and Vicki Gray, Russell and Maria Moore, and Christine Caine, one of my favorite people on earth and a ridiculously generous cheerleader. So many other names deserve to be in this paragraph. These are just a few who have been nearby during these many months of writing. I owe you such debts of love. You have no small part in this memoir. After all, without friends, how good can memories possibly be?

Inexpressibly grateful to my church family. I wouldn't have wanted to miss you for anything in the world. I'll never forget that Sunday.

I began this book with gratitude to each of my siblings, but I cannot draw to a close without echoing it. They didn't volunteer to have a very wordy writer and controversial religious figure in the family. Children who grow up in the same family don't have identical experiences, nor do they witness all the others' most life-shaping scenes. And even when they do, they don't necessarily see those events from the same corner of the room. My siblings' willingness to let me tell any overlapping parts of the Green story from my individual perspective is a mercy and a gift beyond price. I offered to change their names, for what little it was worth, but they declined the offer. So, Sandra, Wayne, Gay, and Tony, I thank you with all of my heart. Lisa, my Wayne's other half, you are one of the dearest people in the world to me and no less my sister than Sandra and Gay. I love all of you.

Uncle Roy, you are our Green family patriarch. Please live long enough to read this book. You are the youngest person in his nineties that I know. We are all so proud to be yours.

Amanda and Melissa, my Sunshine and my Moonshine, you are the only two daughters for me. Your grace toward me after all my mistakes and regrets and love for me in all my weakness and over-the-topness leaves me in tearful gratitude. You are my favorite company. I esteem no one higher. Love no one more. Enjoy no one more. Thank you for being able to deal with this memoir. Curtis, my son-in-law, I don't know how you've dealt with all of us Moores but we're so glad you have. I love you dearly. To my grandchildren: because I adore you, earnestly love you more than my own life and certainly more than my own story, I have very intentionally left your names out of these pages. My hope is that you will grow up free of my public baggage and find your way with Jesus.

Ivan Keith, I come finally to you and find myself at a loss for words. You could not possibly have more skin in this memoir. Your willingness to let me be this transparent about our story is nothing less than heroic to me. We have lived a wild journey together. I reckon, darling, we've been everything but bored. Thank you for enduring. I love you so.

I am grateful beyond any possible measure for Jesus, who saved my soul and who daily saves me from myself. If anything in these pages is of value, if any good dwells in me at all, my blessed Savior, it is you. You have my heart. You are my home. You are my joy.

ABOUT THE AUTHOR

AUTHOR AND SPEAKER BETH MOORE is a dynamic teacher whose conferences take her across the globe. Beth founded Living Proof Ministries in 1994 with the purpose of encouraging women to know and love Jesus through the study of Scripture. She has written numerous bestselling books, including *Get Out of That Pit*; *So Long, Insecurity*; and *Chasing Vines*; and Bible studies, including *Breaking Free, Mercy Triumphs, Entrusted, The Quest,* and *Now That Faith Has Come*, which have been read by women of all ages, races, and denominations.Another recent addition includes her first work of fiction, *The Undoing of Saint Silvanus*.

Beth recently celebrated twenty-four years of Living Proof Live conferences. She can be seen teaching Bible studies on the television program *Living Proof with Beth Moore*, aired on the Trinity Broadcasting Network.

She and her husband of forty-four years reside in Houston, Texas. She is a dedicated wife, the mother of two adult daughters, the grandmother of three delightful grandchildren, an active church member, and a dog-lover-to-the-death.

Join Beth on her journey of discovering
what it means to chase vines—
and learn how to fully embrace God's amazing
design for a fruitful, abundant, and meaningful life.

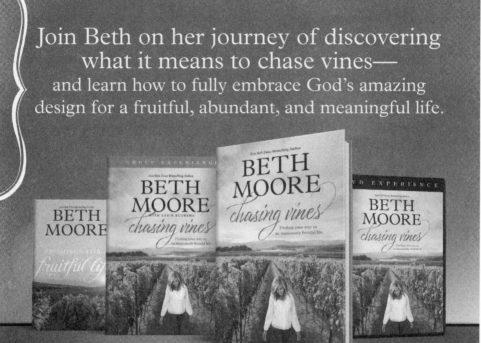

Chasing Vines: Popular teacher and speaker Beth Moore helps us understand how
our life—and our relationship with God—could be different if we better understood and fully embraced His amazing design for making fruitful lives that matter.

Chasing Vines DVD Experience: Designed for use with the *Chasing Vines
Group Experience*, this six-session DVD curriculum based on Beth Moore's book
explores the ways God delights in watching things grow—and how the land of the
vineyard holds the secret for how we can have a fruitful life.

Chasing Vines Group Experience: This is a six-session workbook designed for
use with the *Chasing Vines DVD Experience*, based on the book by Beth Moore.
A great resource for church groups, Bible studies, and anyone who's ever wondered how God makes everything in life matter!

Promises for a Fruitful Life: Drawn from Scripture and passages from Beth
Moore's book *Chasing Vines*, this booklet will help you find new hope for
Kingdom building. With each page, you'll be reminded that your life matters—
and nothing you've experienced will be wasted by the One who created you.

To learn more from Beth and access additional resources,
visit her online at Bethmoore.org.

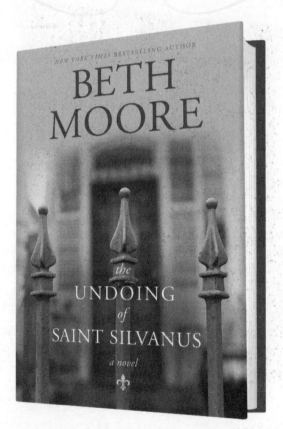

Join bestselling authors Beth Moore and
Melissa Moore for a six-week deep dive into
Paul's captivating letter to the Galatians!

Come to know the letter's original recipients. Study its
original context and embrace its timeless relevance.
Discover—or perhaps rediscover—what makes the
gospel of Jesus Christ revolutionary to those who
choose to believe. Find out how everything has
changed, now that faith has come.